W. L. McCORMICK

WORLD WAR II

World War II

A Concise History

By

Roger W. Shugg, Ph. D.

and

Major H. A. DeWeerd

WASHINGTON

THE INFANTRY JOURNAL

1946

The text of this book was prepared from public sources. Maps 5, 7, 12, 13, 16, 19, 23 and 28 are from *The War in Maps,* by Francis Brown, copyright by Oxford University Press. Maps 29 and 31, copyright by *The New York Times.* Maps 18, 22, 33, 34, 35, 36, 37, 38, 39, 40, 41, 42, 43 and 44, copyright by Infantry Journal, Inc.

FIRST EDITION

January, 1946

FOREWORD

This book is offered to Americans as a brief military history of the war to VJ-day. It aims to tell the whole truth so far as it can be told now in limited space and from public sources. Care has been taken to make the text as accurate as possible, but errors are bound to occur in any attempt to cover such a vast subject. Readers are invited to call these to the attention of the Infantry Journal. Corrections will be made in later editions. While it is largely military, as any account of war is bound to be, the language is not technical.

To know the causes and events of this war and the principles for which we fought, according to General Marshall, "is an indispensable part of military training and merits the thoughtful consideration of every American soldier." The mission of making soldiers aware of the background of the conflict was assigned by order of the War Department, February 9, 1942, to the Army Orientation Course which every soldier takes as part of his basic training. For this course lectures were prepared and published since 1942; and in addition to documentary films and reprints of many books, a special volume, *The War in Outline*, was printed in several editions. WORLD WAR II: A CONCISE HISTORY is an entirely new book. Like its predecessors, however, it has been written exclusively from public sources.

It is hoped that this book will prove useful to soldiers in the field and to citizens at home for both reading and reference. All Americans will observe that as much attention is given to the contributions made by our Allies to winning the war as to the vital part taken by the United States. This book should help us to understand what actually happened, when and where and how, in the greatest war in history, and to see it all in better perspective.

CONTENTS

MAPS

WORLD WAR II

PART ONE

WAR COMES TO AMERICA

1. JAPAN ATTACKS PEARL HARBOR

Japanese bombing planes disabled the United States Pacific Fleet as it lay in Pearl Harbor the morning of December 7, 1941. In a surprise raid lasting two hours a force of 105 bombers crippled the ships and destroyed most of the aircraft in the Hawaiian Islands. All but twenty of the enemy planes flew back to the six carriers which had brought them under cover of bad weather within striking range of the great American naval base. In the smoke, fire, and explosions at Pearl Harbor they left behind them a Japanese declaration of war on the United States.

By this "unprovoked and dastardly attack," Japan won a major victory which her armed forces quickly exploited in the conquest of Southeast Asia, the Philippines, and other islands in the Pacific. Japan did not destroy American naval power at Pearl Harbor. The 86 ships which lay there exposed to attack were not even the entire Pacific Fleet. Two task forces with four aircraft carriers and other vessels escaped because they were at sea. Eight battleships, the new *North Carolina* and *Washington,* each of 35,000 tons, and the *Idaho, New Mexico, Mississippi, Texas, New York* and *Arkansas,* were in the Atlantic, for the fleet formerly concentrated in the Pacific had been divided in 1941 to guard against both Germany and Japan. Most of the ships sunk or damaged were back in service within the following year— except the 26-year-old battleship *Arizona,* which blew up when a bomb plunged down her smokestack and exploded the forward powder magazine.

The disaster suffered at Pearl Harbor, although temporary in its consequences, was grave indeed. Irreparable was the loss of 2,343 American service men dead, 1,272 wounded, and 960 who were never found. Besides the *Arizona,* four other battleships, the *Oklahoma, California, Nevada,* and

1

West Virginia; three destroyers, the *Shaw, Cassin,* and *Downes;* the *Utah,* an old battleship converted into a target vessel; the minelayer, *Oglala;* and a large floating drydock— all these were "either sunk or damaged so severely that they would serve no military purposes" for a year to come. Also heavily damaged, but back at sea much earlier, were three battleships, the *Pennsylvania, Maryland,* and *Tennessee;* three cruisers, the *Helena, Honolulu,* and *Raleigh;* a sea-plane tender, the *Curtiss;* and a repair ship, the *Vestal.* Most of the 273 Army planes on Hickam and Wheeler fields were destroyed; those which might have taken the air against the enemy were pinned to earth by damaged runways. Of the 202 Navy planes, 150 were destroyed in the first few minutes of the Japanese attack. Altogether 38 American planes flew into action against the enemy, but the chief defense of the naval vessels moored at Pearl Harbor was necessarily limited to antiaircraft fire.

Had the Japanese known the extent of their victory, a fact which the American Government took care to conceal, they might have invaded the Hawaiian Islands or followed up their first blow with others, the results of which could not have been so quickly repaired. The United States Army and Navy reacted with haste to secure the defense not only of the exposed islands in the Pacific but of the whole Western Hemisphere.

Within a week after Pearl Harbor, two divisions of infantry rushed by train to the Pacific Coast; aerial reinforcements flew to the Panama Canal; and detachments of Coast Artillery were sent as far as Chile to defend the western coast of South America. All the critical areas on the Atlantic and Pacific coasts of the United States were reinforced within ten days after Pearl Harbor. In the course of six weeks, 600,000 troops with all their equipment were moved by rail to defensive positions.

In this race to man the continental defenses of America, outposts in the Atlantic and Pacific were not neglected. One American division embarked for Great Britain, arriving in Northern Ireland late in January 1942. Two fast convoys left San Francisco for Pearl Harbor during the first ten days of the war. Under radio silence, two transports with 4,500 troops, which had been en route from Hawaii to the Philippines at the time of Pearl Harbor, reached Brisbane, Australia, after fifteen days. The flow of men and supplies to the Southwest Pacific was so fast that by June 1942, the defense of this area was strengthened by 150,000 American ground troops, ready to hold Australia and New Zealand against Japan.

As it happened, however, the Japanese were not interested in doing more than paralyzing American naval power. Their objectives lay not in the Central but in the South Pacific from Australia to India. The tactical success which they achieved by surprise at Pearl Harbor was also a strategical victory because it gave them freedom of action in the Far East. Their advantage did not last long, however, for in the Battle of the Coral Sea [*May 7–8, 1942*], six months later, the American Navy rallied to turn the Japanese back in the South Pacific; and a month later, in the Battle of Midway [*June 3–6, 1942*] to crush the enemy when he again penetrated the Central Pacific. Pearl Harbor was the beginning, not the end, of the war for the United States.

2. AMERICA SURPRISED

The American people were astounded by the incredible news that Japan had bombed Pearl Harbor. What shocked them was the bold treachery of so unexpected an attack, and the fact that Japan rather than Germany had struck first. They were not astonished, however, to find themselves at war. A month before Pearl Harbor, according to polls of American public opinion, it was realized that sooner or later we must fight. Four out of five people thought armed conflict with Germany inevitable; two out of three believed we could not escape war with Japan. Of every ten persons questioned all over the country, seven said that it was more important for us to defeat Germany than to stay out of war, and eight were confident that our Navy would destroy the Japanese Fleet. There were few perhaps who could imagine how or when war would reach America; most people ex-

3

pected that we should go to war rather than wait for it to come to us.

When we were attacked at Pearl Harbor, all doubt of our foreign policy and its relation to National Defense vanished. The fact that we were compelled to fight in self-defense put an end to the long debate which had been carried on between "isolationists" and "interventionists," as the two schools of opinion called each other; one holding that our safety was to be secured by the defense of only the Americas, the other that it was threatened by the German conquests in Europe and by the Japanese in Asia. After Pearl Harbor there could no longer be any question of remaining isolated from or intervening in a war which had come to our territorial shores. Fortunately for the American people, confronted by the strongest enemies in their history, the Japanese attack on Pearl Harbor united them more than ever before. Astonishment gave way quickly to anger, and anger froze in the grim determination to wage war until all enemies were crushed.

The day after Pearl Harbor [*December 8, 1941*] the United States Congress heard President Roosevelt declare that "we will not only defend ourselves to the uttermost, but we will make it very certain that this form of treachery will never again endanger us." The Congress voted, only one member dissenting, that a state of war existed between the United States and the Japanese Empire, and empowered the President as Commander in Chief of the armed forces under the Constitution to wage war with all the resources of the country.

The next evening [*December 9, 1941*], two days after Pearl Harbor, President Roosevelt addressed his fellow-countrymen over the radio, warning them that Japan was not their only enemy:

"The sudden criminal attacks perpetrated by the Japanese in the Pacific provide the climax of a decade of international immorality. Powerful and resourceful gangsters have banded together to make war upon the whole human race. Their challenge has now been flung at the United States of America . . . The course that Japan has followed for the past ten years in Asia has paralleled the course of Hitler and

4

Mussolini in Europe and Africa. Today, it has become far more than a parallel. It is collaboration, actual collaboration, so well calculated that all the continents of the world, and all the oceans, are now considered by the Axis strategists as one gigantic battlefield." Referring to Pearl Harbor, he said, "we must face the fact that modern warfare as conducted in the Nazi manner is a dirty business. We don't like it—we didn't want to get in it—but we are in it and we're going to fight it with everything we've got."

Our cause, he said, and the cause of millions of other people, was "liberty under God."

3. GERMANY DECLARES WAR: THE AXIS AGAINST AMERICA

Four days after Pearl Harbor [*December 11, 1941*] Germany and Italy declared war on the United States. The Tripartite Pact [*September 27, 1940*] which had joined Rome, Berlin, and Tokyo in diplomatic alliance against the United States, became a full-fledged military alliance. By the terms of a new agreement, Italy, Germany, and Japan were now bound to "conduct in common and jointly a war" against the United States and England, and not to make peace separately. "The Tripartite Pact," shouted Mussolini to the crowds gathered in Rome, "becomes a military alliance which draws around its colors two hundred and fifty million men determined to do all in order to win." "A historic revenge," Hitler told the Reichstag, "has been entrusted to us by the Creator, and we are now obliged to carry it out."

It was evident that the Axis Powers had a joint plan for sharing the spoils of a Fascist world to be won by war on two fronts against the United States. The American Congress, without a dissenting vote, immediately recognized that a state of war existed between this country and Germany and Italy. An article in the Selective Service Act prohibiting the use of American armed forces beyond the Western Hemisphere was rescinded. Having tried and failed to defend itself in its own territories and waters, the United States was at last compelled to defend itself everywhere in the world.

5

"We are now in the midst of a war [said President Roosevelt] not for conquest, not for vengeance, but for a world in which this nation, and all that this nation represents, will be safe for our children. We expect to eliminate the danger from Japan, but it would serve us ill if we accomplished that and found the rest of the world was dominated by Hitler and Mussolini. So, we are going to win the war and we are going to win the peace that follows."

4. JAPANESE AGGRESSION IN ASIA

The military reason why Japan struck at Pearl Harbor, as indicated above, was to neutralize the American Navy in the Pacific so that it could not interfere with Japanese troops overrunning Southeast Asia. The political reason why Japan dared to go to war with both the United States and Great Britain was that these nations opposed Japanese expansion in Asia and helped China to resist it. The course of events which led directly to Pearl Harbor covers ten previous years, from 1931 to 1941—ten years of military aggression and conquest by Japan on the Asiatic mainland at the expense first of China and then of France. So it might be truly said that this war first broke out, not in Europe when Germany attacked Poland in 1939, but in Asia when Japan began to encroach on China in 1931. There was never a declaration of war, but it was war, limited to the north until 1937, then spreading south along the Chinese coast up to 1941, and finally sweeping out over the Pacific and Southeast Asia.

The Japanese Army took the warpath in 1931 when it invaded and occupied the Chinese territory of Manchuria. The excuse for this action was the so-called "Mukden Incident" [*September 18, 1931*]. Japan claimed but never proved that Chinese bandits blew up a section of the South Manchurian Railway, owned by the Japanese and heavily guarded by their troops. It was obviously by careful planning long in advance that the Japanese forces, massed in Korea, were able to seize not only Mukden, the capital city, but all the strategic points in Manchuria. By invading and occupying

6

this region, Japan came into control of rich economic resources, which properly belonged to China. Manchuria was reorganized as Manchukuo [*February 18, 1932*], nominally an independent state but actually a puppet of Tokyo, with all its resources exploited for the increase of Japanese armed strength and power.

Chinese Nationalists, growing more united in the face of a common enemy, struck back at Japan with the best weapon they had, an economic boycott which deprived Japanese textile factories in Shanghai of a large market for their goods. There was disorder in the city and some Japanese were mobbed. Punishment was swift and severe. By land, sea, and air the Japanese attacked the native Chapei district [*January 29, 1932*], where a Chinese army was stationed. Thousands of civilians were killed. But the stubborn resistance of the Chinese Nineteenth Route Army, containing an amphibious assault for several weeks, prevented the Japanese from breaking the boycott of their goods or conquering Shanghai.

Japan next attacked the northern provinces below the Great Wall, territory which had always been Chinese. The Kwangtung Army, a Japanese force garrisoned in Manchuria, crossed the Great Wall and moved south on Peiping and Tientsin during April and May, 1933. Lacking both the power and the will to resist alone, the Chinese agreed to a truce at Tangku [*May 31, 1933*], which lost them control of the province of Jehol, adjoining Manchuria, and exposed other provinces to Japanese influence and infiltration. In 1935, Japan struck again, and this time she did not stop until she was supreme in the five northern provinces of Chahar, Suiyuan, Ningsia, Shansi, and Hopeh. Yet China was too vast a country to be subdued by these limited campaigns. Welded together by the relentless pressure of Japan, the Chinese people became stronger in resisting every attack.

In 1937 Japan intensified her effort to conquer China, claiming as provocation what the Japanese called the "China Incident [*July 7, 1937*], an alleged attack by Chinese soldiers at the Marco Polo Bridge in Peiping. The real cause of the struggle was always the adamant refusal of Chiang Kai-shek and the people of China to become Japanese puppets like Manchukuo or to be the victims of an economic monopoly which Japan called the "Greater East Asia Co-Prosperity Sphere." Chinese resistance led to a long war of attrition which has taken the lives of five to ten million Chinese and of nearly one million Japanese in the past seven years. Some forty million Chinese have fled the coastal provinces conquered by Japan, and in a great westward migration to the interior of their vast country they have built up an agrarian society which the Japanese have not been able to conquer. For the Japanese Army the China War has been a training ground and field of maneuvers, the results of which were to be seen, together with new weapons like the Zero fighter plane and new tactics like jungle infiltration, in Southeast Asia after Pearl Harbor.

The Japanese won quick victories in China, but none was decisive. They occupied the old capital of Peiping [*July 29, 1937*] and the next day, Tientsin. After a siege of three months they took the great seaport of Shanghai [*November 8, 1937*]. As Chiang's army withdrew westward, the Japanese pursued them and captured the Nationalist capital of Nanking [*December 13, 1937*], inflicting barbarous atrocities on the civilian population as part of a new policy of terror. An incomplete Japanese blockade began to cut China's trade with the rest of the world and to drive European and American interests out of China.

In 1938 the Japanese marched southwest against the rail center of Hankow, six hundred miles inland from Shanghai and key to the Yangtze River valley, but they were covered by Chinese troops to the northeast at Suchow. In the course of this campaign the Chinese defeated the enemy at Taierchwang, but in October finally lost both Suchow and Hankow. On the southeastern coast the Japanese also captured the port of Canton [*October 21, 1938*], crippling the British port of Hong Kong. Chiang removed his government and army to Chungking, eight hundred miles up the Yangtze from Hankow, where narrow mountain gorges protected his inland-domain.

With the outbreak of war in Europe [*September 3, 1939*], the Japanese gave up their attempt to destroy the Chinese armies and adopted a policy of limited warfare and blockade. They seized the coastal ports of Swatow, Ningpo, and Foochow in 1939, effectively cutting China off from any foreign aid except the small amount which came in over the Burma Road. As the German armies swept over Europe in 1939 and 1940, Japan consolidated her position in northern China and along the coast while preparing to overrun Southeast Asia.

By the time she struck at Pearl Harbor, after four years of sporadic fighting in China, Japan had occupied the largest cities—Shanghai, Peiping, Tientsin, Hankow, and Canton—and ten provinces in the fertile plains of the lower Yangtze and Yellow rivers. Chiang Kai-shek controlled only the five provinces of Szechwan, Shensi, Kansu, Kweichow, and Yünnan, and important parts of Kwangsi and Shensi. Japan dominated about one-quarter of the entire area of China and ruled almost half its population. Three strategic keys Japan did not hold, and without them no conqueror has ever subdued China: Shensi, where the mountains command the North China plain; its barrier, the great elbow of the Yellow River at Tungkwan, gateway to the rich interior of Shensi and Szechwan; and the Han River valley, which the Japanese had four times tried in vain to take.

Japan made the mistake of attempting to conquer China cheaply, with as few men as possible, never using enough to destroy the Chinese armies or to occupy all the country. The largest army Japan had in China probably consisted of 250,000 troops under General Terauchi in the initial campaign of 1937. Many more troops were eventually stationed in China to guard Japanese lines of communication and supply. The vast country swallowed up the men of Nippon wherever they went, and all they really conquered were the railroads and ports. Even in the provinces which they occupied, the Japanese were plagued by Chinese guerrillas, who fell upon their supply trains and garrisons with extraordinary success. The Japanese won battles but failed to conquer China. All they could do was to garrison the coastal ports, shutting China off from her friends, and fight to hold the few railroads and rivers leading into the remote interior. China, like Russia and the United States, is a country of continental size in which distance helps defeat the invader.

9

5. THE UNITED STATES OPPOSES JAPAN

In the ten years before Pearl Harbor, Japan had grossly violated treaties which she had made with other nations, including the United States. At the Washington Conference of 1922, following the First World War, all nations with interests and possessions in Asia or the Pacific Ocean had reached these agreements in an effort to stabilize and assure the peace of the Far East. In the Four Power Pact [*December 13, 1921*], Japan, Great Britain, France, and the United States promised to respect the island possessions which each had in the Pacific and not to extend their fortifications. This treaty Japan violated when she secretly built naval installations in the Marianas and Carolines and when, after the fall of France in 1940, her troops penetrated French Indo-China and seized Hainan and the Spratly Islands opposite the Philippines. The most important agreement concluded at Washington in 1922 was the Nine Power Treaty [*February 6, 1922*], in which all the Pacific Powers, including Japan, pledged themselves to respect the territorial integrity and administrative independence of China, and to keep an "Open Door" in China for the equal opportunity of all nations to trade there without monopolies, special privileges, or discriminatory tariffs. Japan broke this treaty by taking from China first Manchuria, then the Northern Provinces, and finally the eastern coast, and gradually closing the door to the trade of other nations in these regions. Finally, in resorting to force against China, Japan also violated the Pact of Paris, often called the Kellogg Pact, which almost all the nations of the world signed [*August 27, 1928*], agreeing to settle disputes by peaceful methods and to renounce war as an instrument of national policy.

The United States protested each time Japan ignored the pledges made in these three treaties. It tried to apply brakes to Japanese expansion in Asia at the expense of China. A strong China, independent and united, had always been the primary object of American policy in the Far East, because if other nations divided China, whether by annexations or by establishing spheres of influence, their imperial rivalries would lead to war. Since it was to the interest of every

10

American to live in a world at peace, the United States sought to preserve peace in the Far East. And there could be no better guarantee of peace, from the point of view of Americans, than to prevent any nation from attaining complete supremacy in either Asia or Europe.

This policy did not mean, however, that the United States was unalterably opposed to any change in Asia, but rather to arbitrary changes such as Japan made by force. In the past the United States had consented to a considerable increase of Japanese territory and power. When Japan annexed the Bonin Islands in 1876, Formosa and the Pescadores Islands in 1895 after a war with China, Korea in 1910, and the Marianas, Caroline, and Marshall Islands taken from Germany in the First World War, the United States had offered no objection. In all these years our Government never made any attempt to confine the Japanese people to their home islands. So far as the United States was concerned, Japan was free to grow and expand, but not by forcibly carving up China in utter disregard of all treaties made to keep the Far East at peace.

When, therefore, Japan occupied Chinese Manchuria in 1931, the American Secretary of State, Henry L. Stimson, refused to recognize such a change because it was accomplished by force in violation of both the Nine Power Treaty and the Kellogg Pact. His policy became known as the Stimson Doctrine of Non-Recognition. It was the stand taken by the United States toward most of the later conquests and annexations of territory which the Fascist nations achieved by military action. Japan was the first to expand by force, and since nothing was done to stop her, Italy and Germany realized that they could probably extend their empires in Africa and Europe with equal impunity. Hence the Manchurian crisis was the test of whether the march of Fascism could be halted short of war.

In 1931, however, the American people were neither willing nor prepared to curb Japanese aggression at the risk of war. Like all the peoples of Western Europe they were sunk in the depths of an economic depression, and consequently domestic problems of bread and butter weighed more heavily on their minds than the international question of keeping

11

the peace and helping to police the world. Japan, and later the other Fascist nations, took advantage not only of the preoccupation of each nation with its own economic problems but also of their failure to unite against aggression. The League of Nations, at the request of China, investigated the trouble in Manchuria and criticized Japan mildly in the Lytton Report, submitted in September 1932. The United States, although not a member of the League, cooperated in this investigation. Nevertheless, nothing was done, either by the League or by the United States, to compel Japan to change its course, observe treaties, consult with other nations, and expand only with their consent. When the small nations represented in the Assembly of the League passed a resolution condemning Japan and asking for the restoration of Chinese sovereignty in Manchuria [*February 24, 1933*], Japan withdrew from the League of Nations.

The Japanese did not pursue their policy of expansion alone. In an Anti-Comintern Pact [*November 25, 1936*] signed with Germany the two nations struck an alliance, ostensibly against the Communist International of Soviet Russia but actually against any nation which chose to resist their own expansion. Henceforth, like the two ends on a football team, Japan and Germany took turns in running around all opposition in Asia and Europe. Japan no longer disguised her ambition to dominate China, except by the fiction that the collaboration of both countries would be to their mutual benefit in the creation of a New Order in East Asia. Since "the epidemic of world lawlessness [was] spreading" with the use of force, President Roosevelt suggested in a speech at Chicago [*October 5, 1937*] that nations which were waging war should be quarantined by nations which desired to keep the peace. To this bold suggestion there was little response from either the American people or other nations. While Japan was fighting in China to obtain what it wanted, other nations were not ready to run the risk of war for the sake of peace.

Indeed, the fundamental policy of the United States throughout these troubled years was to stay clear of the disturbance and to preserve peace for itself. When the American gunboat *Panay,* on international patrol in China, moved up

12

the Yangtze River to relieve foreigners caught in the besieged city of Nanking, it was bombed and sunk by Japanese planes [*December 12, 1937*]. Japan immediately apologized and paid indemnities of two million dollars. The American people were chiefly disturbed because American lives and property had been exposed to hostile action. According to a poll of public opinion, in January 1938, seventy per cent of the people thought that all American forces should be withdrawn from China.

This was, however, the high tide of sentiment in favor of the United States' isolating itself from the rest of the world. As the war went on in China, the increasing Japanese brutality caused American public opinion to harden. It became evident that Japan and Germany would not halt their expansion if other nations did nothing to stop them. People awoke to the contradiction in our policy of protesting every act of Japanese aggression on the one hand, and on the other supplying Japan with the raw materials to make war. It was estimated that Japan imported nine-tenths of its scrap iron and copper, two-thirds of its oil, and a great deal of its aviation equipment from private sources in the United States. With growing public support for applying economic pressure to Japan, the American Government served notice [*July 26, 1939*] that the commercial treaty of 1911 would be abrogated. On the same day, when Congress granted the President authority, he put the export of oil and scrap iron under Government license and banned the shipment of aviation gasoline to Japan.

The economic support which the United States withdrew from Japan was extended on a growing scale to China. Credits first granted in 1933 and 1934 were renewed in 1938 for $25,000,000 and, with additional loans, reached a total of $170,000,000 by the end of 1940. Small as this aid was, it helped China to sustain its resistance to Japan. The Japanese countered American aid to China by entering a triple alliance with Germany and Italy [*September 27, 1940*], which pledged these countries to come to Japan's support if she were attacked.

As Germany overran Western Europe in 1940, conquering Holland and France and threatening England, Japan pre-

13

pared to move south from China to drive these nations out of their Asiatic colonies. The Japanese spoke no longer of a New Order in East Asia, limited to China, but of a "Greater East Asia Co-Prosperity Sphere" which would include French Indo-China, British Malaya and Burma, the Netherlands East Indies, and the Philippines. Foreign Minister Matsuoka declared that the "white race much cede Oceania to the Asiatics" [*February 25, 1941*]. To obtain freedom of action in Southeast Asia, Japan protected her rear, menaced by planes in Russian Siberia, by signing a pact of neutrality with Russia [*April 13, 1941*].

Then Japan applied increasing pressure to the French and Dutch colonies in Southeast Asia which had been orphaned by the German conquest of their mother contries. Bellicose demands were made on the Netherlands East Indies to sell Japan all their oil. But the United States, afraid lest the war should spread into the Pacific, took the pressure off the Dutch by continuing to supply the Japanese with petroleum products. Meanwhile, in the summer of 1940, Japanese troops entered French Indo-China and, with the acquiescence of the weak Vichy French Government, transformed this strategic region into a Japanese protectorate a year later.

In the face of this direct threat to the Philippines and Southeast Asia, which were outflanked by Japanese forces in Indo-China, the United States took all possible steps short of war to halt Japan. The assets with which she did business in the United States were frozen [*July 25, 1941*]; all her ships were barred from the Panama Canal; and the export of petroleum was severely restricted. Strategic raw materials were purchased from Latin America in order to prevent Japan from getting them. As a result of all these economic restrictions, Japanese war industries slowed down. Their steel production, for example, declined to the level of 1936, their copper supply was cut in half, and altogether about three-quarters of their vital American imports were cut off.

Japan appeared ready to compromise with the United States under this stringent economic pressure, but her diplomatic advances did not mean much. As far back as 1935, Saburo Kurusu of the Japanese Foreign Office told an American diplomat privately [*December 22, 1935*] that "Japan

14

. . . would in course of time be the 'boss' of a group comprising China, India, the Netherlands East Indies, etc.," and that Japan's signing of "treaties for collective security," such as the Kellogg-Briand Pact, was "hypocritical" [*September 12, 1940*]. As Ambassador Grew said of Japan later in a telegram from Tokyo, "the uses of diplomacy are bankrupt in dealing with such powers." Nevertheless, her Ambassador in Washington, Admiral Kichisaburo Nomura, began a long series of diplomatic talks with our Secretary of State, Cordell Hull, and was joined in November 1941, by a special envoy from Japan, Saburo Kurusu, the diplomat who had signed the Japanese alliance with Germany and Italy. In the light of what happened a month later, however, it was obvious that all these talks were but a diplomatic delaying action to screen Japanese preparations for the attack on Pearl Harbor.

The United States and Japan were unable to reach any compromise. The Japanese suggested in August 1941, that they would withdraw from French Indo-China if the United States would persuade China to accept peace terms agreeable to Japan. Secretary Hull refused to be a party to this dishonorable scheme. Finally, in November 1941, Japan submitted her final demands for peace: she would not advance south beyond Indo-China if the United States abandoned China to its fate, resumed trade with Japan, especially in oil, and helped her [*November 26, 1941*] obtain other raw materials. Secretary Hull's reply was a restatement of the conditions which the United States had always believed necessary to assure peace in the Far East: commercial relations would be resumed with Japan if she withdrew all her forces from both China and French Indo-China, joined in a non-aggression treaty to be signed by all the nations interested in the Pacific, and together with the United States abandoned all extraterritorial rights or claims in China. In other words, the United States promised Japan economic cooperation if she would withdraw from China and stop using force in the Far East.

The Japanese reply was delivered at Pearl Harbor. Twenty minutes after bombs began to fall on the American ships stationed there, the Japanese envoys in Washington called

15

upon Secretary Hull to tell him, not that war had begun but that negotiations were at an end. Reading the Japanese note, which alleged that the United States had opposed every attempt of Japan to bring "peace" to the Far East, Secretary Hull declared:

"In all my fifty years of public service I have never seen a document that was more crowded with infamous falsehoods and distortions—on a scale so huge that I never imagined until today that any Government on this planet was capable of uttering them."

PART TWO

ORIGINS OF THE SECOND
WORLD WAR

Americans who fought in Africa, Asia, Europe, and the Pacific knew that the war was a world war. It began long before the Japanese attack on Pearl Harbor. All great nations and most small nations became involved. After the First World War treaties of peace were signed, armies were demobilized, navies were limited, and the reconstruction of devastated lands was undertaken. Multitudes of people believed, or at least hoped, that wars were at an end. Now it is clear that the "peace" of Paris was only a truce, that the twenty years between wars were not really years of peace but years of unrest and of preparation for the new struggle.

Why men and nations fight is not our subject. Our task is to tell how the apparent peace of 1919 became open war. The questions which must be asked are general, dealing with problems too complex and too recent for easy or final solution. Many years must pass before the complete records of governments, statesmen, and generals, on both sides of the battle lines, will be available, before events can be seen in perspective and studied without prejudice. Yet what is happening today can be understood only in the light of what happened yesterday, so we must make what use we can of that part of the record which we now have. Though our knowledge is anything but complete, we nevertheless have to offer answers to the problems of today. These answers are general, relatively simple, and above all, tentative.

In the most general terms, the nations of the world were fighting to settle the differences which some were unwilling or unable to settle by peaceful means. It is possible to outline the sequence of events, from smaller frictions and resentments to larger disagreements, then to isolated acts of violence, and finally to open war. Our incomplete knowledge

17

and limited space do not permit a full and final account of events. We can tell here only the major causes of conflict and their stubborn growth until they led to a world at war.

6. WHY THE LAST WAR DID NOT END WAR

Our fathers fought Germany in the last war with high hopes, to which President Woodrow Wilson gave voice, that they were fighting to end all war and to make the world safe for Democracy. They defeated Germany but were disappointed in their hopes; we often say that they won the war but lost the peace. So deep was our disillusion that we hardly dared expect as much as our fathers. In fact, we seemed to mistrust their ideals and to look upon the war, in the words of President Roosevelt, as a "war of survival." Yet it has always been the faith of many Americans that the world could get rid of war and that a world of democratic nations would be a world at peace. They have been confirmed in this faith by their nation's experience, for Democracy works comparatively well in the United States; ever since the Civil War all the states of the Union have settled their disputes in peace. But Europe is not America, and a system which one nation has worked out slowly and sometimes painfully in the course of nearly two hundred years cannot suddenly be borrowed and operated successfully by other nations, especially when they have only begun to recover from an exhausting war.

The victors of the First World War wanted Democracy to flourish in Europe, but their first aim in writing the Treaty of Versailles was naturally to provide for their own immediate security. For this reason the United States, Great Britain, France, Italy, and Japan reduced the power of their chief enemy, Germany. She was disarmed, except for a force of 100,000 men; she lost her navy, her entire colonial empire, and about one-eighth of her territory in Europe. The Allies held Germany responsible for starting the war and for immense damage to Allied property. They charged her, therefore, with reparations amounting to thirty-three billion dollars, a bill which was later progressively reduced but on

18

which Germany never paid even as much as she borrowed from private banks in the United States. The terms of this peace were accepted under protest in June 1919, by a republican Germany which had overthrown the Hohenzollern monarchy of the Kaiser. The weakness of such a peace became apparent in its aftermath: the German people, beaten but not crushed, nursed a sense of grievance which was later exploited by Hitler. When he sought to evade and finally to undo the restrictions of the Treaty of Versailles, the former Allies of 1919 were unable or unwilling to enforce its terms by united military action.

Postwar German Democracy was born of military defeat and grew up, a friendless orphan, under the burdens imposed by the victors. In the early years, when the German Republic might have been strengthened by the cooperation of its former enemies, it received little international support. In 1923, for example, the French occupied the industrial Ruhr in a vain attempt to enforce the payment of reparations. From the beginning the German Republic lacked internal stability. The Prussian generals and land owners. a professional military caste, retained much power. Under their direction, every private in Germany's force of 100,000 was trained to become an officer of a larger future army necessary for a war of revenge. A disastrous inflation of the currency in 1923 almost wiped out the middle class and multiplied the number of discontented people who were ready to listen to Hitler when he preached aggressive nationalism as a cure for both foreign and domestic troubles. Germany, shorn of considerable power after the last war, was provoked by discontent at home to struggle again for compensation abroad.

The victorious Allies of 1919, having weakened Germany in the hope of making themselves secure, tried to organize peace in Europe on the basis of many small new states. The peacemakers believed, with President Wilson, that the best way to curb aggressive nationalism, which had plagued Europe over a century, was to give each people which considered itself a nation the right to self-government. In pursuit of this ideal of self-determination, they carved Finland, Estonia, Latvia, and Lithuania out of the old Russian Empire; put Poland together again from territory which Germany;

19

Austria, and Russia had taken; and split up the empire of Austria-Hungary, which had fought in alliance with Germany, into the independent states of Austria, Hungary, Czechoslovakia, and Yugoslavia. But the peoples of Europe, especially of central and eastern Europe, could not be divided along racial, linguistic, or national lines; in many geographic areas different peoples had been living for centuries side by side in the same towns and villages. Their national ambitions, sharpened by historic feuds, were not to be settled by increasing the number of nations. Even though some of the new states might contain only one nationality and might govern themselves in greater harmony than the empire they replaced, they were relatively small and incapable of self-defense against the larger nations. It was expected that France and the small countries would cooperate in holding Germany and a revolutionary Russia in check. When French power waned, however, all were at the mercy of their larger neighbors: Germany absorbed Austria and annexed Czechoslovakia; and Poland, which played Germany off against Russia, was eventually squeezed out of existence.

The survival of small nations actually depended upon a League of Nations, proposed by President Wilson, its principal architect, to allay the rivalry of the great powers and provide peaceful means for solving all disputes between nations. Economic and military sanctions, voted by the League, were to be used against any country which broke the peace. But the League was not a super-state; it reflected the distribution of power prevailing among its members and expressed the will of the strongest. Thus, in defiance of the League, Poland seized Vilna from Lithuania in 1920, and Italy bombed the Greek Island of Corfu in 1923. Although every state, strong or weak, was entitled to a voice in the Assembly, nothing important could be done without the assent of the Council, composed of the larger nations which had won the war.

The larger nations could not always agree. Italy, dissatisfied with the territorial settlement, left the peace conference and gradually swung over to the side of the defeated nations. Britain and France failed to see eye to eye on the severity with which Germany should be treated, France being anxious to keep her old enemy weak, and Britain preferring to restore German economic strength and to maintain a balance of power in the European continent.

The League was handicapped not only by the power politics of its members but by the fact that it never included all the nations. The United States refused to join; Germany was not admitted until 1926; and by the time Soviet Russia was allowed to join the League in 1934, Japan, Italy, and Germany had begun to withdraw. The great powers of the world preferred to go their own way rather than to settle disputes and enforce peace through the League of Nations.

7. NAVAL DISARMAMENT AND JAPANESE MILITARISM

Disarmament was one of President Wilson's Fourteen Points for establishing a just and lasting peace. Germany was partially disarmed, and the Treaty of Versailles assumed that the other nations would reduce their armaments. The weapons of war were thought to be a principal cause of war and not simply the means of waging it. Taxpayers everywhere, especially in the United States, resented the financial burden of building and maintaining fleets and armies.

The United States took the lead among nations in moving toward disarmament. It called a conference of the chief naval powers, whose representatives met at Washington in 1921-22 together with delegates from all countries with possessions in Asia and the Pacific. The reason they met was that naval disarmament could not be considered apart from the situation in the Far East, for there the potential rivalry of Japan, Great Britain, and the United States might lead to naval war. The United States was in a fortunate position, because it had built up its navy during the last war to a strength that approached those of the British and Japanese; and it had the economic resources to outbuild either of these nations if they would not agree to some limitation of ships. The

British had no quarrel with us and recognized that we were entitled to a battle fleet equal to their own. The Japanese, although ambitious to extend their power in China, were governed at this time by Liberals who stood ready to cooperate with the nations of the West.

Important treaties were signed at the Washington Conference for the joint purposes of limiting naval strength and assuring peace in the Pacific and Far East. Great Britain and the United States agreed to keep their navies equal, and Japan accepted a fleet inferior to both in the ratio of 5:3. France accepted a ratio of 1.75. No nation was to build any battleships for ten years. Japan, the United States, and Great Britain gave pledges not to strengthen their Pacific islands and bases. All these limitations proved to be a victory for Japan: although she had fewer capital ships, the nations which might oppose Japan were restrained at a time when they could easily have outbuilt her; and with the ban on the fortification of British and American bases in the Far East, Japan's smaller battle fleet, based on home ports, came into control of Far Eastern waters.

The leading naval powers were able to call a halt to their rivalry because the situation in the Pacific, where they all had interests, was stabilized by two treaties. The Anglo-Japanese Alliance was abandoned. This was followed by a Four-Power Pact under which those countries, together with the United States and France, agreed to respect one another's island possessions and to consult in case of trouble. This agreement was a recognition of Japanese rights, without defining them, in the German islands which she had taken in the Pacific during the last war. In return, Japan restored to China the former German properties in Shantung and entered a Nine-Power Pact, signed by all nations with possessions in the Far East, guaranteeing the independence and territorial integrity of China and an Open Door for equal trade. These three conditions promised to protect China from Japan and to give her opportunity to become a strong and united nation.

Japanese militarists were restive under the restrictions which they had accepted at the Washington Conference. They wanted a free hand in the Far East and power enough

22

to have their way in China. When Japan agreed with the United States and other naval powers at London in 1930 to limit cruisers and destroyers, in the inferior ratio of 10:7.5, jingoists in Tokyo assassinated Premier Hamaguchi for humiliating the nation. It was the first of many murders by which secret patriotic societies, all inspired by the militarists, got rid of those in office who opposed them.

Controlled more and more by the Army, the Japanese Government embarked on a program of territorial expansion, seizing Manchuria in 1931 to acquire an "economic life line," attacking China to obtain the benefit of her markets and resources, and finally invading Southeast Asia to gain all the riches of the Far East. In order to conquer these territories, Japan claimed naval equality with the United States and Great Britain, who refused to grant it. Japan then notified them, in 1934, that she would not renew the treaties for naval limitation.

Japan had now disregarded all the treaties negotiated at Washington and London to preserve peace in the Eastern Hemisphere. In order to acquire supremacy in the Far East, she secretly fortified her Pacific islands and built new aircraft carriers and battleships in the yards of the Inland Sea, closed to all foreign eyes after 1937. At the same time that Germany was rearming, Japan converted her industries to war production, and hastened to build a navy and equip an army capable of challenging both America and Britain.

The Japanese militarists, in alliance with the big business trusts which dominated the country, had come into their own. They had, in fact, always been strong in Japan. The Western nations made a mistake in thinking that the Japanese had Westernized all their institutions. The Government, for example, had the apparatus of a constitutional monarchy, and was actually modeled after the Prussia of Bismarck's day, but with three significant exceptions peculiar to Japan. The Emperor did not govern by consent of the governed, nor even by divine right, for he was himself worshipped as a descendant of the Sun Goddess, one who could do no wrong. The Constitution was a gift of the Japanese Emperor, who

23

remained above it and could alter it as he chose; it was neither framed nor won by the people in contest with their rulers as in the West. Actually, however, the Emperor did not conduct the business of government, which devolved upon elder statesmen, the Genro, and a Cabinet. In both these governing bodies the Army and Navy became supreme, because the constitution provided that no Cabinet, for example, could hold office unless the military services were represented by generals and admirals of their own choice. It was, therefore, a dual government in which the Army and Navy did what they wanted and the civilian Foreign Office tried to excuse their actions.

Not only in government, but in social and economic institutions, too, Japan has clung with one hand to her ancient ways and with the other grasped the Western technology of modern times to build up her industrial and military machine. This mixture of the old and the new, so well illustrated by the incongruity of houses and clothes derived from both the East and West, has created discords in Japanese political and social life. Instead of changing feudal institutions to allay economic discontent at home, the people have evaded the problem by increasing their power and wealth abroad. A poverty-stricken peasantry has been conscripted into the Army to conquer new resources for industries owned by a few families.

If Fascism, which can be variously defined, means among other things a military government in the interests of a minority who hold or seek economic power, then Japan was the original Fascist state. Its military government goes back to the twelfth century. All opposition to it in the present century has been suppressed by the transformation of Shinto, a state religion which sprang up long ago with the worship of nature gods, into a patriotic cult of Emperor-worship. In this religion the medieval sin of heresy becomes one with the modern crime of treason; the individual knows only one allegiance, the Emperor, and the citizen's chief reward is to be deified in the Yasukuni Shrine with all the fallen soldiers who have given up their lives for the glory of the Emperor and a truculent, imperialistic Japan.

24

8. RISE OF THE DICTATORS

Mussolini and Hitler were unscrupulous political agitators who rose to power by deception and violence. They appeared in countries where dissatisfaction with the existing weak Democratic governments was rife, and promised to solve social problems at home as well as to achieve national aspirations abroad. They attracted industrialists and landlords by opposing Communism, the unemployed by promising work for all. They organized private armies of the dissatisfied, the ambitious, and the violent. These armies they used to intimidate their opponents and the Government. Eventually each controlled a large political party and was appointed Prime Minister, but neither ever won an election until he was in control of the machinery of government and had the power to eliminate all opposition.

Once in office, they used the authority of government to destroy all rival political parties and to extend their own power until individuals, corporations and societies were reduced to virtual slavery and the state became a military tyranny, more complete and cruel than the past had ever known. Men found that they had lost their freedom to act, to speak their minds, even to think and live. This was Fascism, a system of government by force which could survive only by conquering and plundering other nations. For this purpose all the human and material resources of Italy and Germany were mobilized with the utmost efficiency. If we are to understand the origins of World War II we must begin with the first conquests of Hitler and Mussolini, their subjection of the Italian and German peoples to the bondage of Fascism.

The founder of Fascism was Benito Mussolini, the son of an Italian blacksmith. He was wounded as a corporal in the last war, and later became editor of a newspaper in Milan. Here [*March 23, 1919*] he organized a small political party with an extreme nationalist, anti-Communist program. The party recruited the discontented and violent, and by extravagant promises attracted many war veterans who were dissatisfied with the disturbed political and economic condition of Italy after the war. They wore black shirts as a uniform,

25

used the old Roman greeting of the upraised arm as a salute, and adopted for their badge the *fasces,* a bundle of rods with an axe, ancient Roman symbol for the power of the State.

One of the announced aims of the Fascists was a state powerful enough to maintain order. In the postwar depression, when Socialist strikers occupied factories in the north and the Government failed to restrain them, forty thousand Fascists marched on Rome [*October 28, 1922*]. Mussolini followed his cohorts by train and cajoled the King into appointing him Premier to restore law and order, which had in fact been disturbed as much by his Fascists as by the Communists. A year later Mussolini had consolidated his power sufficiently to decree that any party gaining one-fourth of the votes in the next election should have two-thirds of the seats in Parliament. By such mathematics the Fascists won control of the government in April 1924. When Blackshirts assassinated Giacomo Matteotti, leader of the Socialists [*June 10, 1924*], other parties joined the Socialists in a boycott of the Government, which Mussolini broke by arresting their leaders or driving them into exile. In 1926 he suppressed all political parties but his own and replaced the representative Parliament with a Fascist Grand Council composed of his puppets.

Thus Italy lost all the institutions of political democracy —the individual his civil liberties, the people their right to vote, hold elections, and to participate in a representative government even when opposed to it—and became a one-party state. This party, the *Fascisti,* whose membership reached only one million in 1927, was thereafter limited to boys growing up in the military youth organizations. A small minority of Italians, then, were Fascists, but only Fascists had the power to rule Italy. This power they lodged in the hands of Mussolini by taking an oath to obey him. He was *Duce* (Leader), and his dictatorship, enforced by secret police and the control of education and the press, was complete.

Mussolini set to work building up an army and navy to make Italy strong among the nations of the world. Her destiny, in his imagination, was to conquer an empire in Africa and in the Mediterranean that would revive the glory of Imperial Rome, and exploit, as Rome had done, the resources

26

of other lands to repair the weakness and poverty of Italy. For this imperialist adventure Mussolini prepared the Italian people by abolishing their liberties and regimenting their lives. To secure industrial efficiency, for example, he prohibited strikes and forced all employers and labor unions into Fascist-controlled Corporations. Italy became a Corporate State in theory, but actually it was a semi-military dictatorship with imperialistic ambitions.

Although Mussolini had declared that Fascism was "not for export," since it was exclusively Italian in its ardent patriotism, a similar movement developed in Germany after the last war. Its *Führer* (Leader), Adolf Hitler, proved to be abler and even more ambitious than Mussolini, more dangerous to the peace of the world because he gained control of Germany, a far larger and stronger state than Italy.

Born an Austrian, son of a customs officer, Hitler grew up as a failure, eking out his living by painting postcards in Vienna. During the last war he served as orderly and lance corporal on the Western Front until he was disabled by mustard gas. After the war the German Army hired him to spy on radicals in Munich, where he fell in with malcontents who, like him, were stung by Germany's defeat. They organized a nationalist party to agitate for a stronger and more united Germany. In 1923 they tried to overthrow the government of their state, Bavaria, by staging a revolution which came to nothing more than a street riot. Sentenced to five years in jail, Hitler was released after eight months by the intervention of friends in high places.

In jail Hitler wrote a book, *Mein Kampf* (My Battle), which became the textbook of his party, the National Socialists or Nazis, whose nationalism always overshadowed their socialism. Basic was their belief in a Master Race, the mythical "Aryans" which they considered best represented by the Nordic type of long-headed, blond Germans. This Master Race was threatened with destruction, according to Hitler, by a world-wide conspiracy of Jews either in the role of capitalists who impoverished the people or as German or Russian Communists who plotted revolution and war against the nation. Thus Hitler made the Jews the scapegoat for everything which troubled Germany and called for a relentless persecution to exterminate them.

He was equally vindictive in his attacks upon the nations which had defeated Germany in the last war. Two myths he persuaded many Germans, perhaps the majority, to believe: that their armies were not defeated on the field of battle in 1918, but suffered betrayal by a "stab in the back" from cowardly politicians at home; and that the Versailles Treaty, which the betrayers signed, was the severest peace ever dictated to a nation, reducing Germany to an ignominious position in Europe. Hitler proposed to break the fetters of the treaty, rearm Germany, crush France, and carve an empire out of Communist Russia. For this mission he demanded that the Nazis be made masters of Germany.

At first the Nazis won little support, never polling a million votes until the world-wide depression of 1930. Up to that time intelligent people had regarded Hitler as a demagogue, more ridiculous than dangerous, and deplored the strong-arm tactics of his Brown Shirts as gutter politics. Yet the SA (Storm Troopers), together with the SS (Elite Guard), constituted a private army with which Hitler intimidated his opponents and defied the Government. As economic conditions grew worse, the masses turned to the parties which promised the most drastic changes, the Communists and the Nazis; and these revolutionary parties created a stalemate in the Reichstag (Parliament) by their uncompromising opposition to the Government. In this crisis Marshal Hindenburg, hero of the last war, was reelected President over Hitler by a plurality of four million votes [*April 10, 1932*]. For all their violence, the Nazis were losing ground at the polls when powerful Rhineland industrialists came to Hitler's support to buy the protection of his party against the Communists. These manufacturers were joined by large landowners, the *Junkers,* whose estates in Prussia were threatened by agrarian reforms; and together the landowners and industrialists prevailed upon the aged Hindenburg to appoint Hitler as Chancellor of State [*January 30, 1933*].

Having gained his first public office, Hitler used it, as Mussolini had done, to make his power absolute. He first attempted to secure a mandate from the people by posing as

28

the man who had saved them from a Communist revolution. When the Reichstag building was burned, probably by Nazis themselves, Hitler charged the Communists with plotting against the Government, arrested their leaders, suspended the Constitution of the Republic, and decreed martial law [*February 28, 1933*]. Then he called an election [*March 5, 1933*] to take advantage of this "Red scare," but polled only forty-four per cent of the total vote. Since the people refused to make Hitler Dictator, he obtained the right to rule by personal decree from a Reichstag purged of Communists and beaten into submission [*March 23, 1933*].

With the aid of his secret political police, the *Gestapo*, Hitler consolidated his power. He dissolved all political parties but that of the Nazis [*March 1933*], suppressed the trade unions [*May 2, 1933*], and drove Jews from the civil services and professions and deprived them of citizenship, put education and local government under the Nazis, and subordinated the radical Storm Troopers to the Army by killing their leaders in a Blood Purge [*June 30, 1934*]. Germany became a land where people dared not oppose Hitler for fear of torture and the concentration camp. Not only were they ruled by force, but their whole economic life was reorganized to prepare the nation for war.

9. THE AXIS WAR OF NERVES

When Hitler came to power in 1933, eleven years after the advent of Mussolini, both Germany and Italy were too weak to risk war for the domination of Europe. Even when they combined their growing strength in the Rome-Berlin Axis [*October 25, 1936*], as Mussolini called his agreement to collaborate with Hitler, they were in danger of checkmate by Great Britain, France, and the Soviet Union, if these stronger nations acted together to defend the collective security of Europe. But the Axis divided them, claiming to be the champion of Western Europe against Communist Russia, and paralyzed their will to resist by preying upon the twin fears of another world war and of Communist revolution. In what came to be known as a "war of nerves," the Axis increased its power gradually, never striking directly at the larger nations but conquering or undermining, one by one, their smaller neighbors. Thus Germany and Italy recruited their military power, won strategic positions in Europe and Africa, and weakened their opponents abroad as they had done at home, until at last in 1939 they were strong enough to challenge the world in war.

The first barrier to aggression which Mussolini and Hitler attacked was the League of Nations. The success of Japan in conquering and keeping Manchuria, despite the condemnation of the League and the United States, was a lesson to dictators that they could take what they wanted by armed force. Hitler, failing to obtain the consent of other nations to German rearmament, followed Japan out of the League [October 14, 1933] and established military conscription in violation of the Versailles Treaty. The treaty army of 100,000 Germans was henceforth increased every year by 400,000 newly trained men, and in addition there were 2,000,000 Nazis who had some military training as party Storm Troops or Elite Guards. Upon this growing army Hitler based his aggressive diplomacy.

It was Mussolini, however, with an army already trained, who delivered the final blow to the League of Nations by conquering one of its member states, the independent African kingdom of Ethiopia. He made a border incident the excuse for an imperialistic war and refused to allow the League to settle the dispute peaceably. Half a million Fascist troops crushed the primitively armed tribes of Ethiopia with bombing planes and poison gas [October 2, 1935-May 9, 1936]. The small nations in the League, realizing that what happened to Ethiopia might also befall them, demanded that all the power of the League be used to stop Mussolini. Not only was Italy declared the aggressor in Ethiopia, but economic sanctions were invoked to halt the war [October 7, 1935]. The larger nations, however, failed to cut Italy off from such essential war supplies as iron, coal, and oil. France preferred to conciliate her neighbor, and Great Britain was afraid that Mussolini would make good his boastful threat of a naval war in the Mediterranean.

While these nations were embarrassed by the Ethiopian

crisis, German troops marched into the Rhineland [*March 7, 1936*], a region which had been demilitarized under the Locarno Pact signed by all the nations of Western Europe, including Germany [*November 16, 1925*]. French troops did not oppose the Germans in the Rhineland, as they might easily have done, because on this occasion Great Britain shrank from supporting any move toward war.

The German reoccupation of the Rhine, at a time when Italy was conquering Ethiopia, was the first of the double plays by which these nations, like Japan, scored off the other powers, a technique that became characteristic of Axis diplomacy. It was also the beginning of a disastrous policy of appeasement on the part of France and Great Britain, whose diplomacy became weak and divided as one or the other took the lead in making concessions to the Axis in the hope of avoiding war. Mussolini and Hitler fed their delusion that peace could be preserved by tolerating aggression. Each new move the dictators made they solemnly promised would be the last. While they talked of peace, however, they also shouted threats of war, and so formidable was their growing military power that other nations submitted.

The peace of Europe no longer depended on a concert of nations such as the League, but on the preponderance of military power which nations could establish by alliances. This the dictators understood. Italy left the League [*December 11, 1937*], following Germany, and then sought the alliance of Japan, the third outstanding aggressor. Germany took all Europe, Italy the Mediterranean, and Japan the Far East, for their prospective spheres of expansion. The Axis was now extended to Tokyo through the Anti-Comintern Pact, originally signed by Germany and Japan [*November 25, 1936*], and later indorsed by Italy [*November 6, 1937*], which was ostensibly aimed at the Communist International sponsored by the Soviet Union. Actually the pact had the effect of joining Germany, Japan, and Italy in an alliance stronger than any other existing alliance, and of dividing the nations of Europe by playing on their fear of Communism.

When Spanish Fascists under General Franco rebelled against the Republican Government, and civil war broke out in Spain, the Axis came to the aid of the rebels on the pretext

31

of suppressing Communism, although there were few Communists in Spain and the Government was not Communistic. In the course of two years Italy sent more than 100,000 troops to Franco's assistance, and Germany supplied him with tanks, artillery, aircraft, and the trained men of the Condor Legion. For the Axis, Spain was not only a potential ally, hemming in France on the south and threatening England at Gibraltar, but a testing ground for new weapons. To offset the help which the Axis gave Franco, the Soviet Union and France at first encouraged volunteers with arms and planes to go to the defense of the Republican Government. When it appeared that the Spanish Civil War might involve all Europe, because of the interference of other nations, Russia and France agreed to abstain from further intervention, and obtained a similar pledge from the Axis. Germany and Italy continued to support Franco, hardly troubling to conceal the travesty they were making of the non-intervention agreement. Meanwhile Great Britain and France accepted the delusion, believing that in doing so they were averting the greater evils of Communism in Spain and war in Europe. After two and a half years of bitter fighting in Spain, marked by the prolonged siege of Madrid and a final offensive against Barcelona, Franco won a complete victory [*April 4, 1939*] with the help of the Axis.

While Italy and Germany were having their way in Ethiopia, in the Rhineland, and in Spain, the United States was becoming as apprehensive of war as France and Great Britain were. Many Americans believed that it had been a mistake for the United States to enter the last war. This mood of disillusion grew out of a conviction that we were drawn into the last war solely because of our trade with the Allies and the sinking of our ships by German submarines. The prospect of another great conflict in Europe, and the desire to prevent a repetition of the circumstances which had involved us persuaded the United States Congress in 1934 and 1935 to pass so-called neutrality laws which put an embargo on the supply of credits or munitions to any belligerent nation, and prohibited American ships from venturing into war zones. These laws, renewed in 1937, were not relaxed until November 4, 1939, when the embargo on munitions was lifted to permit other nations to buy them on a "cash-and-carry" basis. To many Americans, the neutrality laws appeared to be the only way to stay out of war; but to the peoples of Europe and Asia they signified that the United States had retreated into complete isolation, preferring peace for America even if it meant the triumph of Fascism over the rest of the world.

The American Government, however, based its diplomacy from the summer of 1937 on the conviction that the joint ambitions of Germany and Japan were to conquer Europe and Asia. "Since August a year ago," the Secretary of State, Cordell Hull, told the Canadian Minister [*September 21, 1938*], "I have proceeded here on the theory that Japan definitely contemplates securing domination over as many hundreds of millions of people as possible in eastern Asia and gradually extending her control through the Pacific islands to the Dutch East Indies and elsewhere, thereby dominating in practical effect one-half of the world; and that she is seeking this objective by any and every kind of means; and . . . at the same time I have gone on the theory that Germany is equally bent on becoming the dominating colossus of continental Europe." Taking this point of view, the American Government was hampered by the neutrality laws. It "had to move," according to the State Department,"within the framework of a gradual evolution of public opinion in the United States away from the idea of isolation expressed in 'neutrality' legislation and toward realization that the Axis design was a plan of world conquest in which the United States was intended to be a certain, though perhaps ultimate, victim, and that our primary policy therefore must be defense against actual and mounting danger." The American people did not fully awaken to the need for defense until Hitler had conquered France; and in a democracy like the United States, the Government could move no faster than the people.

The growing military power of Hitler made him bold. He spoke no longer, as he had at first, of obtaining for Germany nothing more than a position of equality with the other nations of Europe. His ambitions now were to unify all Germans living in Austria, Czechoslovakia, and Poland, and to find for them what he called *Lebensraum* (living space) in other countries. To pave the way for the expansion of Germany, Hitler

33

inspired Nazi movements abroad in order to create dissension in foreign governments and eventually overthrow them under the pretext of rescuing his followers in those countries.

A Nazi party in Austria agitated for *Anschluss* (union with Germany) and the Austrian Government was too weak, after it suppressed the Socialists and lost the support of Italy, to resist Hitler. German troops invaded and annexed Austria [*March 12, 1938*]. Europe was stunned, but no country dared risk war to compel Germany's withdrawal. Hitler declared, as he had after the reoccupation of the Rhineland, that he had no further territorial ambitions in Europe.

The next country to fall prey to his tactics of fomenting disorder within its borders by the clamor of a native Nazi party, and then sending his army to occupy it, was Czechoslovakia. The Sudeten Germans on its strategic northern frontier at first demanded autonomy or home rule, but when the Czech Government granted this upon the mediation of Great Britain, the Sudeten Nazis cried out for annexation to Germany. As Hitler mobilized his forces, threatening war, Czechoslovakia stood fast with a strong army on its fortified frontier, depending for support on an alliance with France. The French called up reserves, and Great Britain warned Hitler that she would aid France if the latter went to the defense of Czechoslovakia. The Soviet Union, whose earlier proposal for consultation among the non-Axis powers to assure the collective security of all had been rejected by Great Britain, was joined to France and Czechoslovakia by mutual assistance pacts. In view of these pledges and understandings, all pivoting on Czechoslovakia, the European crisis in the summer of 1938 was the supreme test of the power of the Axis to break all opposition.

The opposition was weak, however, because neither Great Britain nor France was as well prepared for war as Germany, and the failure of France to implement its pact with the Soviet Union, as the latter had requested, made their alliance fragile. France leaned heavily upon Great Britain, whose Prime Minister, Neville Chamberlain flew twice to Germany to confer with Hitler in an effort to appease him. Both the British and the French exerted tremendous pressure upon Czechoslovakia to reach a settlement satisfactory to Ger-

34

many. Mussolini intervened at what appeared to be the last minute to arrange a conference at Munich [*September 29, 1938*], from which the Soviet Union and Czechoslovakia were excluded, and Hitler won the assent of Great Britain and France to his demands.

The triumph of the Axis at Munich saved the peace of Europe for the time being but made war inevitable. Not only was Czechoslovakia robbed of its strong defenses and exposed to the power of Germany, but all the smaller nations of Europe lost faith in their protective alliances with France. The only bulwark they had against the Axis, after the failure of the League of Nations, was gone. Even more disastrous to the peace of Europe was the fact that the Axis had divided its strongest opponents by the exclusion of the Soviet Union from the Munich Conference and the pact made there to guarantee the diminished borders of Czechoslovakia. The Russians looked with suspicion upon Franco-British appeasement of the Axis as deliberate encouragement of Germany to expand eastward. When Prime Minister Chamberlain returned from Munich with a gentlemen's agreement pledging Germany and Great Britain to consultation, the English people hoped that it would mean, as he said, "peace in our time," but the Russians wondered at whose expense.

Great Britain was soon disabused of its trust in Hitler when his troops in the following spring marched into Prague [*March 15, 1939*] and occupied all that was left of Czechoslovakia. It was evident that Hitler had only been appeased, not satisfied, at Munich.

Two weeks later, on April 7, 1939, in another Axis double play, Italy invaded and occupied Albania. Mussolini dared to attack his weak neighbor across the Adriatic because on January 30, 1939, Hitler had promised to support him if any other nation interfered. Of the nations conquered by the Axis, only Czechoslovakia had received so comprehensive a guarantee as Germany now gave Italy.

The destruction of Czechoslovakia wakened Great Britain and France to the insatiable ambitions of the Axis. They abandoned the policy of appeasement and sought desperately to establish a "Peace Front" of the smaller nations as a barrier to German expansion. Turkey, Greece, Rumania, and

35

Poland were promised armed support if the Axis attacked them [*April 6–13, 1939*]. Hitler singled out his next victim [*April 28, 1939*] by denouncing the non-aggression pact which he had made with Poland in 1934 and the naval treaty of 1935 with Britain, the new ally of Poland. Then he entered a full military alliance with Mussolini [*May 22, 1939*].

"With united strength to secure their *Lebensraum*," Italy demanded Corsica, Nice, Savoy, and Tunisia from France, and Germany called upon Poland to yield control of the Polish Corridor, only one-tenth of whose population was German, including the Free City of Danzig. The Poles had been willing to negotiate their differences with Germany, having profited from the partition of Czechoslovakia, until they realized that Hitler was playing the same game with them that had cost the Czechs their existence as a nation. Just as Hitler had protested violently about the outrages which he alleged the Czechs perpetrated upon Sudeten Germans, so now he stormed against the treatment which the Poles, acting in self-defense, were meting out to the Nazis in the Corridor.

The Anglo-French guarantee of military aid to Poland depended upon the cooperation of the Soviet Union, for only Russian troops could conceivably protect Poland against Germany. A Russian proposal, made in March, that all the nations of the Peace Front meet with the Soviets to organize their strength for collective security was rejected by Great Britain. All that Britain desired was consultation in case of attack. As Hitler threatened war on Poland, her new allies, Great Britain and France, made belated and half-hearted efforts to close the breach which Munich had opened between them and the Soviet Union [*August 10, 1939*]. But these dilatory attempts to reach a military understanding with the Russians came to nothing, because Poland had refused to admit Soviet troops, even in a war against Germany, and the Russians had insisted upon a guarantee of the Baltic border republics, Estonia, Latvia, and Lithuania, which Britain and France were loath to give. Mutual suspicions and recriminations, not only between the Russians and the western nations but also among the smaller eastern nations and their giant neighbor, prevented the formation of a common front against the Axis.

36

In August the Soviet Union suddenly abandoned its vain efforts to collaborate with other nations menaced by the Axis and went into isolation, preferring to assure its own safety rather than to risk the chance of becoming involved alone in a war with the Axis. Ever since Munich, the Russians had been afraid that Great Britain and France were seeking peace for themselves by encouraging Hitler to expand eastward. Now they turned the tables upon the western nations, making a trade agreement with Germany [*August 19, 1939*] followed by a nonaggression pact [*August 23, 1939*] which pledged both countries to settle all disputes for ten years by peaceful consultation. The Soviet Union made no alliance with the Germans, but its pact had much the same effect. It left Poland to the mercies of Hitler and assured him that the Russians would not join France and Great Britain, as in the last war, to fight Germany on two fronts. Hitler was free to act as he chose against the divided nations of Europe. Weak, and ill-prepared for war, they would fight back, but each for its own survival.

PART THREE

THE AXIS THREATENS AMERICA

10. HITLER CONQUERS EUROPE

In 1939 Hitler was ready to wage war for the conquest of Europe. The armed forces which he had always threatened to use in his war of nerves were made ready for a showdown in the year following Munich. He no longer resorted to a show of diplomacy. The ancient stratagem of "divide and rule" which had inspired his bargaining with the nations of Europe would now be tested on the battlefield. To conquer a united Europe was impossible. Even to fight on two fronts against a coalition of powers, as Germany learned in the last war, could be disastrous. But war on one front at a time promised the conquest of every country in its turn. Hitler's diplomatic policy in the years of peace had been to gain one objective at a time; now it was his military strategy in a war of conquest. Poland was the first victim.

I. BLITZKRIEG IN POLAND

German troops invaded Poland without a declaration of war [*September 1, 1939*]. The night before they marched, Hitler dropped any pretense of getting Danzig and the Polish Corridor by diplomacy. His "sixteen points" were broadcast for propaganda to the German, not the Polish people, as he ordered his armies to march. The two air fleets of Kesselring and Löhr delivered Hitler's ultimatum to the Polish people in the form of bombs. They struck at thirty-six towns in Poland, caught a small air force on the ground, cut all railroads, and crippled the mobilization of reserves.

Within sixteen days the Polish armies were completely broken, and in less than a month Poland was overrun by Nazis. This quick victory surprised the world, for the Polish Army was the fifth largest in all Europe. But it was not prepared to fight an enemy equipped with the tanks and planes of the Nazis. The Poles looked for rain, which never came, to bog down the tanks in mud, and depended on eight brigades of cavalry to stop fourteen mechanized divisions. Such forces as the Poles had, twenty-two divisions of infantry, they failed to concentrate, but spread them out along the frontiers which Germany enclosed on three sides.

German strategy was designed to annihilate the Polish forces in one decisive battle by a maneuver known as the double envelopment. It has been the aim of all strategists, but of none more than the German General Staff. In the Battle of Poland they applied it on a grand scale, not once but twice, and the second double envelopment trapped forces escaping the first. Bock's armies in the north, descending from East Prussia and striking across the Polish Corridor from Pomerania, joined with Rundstedt's armies from Silesia and Slovakia in the south to forge two rings of steel around Warsaw.

New weapons gave Germany the tactical power and speed to carry out this strategy. Planes and tanks supported the infantry in breaking through enemy lines and rolling up their flanks. Wherever Polish defenses were weak, Nazi infantry punched holes in them with tanks, then exploited by driving through and enveloping the flanks on either side of the gap. Stukas—dive-bombing planes—ranged the skies as a flying artillery; and fast-moving infantry, often motorized, swept forward as much as forty-five miles in a day. This was *Blitzkrieg*—lightning war. The internal-combustion engines, armor, and fire power of planes and tanks worked miracles until defense was improved to foil them.

The Battle of Poland first demonstrated the offensive power of the armored division which, with its supporting units, was an effective combination of tanks and motorized infantry. The Nazi panzer (armored) division of 14,000 men, 450 tanks, and 3,000 motorized vehicles was organized in three echelons. For reconnaissance there were a battalion of fifty armored cars and a company of motorcycle infantry. Two regiments of tanks made up the shock force. The ground-holding force comprised two regiments of motorized infantry, one of artillery, and engineer, signal, and antitank companies. The Germans did not rely so much on tanks in the battle of Poland as on the old horse drawn artillery and on infantry divisions whose fire power they increased tremendously with 442 machine guns, 135 mortars, 72 antitank guns, and 24 howitzers. It was the infantry, supported by tanks and planes, which won the Battle of Poland.

In this campaign Rundstedt's armies in the southwest delivered the main blow toward Warsaw. One of his armies, the Tenth under Reichenau, trapped sixty thousand Poles west of Radom, and penetrated with tanks to the outskirts of Warsaw in a week [*September 8, 1939*]. From the north the Third and Fourth Armies converged under Küchler and Kluge to cut off eighty thousand troops in the Polish Corridor and then swept forward to Warsaw.

Against these three drives the Poles fought in vain. Dive bombers broke up their retreat and prevented reserves from coming to their rescue. At Kutno over 170,000 soldiers of the Posen Army were encircled and captured [*September 15, 1939*]. The northern Nazi forces pierced the heart of the country when they crossed the Narew River near Modlin and swept behind Warsaw [*September 14, 1939*]. From Slovakia in the south, List's army enveloped the Polish industries of Silesia, taking care not to destroy war plants, and thrust out an arm to Lwow to shut off any escape into Rumania. Two nets were thus cast around Warsaw as Küchler's troops met Reichenau's tanks at Siedlce [*September 17, 1939*], and List's advance units farther southeast at Brest-Litovsk [*September 28, 1939*]. Although Warsaw did not surrender until large parts of the city were destroyed by bombardment, effective Polish resistance came to an end when the northern and southern German armies drew their nets tight around the capital and caught the remnants of the Polish armies.

Partition of Poland

Halfway through the Nazi campaign the Russian Army marched into Poland [*September 17, 1939*], without meeting any opposition to secure a strategic frontier against Germany. The Nazis agreed [*September 28, 1939*] to a new boundary between Russia and the territory they now dominated, the line flanking East Prussia and running south along the Bug River and west of Lwow to include eastern Galicia. Except for strategic salients this frontier followed the Curzon Line proposed in 1919 by the Allies on ethnic grounds. Although a majority of the inhabitants in the area taken over by

40

Russia were White Russians, Ukrainians, and members of smaller non-Polish groups, Poland did not accept the Curzon Line, and in a war against the Soviet Union in 1920 had regained much of the territory now taken once more by Russia. When Russian plebiscites showed a majority of voters in favor of annexation [*November 3, 1939*], eastern Poland with a population of twelve million was incorporated into the Soviet Union, providing it with a buffer zone of defense and setting a limit to Nazi expansion eastward.

Hitler had his triumph in Warsaw [*October 5, 1939*]. He added western Poland, with a population of ten million to Germany and assumed a "protectorate" over central Poland, to which all Poles and Jews in the west were to be transferred. Here the Poles were reduced to slavery, and the Polish Jews were confined to ghettos and gradually exterminated. In the course of the next two years over a million Poles were forced to work in Germany. The Polish Government fled to Rumania, and finally to London, where several thousand Polish soldiers and fliers were to carry on the war from England. A strong Underground movement developed in Poland which the Nazis were unable to crush even by torture and mass murder.

Sitzkrieg

When Germany attacked Poland, Great Britain and France declared war [*September 3, 1939*], fulfilling their pledge to defend Polish independence. They took up the fight against what Prime Minister Chamberlain called the "evil things" of Fascism. But they were not ready to give Poland effective help. France mobilized fortress troops in the Maginot Line, pushed forward patrols, made a limited attack on the Saar Basin, and spent the winter in a vain attempt to produce planes and tanks for her badly equipped armies. No offensive was launched on a second front to relieve Poland.

Nor was Great Britain able to rally as quickly as in the last war. A month went by before a small expeditionary force took up defensive positions in France. There was almost no aerial bombing of Germany, perhaps for fear of reprisals, since the Nazis boasted many more bombers than the Allies. Both France and England thought of war as passive self-defense

41

and neither nation was mobilized to take the offensive. They established a naval blockade to starve Germany out, as they had done in the last war, while they tried to produce enough tanks and planes to meet Hitler whenever he should choose to attack them.

Cynics accused England and France of opposing *blitzkrieg* with *sitzkrieg*, a sitting war, and some Americans called it a "phony war" because there were no major actions through the winter of 1939-40. The critics overlooked the fact, however, that Great Britain and France had declared war on Hitler, refused his offer of peace after Poland was conquered [*October 12, 1939*], and insisted that the war must go on until both Czechoslovakia and Poland were set free. There was to be no more appeasement. Hitler had conquered Poland; but he could not keep his spoils without conquering France and Great Britain too.

II. INVASION OF DENMARK AND NORWAY

Denmark and Norway remained neutral through the last war, but now their geographic position to the north of Germany robbed them of peace in this great struggle. Because these countries outflanked Germany, it was essential for the Allies to prevent German use of them, and mines were finally laid off the Norwegian coast by the British Navy [*April 8, 1940*]. This coast offered Germany an extended maritime front from which to attack Britain with planes and U-boats, and the ice-free port of Narvik in the north was an outlet for the Swedish iron ore so necessary to German war industries. Hence the Nazis occupied Norway [*April 9, 1940*]. They also turned on Denmark because it lay in their path and bordered the waters of the Skagerrak and Kattegat controlling the sea routes to the Baltic, Sweden, and the northeast coast of Germany.

The Nazi conquest of these maritime countries called for tactics different from those of the Polish campaign. Since airplanes could span both sea and land, the Nazis oriented their strategy to the air, seized airfields, and brought in mortar and machine-gun troops by plane. In this daring operation Nazi airborne infantry and parachute battalions weathered their first test. Although the Germans commanded

42

the air, they did not rule the seas. To prevent a superior British Navy from carrying out the expectation of every Englishman and making Norwegian and Danish waters impassable, the Nazis mined the Kattegat, patrolled the North Sea with submarines in force, and drove off hostile warships with land-based bombers. It was the first campaign of the war in which air power successfully challenged sea power and proved that aerial cover was essential to ships operating in coastal waters.

What startled Norway and the whole world was not only the Nazi invasion, but the tactics by which a "fifth column" made it a success. The name had been coined by Franco's General Mola in the Spanish Civil War when he boasted that the four Fascist columns advancing on Madrid would be helped by a fifth column of sympathizers within the Loyalist capital. In Norway the Nazis recruited a powerful fifth column among discontented natives and German residents. Chief was Major Vidkun Quisling, leader of a small Nazi party, whose name became the epithet for traitorous leaders in every land. Once the invasion of Norway began, the fifth column seized radio and telephone communications to send counterfeit orders which confused the small army of defenders, paralyzed mobilization, and directed forts and ships to surrender.

Nazi Invasion

German forces under General Nikolaus von Falkenhorst seized both Denmark and Norway at once [*April 9, 1940*]. For the amphibious tactics required by this operation reserve divisions had been carefully rehearsed during the winter in East Prussia. They overran Denmark in a day. The country could offer no resistance with a land frontier open only to Germany, a population of scarcely four million, and a weak militia. Naval landings took place at Copenhagen and Middelfart [*April 9–11, 1940*]. From these ports and the airfield at Aalborg reinforcements flowed north to Norway.

The Nazis caught three million Norwegians off guard. Their little army of 114,000 men was never wholly mobilized, and the six divisions which took the field were confused and unprepared. Oslo, the capital city commanding a strategic

43

fjord, woke up on the morning of invasion to find its two airfields in the hands of the German agents, with transport planes already landing an infantry force of three thousand men, and its coastal batteries under fire from Nazi warships. The powerful guns at Fort Oskarsborg, were supposed to have been spiked by fifth columnists, but they sank the heavy German cruiser *Blücher,* and a Norwegian minelayer crippled the *Emden* before fifth column signals stopped their fire. From Oslo three divisions of German infantry fanned out in spearheads to occupy southern Norway, make contact with forces holding western ports, and strike the rear of such Norwegian troops as gathered in the mountains to the north. Oslofjord was soon won [*April 15, 1940*] and the first Norwegian division to muster its forces was threatened with a double envelopment as it retreated eastward into Sweden.

At the start of the invasion, amphibious units also landed at the secondary ports of Kristiansand on the Skagerrak, and at Bergen, Trondheim, and Narvik on the Atlantic coast [*April 9, 1940*]. The North Sea port of Stavanger fell to five thousand airborne infantry. Serious resistance was met only at Kristiansand, where a fort battery sank the cruiser *Karlsruhe.* In one day the Germans had seized Norway's principal harbors and—like a spider spinning its web—connected these ports and strengthened their lines with airborne reinforcements and supplies.

British Counterattacks

The British Navy had failed to forestall the invasion of Norway. Allied troops tried too late to undo it. Trondheim, center of a railway network extending across the mountains to Sweden, was the objective of an expeditionary force of about thirty thousand men. They landed at Namsos and Andalsnes [*April 14–20, 1940*], one hundred miles north and south of the city, with heavy losses from German bombers. It was an ill-fated expedition, lacking both air cover and antiaircraft artillery, and its supply bases like its advance columns were always under bombardment by the Luftwaffe. As the Allies moved inland to Dombaas, German troops struck at them from three directions [*April 30, 1940*], out of Trond-

44

heim, up the valleys from Oslo, and in a surprise flanking blow through the mountain passes in the east. Norwegian divisions were cut off one by one [*May 1–2, 1940*] as the Allies fell back from Dombaas to Stören and evacuated Namsos and Andalsnes under furious bombing.

The last desperate effort of the British in Norway was to take and to hold the iron port of Narvik in the north, which had been captured the first morning of the invasion by nine German destroyers and occupied by infantry smuggled aboard a freighter. Five British destroyers stormed the port next day and two were lost. The battleship *Warspite* led nine destroyers back to avenge their loss and sank all the German craft [*April 13, 1940*]. Then British troops landed south and north of Narvik but could not maneuver in deep snow against German units reinforced by air from Trondheim [*May 27–28, 1940*]. Another British landing nearer Narvik secured the port for a brief spell until German planes based on Trondheim compelled the British to abandon [*June 8–9, 1940*] this beleaguered spot, taking with them the King and Crown Prince of Norway. Nazi occupation of the country was complete [*June 10, 1940*], and Great Britain was outflanked in the north.

"Blood, toil, tears, and sweat"

Hitler did not conquer Norway without losses. German casualties were slight, running from 35,000 to 55,000. But the Navy suffered severely on convoy duty, with the sinking of one heavy and two light cruisers, eleven destroyers, and six submarines. Germany's naval force never had been adequate for fleet action, as in the last war, but now it was weaker than ever. At least nine-tenths of the Norwegian merchant marine escaped Hitler's clutches. When he invaded their ports, everyone of the 1,024 ships at sea obeyed their Government's orders to put in at British ports, where they later became a valuable addition to Allied supply convoys, some two hundred Norse tankers carrying two-fifths of the gasoline which the Royal Air Force consumed in the Battle of Britain. The most ominous misfortune which befell Hitler as a result of his success in Norway was that the British lion was aroused. Neville Chamberlain, the Prime

45

Minister who failed to secure "peace in our time" at Munich, gave way to Winston Churchill, First Lord of the Admiralty [*May 10, 1940*], and to a coalition cabinet of war-minded Conservatives, Liberals, and Laborites. All that Churchill could promise his countrymen was "blood, toil, tears, and sweat." "Our only aim is victory," he said, "for without victory there is no survival" [*May 13, 1940*].

III. FALL OF FRANCE AND THE LOW COUNTRIES

Great Britain and France were not yet ready to fight when Hitler's armies turned west to crush them [*May 10, 1940*]. Nazi forces swept across the borders of Holland, Belgium, and the little state of Luxembourg on a swift drive into France which brought them complete victory in one month. This campaign, Hitler told his troops, was to "decide the fate of the German nation for the next thousand years." He swore vengeance for the defeat Germany had suffered in the last war. The hereditary enemy, France, was to be destroyed. The Nazis planned to repeat the victory won in the Franco-Prussian War, but on a far grander scale with the conquest of both France and England. Then Germany would be supreme in Europe. This was Hitler's ambition in 1940.

Weakness of France

To achieve it the Nazis had mobilized an overwhelming force. Between six and seven million Germans were organized in 240 divisions, of which at least twelve were armored and the rest were infantry and artillery. The Luftwaffe boasted about nine thousand combat planes. French Intelligence estimated that of this huge army more than a hundred infantry divisions, all tank units, and two air fleets with an array of 1,500 fighters and 3,500 bombers were massed on the Western Front.

To oppose them the French had mobilized ninety-five divisions. About one-third of these units were made up of older reserves with only a year of training; thirteen divisions garrisoned the Maginot Line, and three were armored with 480 tanks, little more than the strength of one panzer division. Other battalions had light tanks left over from the

46

last war. The French Air Force in action did not exceed one thousand planes. Ground units had no antitank and not enough antiaircraft guns. The allies of France were even less prepared. Britain had sent to France an expeditionary force of thirteen divisions, with three still in training, seven regiments and two battalions of light tanks, and air squadrons of about seven hundred planes. The Belgian Army, poorly trained and badly equipped, was organized in twenty-one regular divisions with twelve of them along the fortified Albert Canal. The Dutch Army enrolled 400,000 men on paper, but had no machines with which to fight a mechanized war.

It was not only this lack of planes, tanks, and guns which made France weak. The French did not even concentrate all their force and matériel against Germany. They kept many of their best troops in Syria and Africa, nearly half of their planes on the border of Italy in fear of an attack from the Italians, and dispersed tanks and planes alike in "little packages" among their divisions.

What led the French to defeat was their strategy, leadership, and internal class strife. They had lost the offensive spirit which saved them in the last war. Their strategy was to hold the Maginot forts and to fight a long war of position on a continuous front, with massed infantry for defense, until attrition should sap the strength of the enemy. Military leadership suffered from the "Maginot mentality"; the fate of France was staked on the forts, which had been built at a cost of two million dollars a mile, with their big guns pointing east. Premier Daladier, General Gamelin, Marshal Pétain, like the people whom they led, were tired victors who wished only to keep what France had and to be left alone in peace.

French patriotism was so paralyzed by class hatred that some leaders of business and politics thought of their pocketbooks before their country. There was a fifth column in places of power: men who preferred to collaborate with Hitler, or even to have him rule France, in order to avoid the Communism which they feared would be the result of Labor gains like the forty-hour week. France was weak on the field of battle because it was so badly divided and poorly led at home.

Nazi Strategy and Tactics

German strategy, true to the teachings of Clausewitz, did not aim to capture Paris but to annihilate the opposing armies. This same attempt had been made in 1914 under the Schlieffen Plan of outflanking the French Army through Belgium. In 1940, however, with an extension of the Maginot Line reaching the sea, France could be outflanked only through Switzerland, too limited and mountainous a terrain for maneuver. Hence the Germans decided upon a strategic penetration of the center to expose flanks which could be enveloped. Such attacks had bogged down in the last war because infantry lacked the speed to exploit a breakthrough before it was closed with defensive reserves. But the strength of defense to obstruct maneuver had been broken in Poland. There heavier mortars and howitzers had demonstrated how they could increase the offensive fire power of infantry, while tanks gave them mobile support or with dive bombers made up a flying wedge, the armored spearhead.

With the tactics made possible by these weapons the Germans chose to surprise the French at the weakest point of their fortifications. This was at the hinge of the Maginot Line in the Ardennes Forest along the Meuse River, where the main works ended and lighter defenses ran northwest to the sea between France and Belgium. The Nazis knew that if they penetrated French defenses at this point and pressed forward to the Channel coast, they could drive between the Allied forces which moved north to hold Belgium and those which remained in France, and hence open the flanks of both to envelopment. After the destruction of the Allied forces in Belgium, the Germans could swing south on either side of Paris, overrun the west, and take the Maginot Line in the rear. In support of this plan the Netherlands were to be occupied, to prevent British landings and counterattacks on the Ruhr, and Belgium was to be invaded to draw the Allies north to its aid. As Hitler explained the strategy of his generals, in July 1940, after it had proved successful: "I feinted to the north and moved my main

48

mass against the left wing in contrast to the Schlieffen Plan [which moved by the right wing in 1914]. The feint succeeded."

Fall of Holland and Belgium

The German feint was the more effective because the defensive plans of France and England changed often during the year of stalemated action, and never really covered the exposed flank of Belgium and the Netherlands. These small nations remained aloof from friend and foe, hugging the illusion that neutrality would preserve them. When they found themselves outflanked by the Nazi occupation of Norway and Denmark, it was too late to close the natural corridor which their lowlands opened to a German attack on France and England. When it came, British and French forces moved north to fight a delaying action in the Netherlands and to strengthen the strong Belgian defenses along the Albert Canal. But they moved too late and with too little.

In the first week of invasion [May 10–16, 1940] the Nazis compelled the Dutch to surrender and drove the Belgians from the Albert Canal. Parachute troops seized Dutch airfields, bridges, and highways, and with reinforcements of airborne infantry secured the bridges over which German motorized troops quickly reached Rotterdam. This port was almost destroyed [May 14, 1940] by Nazi bombers to terrorize the Government and people into surrender. Utrecht, The Hague, and Amsterdam were threatened with destruction from the air. Resistance became hopeless and the Dutch surrendered [May 16, 1940].

In Belgium, where many bridges remained undemolished, the Germans reached the Albert Canal in two days [May 11, 1940] and captured its chief strongpoint, Fort Eben Emael, by investing it with parachutists while specially trained engineers made a frontal assault with explosives and flamethrowers. As the Nazis threw bridgeheads across the Albert Canal, the Belgians retired to stand with British and French forces on the main defense line of the Dyle River. Their situation soon became desperate, however, because of the German breakthrough to the south.

49

There, in France, was the crucial attack. Kleist's armored divisions had crossed Luxembourg and southern Belgium [*May 10–11, 1940*] through the dense Ardennes Forest under orders that "this side of the Meuse River there can be no rest or halt for a man of this column." They turned back mechanized French cavalry which was advancing to cover General Corap's Ninth Army as it pivoted north of Sedan to swing eastward and defend the Meuse. This French maneuver was forestalled by a surprising onrush of German tanks. A division under Rommel crossed the Meuse at Houx in the north [*May 13, 1940*] with tank fire to support infantry, and drove a wedge between the French First and Ninth Armies. The same day, south at Sedan, hundreds of dive bombers blasted a bridgehead across the river for Guderian's tanks which raced between the Ninth and Second Armies and crossed the Ardennes Canal before its bridges could be destroyed [*May 14, 1940*]. Other tank units under Reinhardt jumped the Meuse farther north at Montherme and cut up the whole defensive sector of Corap's isolated Ninth Army. There was a gap fifty miles wide in the French lines which List's infantry occupied [*May 16, 1940*] as it came forward at the rate of thirty miles a day with 45,000 vehicles in its columns. The French committed their reserves all too slowly in a belated counterattack to unite their First and Second Armies.

Meanwhile Nazi armored spearheads drove toward the English Channel in two columns, one up the valley of the Somme, the other along a northern ridge, both following good highways. In eleven days these tanks raced 220 miles through the enemy's rear to the English Channel [*May 21, 1940*]. Motorized infantry followed the tanks to protect their southern flank, and Rundstedt's main infantry force marched up the panzer corridor which now divided the combined British and Belgian armies from the bewildered French.

General Weygand, who replaced Gamelin in command [*May 19, 1940*], sought to reunite these armies by joint counterattacks from north and south upon the German corridor. But in France the Nazis could not even be dislodged from their bridgeheads on the Somme [*May 29, 1940*], and in Belgium the British were hard pressed on both flanks. So the French tried to improvise a defense in depth, the Weygand Line, with strongpoints where 75 mm. field guns were sited for point-blank fire against tanks.

Evacuation of Dunkirk

In Belgium the British Expeditionary Force could not hold a defensive triangle based on the Channel against Nazi tanks and planes. Belgians on the left flank abandoned Antwerp [*May 18, 1940*] and defensive lines were drawn back from the Dyle River to the Scheldt (Escaut). The British Cabinet ordered withdrawal southward to join the French armies, but the German corridor cut off this escape. Since counterattacks failed to close the gap, the British retreated west to the Lys River [*May 21, 1940*]. When the Channel ports of Boulogne and Calais fell into enemy hands, only Dunkirk was left for a base [*May 22, 1940*]. The Belgians were driven northwest to expose the flank joining the British at Ypres, and there were no reserves to cover it. In this plight the King of the Belgians surrendered his Army [*May 27, 1940*]. Unless the British were to be annihilated, they had no choice but to leave the continent of Europe.

Then began the last retreat to the beaches around Dunkirk [*May 28, 1940*], a race against time. The difficulty of this operation was increased by streams of civilian refugees who crowded the roads and became panic-stricken under the strafing of Stukas. The threats of German tanks at Nieuport to cut off the retreat hurried the withdrawal. R.A.F. fighters from England soon raised an umbrella over the beaches, and No. 11 Fighter Group shot down 603 German planes with a loss of but 130. In the dark hours of five nights [*May 29–June 2, 1940*], 224,585 British and 112,-546 French and Belgian soldiers were evacuated to England. The Royal Navy commanded their rescue, but hundreds of small boats which could run close in shore did the work. Thirty thousand British troops were lost in the whole campaign, and after six days of evacuation not a man was left on the beaches. Then the RAF gave up the skies to the Germans. The Battle of Flanders was lost, and the Nazis were free to swing their forces southward to destroy the French.

Battle of France

Only thirty-seven divisions remained on the Weygand Line to defend France, and the Germans needed but forty to crush them. "The French front consisted," as Weygand later said, "of a line of troops without depth or organization." Bock's armies started the attack [*June 5, 1940*] in a secondary sweep designed to close the French coast to British aid. An armored division crossed the Somme and quickly struck westward to encircle the French Tenth Army [*June 9, 1940*]. Above Paris the Seventh was forced to retreat southeast to the Oise, which in turn required the Sixth on its right to fall back. The main German attack [*June 9, 1940*] across the Oise east of Paris was made by infantry which established a bridgehead for tanks to fan out and push the defenders back to the Marne. The rapid development of these attacks disorganized the French armies. With their communications gone they lost all power to resist. The defenses of Paris were abandoned; it was declared an open city to escape bombardment, and was finally occupied by Nazis [*June 12–14, 1940*].

The Germans did not halt their swift and thorough pursuit. While Leeb's armies made holding attacks in front of the Maginot Line, the main German forces attacked it from the rear, pushing forward to Belfort [*June 17, 1940*]. This envelopment, together with a frontal penetration from Colmar, divided the French forces in the east and trapped them in two pockets behind the Maginot Line. Retreating columns in western France were overwhelmed by armored Nazi forces which fanned out to Cherbourg and Brest. French divisions in the center were pursued south of the Loire as their ranks melted away [*June 25, 1940*]. "Generals are commanding battalions," Premier Reynaud wrote President Roosevelt when Paris fell; many of these battalions fought doggedly to the last. There was no organized rear-guard action; for the moment France was stunned by the disaster. Soon, however, bands of patriots began to wage guerrilla war and the Underground movement was born. In the African colonies were many Frenchmen who never admitted defeat and carried on the fight.

Italy Enters the War

"The hand that held the dagger has struck it into the back of its neighbor," was President Roosevelt's description of Italy's coming into the war [*June 10, 1940*]. Not until France was staggering to its fall did Mussolini leap to the kill. Then his Alpine troops had so much trouble penetrating a few miles into France that it was evident he wanted the spoils of victory without fighting for them. Upon the outbreak of war in Poland, Italy had declared itself non-belligerent, not neutral, for it was free to choose its role by a secret provision in the pact with Germany which pledged both countries to avoid war for three years (1939–1942). During these years Mussolini expected to force France by diplomacy to give up Tunisia, Corsica, Nice, and Savoy. Hitler called the game off by plunging into war. Until the fall of France the Italian peninsula served him as a loophole in the Allied blockade. Italy entered the war too late to get anything from France except demilitarized zones between the French and Italian border and between Libya and Tunisia. But the war was extended to the Mediterranean and Africa as the Italian Army and Navy joined the victorious Germans. Great Britain rather than France stood the brunt of the Axis attack southward.

The French Surrender

When the French armies were routed on the field of battle, the French Government lost the will to resist and surrendered. It was a political as well as a military collapse. At Tours, where the French Cabinet sought refuge after leaving Paris, Premier Raynaud asked Churchill [*June 11, 1940*] to release France from a joint pledge never to seek separate peace except by mutual consent. Churchill refused, and the English Government declared for itself that the war would go on. Reynaud tried to buoy up his faint-hearted colleagues by an appeal to President Roosevelt [*June 13, 1940*] to send "clouds of war planes . . . to crush the evil force that dominates Europe." The President promised aid "so long

53

as the Allied Governments continue to resist" *[June 15, 1940]*, but pointed out that only Congress could make military commitments.

England finally consented *[June 16, 1940]* to France's making peace provided that the French Navy was ordered to British ports. Churchill urged that France should join with Britain to carry on the war from Africa in a political union with one war cabinet, associated parliaments, and common citizenship, a pooling of resources, manpower, and colonies which might have made the two nations one and given them the strength to oppose Hitler. The French Cabinet, however, voted thirteen to eleven for an armistice with Germany. Reynaud resigned and President Lebrun asked Marshal Pétain to form a new cabinet. The old Marshal, a defeatist like General Weygand, at once sued Hitler for peace *[June 17, 1940]*.

In the railway carriage at Compiègne, where Marshal Foch granted Germany an armistice in 1918, Hitler had his revenge *[June 21, 1940]*. France was divided, and the rich industrial north, over three-fifths of the country, was occupied by the Nazis. The French were charged with the costs of occupation at the rate of twenty million marks, or eight million dollars a day. French prisoners of war remained in Germany, hostages of Hitler, and the French Navy was disarmed with the assurance that neither Germany nor Italy would use it themselves.

Marshal Pétain became Chief of State *[June 12, 1940]* over what was left of France, the unoccupied south; and a rump session of the Parliament voted him full power to make a new constitution. He abolished the political system of the Third Republic, established in 1871, suppressed all political parties and trade unions, and tried to wipe out the memory of the French Revolution of 1789, exhorting his countrymen to take Work, Family, and Fatherland as their watchwords instead of Liberty, Equality, and Fraternity. If the government at Vichy was not Fascist, at least it must collaborate with Fascism, for there was no longer any power left Frenchmen to resist Hitler. General Charles de Gaulle escaped to London and raised the Cross of Lorraine as a

54

standard around which Frenchmen in the colonies and Underground patriots in France could rally.

IV. BATTLE OF BRITAIN

Back in the dark days of Dunkirk, the British people had resolved to die on their feet rather than live on their knees. "We shall defend our Island, whatever the cost may be," declared Prime Minister Churchill [*June 4, 1940*]. "We shall fight on the beaches, we shall fight on the landing grounds, we shall fight in the fields and in the streets, we shall fight in the hills; we shall never surrender, and even if, which I do not for a moment believe, this Island or a large part of it were subjugated and starving, then our Empire beyond the seas, armed and guarded by the British Fleet, would carry on the struggle, until, in God's good time, the New World, with all its power and might, steps forth to the rescue and liberation of the Old." Americans took comfort from this declaration that if worse came to worst, the Royal Navy would move to their side of the Atlantic, although they saw no need to rally to Churchill's summons to cross the ocean and free Europe.

Why Hitler never put Churchill's brave words to the test when England was least prepared is a mystery. It was an opportunity which once lost was never to be recovered. Perhaps he expected England to surrender like France; possibly he had counted on annihilating the Allied forces at Dunkirk; certainly his timetable of conquest did not allow for immediate invasion.

In any case Hitler prepared to conquer his last enemy, who, with the surrender of France, now stood alone. Only the Royal Navy and Air Force guarded Britain's shores. An army of nine divisions but none of their weapons had been saved at Dunkirk, and a month passed before they could be reorganized for the defense of the British Isles. To help arm this force anew, the United States sold Britain what weapons could be spared from the stock piles of the last war: old Enfield rifles, Browning machine guns, and 75-mm. field artillery. In all of Britain there were less than one hundred tanks.

Against such arms it was apparent in the summer of 1940 that Hitler could invade England. The divisions he had used in Norway were trained to amphibious assault. He lacked sea power but he had planes to transport troops. From the inland canals of Europe he brought over three thousand barges to the coastal ports between Rotterdam and Cherbourg, where they became the summer targets for English bombers. The Nazis built bases for their bombers in France and the Low Countries, and set out to win full command of the air and temporary command of the sea, to cover the crossing of their troops. This vain attempt to conquer the English skies was the Battle of Britain, the first battle that Hitler lost. It was an action traced by the white vapor trails which earthbound people saw four and five miles up in the sky as hundreds of planes, often invisible, fought at the furious speed of five miles a minute. The battle area, limited by the range of Nazi fighters escorting their bombers, extended from Hull and the Humber across to Bristol and the Severn. Never had there been so great a struggle in the air to decide the fate of any land.

The Battle of Britain fell into four phases. In the first two phases the Luftwaffe sought to secure the Channel, ground the RAF, and destroy its airfields in order to prepare the way for invasion. Since none of these objectives was attained, in the last two phases the Luftwaffe resorted to a desperate aerial blitz to destroy London, cripple English transport and supply, and paralyze the British will to fight on alone.

Triumph of the Spitfire

The battle began over the English Channel [*August 8–18, 1940*]. Coastal towns and ships were bombed all through the summer, but mass attacks started with four hundred planes swooping down on a convoy [*August 8, 1940*]. Soon other attacks were directed at the coastal ports and airdromes from south of Brighton to Portland. Armored Hurricane and Spitfire fighters took heavy toll of the unarmored Messerschmitts, coming in on their tails and shooting them down. The Heinkel and Junkers bombers, slow and under-armed, blew up and fell like clay pigeons. Nazi losses mounted as the attack reached its first peak, 180 planes being shot down one day [*August 15, 1940*], 153 three days later, for a loss of only

56 British planes and 27 pilots. Altogether, in the first ten days the Germans lost 697 planes, the British 153.

Even the Luftwaffe could not survive attrition at this rate. So Goering gave his airmen a brief rest, reorganized his squadrons, and in the second phase [*August 24–September 5, 1940*] sent them after the stout British fighters and their airfields. Nazi bombers flew over a wider front with increased fighter protection; in one day as many as eight hundred planes sallied forth against the RAF [*August 30, 1940*]. But the airdromes in the Home Counties around London were too scattered, the pilots too tough, and warning too quick for the RAF to be grounded. Again the box score of aerial combat showed the Nazis to be heavy losers: 562 German to 219 British planes, and from the latter 132 pilots parachuted to safety and took up other planes. Because Nazi bombers could not face the British fighters in daylight, they began to come over more frequently at night.

Bombing of London

In the third phase of the battle [*September 6–October 5, 1940*], Goering concentrated his attack on London, nerve center of the British Empire, as if the RAF were out of the way and the British ready to be softened up for invasion. London was a political rather than a military target; it was pounded in thirty-eight daylight raids to paralyze communications and morale. Goering himself flew in command of this attack, for it was intended to be the knockout blow. London antiaircraft batteries had first opened fire on stray raiders a month before. Now the Nazi bombers came over day and night, alone in the dark, in waves of 20 to 250 when it was light, with as many fighters boxing in their flanks and tails, flying escort upstairs and down. Docks, railways, factories, gas and electric light plants, and thousands of homes were ruined. In September over one thousand tons of high explosives, altogether some ten thousand bombs, fell on London, visiting more destruction than any city had ever endured. In three months 12,696 London civilians lost their lives. The Spitfires and Hurricanes ranged in three great semicircles around the battered British capital to intercept the best yellow-nosed planes of the Luftwaffe. Spitfires dashed into the high fighter screens of Messerschmitts, while Hurricanes stampeded the Heinkel and Junkers bombers below.

In desperation the Nazis protected these bombers with more fighters until there were sometimes four Messerschmitts to guard one Heinkel. Yet in the first great daylight raid on the London docks [September 7, 1940] they left 103 of their 350 planes in the smoke and flame which swept the Thames. A week later, when 500 planes raided London in two waves, coming before and after Sunday dinner, 185 never returned. On another raid [September 27, 1940], No. 11 Fighter Group of the RAF, which destroyed 442 enemy planes in this phase, brought down 99 Nazi craft with a loss of only 15 of its pilots.

Churchill spoke their citation: "Never in the field of human conflict was so much owed by so many to so few." No less credit was due their machines, the deadly Spitfires, and the controllers who plotted their paths, and the weary thousands of men and women who kept watch in Air Raid Precautions, fought fires, and dug their neighbors out of the smoking rubble. They were all soldiers of the army, civilian and military, which saved Britain.

Defeat of the Luftwaffe

The last phase of the battle [October 6–31, 1940] was marked by the Luftwaffe's retreat to night raids on London, and later on other cities and towns. The bombing now was blind, carried on for the sake of terror and destruction. Large formations of bombers came over London at thirty thousand feet, and speedy Messerschmitts fitted up with bombs made hit-and-run raids. All these attacks failed, with losses too heavy for the Luftwaffe to bear. In day raids alone during the Battle of Britain the Nazis sacrificed 2,375 planes and their crews, while the British lost altogether only 375 pilots.

Because of such losses, amounting to ten per cent of the planes engaged, the Luftwaffe lost the Battle of Britain. Operating [August 8–October 5, 1940] with a force estimated at 1,500 bombers and 1,000 fighters, the Nazis made about 22,000 sorties, an average of 400 a day, against a British force of some 800 fighters, each one flying several sorties a day to compensate for inferior numbers. Thus at the height of the battle the Luftwaffe made 900 sorties in a single day [*September 15, 1940*], and the RAF flew only one less. Although the total German air strength was far greater than the British, it was actually much weaker in the decisive element—fighter planes. The four-cannon Hurricanes and six-gun Spitfires, outnumbered by the Messerschmitts, nevertheless outfought them two and three to one.

Nazi bombers failed no less than their fighters. Unlike such British and American heavies as the Lancaster, Liberator, and Flying Fortress, they did not have the armor, fire power, and bomb capacity to undertake strategic bombing by themselves. When British bombers began their offensive against Germany [*May 30, 1942*], they blasted Cologne in an hour and a half with three times the weight of high explosives dropped on London by the Luftwaffe during the worst month of the Battle of Britain. Want of efficient ground crews and of stockpiles of spare parts for repair robbed the Nazi bombers of the staying power necessary to deliver a knockout blow. Goering's proud Luftwaffe was found to be only a tactical auxiliary to the Army, and air power no substitute for power on land. The Luftwaffe had its chance and suffered a decisive defeat in the Battle of Britain. Never again did the German command rely on air power alone to crush an enemy.

Continued Bombing of Britain

The bombing of Britain did not stop. It went on through the winter and into the summer of 1941, until the bulk of the Luftwaffe was transferred to the Russian front. Industrial cities in the Midlands and the north of England suffered from the sporadic night raids of one hundred to four hundred bombers. About four hundred Nazi planes dropped more bombs on Coventry in one night [*November 14, 1940*] than any part of London ever received. Birmingham, Manchester, Liverpool, and the ports of Hull, Plymouth, and Bristol were repeatedly bombed in the spring of 1941. But of all English cities, London was struck most often. Incendiaries were first dropped in the City on a massive scale [*December 29, 1940*] when one hundred Nazi planes started fifteen hundred fires in a three-hour raid. Through 1940 over a million houses in

59

London were damaged. Up to the end of 1941 it was estimated that the Nazis dropped 190,000 tons of bombs on all of Britain, killing 43,667 civilians and seriously wounding 50,387, inflicting more casualties on the "home front" than British troops had then suffered in battle.

11. THE UNITED STATES IN DANGER

The fall of France in 1940 brought Nazi troops to the Atlantic coast of Europe, where they were to stay until American and British armies drove them back in 1944. The French Army, which had stood between Germany and the United States in the last war, was gone. For the first time since Napoleon the continent of Europe was dominated by one military power, and consequently the United States was in danger. Its safety in the nineteenth century, the freedom it enjoyed to expand its territory westward, keep out of European wars, and raise its standard of living to new heights of comfort and prosperity, had rested at bottom on the fact that no single power threatened it with the organized might and resources of Europe. When Germany and her allies fought to control Europe in the last war, the United States entered the struggle which had ended in German defeat. By the summer of 1940, however, Germany had conquered Western Europe, and the Germany of Hitler was a far stronger nation, much more dangerous and ambitious than the Germany of 1917. Only the British fleet and air force barred the way to the west.

The swift and overwhelming success of the German armies aroused the American people from a complacent trust in their own security. To their earlier complacency, public opinion polls testified. In the summer of 1939 a majority of Americans did not anticipate any war in Europe. When asked what we probably would do if war broke out, one-third of the people thought we would remain neutral; one-fourth, that we would enter the war and send troops overseas; and almost one-half, that we would furnish supplies but not men. Most Americans, of course, sympathized with England and France rather than with Germany, and when war actually broke out,

60

they believed that these countries would defeat the Nazis. Half the Americans canvassed in polls of opinion thought at first that the war would not last over a year. If it appeared that England and France were to be beaten, however, almost half believed that we should declare war on Germany and send troops to aid the democratic nations.

In short, before war broke out, we did not as a people think there would be any war; when war came, we expected it to be over soon, with France and England triumphant. In the unlikely event that they were not to win, we rather easily imagined that we ourselves would fight, and win victory. The natural optimism of the American people was reflected in their opinion, so far as it could be accurately registered by sample polls, and what they wished strongly colored what they thought. But the swift march of events woke them up with a shock.

The conquest of France was the greatest lesson Hitler ever taught the American people. Before France fell, not half of us imagined that we would be personally affected by a German victory. The New World said of the Old, "It is *their* war." With the collapse of France, however, two-thirds of the American people realized that the triumph of the Nazis would affect their individual lives, and they grimly prepared for it. Although no longer confident that Britain would win the war, a majority believed that it was more important for the United States to stay out of war than to help Britain. If Germany won, they thought we could still carry on friendly diplomatic relations and trade with the Nazis. The immediate problem was to look to our own defenses. About three of every four Americans said that all able-bodied men should serve one year in the Army, that the National Guard should be called up for intensive training, and that production for defense should be increased.

America Prepares

With the evident support of an enlightened public opinion both the President and Congress heeded the pleas of the Army and Navy to improve our defenses. The American Navy, although second to none at the start of the war, had been kept for the most part in the Pacific Ocean to guard

61

against the danger of Japanese expansion. It was essentially a one-ocean Navy, but the alarming situation in Europe made it clear that protection was needed in two oceans, against Germany as well as Japan. The British Navy still held the Atlantic, but not securely against submarines and airplanes. If its ships were dispersed or destroyed, and its English bases lost in the Battle of Britain, a prospect that no one could discount in the summer of 1940, then we would be face to face with a triumphant Hitler. As extra insurance Congress passed the Two-Ocean Navy Bill [*July 19, 1940*], appropriating money to add some two hundred warships to our fleets. This was the greatest naval expansion ever authorized up to that time by any country. It promised to increase our combat tonnage by seventy per cent or 1,325,000 tons, and to give us a navy equally strong in the Pacific and the Atlantic, but not until 1943 or 1944.

In the production of military armament the most startling increase was planned for airplanes. The United States Army Air Forces hardly deserved the name and had to be enormously expanded almost overnight. The Army was limited by law to a strength of 2,300 planes, the Navy to 1,000, and neither service was up to its authorized strength. In 1939 the American aircraft industry produced only 2,100 military planes, the bulk of which were for training; production had been doubled to reach even this small output, and in the absence of American orders the industry had been enlarged by English and French purchases. Nevertheless, six days after the Nazis began their invasion of France, President Roosevelt sent a message to Congress [*May 16, 1940*] asking for the production of fifty thousand planes in one year. At that time nothing short of a miracle could have achieved the goal, but we surpassed that figure in 1943. With increasing American orders in 1940–41 the aircraft industry grew rapidly. Production soared from 561 military planes in July 1940, to 1,914 fourteen months later.

Essential to the manufacture of planes, tanks, ships, and ordnance, the blue prints for which were drawn in 1940, were the tools to make them. Almost unnoticed by the public, the manufacture of machine tools increased sharply. Normal production ran about 25,000 units a year, but in 1940 it mounted to 100,000, the best guarantee of far greater industrial output in the next few years. In terms of dollars, however, the nation still saved on defense and spent for peacetime living. In 1940, articles manufactured for civilian use cost about twenty-four billion dollars, and those for defense only one and a half billions. But money was appropriated and orders were being placed for the greatest war production ever known in the United States in times of peace. The defense program which got under way with the fall of France called for an expenditure of twenty-eight billion dollars, only twelve billions less than our entire national debt. This was the initial cost of building a navy and training an army to protect the United States against Hitler's forces.

Mobilization by Selective Service

The authorized strength of the Regular Army early in 1940 was 227,000, and of the National Guard, 235,000, a total of half a million men, less than Poland or Belgium mustered against Germany. This small army was regarded as the initial protective force, according to the American military policy adopted after the last war in the National Defense Act of 1920. It was expected that in any emergency there would be time to train a mass army behind the protective screen of the Regular Army and National Guard. But the collapse of the French Army left us no time in which to prepare as in the last war. For the defense of the Western Hemisphere. which we had to assume at once, the General Staff believed that three to four million men should be trained. An initial protective force of half a million was no longer enough; it was imperative for the U. S. to begin mass mobilization in order to be safe.

To start the necessary training, the War Department requested in May 1940, that the National Guard should be called to duty and "federalized" as part of the active army. Congress not only granted this request [*August 27, 1940*] but after a summer of debate passed the Selective Service Act [*September 16, 1940*] to mobilize the manpower of the nation for military service. Sixteen million men between the ages of twenty-one and thirty-six were registered [*October*

63

16, 1940] by voluntary boards of their fellow citizens. The number of men to be called up for training each year was first set at nine hundred thousand, and their period of training was limited to one year. Nine months later [*June 30, 1941*] nearly a million and a half men, including the Regulars and National Guard, were serving in the Army. Their number was limited chiefly by the slower increase of officer personnel to train them and of supplies with which to equip them. It was significant that for the first time in its history the United States had adopted compulsory military training while the country was still at peace. The fact was a measure of the danger which the American people felt as a result of the fall of France and the sweep of Hitler's armies over Europe.

"We are in the presence not of local or regional wars," declared the Secretary of State, Cordell Hull [*October 26, 1940*], "but of an organized and determined movement for steadily expanding conquest. Against this drive for power no nation and no region is secure save as its inhabitants create for themselves means of defense so formidable that even the would-be conquerors will not dare to raise against them the hand of attack."

12. THE AXIS ON THE OFFENSIVE

Hitler's armies did not overrun all Europe in one year of war, but in that time the continent west of Russia fell under his sway. Nations which remained independent in name were nevertheless dependent on Hitler's will because they lacked either the strength or the resolution to oppose it. German military power overawed Fascist Italy, outflanked Sweden, and surrounded Switzerland. Governments friendly to Fascism ruled Spain, Rumania, Bulgaria, and Hungary. Yugoslavia, Greece, and Russia, the only European nations besides Great Britain which still resisted the New Order, soon felt the tramp of Nazi boots across their lands.

The influence of Hitler extended far beyond Europe, for his military success was a most frightening recommendation. What he had done, democratic peoples were afraid could never be undone, and Fascists in other countries thought they might do the same. The Nazis, according to one widely-read American author, were riding the "wave of the future." A few thousand people in this country dressed themselves up in uniforms like those of Hitler's Brown Shirts, organized a *Bund*, and gave the Nazi salute; many more thousands of Americans expressed Fascist sentiments in the pattern set by the Ku Klux Klan, venting their spleen on Jews, Negroes, Catholics, and "furriners." In South America, Nazi agents plied their trade with governments and groups which disliked the United States and admired the mother-country of their language, Fascist Spain. In the Far East another militaristic country became the ally of Germany and Italy, extending the Rome-Berlin Axis to Tokyo.

Even after Hitler had lost the Battle of Britain, the power and influence of Fascism were terrifying. Capitalizing on this prestige, Hitler offered in a speech to divide the world with Britain, the United States, and Japan, choosing Europe, the Middle East, and most of Africa for the Axis. When neither Great Britain nor the United States took up this offer to share a world he did not yet possess, he set out to conquer it alone. To assure his domination of Europe, he first had to subdue the two great powers which had not yielded to his will, Great Britain and Russia. Britain was besieged with both airplanes and submarines. These arms enabled the Nazis to escape the limitations of ground troops and to reach out beyond continental Europe.

I. BRITAIN BESIEGED

The Battle of the Atlantic, as the war between German submarines and Allied ships came to be called in 1942, really began the first day war broke out between Great Britain and Germany. This struggle was crucial because the British Isles depended on Atlantic sea lanes for existence. The Royal Navy, starting in where it had left off in the last war, established a blockade of Germany, and the Germans likewise resumed their undersea counterblockade with submarines. During 1939 and 1940 the British Admiralty reported the loss of 677 merchant ships, and a total loss, including Allied and neutral ships, of 4,525,228 tons. With an annual shipbuilding capacity of 1,500,000 tons, Britain could not hope to replace vessels at this rate of destruction.

The situation grew critical for England because, with the fall of France, Germany became an Atlantic power with greater undersea strength than the Royal Navy could handle. British coastal waters were protected by minefields and flying-boat patrols, and trans-Atlantic ships were herded into convoys, which were first used to defeat the submarine in 1917. The British did not have enough destroyers to escort convoys across the Atlantic and through the Mediterranean or around Africa. Furthermore, the French Navy, which had policed the Mediterranean, was out of the war. In this sea Germany had gained the advantage of assistance from the Italian Navy. Thus the Axis acquired offensive power in two seas which Britain could not control single-handed.

American Aid

The United States came to the aid of the British. Britain had lost ten destroyers at Dunkirk, and in the evacuation of troops seventy-five more were damaged and laid up for repairs, disabling almost half their destroyer fleet. By Executive Agreement [*September 3, 1940*] the United States traded 50 four-stack, flush-deck destroyers, veterans of the last war, in exchange for 99-year leases of British bases in the West Indies, on Antigua, Jamaica, St. Lucia, the Bahamas, British Guiana, and Trinidad; in addition we received as gifts the right to bases on Newfoundland and Bermuda. By this deal Britain recruited her naval strength against Nazi submarines, and America came into possession of bases adequate to protect her Atlantic shores.

U-Boat Campaign, 1941

The German undersea drive against British shipping reached a new peak early in 1941. Losses for the year mounted to 3,708,000 tons, the heaviest toll being taken in the winter and spring months. In May, the worst month, the sinkings amounted to 658,000 tons. Although these losses never ran as high as in the last war, when 834,000 tons were sunk in April 1917, the future looked dark because of the low rate of replacement and the more successful tactics of German submarine warfare. The combined shipbuilding production of British and American yards in the spring of 1941 was only two million tons a year, little more than half the current losses.

With a fleet of U-boats variously estimated at 180 to 400, oceanic submarines of over 1,000 tons and coastal "minnows" of 250 tons, the Nazis perfected new and more efficient tactics. Their U-boats no longer scouted the seas half-blind and alone, as in the last war, but hunted in wolf-packs with aerial observers to spot convoys. U-boats trailed their quarry by day and lay in wait to make the kill at night. They attacked swiftly from the surface by night, combined their torpedo fire along the flanks of convoys, cut out stragglers, and made feints to divert escort warships. Against such tactics the British had little success at first. Only seventy-one U-boats were sunk from the beginning of the war to April 1941. During all of 1941 the press estimated that twenty-three were sent to the bottom. While the British lost ships faster than they could replace them, the Germans did not lose as many U-boats as they were building.

More American Aid

In this crisis the United States again came to the aid of Britain. President Roosevelt put at the disposal of England the Axis ships seized in American ports [*March 30, 1941*]. The United States took over British shipping routes in the Pacific Ocean and in June released vessels for service in the Atlantic. U.S. Marines landed in Greenland [*April 9, 1941*], with Danish permission, to forestall Axis raiders, and later in Iceland [*July 7, 1941*] to protect the easternmost approaches to American waters. The U.S. Navy established patrols [*April 30, 1941*] between the Atlantic coast and island outposts and, following the occupation of Iceland, along the western convoy routes. British naval forces were released to concentrate their strength in the dangerous waters between Iceland and Eire. When a Nazi submarine fired on the *Greer*, a U. S. destroyer delivering mail to Iceland [*September 4, 1941*], American naval patrols were ordered

67

to "shoot on sight" any hostile craft. Nazi torpedoes disabled the destroyer *Kearny* [*October 15, 1941*] and sank the *Reuben James* [*October 15, 1941*] west of Iceland. Even before Pearl Harbor the Battle of the Atlantic cost American lives.

The destruction of shipping abated sharply in the middle of 1941, and from July through October only 750,000 tons were sunk. This improvement was the result not only of American aid but of an increase in British flying patrols, corvettes, and bombing raids on submarine yards and bases. When the Nazis threw all their strength against Russia, moreover, they became weaker in the Atlantic. U-boats were concentrated in the Gulf of Finland and the Barents Sea, and the Luftwaffe shifted over most of its strength to the Russian front.

II. BRITAIN DEFENDS THE MIDDLE EAST

The war in the Middle East was a struggle for control of important waterways and land routes centering at the Isthmus of Suez. The shortest shipping route from Europe to India runs through the Mediterranean and the Suez Canal, the life line of the British Empire. At the head of the Persian Gulf, flanking this route, are the richest oil fields outside America and the East Indies. The isthmus itself, a waste of sand and stone, is the land bridge between Africa and Asia. The tanks which dug their treads into the sand and soil of Libya, Egypt, Abyssinia, Syria, and Iraq were fighting for an area strategically vital since history dawned. Who won the Middle East, as Napoleon realized, might win the world.

Italian Pincers in Africa

Here the British, hard pressed at home, mustered an army of one hundred thousand Imperial troops. These men were drawn from Australia, New Zealand, South Africa, and India, as well as from England, Scotland, and Wales. Early in the war they had only old planes and less than two hundred light tanks. Against these British forces Italy put in the Middle East two armies totaling half a million men with all their tanks, planes, and trucks. One army in Ethiopia under the Duke of Aosta was to advance upon Egypt from the south, while the other under Marshal Rodolfo Graziani was to drive east from Libya. General Sir Archibald Wavell destroyed these armies, first in Libya and then in Ethiopia, in the course of six months. Yet this swift double play was only the beginning of three long years of war in the Middle East; the small British garrisons were robbed of men and planes to reinforce Greece, hold Crete, and conquer Syria, while Hitler sent the Afrika Korps across the Mediterranean under Field Marshal Erwin Rommel to renew the struggle which the Italians had almost lost.

Wavell Defeats Graziani in Libya

The war in Africa began when Graziani's forces struck at Egypt [*September 13, 1940*]. The fall of France had secured their rear in Tunisia; England was fighting for its life in the Battle of Britain; and the Italians advanced safely into Egypt as far as Sidi Barrani. Here they sat down in rockbound camps before reaching the main British line of resistance at the railhead of Mersa Matruh. The Italians feared the desert and hugged the coast, though the British Navy shelled the coastal positions. They were often sick and always homesick. It was the greatest opportunity Italy had to increase her empire, for these troops might have raced east through the desert to Egypt, joining with the army in Ethiopia.

But General Wavell caught the Italians in their African siesta when his brilliant tactician, General O'Connor, surprised them at Sidi Barrani [*December 9, 1940*]. British tanks raced along the Libyan coast, and in two months took El Sollum, Bardia, Tobruk, Derna, and Bengasi. From a gasoline depot set up at El Meckili, deep in the desert southwest of Derna, a column of twenty-five tanks with motorized infantry crossed 150 miles of unmapped desert to cut off the Italians retiring from Bengasi. The British reached their objective scarcely two hours before the enemy. The Italian army was trapped. Over 133,000 prisoners were captured by the British Imperials, who lost only 604 men in their lightning drive. They occupied Cyrenaica [*February 8, 1941*], eastern half of Libya, as far as El Agheila.

The British owed their success to surprise, mobility, and

bold bluff. The Italians made many mistakes. Their intelligence was poor; their planes were destroyed on the ground; and Marshal Graziani made each coastal town a fortress, walled with guns, wire, and antitank ditches, behind which his troops were trapped by British infantry and tanks. Fixed forts scattered over the vast Libyan desert could not hold it against fast-moving tanks. The sands like the seas presented no obstacles to ships equipped to navigate them, and armored trucks or tanks ranged the desert with speed and surprise. With their Long-Range Desert Patrols, based on the Siwa Oasis, the British raided enemy garrisons and communications across hundreds of miles of desert wastes and compelled the Italians and Germans to convoy all their supplies.

Liberation of Ethiopia

General Wavell's victory in Libya protected Egypt on the west and left him free to destroy the Italian army in Ethiopia, though few men could be spared for this operation. Against Italian garrisons of some 200,000 troops in Eritrea, Somaliland, and Ethiopia, the British mustered about 30,000 men. They depended on naval support along the coast, superior plane and tank arms in the interior, and an uprising of native tribes to subdue the Italian forces. The blitzkrieg and fifth column tactics of the Germans were turned against their Axis partner.

The British attacked from three directions, converging toward Addis Ababa, inland capital of Ethiopia, as they advanced over highways built by the Italians and cut the two railroads to the coast. In Eritrea, to the northeast, British Imperials captured the mountain fortress of Keren [*March 26, 1941*] after a siege of seven weeks. In the southeast, amphibious forces landed at Berbera [*March 26, 1941*] and cut the railroad from Addis Ababa north of Harar. The main attack came from Kenya in the southwest whence armored forces took Addis Ababa [*April 5, 1941*] after covering 1,725 miles in fifty-three days, one of the fastest sustained advances of the war. Under orders from Rome, the Duke of Aosta made a last stand to prevent British troops from reinforcing Libya. A month later all Italian resistance ended [*May 19, 1941*].

Ethiopia, first of the Fascist conquests, was liberated; the Emperor, Haile Selassie, returned to his kingdom. Italy lost control of the Red Sea coast, and American Lend-Lease supplies could reach Egypt.

Rommel's Advance to Egypt

In Libya the British had been compelled to halt at El Agheila [*February 8, 1941*] because troops and planes were needed in Greece against the impending German invasion. While the British forces were depleted, the Axis was reinforced by the arrival in March of the Afrika Korps. This corps comprised two highly trained armored divisions (the 15th and 21st) each with eight thousand men and 135 tanks, and the 90th Light Infantry Division, which made history with brilliant tank forays under Field Marshal Erwin Rommel. Special equipment provided by the Tropical Institute at Hamburg included food, clothes, shelter, and medicines, scientifically prepared for troops fighting in the desert. To support the Afrika Korps and hold its supply lines there were seven Italian divisions, one of tanks and six of infantry.

Rommel's superior force ran through the weak British defenses [*March 24, 1941*], manned by only two divisions, and drove them back into Egypt. One Australian division was left behind to hold the fortified harbor of Tobruk on the German supply line. Rommel contained Tobruk as he built up a deep triangular zone of defense, from Halfaya Pass to Sidi Omar and Bardia, in order to secure Libya. An effort to relieve Tobruk [*June 15–17, 1941*] was disastrous to the British tanks which were used piecemeal against Rommel's concentrated counterattacks. During a siege of eight months the "Rats of Tobruk" were supplied by the Navy and RAF despite heavy losses from enemy bombers. If the German invasion of Russia had not deprived Rommel of the reinforcements he needed to continue his advance, Egypt might have fallen in 1941. In July the British took advantage of German preoccupation with Russia to build up a strong army under General Sir Claude Auchinleck, who followed Wavell in command of the Middle East.

71

Safeguarding Iraq

Meanwhile disorders in Iraq [*May 2, 1941*], inspired by Nazis, threatened the oilfields and pipe line to Haifa on which the British Mediterranean Fleet depended for fuel. Iraq was bound by an alliance with England, made in 1930, to admit troops to guard these oil lines, and a small British force had landed [*April 17–18, 1941*] at Basra in the Persian Gulf to march on Bagdad. But Arab forces surrounded the western airfield of Habbaniya and seized the oil wells of Kirkuk and Mosul. Troops were flown from India to relieve the Habbaniya garrison, and other units destined for Egypt were diverted to Iraq. General Wavell finally crushed the revolt [*June 1, 1941*] by sending a force in armored cars four hundred miles across the desert from Palestine. Thus the British confirmed their treaty rights and secured their oil supply. For the Nazis it was a serious loss of prestige among the Moslems in the Middle East.

French Civil War in Syria

In the Mediterranean, Nazi ambitions to strike at Suez and move toward India led the Luftwaffe to export planes and technicians to the Vichy French mandate of Syria. This was a key position because it threatened Egypt and the Canal. When Germany persuaded the Vichy Government to provide bases in Syria, even the United States protested [*May 15, June 5, 1941*] that such collaboration in the French colonies menaced the peace and safety of the Western Hemisphere and made France an instrument of aggression.

To forestall the Nazis, a mixed British force supported by the Free French invaded Syria from Palestine and Iraq [*June 8, 1941*]. They hoped to occupy the mandate without much bloodshed lest the Arabs be aroused and the French Government provoked into handing its fleet over to Germany. Civil war broke out as Vichy troops fought the Free French, each regarding the other as traitorous to France. Damascus fell in two weeks [*June 21, 1941*] and the advance continued slowly for another three weeks before the Vichy French sued for an armistice [*July 12, 1941*]. British occupation of Iraq and Syria secured one flank of the Middle East and of the main highways to India.

In Libya the British prepared another drive, the "Crusader" campaign, to relieve Tobruk. The famous Eighth Army came into existence with six divisions: the 7th and 70th Armored; two infantry divisions from South Africa; one from New Zealand; and another from India. They had enough tanks and planes, thanks to American Lend-Lease, to destroy Rommel's Afrika Korps if the tanks were concentrated and if the planes gave them tactical support.

The British launched their offensive [*November 17–18, 1941*] with a holding attack in the north, a diversion deep into the desert from Giarabub to Gialo, and a sweep southward around Axis positions to take the airfield at Sidi Rezegh. At first the British wasted their armored strength, dispersing three tank brigades, each of which Rommel defeated in detail with his massed armor [*November 18–26, 1941*]. Later, when the British concentrated their tanks at Sidi Rezegh, they won. But they could not pursue the Germans because the 50mm. and 75mm. guns of the Mark III and Mark IV tanks outranged the British and American light machines.

With this qualitative superiority in tanks and extraordinary skill in using them both strategically and tactically, Rommel seized the initiative. With a force of one hundred tanks he cut up the British rear and boldly swept into Egypt [*November 24–27, 1941*]. In this crisis British armor was regrouped to stab at Rommel's extended lines. A New Zealand division sped to the relief of Tobruk through a corridor opened up from the west by Lieutenant General B. C. Freyberg. Rommel won in a dash for Tobruk himself. [*November 30–December 1, 1941*]. But he had lost so many tanks and reserves that he had no force left to continue his offensive. He fell back [*December 16–17, 1941*] before a threatening British envelopment, broke it up with dive bombers, and withdrew his Italian infantry all the way to El Agheila. Here, reinforced by tanks, he twice surprised the British covering forces with reconnaissance raids northward which destroyed two of their tank brigades around Msus [*December 28, 1941, and January 23, 1942*]. The British abandoned Bengasi [*January 28, 1942*] to stabilize their defenses farther east, planting minefields from Gazala south to Bir Hacheim. Both sides settled down to repair their losses.

What saved the British in this disappointing campaign was the stand of the Tobruk garrison, the 25-pounder used as an antitank gun under cover of which their inferior tanks moved within range of the Nazis, and the swift mechanized patrols which destroyed enemy supply dumps. Yet the British had not learned to use tanks with the speed, concentration, and economy of which Rommel was now a past master. The "Desert Fox" still threatened Egypt and the Middle East.

Lend-Lease Aid to the Middle East

American supplies also helped to save the Middle East from the Axis in 1941. Lend-Lease began to supplement British purchases, and American supplies were a crucial factor in maintaining the defenses of the Middle East. During the year 2,400 planes were sent abroad to British forces at home and in Egypt, of which less than one hundred went under Lend-Lease, the remainder being bought by the British for cash. Over half the production of light tanks in April, May, and June for the U. S. Army, 280 in all, were hurried overseas by Lend-Lease to slow down Rommel's drive into Egypt. Before the end of the year a total of 951 light tanks and 13,000 trucks was exported to Egypt, of which 786 and 4,000, respectively, went under Lend-Lease, the balance for cash purchase. With these machines General Auchinleck launched his winter offensive to roll Rommel back through Libya and with them held the Germans when the drive failed. Lend-Lease came too late to save Greece and Yugoslavia, but in time to help defend the Middle East.

III. NAZI INVASION OF THE BALKANS

Hitler conquered the small countries of the Balkans as he subdued the rest of Europe, by political and economic coercion of rulers who would yield and by war against nations which resisted. He always applied diplomatic pressure first, advertising the success of his armies in Poland, Norway, and France as proof of what happened to peoples who disobeyed his will. Military force he used only as a last resort.

Húngary, Rumania, and Bulgaria were gathered into the Axis camp without fighting; Yugoslavia and Greece were crushed for daring to remain independent.

Hungary, Rumania, and Bulgaria Join the Axis

The Nazis extended their rule over the Balkans in order to close this corner of Europe to their enemies and to obtain oil, foodstuffs, and manpower. Hitler's diplomacy divided the Balkans by favoring Hungary and Bulgaria at the expense of Rumania and Yugoslavia, former allies of France. Then the countries which yielded were reduced to the position of satellites and used as bases from which Yugoslavia and Greece were outflanked, invaded, and conquered.

Hitler's first step toward control of the Balkan area was the Vienna Award [*August 30, 1940*] by which the Axis stripped Rumania of spoils from the last war, returning northern Transylvania to Hungary and the southern Dobrudja to Bulgaria. When Rumanians rioted in protest, King Carol abdicated the throne [*September 3, 1940*]. General Ion Antonescu, supported by the Iron Guard, his only political party, became Dictator, and Nazi troops marched in [*September 14, 1940*]. Rumania then joined the Axis [*November 23, 1940*]. Hungary also entered the Rome-Berlin-Tokyo alliance, along with Slovakia, the rump state of Czechoslovakia [*November 20, 24, 1940*]; Bulgaria was occupied by German troops as its Premier signed on the dotted line of the Axis pact [*March 1, 1941*]. The stage was set for the partition of Yugoslavia and Greece.

Mussolini's Defeat in Greece

Italian troops were snowbound in Greece after a winter campaign in which they tried to carve the country up single-handed. Mussolini had attacked Greece not only to extend his empire but to secure other points from which he could threaten Egypt, the prize which his troops in Libya sought. The attack on Greece was launched from Albania [*October 27, 1940*] with five columns pushing through the mountains toward the main railroad leading to Athens. In two weeks the Italians advanced as far as the River Acheron, south of

Yanina, but there Greek mountain troops beat them back into Albania.

Heavy snowstorms in the mountains suspended the Greek counteroffensive and saved the Italian troops. The Greek mountain infantry, without tanks or antitank guns, lived on coarse bread and packed their supplies on mules. For ordnance they depended chiefly on captured Italian arms, some taken by General Wavell in his Libyan advance, the rest seized by the Greeks themselves. Despite lack of equipment and air power, the Greek Army more than held its own. Italian troops hugged their winter quarters in the mountains of Greece and Albania until the Nazis came to their rescue.

The Balkan Campaign

In a swift campaign of three weeks [*April 6–30, 1941*] the Nazis overwhelmed Yugoslavia and Greece, the only Balkan countries yet unconquered, and added the southeastern corner of Europe to their continental fortress. They conquered sixteen million Yugoslavs, ill-equipped, never fully mobilized, and divided among themselves by feuds of the Serbs, Croats, and Slovenes. Patriots rallied as the Poles had done, to defend their long frontiers, instead of concentrating in the mountains as the guerrillas later learned to do. The seven million Greeks were also conquered by Nazi planes and armor after the Italians had been fought off by the almost weaponless Greek Army.

From Egypt came a British Expeditionary Force of some 74,000 men, under General (now Field Marshal) Sir Henry Maitland Wilson, to fight a delaying action, hold Greek air bases, and honor their pledge to protect Greece. Too small to save the Balkans, this expeditionary force was nevertheless too large to be moved from Africa without seriously endangering Britain's position there. While the Royal Navy convoyed these troops to Greece, the Afrika Korps crossed the Mediterranean to start its drive from Libya under Rommel.

To crush the Yugoslavs and Greeks, the Nazis assembled about thirty divisions, chiefly in Bulgaria, equipped with new light tanks suitable for mountain warfare, and two fleets of three thousand planes. Mountains did not stop the

German war machines, which made strategic penetrations through the passes. Armored units worked even closer to the infantry than in Poland or France, and dive bombers gave tactical support to ground troops. This blitzkrieg in the mountains repeated the successes of Poland and Norway.

Nazis Conquer Yugoslavia

From east of the Struma River in Bulgaria, three mechanized armies struck west through the mountain passes [*April 9, 1941*]. The capture of Nish and Skoplje by the two northern forces divided the Yugoslavs, cut them off from their allies, and opened the Vardar River valley to Greece. The southern army advanced through the Strumitca Gap to the lower Vardar and turned southward to Salonika. These crucial penetrations decided the issue of the whole campaign within seventy-two hours after it was begun.

Yugoslavia was conquered in eleven days [*April 17, 1941*]. Belgrade, the capital, although declared an open city, was devastated by bombers and captured by a pincers movement converging from the borders of Austria, Rumania, and Bulgaria [*April 14, 1941*]. From Belgrade the Germans dominated northern Yugoslavia; Skoplje was their center in the south. Italian forces met in the west at Ragusa to close the Adriatic coast to Allied intervention and to cut the Yugoslavs off from any such escape as they had made in the last war.

Nazis Overwhelm Greece

In Greece the Nazi assault on the Metaxas Line, protecting Greece from attack through Bulgaria, was resisted for two days. But the enemy breakthrough in the Strumitca Gap to the west had compelled Yugoslav forces to withdraw and expose the Greek left flank. A panzer division raced through the Vardar Gap to Salonika [*April 8, 1941*], outflanking the Metaxas Line and isolating three Greek divisions. Defense now rested mainly on the British troops, because the bulk of the Greek Army held their old positions in Albania to contain the Italians. Two Nazi armored divisions pressed south through the Monastir Gap toward Florina, splitting the British and Greek forces. To avoid being outflanked the

British had to fall back to a highland defense anchored on the east at Mount Olympus.

The Luftwaffe, which had been held in leash by stormy weather, attacked strongpoints, strafed retreating columns with dive bombers, cut up the British rear, and smashed the Athenian supply port at Piraeus. British fighter support had to cease when it was most desperately needed because forward airfields were lost to the advancing Germans. The superior German armor threatened to surround the British on both flanks and forced them to shorten lines by retreating across the plains of Thessaly. At Thermopylae the Adolf Hitler SS Motorized Division was halted, but it turned westward to cut off and capture the Greek army at Yanina. A day later [*April 20, 1941*] the Greek Government advised the British to evacuate: "You have done your best to save us. We are finished. But the war is not lost. Therefore save what you can of your Army to help to win elsewhere."

Evacuation was no easy task for the British because they lacked the air cover of Dunkirk. The Luftwaffe dominated the skies, its planes hovering like vultures over troops withdrawing southward to the Peloponnesus. To protect their retreat, Anzac units held a thirty-mile line from Thermopylae to the Gulf of Corinth against six enemy divisions. In the west the Hitler Division raced southward through Epirus, crossed into the Peloponnesus at Patras, and threatened the British rear. In the east, Nazi paratroopers seized the Corinth Canal only a few hours after General Wilson's headquarters had crossed over. Once the British troops reached Raftis, Navplion, and the southern beaches, a lucky series of moonless nights [*April 24–30, 1941*] hid their evacuations from the Luftwaffe. Some 44,000 men were taken to Crete and Egypt with the loss of only two destroyers and four transports. But in Greece the British alone had lost about 30,000 Imperial troops.

Nazi Occupation of Crete

The world gasped when German airborne infantry from bases in Greece, 180 miles away, captured the island of Crete in ten days [*May 20–30, 1941*]. It was the first time in history that airborne troops without heavy weapons overcame superior land and sea forces. Twice the British East Mediterranean Fleet destroyed Nazi convoys [*May 21–22, 1941*], but hundreds of enemy land-based bombers and torpedo planes sank or damaged so many ships that the Fleet withdrew from Cretan waters. Most of the 3,500 Nazi shock troops who dropped by parachute were killed, but nothing could stop the glider trains and troop-carrier planes once airfields had been seized for their landing. The British garrison under Lieutenant General Sir Bernard Freyberg had abandoned most of its antiaircraft artillery in Greece. Hurricane fighters in Africa, 350 miles south, were too far away to give support. In a few days the Germans landed in Crete about 35,000 airborne troops.

Maleme, strategic airfield in the northwest commanding the British base at Suda Bay, was surrounded by paratroopers and finally captured by airborne reinforcements [*May 20–25, 1941*]. Although garrisons at the other airdromes, Retimo and Candia, stood their ground, they could not join forces because German parachutists cut their communications along the northern coastal road. Enemy reinforcements soon threatened Candia, and the island was lost.

The evacuation of Crete took three days [*May 27–30, 1941*] and proved more difficult than Dunkirk or Greece. Troops beat their way to Skafia on the southern coast, hid by day in caves, and at night boarded destroyers which carried them to Alexandria under a rain of enemy bombs. Over half the British garrison of 27,000 men was saved. The Germans suffered 17,000 casualties to win Crete, but the victory protected their shipping and bases in Greece, interfered with the British Mediterranean Fleet, and threatened Egypt, Suez, and the Middle East from the air.

Though the battle was a tactical defeat for the British, the island had not fallen in two days as Germany hoped. It was expected that the Luftwaffe would fly from Crete to Syria, to dominate the Middle East with the connivance of the Vichy French. Syria could serve as base for attacks on Iraq, and Iran in the summer of 1941 and perhaps for a later advance to meet the Japanese in India. The failure of the Nazis to carry out this obvious strategy, which would have divided the British Empire, was in part due to the fight

79

Britain put up in Greece, Crete, and Africa. Every battle, even though a defeat, delayed the enemy's advance and reduced his striking force. For the British, the Balkan campaign was a retreat to victory.

IV. GERMANY ATTACKS RUSSIA

On June 22, 1941, Nazi armies invaded the USSR (Union of Soviet Socialist Republics), first by air and a few hours later by land. The attack brought immediate aid to Britain, for the two strongest military powers in Europe were now at grips, and the war's strategic center of gravity would shift from Britain and the Mediterranean to Russia. Both Germany and Russia were organized for total war. After nearly two years of conquest, the Axis commanded the population and resources of fifteen European countries. The USSR had a population of 192,000,000, more than Germany and all her unwilling vassals combined, and the Soviet peoples were spread over one-sixth of the earth's surface, a continental territory so vast that even the Nazis must have doubted the possibility of conquering it.

How Russia Prepared for Defense

While Hitler was busy conquering Poland, Western Europe, and the Balkans, the USSR prepared to resist him. The Russians pushed their frontier westward at every opportunity to gain a buffer zone of defense against invasion. Eastern Poland was annexed to the geographic frontier of the Bug River [*September 17–29, 1939*]. Bessarabia and northern Bukovina were taken back from Rumania [*June 27, 1940*]. The Baltic states of Estonia, Latvia, and Lithuania were occupied and incorporated in the Soviet Union [*August 29, 1940*]. A war against Finland won defensive space for Leningrad and control of the Gulf of Finland.

Russo-Finnish War

The winter war against Finland improved the strategic defenses of the USSR. The Finnish border came within sixteen miles of Leningrad; Hangö and other naval bases in the Gulf of Finland covered a seaway for invasion; and Petsamo in the far north was only sixty miles from Russia's ice-free

80

port of Murmansk. When Finland refused to yield control of these vital places, Russia went to war to get them.

The Russians invaded Finland [*November 30, 1939*] with reserve troops, expecting little resistance, but their attack was halted fifty miles above Lake Ladoga. Fighting froze to a standstill in the cold winter with temperatures of seventy below zero. For a month the Red Air Force systematically bombed Finnish railroads, ports, and airdromes [*January 13, 1940*]. Then massed howitzers blasted the reinforced concrete blockhouses of the Mannerheim Line on the Karelian Isthmus and threw its guns out of alignment [*February 11, 1940*]. Voroshilov brought up his best infantry and tanks to storm the Viborg fort, bypass and then surround Koivisto, and smash Finnish resistance [*March 2, 1940*]. The Finns signed a treaty of peace which gave the USSR the frontier it wanted [*March 12, 1940*].

In the Russo-Finnish War the popular sympathies of France, England, and the United States went out to the smaller nation, for the USSR seemed at that time to stand closer to Germany than to the Allies. The United States discouraged the export of military supplies to Russia. France and England planned to send an army to Finland's aid, but Norway and Sweden would not permit the crossing of their borders [*March 2, 1940*].

The Finnish War was generally regarded as a proof of Russian military weakness; actually, it was a demonstration of strength. The USSR used about 600,000 troops against an equal number of Finns, supplied a 700-mile front over a single railroad, and broke through one of the greatest fortifications in the world, the Mannerheim Line. As a result of the poor start Russia made in Finland, however, Stalin overhauled the tactics, supply, and command of the Red Army, relieved Voroshilov of command, and hastened preparations to withstand a Nazi invasion.

Why Germany Invaded Russia

Russia was alarmed by the sudden fall of France because it left Germany free to attack her in the east [*June 26, 1940*]. Industry was converted entirely to war production and labor was speeded up. Soviet troops held maneuvers on

81

the border of East Prussia to the great alarm of Hitler, who was then fighting the Battle of Britain. He was dissatisfied with the scanty supplies obtained from Russia under the trade agreement of 1939, and frightened by the expansion of the Russian frontier westward. The showdown came in a conference between Hitler and Molotov in Berlin [*November 12, 1940*] which revealed that Germany and Russia were no longer friendly enemies and that both wanted to be supreme in the Balkans. When Germany swept through the Balkan region [*March 3, 1941*], Russia denounced Bulgaria's union with the Axis and signed a nonaggression pact with Yugoslavia [*April 5, 1941*], hoping to encourage her resistance against Nazi invasion.

Soviet preparation for war reached its final stages. The quick triumph of Germany over the Balkan countries pushed Russia into signing a neutrality pact with Japan [*April 13, 1941*] to secure her Siberian frontier and escape a war on two fronts. The best trained of all Russian generals, Gregory K. Zhukov, became Chief of Staff in February 1941; in May, Stalin publicly centralized all power in himself by taking the title of Premier. Russia was warned in the previous winter by both Churchill and Sumner Welles, then American Under Secretary of State, that Hitler plotted attack.

There is no mystery about the reasons for the Nazi attack on Russia. Hitler had always looked on Russian Communism as his worst enemy and had long coveted the resources of the Soviet Union to make Germany self-sufficient. In *Mein Kampf* he wrote: "If the Urals, with their immeasurable treasure of raw materials, Siberia, with its rich forests, and the Ukraine, with its limitless grain fields, were to lie in Germany, this country under National Socialist leadership would swim in plenty." The dream of this wealth inspired Hitler to resume the old *Drang nach Osten,* the push to the east which the Kaiser had pursued before him.

The Nazis had reached the conclusion that it was necessary as well as desirable to conquer Russia. "In my rear," explained Hitler [*October 3, 1941*], "there stood a State which was getting ready to proceed against me." He believed that Germany was not safe so long as another great power in Europe had the potential strength to defeat her.

Britain, the only other great European power which Hitler had not conquered, was already under attack. From the summer of 1940, when the USSR had frightened him with a passive second front and contained so many of his troops, he looked upon Russia as his enemy. His plan was to strike at Russia, whose power was stronger on land, before Britain could invade Europe, or American Lend-Lease supplies added too greatly to their strength. Hitler hoped to neutralize Britain and America by presenting his attack on Russia as a crusade against Bolshevism. His political heir, Rudolph Hess, flew to Scotland on this mission [*May 12, 1941*]. It was the old dream of Munich, but Hitler found that his enemies could no longer be divided by the specter of Communism.

The Nazi Invasion, 1941

Until the Russian invasion the Nazis had never engaged in a campaign longer than two months, or fought on a front of over three hundred miles. In their attempt to conquer Russia, however, they had to spread their forces along a broken front of 1,800 miles from the Arctic Ocean to the Black Sea. Instead of carrying off another blitzkrieg, they involved themselves in a grim war which sapped their strength for three long years.

Nazi prospects were brightest when Hitler attacked Russia. He massed so much manpower and fire power that he threatened the quick destruction of the Red armies. The Nazi forces were organized in three groups: the northern armies under Leeb to advance on Leningrad through the Baltic states; the central armies of Bock to move on Moscow with the largest force; and the southern armies led by Rundstedt to sweep through the Ukraine and take Kiev. Five air fleets totaling more than 3,200 planes and 20 armored divisions of 8,000 tanks were part of the 180 divisions mobilized by Hitler for the invasion of Russia.

The Red Army had 158 infantry divisions ready to meet their attack. Red air strength was estimated at 6,000 combat planes, and of tanks there were 54 brigades, each with 200 armored machines. Some 300 new divisions of reserves were mobilized within a half a year after the invasion began. The

83

potential power of the Red Army was seriously underestimated by the Nazis.

The invasion of the Soviet Union fell into five phases, each an attempt at decisive victory which was never achieved. In the first phase [*June 22–July 10, 1941*] the German armies made rapid progress as tanks paced infantry, and motorized troops in the center drove forty miles a day into the heart of Russia. They overran Lithuania in the north, encircled Bialystok and Minsk in the center, and captured Lwow in the south. There was no "Battle of the Frontiers" in which the Russians could be destroyed like the Poles, for the Red armies retreated to the Stalin Line, trading space for time.

In the second phase [*July 11–August 8, 1941*] the invaders penetrated the deep defenses of the Stalin Line, advanced to Leningrad, besieged Odessa on the Black Sea, pushed to Kiev in the Ukraine, and fought the great battle of Smolensk. Again the main Russian forces escaped destruction, though the invaders pressed them hard and never relaxed the strategical and tactical offensive.

After Smolensk, in the third phase [*August 9–September 30, 1941*], the weight of the Nazi attack shifted southeast to Kiev. The central and southern armies joined in the encirclement of Budyenny's forces and exploited this victory rapidly through the Ukraine. In the north, however, the Germans failed to break the defenses of Leningrad and settled down to a siege which lasted two years. In front of Smolensk the Nazis first gave ground in a tactical defensive against Timoshenko's counterattacks. Blitzkrieg could not be fought without pause in the vast spaces of Russia.

The fourth phase [*September 30–October 15, 1941*] of the German invasion, part of the drive on Moscow, was the largest tactical operation ever planned by the Nazis. It took the form of two gigantic double envelopments of Vyazma and Bryansk to trap the forces defending Moscow. A battle more violent but less conclusive than Smolensk was the first result, and the struggle for Moscow followed. In the north the invaders spread eastward from the Valdai Hills to the headwaters of the Volga and from Velikie Luki to Rzhev; in the south they drove deep into the Dnieper Bend. The situation became critical along the whole front.

The fifth and final phase of the invasion fell into three stages, each a more furious battle than the last. First came the battering at the gates of Moscow [*October 15–November 1, 1941*], then a rush in the south to Rostov on the Don [*November 1–21, 1941*], and finally a series of smashing blows on three sides of Moscow [*November 21–December 7, 1941*]. Hitler hailed the Battle of Moscow as a deathblow to the Red armies, but Russia reserves sprang to a counter-offensive while the Germans went into winter defense. The saving of Moscow doomed Nazi hopes of destroying the Soviet Union. The Red Army proved that it could stand every blow of the invaders, come back for more, and counter with heavier blows of its own.

Race to Smolensk

The Nazi invasion of Russia started with the main drive from Poland toward Moscow [*June 22, 1941*]. Marshal Bock sent the panzer armies of Hoth and Guderian racing ahead of his infantry in a double envelopment of Bialystok, which was surrounded from Grodno and Brest-Litovsk. As the infantry came forward to reduce these positions, motorized forces with armored spearheads swept on to envelop Minsk [*June 30, 1941*]. From these encirclements the Nazis claimed the capture of 323,898 prisoners, 7,615 armored vehicles, and 6,633 planes [*July 10, 1941*]; signifying, if true, the annihilation of a Russian army. The Russians in their forward positions were not overcome for three weeks; they maintained an active defense, counterattacked the flanks of Nazi spearheads, and fought stubborn delaying actions, using tanks and eight to twelve firing lines of infantry disposed in depth. Such were the aggressive tactics of the Russian retreat that the Nazis were halted for almost a week at the Berezina River [*July 3–8, 1941*].

But the power of the German drive appeared to be irresistible. Armored units lived off the country, abandoning their supply lines except for munitions and gasoline brought forward by air, and the infantry mopped up Russian forces left in the rear of the panzer advance. Nazi tanks crossed the Dnieper River and breached the Stalin Line [*July 12, 1941*], bypassing such strongpoints as Mogilev and Vitebsk, which fell to infantry assaults, and reached the defenses of Smolensk, only 230 miles from Moscow. In this swift advance Bock's motorized infantry covered 360 miles from Bialystok to Smolensk in nine days, divisions leapfrogging those at rest to keep a force moving night and day.

The great battle of Smolensk raged for three weeks [*July 20–August 9, 1941*] in an arc extending from Nevel to Mogilev and along the road west to Orsha. From north and south the Russians counterattacked the German flanks and rear in an effort to encircle the invaders. These counterattacks lost cohesion under the combined assault of Nazi infantry in front and tanks in the rear. Russian communications were cut by a panzer thrust to Vyazma [*July 27, 1941*]. The battle ended with the Germans claiming the annihilation of another Russian army as they announced the capture of 310,-000 prisoners, 3,205 tanks, 3,120 guns, and 1,098 planes. In this battle of encirclement which lasted three weeks the Nazis had not destroyed all the "encircled" Russians. Many divisions withdrew; others took greater toll of the enemy than the enemy could take of them; and all the defenders carried out their mission of slowing down the Nazi advance. As they evacuated Smolensk the Russians destroyed most of the city and left behind only 20,000 of the 160,000 inhabitants, "scorching" the earth of both city and country in the wake of their retreat.

At Smolensk German forces reorganized [*August 10–15, 1941*], and some units went south to join others moving north from the Ukraine. They applied a pincer to twenty-eight Red infantry and armored divisions which had retired from Smolensk to Gomel. Although these units were enveloped [*August 19, 1941*], many elements evacuated Gomel in a general Russian withdrawal all along the line to the east bank of the Dnieper [*August 22, 1941*].

Southern Advance in the Ukraine

Rundstedt's southern armies made slow progress in a secondary drive from southern Poland toward Kiev [*June 22, 1941*]. Hungary entered the war [*June 24, 1941*] and joined the attack across her narrow Carpathian frontier. After armored counterattacks failed to save the fortress of Lwow, the

Russians withdrew to the deep defenses of the Stalin Line [*June 30, 1941*]. The Germans bypassed Tarnopol, a strongpoint which was later turned by Hungarian motorcycle troops, and swept forward to Zhitomir, bastion of the Stalin Line covering Kiev [*July 9, 1941*]. Here for almost a month German and Russian tanks fought a duel over Zhitomir [*July 6–August 2, 1941*], an action comparable to that at Smolensk in retarding the Nazi advance. Reichenau's panzer units meanwhile reached the Dnieper below Kiev [*July 21, 1941*]. Far to the south the Rumanians advanced through Bessarabia and forded the Dniester; the Hungarians connected the Rumanian left flank and the German right [*July 2–19, 1941*].

Zhitomir fell, and Kleist's panzer army swept south to join Rumanian troops who had now crossed the Bug in an encirclement of three Russian armies around Uman. This battle was another Russian disaster, according to the Germans, who claimed the capture of 103,000 prisoners, but the bulk of the Russian forces retired across the Dnieper River [*August 1–8, 1941*]. Plunging deep into the Dnieper Bend, the Germans took up the pursuit, occupying Nikolaev on the Black Sea after its naval base had been destroyed. As the Germans reached Cherkassy and the Hungarians advanced to Kremenchug [*August 26–September 6, 1941*], both key points on the Dnieper, the Russians evacuated Nikopol and Dniepropetrovsk [*August 26, 1941*], blowing up the largest power plant and dam in Europe. One Rumanian army laid siege to Odessa [*August 31, 1941*]; another pushed ahead to capture Perekop and invade the Crimea [*September 17, 1941*]. Except for Kiev and Odessa, the Ukraine was in Nazi hands.

Battle of Kiev

Although Reichenau's armored spearheads had reached Kiev [*July 21, 1941*] one month after the invasion began, the Nazis were held up within sight of the city for two months, a crucial delay in their timetable of conquest. Red artillery commanded the crossing of the Irpen from wooded heights, and westward along the Pripet Marshes the infantry harassed the extended northern flank of the invaders.

East of Kiev, Budyenny massed 750,000 Russian troops for a counteroffensive.

The Nazis planned to destroy the Red forces and take the city by encirclement. This maneuver was conceived on a scale so great that it required armies of the south and center to join hands; they fought the battles of Uman and Gomel as they moved toward each other. From the center Weich's Second Army, which had been kept in reserve during the struggle at Smolensk, advanced south to meet Stülpnägel's Seventeenth Army coming north [*August 26, 1941*]. Meanwhile the panzer armies of Guderian and Kleist swept east to form the outer arms of the double envelopment. The trap for the Russian reserves was set at Lubny, and Reichenau's Sixth Army sprung the trap by attacking Kiev from the West [*September 14, 1941*].

The Russians withdrew from the city, consolidated all their forces in a hollow square with hedgehog defenses, and launched furious counterattacks to break the encirclement. The Germans struck them from all sides, cutting armies into corps and corps into divisions, and using two air fleets to disrupt communications and provide quick reconnaissance. Russian units escaping east toward Kharkov were caught by Hungarian and Italian troops whom Hitler had brought into the line. Budyenny's southern armies were decisively defeated [*September 26, 1941*]. The Nazis claimed the capture of 675,000 prisoners. Kiev was taken and the whole Ukraine down to the Dnieper Bend lay open to the invaders.

Meanwhile the Russians challenged the enemy with a counteroffensive on the central front [*September 5–27, 1941*] to divert his strength from Kiev and save Moscow from the main German forces. With fifty divisions Timoshenko pushed west almost to Smolensk [*September 14, 1941*], making the Nazis yield ground for the first time during the invasion. A pincers attack on Smolensk soon exhausted itself [*September 27–29, 1941*], without disturbing the German preparations for resuming their offensive. Moscow was safe for the moment, but the reserves at Kiev had been lost, and German forces swung north from the Ukraine to join the attack on the Soviet capital.

Southern Advance to Rostov

While Bock's armies fought in vain to take Moscow, Rundstedt's southern forces advanced into the Crimea and the Donbas (Donets Basin), taking Kharkov, Belgorod, Kursk, Odessa, Stalino, Kerch and Rostov on the Don. Kharkov a city of 840,000 people, an industrial center like Pittsburgh, was defended by six lines of pillboxes which the Nazis penetrated with special combat teams using flame-throwers and dive bombers [*October 23–24, 1941*]. Kursk and Belgorod, rail junctions above Kharkov on the main line from Moscow to the Crimea, were outflanked [*October 24–November 1, 1941*]. The Nazis organized the upper Donets for winter defense.

Farther south, however, they pushed beyond the Dnieper Bend into the Donets Basin. The left wing of Manstein's forces circled toward Rostov and the right spread over the Crimea [*October 15–16, 1941*]. Their advance cut off Odessa. A Russian army besieged there by Rumanian troops secretly evacuated the garrison and crossed the Black Sea to Caucasia after destroying all the shipyards and factories of Odessa. Manstein's forces entered the Crimea by storming five lines of concrete fortifications on the narrow isthmus below Perekop [*October 29, 1941*]. Then they fanned out south and east, took the capital of Simferopol [*November 13, 1941*], contained the naval fortress of Sevastopol [*December 7, 1941*], and bottled up a Red army in the Kerch Peninsula. Kerch, guarding the exit from the Sea of Azov and the passage across the strait into the Caucasus, was reduced by siege artillery. In the Crimea only Sevastopol was left to the Russians.

While Manstein's right wing swept the northern coast of the Black Sea, his left wing trapped Russian reserves between Perekop and Berdyansk on the shores of the Azov Sea. Kleist's tanks cut off their retreat by racing northeast toward Stalino. The fall of this industrial city threatened Rostov [*October 20, 1941*]. Instead of defending Rostov, Timoshenko withdrew most of his troops from the city and organized a counteroffensive in the Donbas on a broader front. The Nazis took Rostov but they could not keep it [*November 21, 1941*].

Timoshenko unleashed a powerful counteroffensive [*November 24, 1941*] on a 120-mile front, in which his three armies not only recaptured Rostov but also relieved Moscow. As far north as Kharkov one Red army struck the Nazis; another descended on Rostov from the Donets; and a third, organized in Caucasia from troops who had evacuated Odessa, attacked Rostov directly across the Don [*November 28–29, 1941*]. The Nazis retreated over one hundred miles to avoid encirclement and could not rally to halt the Red drive until they were west of Taganrog [*December 3, 1941*]. For the first time in the war Hitler had met an enemy who counterattacked in strength and robbed him of his conquests. Although the Russians had lost the bread basket of the Ukraine and the war industries of the Donbas, they had evacuated heavy machinery and skilled workers to the Urals, destroyed whatever they could not take with them, and literally scorched the earth as they retreated. The Nazis conquered little but the land, thousands of square miles of it, and the sudden counteroffensive out of Rostov had shown that even these conquests were as insecure as they were barren.

Northern Advance to Leningrad

In the meantime, Leeb's armies in the north made the third great drive of the invasion [*June 22, 1941*], sweeping up through the Baltic states from East Prussia to Leningrad. At the start they overran Lithuania and Latvia without much opposition, and reached Dvinsk [*June 26, 1941*] after advancing a distance of 175 miles in five days. Occupation of Riga [*June 29, 1941*] gave them a large supply port on the Baltic Sea. Through the summer the Nazi left wing under Küchler reached the Gulf of Finland, splitting the Russian forces west of Lake Peipus and driving them into Tallinn, which was finally reduced by siege and assault [*August 29, 1941*]. The right wing under Busch advanced northeast to Lake Ilmen, taking Polotsk, Nevel, Velikie Luki, Kholm, and closing in on Leningrad [*August 21, 1941*].

In the heavily wooded marshlands south of the city, the defenders checked the enemy from a maze of bunkers and tank traps. Unable to hold these positions, they were pushed back to the Valdai Hills in a great arc from Tallinn to Velikie Luki, and finally contained within the fortifications of Leningrad. Beginning the assault on the city [*September 4, 1941*] with a tremendous artillery duel, the Germans captured Krasnoye Selo, stormed two hills, and claimed to have penetrated the inner line of forts. They crossed the Volkhov River and partially encircled the city [*October 21-November 8, 1941*], only to be stalemated. Leningrad held, though for two years the Nazis shelled the beleaguered city and waited for its starving inhabitants to surrender.

Four days after the German invasion began, Finland entered the war against Russia [*June 26, 1941*] to regain the territory lost in 1940. Mannerheim's armies attacked southeast toward Leningrad, gradually reconquered the lost ground, and established a blockade of the city along the Svir River. The chief accomplishment of these Finnish troops was to immobilize Soviet forces. In the far north fourteen Finnish and seven German divisions under Falkenhorst succeeded in cutting the railroad to Murmansk, but were unable to take the city. This vital ice-free port was kept open for supplies from America and Britain.

But no Lend-Lease matériel was to be shipped to Russia until an accord had been worked out [*October 1, 1941*] by an Anglo-American mission to Moscow, and ratified by President Roosevelt and Premier Stalin [*November 4, 1941*]. Some planes and tanks arrived from England, but never enough to replace those that were lost. The Russians admitted that in the first month and a half of the Nazi invasion, they had lost seven thousand guns, five thousand tanks, and four thousand planes—more tanks than they would receive by Lend-Lease in the next three years and nearly half as many planes. In the fall of 1941 their situation appeared desperate.

Battle of Moscow

After the encirclement of Kiev the armies of Bock turned against Moscow in the greatest offensive of the invasion. The best troops of the USRR were concentrated before the Soviet capital, the focal center for all the main highways and railroads of Russia. To Hitler its capture was necessary for political as well as military victory.

If Moscow was to be taken, the defending armies must be driven off or destroyed. For ten weeks the struggle raged [*October 1-December 5, 1941*] marked by the heaviest antitank battle of the war. The Red Army, attacked by five panzer armies, each with a thousand tanks, met the assault by massing guns of every type to support its infantry. A vast network of antitank ditches and trenches, strengthened with pillboxes and minefields, perfected the defense in depth. The total strength of Moscow, civilian as well as military, faced the invaders. Trained soldiers and the people of the city fought side by side. Battalions of workmen, young and old, untrained and almost unarmed, filled the line at Tula; divisions of volunteers marched out of Moscow to throw themselves at the enemy tanks. As week after week of fighting went by, Russian manpower proved stronger than German fire power. The Nazi machine lost momentum, stopped, and finally rolled back. The Russians had saved Moscow and won a defensive victory which put an end to the Nazi invasion of 1941. The victory came after a series of defeats. Before the Germans reached Moscow they had to drive through Russian lines, splitting them apart and forcing them to a last stand before the city. The great offensive began with assaults on Bryansk and Vyazma.

Encirclements of Bryansk and Vyazma

The first objective of the Nazi drive toward Moscow was to break the armies under Timoshenko which had moved forward in their counterattacks on Smolensk as far as Vyazma and Bryansk. To annihilate these Red forces the Nazis planned the most complex operation of the Russian war, two gigantic double envelopments of both wings, with two secondary envelopments, all to be accomplished in rapid sequence before the defenders were aware of the threat. These maneuvers started with Hitler's order to his troops [*October 1-2, 1941*]: "Today is the beginning of the last great decisive battle . . . which . . . will annihilate this enemy."

The battle began with the sweep of Guderian's tank army from the Kiev front northeast to Orel [*September 30–Octo-*

92

ber 3, 1941]. The German capture of this rail junction, seventy miles east of Bryansk, divided the armies in central Russia from those in the south and threatened to cut off retreat from Bryansk. From the north Höppner's tanks rolled south to Gzhatsk between Moscow and Vyazma [*October 10, 1941*]. These armored arcs drawn by Guderian and Höppner were the outer arms of encirclement. In the center Kluge's infantry, with the panzer armies of Reinhardt and Hoth, drove forty miles into the Russian rear, divided, and then circled the flanks north and south [*October 2–6, 1941*]. The Germans boasted that the Red armies at Bryansk and Vyazma were split apart like an apple and each half seized and crushed in the armored jaws of the panzers. The circumference of each encirclement, however, was over 124 miles, too great an area to be mopped up quickly. The Russians adopted a hedgehog defense and launched ferocious counterattacks to break out. After nearly three weeks of continuous fighting the Nazis claimed the annihilation of eight armies of defenders with the capture of 648,196 prisoners. But the Russians had abandoned Bryansk and Vyazma several days before [*October 12, 13, 1941*], and while many divisions were lost, many more fell back to form an unbroken front before Moscow. The envelopments of Bryansk and Vyazma, chiefly the work of Kluge's army, were maneuvers preliminary to the assault on the Moscow front.

Advance on Moscow

For the main drive to the city Field Marshal Bock had two army groups; the Seventh, on a line about forty-five miles north of the Smolensk-Moscow highway; and the Fourth under Marshal Kluge along a line some sixty-five miles in the south. It was estimated that these forces consisted of thirty-three infantry divisions, comprising half a million men, thirteen panzer divisions, each with about four hundred tanks, and five motorized divisions. They jumped off along a line running from Yartsevo to Roslavl, about two hundred miles from Moscow [*October 3, 1941*]. Within three weeks they had smashed forward until their most advanced elements were at Mozhaisk, only sixty-five miles short of the city. This drive was an attempt to encircle the whole central front in an arc from Kalinin through Rzhev to Kaluga. The crisis came when Nazi tanks, followed by motorized infantry, broke through the center to Mozhaisk [*October 15, 1941*]. Russian counterattacks threw them back fifteen miles beyond Borodino but lacked the strength to hold them, so the Nazis recovered Mozhaisk [*October 16, 1941*] and swept southeast to Maloyaroslavets. The outer defenses of Moscow were dented.

Stalin gave the order [*October 19, 1941*]: "Moscow will be defended to the last." He declared a state of siege, charged Marshal Zhukov with the defense, made Marshal Shaposhnikov Chief of Staff, sent Timoshenko south to defend Rostov, and Voroshilov and Budyenny to the rear to organize new armies. Trained reserves, including divisions from the Urals and Siberia, were arriving in the birch forests behind Moscow, but they were not flung prematurely into battle. Instead, the citizens of Moscow, even those who had no military training, were called to volunteer, and four Communist divisions went into action, without any weapons heavier than machine guns, while other citizen divisions, with women in their ranks, dug trenches and tank ditches. The improvised army slowed down the Nazis but could not stop the advance. In the last ten days of October the enemy made slow progress, pushing ten miles beyond Mozhaisk in the center, twenty miles toward Tula in the south, and halting at Rzhev before the fortified northern bank of the Volga.

The Assault

Having failed to encircle the whole central front at Moscow, Marshal Bock reorganized his forces for a concentrated envelopment of the city proper. He kept the bulk of his infantry with two tank divisions in the center, and strengthened his northern arm with seven tank divisions, three infantry divisions, and two motorized divisions. To his southern arm he gave speed and mobility, with four tank and two motorized divisions, reinforced by one infantry division. His plan was to use most of his infantry to hold the center under pressure while three columns from the north and four from the south encircled the city, the tanks to meet near Orekhovo-Zuevo, fifty miles in the rear. During the two

94

weeks Bock spent in preparing this assault, Marshal Zhukov brought some of his trained reserves into line. The Russian forces consisted of seven armies and two cavalry corps concentrated on a front of two hundred miles. Red tank forces had been so heavy that units of 360 tanks were now reduced to brigades of 96 or even 60.

In this final assault [*November 16–December 5, 1941*] the Germans in the north took Klin on the Moscow-Leningrad highway, pushed twenty-five miles east to Dmitrov, broke through from Rzhev to Volokolamsk, and came to within twenty-five miles of Moscow at Krasnaya Polyana. In the south two Nazi columns were stopped at Serpukhov on the Moscow-Tula road and at the Nara River. The whole population of Tula held the town by taking to trenches in support of Siberian divisions. Guderian bypassed them with three tank and two infantry divisions, swept forward to Kashira, turned northwest in the rear of Tula and covered it with fire from all sides. The Russians here fell back, regrouped their forces, adding reserves, and struck at Guderian's exposed flank [*December 1–4, 1941*]. In the center the crisis came when the Germans tried to envelop the defenders' flanks on the Smolensk-Moscow road; they succeeded in breaking through in the south but were repulsed by reserves in the north, and this smaller envelopment collapsed.

After the first fury of the assault was spent, Marshal Zhukov moved from passive to active defense, committed his strategic reserves to prevent encirclement of the flanks north and south of Moscow, and launched a counteroffensive on all sectors against the dangerously extended enemy. [*December 6, 1941*]. The German lines had been flung eastward in two great arms, curving to inclose Moscow. But the grasping hands never met. In the rear of the city, a distance of 140 miles separated the Nazi forces. Heavy snow covered the roads around Moscow, the temperature fell below zero, tank engines stalled as the lubricating oil failed, and the Luftwaffe was grounded. The Russians with skis on their planes and stoves to warm the oil for tanks were better equipped for winter fighting, and consequently gained superiority over the Germans in air power, armor, and fire power. The swift

Russian counteroffensive consisted of a series of small punches planned on a scale so great that the enemy had no chance to recover. One night a Red force knocked out a Nazi battalion, the next day partisans in the rear cut off a division's supply train, and always the Russians pressed the flanks of the retreating Germans. Guderian was beaten back in the south from Tula, and in the north Klin and Kalinin were retrieved.

Moscow was safe; Leningrad held out; and only in the south of Russia did the Nazi invasion make headway again. In the Battle of Moscow the Germans were superior to the Russians in maneuver, mobility, and armament. Their tanks, two and a half times as many as the Russians had, failed to take Moscow. The Red Army held the city and won the battle by saving their reserves until the enemy was exhausted and then hurling them at his exposed flanks. These tactics marked the opening of the first Red Army winter offensive.

13. AMERICA THE ARSENAL OF DEMOCRACY: LEND-LEASE

Although the United States was technically at peace in the fall of 1940, busily preparing its own defenses while Great Britain was fighting for its life, the shadows of war spread across America from both the Pacific and the Atlantic. The sweep of Hitler's forces through Europe threatened this country from the east, as Japan's joining the Axis threatened it from the west. For the first time in its history the United States was confronted by the menace of war on two fronts.

The Rome-Berlin Axis was extended to Tokyo when Japan signed the Pact of Berlin and became partner to a military alliance directed against the United States [*September 27, 1940*]. In this treaty Japan recognized "the leadership of Germany and Italy in the establishment of a new order in Europe." On their side, Germany and Italy gave equal recognition to "the leadership of Japan in the establishment of a new order in Greater East Asia." The Fascist powers were thus united for the conquest of Europe and Asia. The most

96

significant article in their treaty was an undertaking "to assist one another with all political, economic, and military means if one of the three Contracting Powers is attacked by a Power at present not involved in the European War or in the Chinese-Japanese conflict." This could refer only to the United States, which was to be neutralized and isolated while the Fascist Powers won the war. As Secretary Hull described it, "If you stepped on the tail of one of them, the other two would holler."

The United States stepped on the tail of the Nazis in order to relieve the shortage of supplies from which Great Britain was beginning to suffer. All during the summer and fall of 1940 it was apparent that Britain would soon be embarrassed for want of matériel with which to defend its home islands and the Middle East. Not only did British production diminish under the persistent German bombing of towns and factories, but American production was taxed by the demands of our own defense program. Only 2,100 of the 23,000 planes which the British had ordered or planned to obtain in the United States were delivered by the end of 1940. Worst of all, British purchasing power was nearly exhausted, for they could not offer goods or services to compensate for what they needed from us, and of private stockholdings in American companies they had already sold a third of a billion dollars. Loans of money might have been advanced; but it was war goods they wanted, and Americans still remembered that what they had lent their allies in the last war had not been repaid.

In this crisis, which threatened to leave the United States to face the Axis alone on two fronts if Britain collapsed, the United States Treasury proposed to lend or lease weapons of war to nations fighting the Axis. From this proposal President Roosevelt eliminated the dollar sign, as he said, by balancing the defense of the United States against the cash value of weapons and supplies. Over the radio he told the American people that if Britain collapsed, "all of us in the Americas would be living at the point of a gun—a gun loaded with explosive bullets, economic as well as military." To prevent the triumph of the Axis and to keep the war from our shores, he proposed to Congress that we become "the great

97

arsenal of Democracy." After two months of debate [*January 6–March 11, 1941*], Congress passed the Lend-Lease Bill by large majorities in both houses, and two weeks later voted seven billion dollars to meet the first installment of the costs.

Under Lend-Lease the President was empowered to manufacture, sell, lend, lease, or exchange any war matériel to "the government of any country whose defense the President deems vital to the defense of the United States." The terms and conditions upon which foreign governments received such aid were "those which the President deems satisfactory," and the benefit to the United States might be "payment or repayment in kind or property, or any other direct or indirect benefit which the President deems satisfactory." In short, the President was given complete discretion to aid any country resisting the Axis, because its resistance was of aid to the defense of the United States; there need be no repayment, if the President wished none, beyond this contribution to American defense.

Lend-Lease was restricted at first by a special time limit and a fixed maximum of expense, but it was subsequently renewed and additional appropriations were voted; thirty billion dollars had been spent by April 1944. Of this amount, nearly twenty billion went in war goods and services to the British Empire; over four billion to the Soviet Union; over two billion to Latin America, chiefly to Brazil; and half a billion to China. More than half of all this money was spent after the middle of 1943, when American production had at last expanded sufficiently to satisfy both our own needs and those of our allies. Up to the middle of 1943, the actual cost of Lend-Lease was nearly thirteen billion dollars; almost half of this amount was spent on planes, tanks, ships, guns, munitions, and trucks, and the remainder for raw materials, machinery, food, clothes, and services.

To the question, "Have we got our money's worth?" Lend-Lease Administrator Edward R. Stettinius, Jr., replied: "I think that we have in more than double measure . . . If we had not had Lend-Lease, . . . if Britain had gone under, Hitler had isolated Russia, Japan had completed the conquest of China, and finally we in the Western Hemisphere had stood alone against an Axis-dominated world, who can

98

measure the expenditure of men and of our material wealth we would have had to make if our liberties were to survive?" The answer to this question may be guessed from the fact that three years of Lend-Lease cost the United States thirty billion dollars, but every month of fighting in 1944 cost this country alone eight billion dollars.

Lend-Lease did not confine the United States to a spending program. Quite apart from the contributions made to American defense by Great Britain, the Soviet Union, and China in fighting against the Axis, there was also Reverse Lend-Lease which increased steadily as the war went on. By the middle of 1944, Great Britain and the Dominions had repaid over two billion dollars in supplies given to our troops abroad. For all the aid granted the Soviet Union, wrote Mr. Stettinius, "the Russians have already made a return far beyond any measurement in dollars or tons. It is in the form of millions of Nazi soldiers dead or in Russian prison camps, of Nazi tanks reduced to scrap on the battlefields, of Nazi guns and trucks left behind by the retreating German armies . . . The war will be much the shorter for it."

In a report to Congress in the spring of 1944, President Roosevelt reviewed the results of Lend-Lease. Of every dollar spent by the United States in fighting the war, fourteen cents had gone to Lend-Lease. Out of this small proportion of our total war costs we had shipped to our Allies over twenty-three thousand planes, as many tanks, and more than half a million motor vehicles. In addition, the Allies had bought in cash seven thousand planes, two thousand tanks, and a quarter of a million motor vehicles.

To the Soviet Union, for $4,750,000,000, went 8,800 planes, 5,200 tanks and tank destroyers, 190,000 military trucks, 36,000 jeeps, 30,000 other motor vehicles, 7,000,000 pairs of military boots, 2,600,000 tons of food, 1,450,000 tons of steel, 420,000 tons of aluminum, copper, nickel, zinc, and brass, 200,000 tons of high explosives, and $200,000,000 worth of machine tools. Two-thirds of all these supplies were shipped to Russia late in the war, between March 1943, and March 1944.

The great stream of supplies flowing to the United Kingdom included over one billion dollars' worth of ordnance, nearly as much in tanks and military vehicles, two hundred million dollars' worth of landing craft for the invasion of Europe, 5,750,000 tons of steel, 500,000 tons of other metals, and several hundred thousand tons of high explosives for bombs to mount the air offensive against Germany. The larger part of these supplies for Britain, like those for Russia, were shipped overseas in 1943 and 1944 to prepare great offensives.

A considerable volume of Lend-Lease aid went to the Middle East and Pacific earlier in the war, because of the urgent need to hold and defend these theaters. With this assistance, British and French forces turned the tide of battle in the Middle East and made possible the British and American invasion of North Africa in 1942. French Colonial forces in this region were trained and equipped with $300,000,000 worth of Lend-Lease supplies. In the Pacific, Australia and New Zealand received $200,000,000 worth of planes, tanks, and military vehicles valued at the same amount. Two billion dollars in matériel went to these British Dominions, and to India, China, and the Netherlands East Indies, three-fifths of it military equipment for fighting the enemy. In India, two Chinese divisions were trained and equipped under Lieutenant General (now General) Joseph W. Stilwell for the campaign in Burma.

The contribution which American Lend-Lease made toward winning the war was to be found on every battlefield of the United Nations after 1941. The tragic weakness of all the nations fighting the Axis in the first two years of war—too little, too late—was slowly transformed into an overpowering superiority of armament, fire power, mobility, and supply. This was due in part to Lend-Lease. Even in the darkest days of the war American equipment helped to hold the enemy in the Middle East, in Russia, in China, in India, and in the South Pacific; now it was a firm foundation of victory.

14. WHAT AMERICA DEFENDED

In his message to Congress proposing Lend-Lease aid to the democracies fighting the Axis [*January 6, 1941*], President Roosevelt declared that our policy was "all-inclusive national defense." The defense of a nation, he implied, should safeguard more than the land and water which make up a country. It should give security to a people and to their way of life. The American way of life is essentially democratic in spirit and ideals. It cannot easily be defined, but is implicit in our whole history and forms part of the experience of every American. It would not be safe, said the President, if we consented to "a peace dictated by aggressors and sponsored by appeasers," for "enduring peace cannot be bought at the cost of other peoples' freedom."

Warning the Fascist powers that we would not live in a world divided between tyranny and democracy, the President proclaimed that we looked "forward to a world founded upon four essential freedoms." To call for a peace based upon these freedoms wasn't to envision a distant millenium. "It is a definite basis," he said, "for a kind of world attainable in our own time and generation. That kind of world is the very antithesis of the so-called new order of tyranny which the dictators seek to create with the crash of a bomb. To that new order we oppose the greater conception—the moral order."

Four Freedoms

The President proposed that four freedoms, born of American experience, should prevail "everywhere in the world." They were of two kinds, positive and negative, the right to do something, which could be done only if something else did not interfere. "Freedom of speech and expression" and "freedom of every person to worship God in his own way" were individual liberties essential to Democracy. Without them no man could call his soul his own; without them he would not be a free human being. But these liberties could not exist unless there were prosperity and peace in the world—freedom from want and from fear. The third—"freedom from want"—was translated by the President into world terms to mean "economic understandings which will secure to every nation a healthy peacetime life for its inhabitants." The fourth—"freedom from fear"—he defined as "a worldwide reduction of armaments to such a point and in such a thorough fashion that no nation will be in a position to commit an act of physical aggression against any neighbor." These, then, were the four freedoms: the right of every person to think, speak, and worship as he pleased, secured by preserving the prosperity and peace of every nation.

The Atlantic Charter

The four freedoms were incorporated, not in so many words but in their essence, in the document called the Atlantic Charter which President Roosevelt drafted with Prime Minister Churchill at their first meeting aboard American and British warships anchored off Newfoundland in the summer of 1941 [*August 3-14, 1941*]. They met with their staffs to discuss problems of Lend-Lease supply and to arrange for the support of the Soviet Union in its war against Hitler. But they also "considered the dangers to world civilization arising from the policies of military domination by conquest upon which the Hitlerite government of Germany" had embarked. In the Atlantic Charter they drew up a "declaration of principles" to which all men unwilling to compromise with the Nazis could subscribe, "a goal which is worth while for our type of civilization to seek." Before the United States entered the war, it reached an agreement with Great Britain on the basic terms of peace.

In the Atlantic Charter, the President of the United States and the Prime Minister of Great Britain set down "certain common principles in the national policies" of their countries "on which they base their hopes for a better future for the world." There were eight principles:

> *First*, their countries seek no aggrandizement, territorial or other;
> *Second*, they desire to see no territorial changes that do not accord with the freely expressed wishes of the peoples concerned;
> *Third*, they respect the right of all peoples to choose the form of government under which they will live; and they wish to see sovereign rights and self-government restored to those who have been forcibly deprived of them;
> *Fourth*, they will endeavor, with due respect for their existing obligations, to further the enjoyment by all states, great or small, victor or vanquished, of access, on equal terms, to the trade and to the raw materials of the world which are needed for their economic prosperity;

Fifth, they desire to bring about the fullest collaboration between all nations in the economic field with the object of securing, for all, improved labor standards, economic advancement, and social security;

Sixth, after the final destruction of the Nazi tyranny, they hope to see established a peace which will afford to all nations the means of dwelling in safety within their own boundaries, and which will afford assurance that all the men in all the lands may live out their lives in freedom from fear and want;

Seventh, such a peace should enable all men to traverse the high seas and oceans without hindrance;

Eighth, they believe that all of the nations of the world, for realistic as well as spiritual reasons, must come to the abandonment of the use of force. Since no future peace can be maintained if land, sea, or air armaments continue to be employed by nations which threaten, or may threaten, aggression outside of their frontiers, they believe, pending the establishment of a wider and permanent system of general security, that the disarmament of such nations is essential. They will likewise aid and encourage all other practicable measures which will lighten for peace-loving peoples the crushing burden of armaments.

PART FOUR

THE UNITED NATIONS ON THE DEFENSIVE

15. AXIS AND ALLIED STRATEGY AFTER PEARL HARBOR

All "hopes for a better future for the world" expressed in the Atlantic Charter became doubly difficult to achieve when Japan attacked in the Pacific. No longer was Hitler the only enemy, with Europe and Africa the only battlefields; the Nazis were reinforced by the Japanese, and war swept over the whole world. The Axis powers, leagued together in military as well as diplomatic alliance, fought to complete the world conquest upon which they were already well advanced, Germany in Europe and Japan in Asia.

In this vast undertaking the aggressors enjoyed two great advantages over their enemies: they were already well prepared and fully mobilized. Interior lines of supply also favored their operations. At the peak of its military and naval power early in 1942, the Axis controlled a force so tremendous that it could mount offensives simultaneously in Europe, Africa, Asia, the Pacific, and the Atlantic. Under attack by land, sea, and air, the United Nations were everywhere on the defensive. For a year or more they would have to struggle to hold what they had, to keep lines of communication open around the world, and to lose no time in transforming their superior industrial resources into fighting strength. The great question they had to answer was how soon they could assume the counteroffensive. If they took too long, they would be defeated before they were ready to fight with all their strength. A quick victory was impossible for the Allies because, quite apart from lack of preparation, they depended on exterior lines of supply. Germany and Japan each held a central military position at the hub of its continental wheel. The United Nations and their possessions were scattered around the rims.

Yet the space that separated the chief Axis powers and limited each to its own radius, was their main weakness, preventing the pooling of Japan's naval strength with Germany's land and air power and the combining of all their resources. The Axis realized the power to be gained from a union of force. Their offensive strategy in 1942 may have anticipated the ultimate goal of locking arms in India, toward which both converged—Japan by enveloping Southeast Asia and Germany by attacking eastward through the Russian Caucasus and Egypt. If their armies should meet, they would outflank and isolate both Russia and China; Great Britain and the United States would be cut off from their allies and besieged. This was the offensive strategy of the Axis in the long run; the immediate defensive plan behind Japan's entering the war was, as was pointed out earlier, to engage the United States on two fronts.

For the United Nations a fateful decision had to be made in the days following Pearl Harbor, when Prime Minister Churchill met President Roosevelt in Washington. Which front was the more important, Europe or Asia? Who was, in the language of the American police, "Public Enemy No. 1," Hitler or the Japanese militarists led by General Tojo? Upon the answer to these questions of strategic priority depended the length of the war and possibly even the victory of the United Nations, none of whom, not even the United States, was strong enough to fight both Germany and Japan with equal power. The military principle of economy of force required that sufficient power should be concentrated against first one enemy, then the other, splitting up and defeating them in detail. Opinion among the peoples of the United Nations was somewhat divided in selecting the more dangerous enemy, Germany or Japan. In China, Australia, New Zealand, India, throughout the Pacific, and on the American West Coast public opinion naturally feared Japan who was already close and coming closer. But the people of Great Britain, Russia, and occupied Europe looked on Hitler as their chief enemy because they were already at grips with him.

After Pearl Harbor the fundamental decision of the Combined Chiefs of Staff in Washington was to beat Germany

105

first, while holding Japan at bay. They planned to launch major offensives as soon as possible on the primary fronts in Africa and Europe and limited offensives on the secondary fronts of the Pacific and Asia. "The defeat of Hitler and the breaking of German power," as Churchill said later, "must have priority over the decisive phase of the war against Japan." This decision, reached early in 1942, was never changed. Events which no man could then foresee have since justified it. Fortunately for the United Nations, however, the speed and magnitude of American production enabled the United States to assume an unlimited offensive in the Pacific even before Germany was fully crushed.

The reason Allied strategy was concentrated first against Germany rather than Japan was that the Nazis presented a more serious immediate threat. The industrial war potential of Germany, with the resources of occupied Europe at her command, surpassed that of Japan even with her control of Asia. German-ruled Europe produced four times as much steel as Japan. The annual Japanese output could never exceed ten million metric tons, for all the raw materials and labor conquered in Asia had to be fed into the limited industrial machine of Japan itself. Once Germany was defeated, Japan could not hope to match the United Nations in production.

Another consideration in Allied strategy was the fact that Germany was nearer than Japan to the three strongest Allies—the United States, Great Britain, and the Soviet Union. They could strike much more quickly and directly at Germany; indeed, there were already two fronts established against the Nazis in Russia and Africa. A front against Japan, except in China and over the far distances of the Pacific, had yet to be set up. Britain, Russia, and Africa, already far stronger than Australia or India, were comparatively accessible bases from which to prosecute the war.

Unlike the Axis, the United Nations could reinforce one another by sea and concentrate their strength where needed. Determining the most economical use of that force was a final concern in their strategy. Hitler's defeat was prerequisite to victory over Japan, for if he could add the resources of Russia to his empire, his power would be irresistible. No such

106

reserve of power was within reach of Japan. With relatively small forces, largely air and naval, Japanese expansion might be checked until Allied strength could be shifted from Europe to the Pacific. Then overwhelming strength could be concentrated to drive the Japanese back to their home islands and crush their power at its source.

So the United States made the wise decision to join her Allies in fighting a global war on all fronts in the order of their strategic importance. To concentrate American force in the Pacific apart from our Allies would be to throw away the obvious advantages of a coalition, to let the Axis once more "divide and conquer." The strategy of uniting with our neighbors, first worked out in Lend-Lease, when any Axis attack on another nation was seen to endanger the United States, had proved its wisdom. The direct attack of Japan upon Pearl Harbor had aroused the fighting temper of all Americans. They were impatient to avenge it. But they were wise enough to keep their powder dry, and bide their time in the Pacific, so that they could defeat all their enemies, each in his own time and, it was hoped, for all time.

16. RISE OF THE UNITED NATIONS

With almost the whole world at war, the United States proposed that all the nations hostile to the Axis pledge their cooperation in waging war and agree not to make a separate peace or armistice. A declaration to this effect was signed at Washington [*January 1, 1942*] by the representatives of twenty-six governments: the United States of America, United Kingdom of Great Britain and Northern Ireland, Union of Soviet Socialist Republics, China, Australia, Belgium, Canada, Costa Rica, Cuba, Czechoslovakia, Dominican Republic, El Salvador, Greece, Guatemala, Haiti, Honduras, India, Luxembourg, the Netherlands, New Zealand, Nicaragua, Norway, Panama, Poland, South Africa, and Yugoslavia. They were joined later in 1942 by Mexico, the Philippine Commonwealth, and Ethiopia, and in 1943 by Iraq, Brazil, and Bolivia. General Charles de Gaulle, representing the Free French, had also subscribed his name. Thus thirty-three governments in the New and Old Worlds were united in the war.

In the Declaration of Washington all the United Nations subscribed to the "purposes and principles" of the Atlantic Charter. Their indorsement transformed it into a world charter. The United Nations further declared in the Charter "complete victory over their enemies is essential to defend life, liberty, independence, and religious freedom, and to preserve human rights and justice in their own lands as well as in other lands." For the survival of these values they "engaged in a common struggle against savage and brutal forces seeking to subjugate the world." To carry on this struggle, each government promised to employ "its full resources, military or economic," against the Axis powers with which it was at war, to cooperate with the other United Nations, and "not to make a separate armistice or peace with the enemies."

These pledges among the United Nations, the statecraft of war, were formulated slowly and painfully at the conferences of diplomats, but their actual working out was swift and efficient on the fields of battle. Inevitably the more powerful countries took the lead, both in diplomacy and war, and the very loose military alliance of the United Nations found its voice and strength in the United States, Great Britain, the Soviet Union, and China. The agreement of these four powers gave promise of a coalition of manpower, resources, and strategy sufficient to defeat the Axis, and if the Atlantic Charter were observed, to crush Fascism and extend Democracy.

Joint Anglo-American strategic command, to insure "full British and American collaboration with the United Nations," was vested in the Combined Chiefs of Staff, appointed in Washington by President Roosevelt and Prime Minister Churchill at their first conference following Pearl Harbor [*February 6, 1942*]. The United States was represented by Generals (now Generals of the Army) George C. Marshall and Henry H. Arnold, and Admirals (now Fleet Admirals) Ernest J. King and Harold R. Stark; Great Britain by Field Marshal the late Sir John Dill, Admiral Sir Charles Little, Air Marshal A. T. Harris, and Lieutenant General Sir Colville Wemyss. These eight men became responsible for planning the Anglo-American war effort at the highest levels of military strategy, and their advice was the foundation of all the military decisions made by Roosevelt and Churchill. The fact that the Combined Chiefs of Staff sat together in almost daily sessions in Washington gave Britain and America the benefits of unified strategic command; neither country fought the war alone, but could rely on combined manpower and resources in all theaters of operations. Liaison was maintained with the Soviet Union through an Allied Military Mission to Moscow, and with China by the Allied Military Council at Chungking. Each of the four leading United Nations was fighting the enemy on a major front.

17. THE JAPANESE OFFENSIVE IN THE PACIFIC

The strategy of Japan's amphibious warfare, which swept over the islands of the southern Pacific in 1942 as the German blitzkrieg had overwhelmed western Europe in 1940, was to win control over the rich resources and numerous populations of Asia. Five hundred million Orientals, more easily exploited than the politically conscious peoples of Hitler's Europe, offered a labor power with which Japan could hope to achieve world dominion. In Malaya and the Netherlands East Indies she would gain not only all the oil she needed, but eighty-five per cent of the world's rubber and sixty-five per cent of its tin, and her gains would be at the expense of democratic nations, making the United States weak and Japan strong. It was no idle dream of Japanese imperialists that with these advantages the "eight corners" of the world might eventually be brought under the roof of the Mikado's palace.

Nor were the Japanese war lords completely irrational when they struck at the United States and Great Britain. The year 1941 and even 1942 promised to be Axis years. Great Britain was fighting for her life in the Middle East; Soviet Russia was staggering under the impact of the Nazi invasion; and the United States, unprepared for a war on two fronts, was desperately trying to support Britain and Russia with Lend-Lease supplies. Timing meant everything if Japan were to dominate Asia while the other Great Powers of the world had their hands tied by Hitler.

Hence the Japanese launched a centrifugal offensive from bases in Formosa, French Indo-China, and the Pacific islands, with simultaneous blows at almost every point of the compass—Pearl Harbor, Midway, Wake, Guam, the Philippines, Hong Kong, Malaya, and Singapore. Germany had fought on one front at a time; Japan struck all fronts. Pearl Harbor came first because it was essential to neutralize the United States Pacific Fleet and free the route of conquest to Malaya, the Netherlands East Indies, and the islands of the Pacific. These Asiatic treasure houses were isolated by the temporary crippling of the American Navy at Pearl Harbor, where the United States was caught unprepared and compelled as a result to fight on the defensive for a year, until American men and industries were mobilized for action. The situation in Europe gave Japan her opportunity in Asia.

Japanese Envelopment of Southeast Asia

The fall of France and the Netherlands in the spring of 1940 had diverted Japan from China to rich but defenseless French Indo-China and Netherlands East Indies, which now promised easy pickings. Under pressure from Hitler as well as Japan, the French Vichy Government opened Indo-China to Japanese agents [*June 20, 1940*], and by a pact signed at Hanoï, conceded three airfields and admitted a garrison of sixty thousand Japanese troops [*September 22, 1940*]. Japan then gained control of Saïgon, only 650 miles north of Singapore, and converted it into a naval base. Thailand, formerly known as Siam, fell under Japanese domination early in 1941 when Tokyo dictated a settlement of her dispute with Indo-China to the advantage of the Thai—and the Japanese. From bases in Indo-China and later in Thailand, Japan was ready to swoop down upon Malaya, Singapore, the Netherlands East Indies, and Burma.

Great Britain could not hold these regions, the richest part of which belonged to her, because, as Churchill said, she

110

was "engaged in a life-and-death struggle" in Europe and the Mediterranean. In order to appease Japan, Britain had in January 1939, suspended the supply of China through Hong Kong and, for three months, closed the Burma Road. Not only did Britain lack the air power in the Far East to resist Japan, but with the paralysis of the U. S. Pacific Fleet at Pearl Harbor and the sinking of the *Prince of Wales* and *Repulse* three days later, no power was available to stop Japan north of Australia and east of India. The Netherlands East Indies, reinforced at the last moment by limited American supplies, could do no more than fight a delaying action.

Taking advantage of this military and naval situation in the far distances of the Pacific, a situation created partly by her own diplomacy but above all by Hitler's success in Europe, Japan overran the colonies of Southeast Asia in four short months. With a force estimated by Churchill at twenty-six divisions, the Japanese enveloped East Asia and conquered all the aslands of the Southwest Pacific between Australia and the Asiatic mainland.

I. HONG KONG, MALAYA, SINGAPORE, BURMA

The main force with which the Japanese enveloped Southeast Asia was an army of some 200,000 troops in French Indo-China. Their intentions were hidden behind the diplomatic smoke screen which their envoys raised in Washington, where they pretended to be negotiating a peaceful settlement of all differences. When the Japanese carrier force struck Pearl Harbor, well supplied armies were prepared to move on Thailand, Malaya, Singapore, and Burma. Additional troops, specially trained in jungle warfare and in all the requirements of their different missions, were ready in the island of Formosa and on the coast of occupied China. Not only the Pearl Harbor attack but the many others made in Asia and the Pacific by the Japanese had been carefully planned long before their execution. Tactical success depended on speed and surprise, and the enemy achieved both by striking Hong Kong, Manila, Thailand, Singapore, Midway, Wake, and Guam at the same time that they raided Pearl Harbor.

111

Hong Kong

The British crown colony of Hong Kong, deep-water port of Canton in southeastern China, was the apex of a triangle based on Singapore and Corregidor, within which Anglo-American power in the Far East was concentrated. The Japanese occupation of Canton in the war against China, and of French Indo-China and Hainan Island in 1940-41, had enclosed Hong Kong and would be able to cut it off from Singapore, fourteen hundred miles south, on the outbreak of the war. Though Hong Kong was doomed, a delaying action fought in its defense would give Britain and America time to reinforce other positions in the Pacific. Late in November, some three thousand Canadian reinforcements landed, bringing the total strength of the Anglo-Indian garrison to about twelve thousand men, poorly equipped, burdened with crowds of Chinese refugees, and without any liaison with Chinese troops on the mainland.

Japanese dive bombers opened the attack on Hong Kong at the same hour that other planes were striking Pearl Harbor [*December 8, 1941*[1]]. Air strip, hangars, and old training planes—all the air power of the garrison—were destroyed and Hong Kong was at the mercy of Japanese bombers. Ground troops penetrated Kwangtung Peninsula and overcame the strongpoint of the inner line of resistance on Kowloon. As the British withdrew to the island of Hong Kong, the Japanese bombed and shelled reservoirs of the colony until there was only one day's water supply left [*December 18-24, 1941*]. The British surrendered the next day. Even if there had been water they could not have resisted much longer, for Japanese troops had crossed the harbor, had landed, had expanded a bridgehead, had infiltrated the British lines, had survived all counterattacks, and had narrowed the siege to Victoria Peak. With the fall of Hong Kong the last major port into Free China was closed [*December 25, 1941*].

Malaya

From the frontier of Thailand, which had surrendered

[1] Dates west of the International Date Line, following 180° West Longitude, are one day later than those in the United States.

112

after token resistance [*December 8, 1941*], and French Indo-China the Japanese moved swiftly south through the British Malay States to Singapore, 580 miles away. The Malay States not only provided a highway to Singapore but were a rich prize in themselves, for they produced nearly half the world's rubber and over a quarter of its tin. Against the British Imperial III Corps, consisting of Scottish, Australian, and Indian units, holding the main roads, the Japanese sent their best troops, a force of four or five divisions trained to advance through the rice-field swamps, traveling light, sometimes clothed only in loin cloths, and easily mistaken for Malay natives as they infiltrated British lines. In a global war of machines Japan's armies perfected the tactics of jungle warfare.

Since the Japanese required air cover for their overland advances, they always seized airfields first. Thus the attack on the long, narrow Malay Peninsula began with landings on the east coast and in Thailand [*December 8–9, 1941*] to pinch off the airdrome at Kota Bharu, and to take the fields at Singora and Patani. From the latter points a division equipped with light tanks and armored cars cut across the neck of the peninsula to the west coast and threatened to envelop the British Imperial 11th Division, which fell back, uncovering Penang. After the capture of this important island port, evacuated by the panic-stricken white residents, the Japanese pressed steadily down the west coast, turning strongpoints by amphibious hops and outflanking British positions with a series of surprise raids in which the defenders suddenly found themselves behind enemy lines. From the east coast, after overcoming strong resistance at Kota Bharu, the Japanese advanced southward along an inland railway, pushing the British Imperial 9th Division before them. The mobility of Japanese units enabled them to infiltrate and envelop each receding line of British defense. Another enemy force drove down the east coast. All three Japanese drives converged on a common front in Johore, less than one hundred miles above Singapore [*December 29, 1941*].

The fate of the great naval base, and of the troops covering it in Malaya, was sealed by the early sinking of the bat-

113

tleship *Prince of Wales* and the battle cruiser *Repulse* [*December 10, 1941*], caught without air cover by Japanese torpedo planes off Kuantan on the east Malay coast. The destruction of these mighty British warships was a triumph of air power. It deprived the combined forces of the British, Dutch, and Americans of any effective naval strength in Southeast Asia, reduced the conquest of that region to a land-and-air problem for the Japanese, and freed them to sweep the seas south through the Indies to Australia. To the Allies it was a tactical misfortune no less serious than the strategic blow suffered at Pearl Harbor.

In a desperate effort to save the situation in Malaya, the Allied command in Southeast Asia was reorganized and unified, the result of British-American discussions in Washington. General Sir Archibald Wavell assumed supreme command [*January 3, 1942*]; his deputy, Lieutenant General George H. Brett, directed the weak air forces, and Admiral Thomas C. Hart took charge of such naval forces as were left. Generalissimo Chiang Kai-shek was head of all land and air forces isolated in China. But this change of command came too late and was not of sufficient force to relieve the British forces in Malaya. At the Slim River they were defeated by about thirty enemy tanks [*January 7, 1942*] and driven relentlessly south from Kuala Lumpur to the Johore Causeway connecting Malaya with the island of Singapore. Scottish Highlanders and Australians covered the withdrawal [*January 30–31, 1942*] of remnants of British III Corps which had rallied to the defense of Singapore. The land approaches to this naval base had been conquered by the Japanese in less than two months; they had swept south through Malaya over five hundred miles, waging blitzkrieg in the jungles, rice swamps and rubber forests in which superior forces and tactics caught the British off guard and swept them aside.

Singapore

The naval base on Singapore Island was prepared to resist assault from the sea, but not from the jungles in the rear, or from the skies. All fighter planes had been recalled from Malaya before Christmas to beat off the flights of

114

thirty to ninety Japanese bombers which raided Singapore three times or more every day. Air defense, even when reinforced by a squadron of Hurricanes recently arrived at Singapore, was inadequate. The Japanese aerial siege persisted for over a month [*December 29, 1941–February 8, 1942*], and by that time enemy ground troops were in position to launch their assault across the river-like Strait of Johore. Under cover of intense artillery bombardment the invaders secured a bridgehead at Kranji, made two other landings east and west [*February 8–9, 1942*], and converged on the city of Singapore in the south after isolating the naval base and water reservoirs. The defenders were hopelessly cut up.

Singapore surrendered unconditionally seventy days from Japan's first attack on Malaya [*February 15, 1942*]. The enemy had not only reduced a naval fortress once considered impregnable, but had captured some seventy thousand British Imperial troops. The fall of Singapore, according to Prime Minister Churchill, was "the greatest disaster to British arms which history records." It was likewise a death blow to Allied forces left stranded in Southeast Asia, for it compelled them to fall back to the Netherlands East Indies, and eventually to Australia. Worst of all, the way lay open for the Japanese to attack Burma and India.

Burma

The Japanese invaded lower Burma from Thailand early in the Malaya campaign. Their object was to protect the right flank and rear of troops pushing south to Singapore by neutralizing the Burmese airfields. But the RAF and the American Volunteer Group of "Flying Tigers" retained local control of the air against a superior force of enemy bombers. Japanese ground troops, however, soon gained possession of lower Burma. The British evacuated Moulmein, fell back on the main port of Rangoon, where supply was badly disorganized by enemy bombing, and prepared to defend upper Burma on the line of the Salween River [*January 31, 1942*].

Foreseeing the fall of Singapore, the main Japanese forces in Thailand entered Burma to cut the Burma Road and isolate China [*February 8, 1942*]. They enveloped the southern flank of the British position by landings across the Salween

115

River and drove the defenders west to the Sittang [*February 23, 1942*], cutting up some British units as they crossed the river. Rangoon was evacuated after heavy bombing and a Japanese thrust to Pegu had made the great port appear untenable [*March 8, 1942*]. The loss of Rangoon cut the supply lines of the British and Chinese forces in Burma; the only remaining means of communication with India was by air. British troops retreated north to Prome, fighting their way through enemy lines.

Large Chinese forces under Lieutenant General (now General) Joseph W. Stilwell were sent into north Burma by Generalissimo Chiang Kai-shek. The Japanese moved north so rapidly in pursuit of the British, however, that the Chinese were left in the position of covering the withdrawal of Imperial troops to India. Their own withdrawal became necessary [*April 26, 1942*] when Japanese motorized troops penetrated to Lashio, split the Allied forces, and cut the Burma Road. As the enemy continued north to Bhamo and Myitkyina, the British escaped west over jungle trails to Imphal in India, while the Chinese retreated north up the Salween River into their own country. By the end of May the Japanese had occupied all of Burma, a land a little larger than France, and cut off all connections between China and her allies, except by air over the hazardous Himalayan "hump" to India.

Even India was threatened by a large Japanese naval force of three battleships and five aircraft carriers screened by cruisers and destroyers, which entered the Bay of Bengal and struck the island of Ceylon [*April 4, 1942*]. Japanese planes raided Colombo in force [*April 9, 1942*], and sank two heavy British cruisers, the *Cornwall* and *Dorsetshire,* and the carrier *Hermes.* Nearly all the British planes attacking the enemy carriers were shot down. As Japanese submarines sank numerous merchant ships and the carrier force raided the mainland of India, the British rushed naval reinforcements to the East to hold the Indian Ocean. By early summer the British had three battleships and an aircraft carrier in the Bay of Bengal to thwart any Japanese attack. The onset of heavy monsoon rains protected the peninsula from overland invasion through Burma.

The defense of the Philippine Islands was a gallant delaying action which slowed down the Japanese advance into the South Pacific. It was never intended to hold the Philippines at all costs. Since the islands were untenable for long, American supply was directed to building up trans-Pacific lines to Australia in order to keep the continent "down under" as a base from which a counteroffensive could later be launched for the reconquest of the Philippines.

The fate of the Philippines was settled before the war began. They were almost surrounded by the Japanese, who were north in Formosa, west in the Spratly Islands and Indo China, and east in the Mariannas, Caroline, and Marshall Islands. Since the U. S. Congress had voted in 1934 to make the Philippines independent in 1946, little had been done to protect them. General (now General of the Army) Douglas MacArthur was appointed in 1937 by the Filipino government to train a native army, but when war broke out, not more than one hundred thousand Filipinos had become soldiers. Twelve thousand Philippine Scouts, the best trained of these men, together with the U. S. 31st Infantry, bore the brunt of the fighting. Altogether, nineteen thousand U. S. Army troops defended the islands at the time of the attack. Included in this number were some eight thousand Army Air Forces personnel, equipped with about 250 aircraft, of which 35 were Flying Fortresses and 107 were P-40 fighters. Among the ground troops were National Guard units from New Mexico, California, Kentucky, Ohio, and Illinois. The 4th Marine Regiment, recalled from Shanghai, was also stationed in the Philippines at this time. In addition, during the final stand on Bataan, there were one thousand sailors without ships, eighteen thousand civilians evacuated from other areas, and some six thousand laborers. The situation in the other islands was much worse. In Mindanao, second to Luzon in size, Brigadier General (now Major General) William F Sharp did not have enough small arms for the thirty thousand Filipinos who could be called into service; in the island of Cebu only fifteen hundred old rifles were on hand. In the first two months of war, munitions and supplies from New

117

Zealand were run in through Japanese blockade, but for every ship which arrived safely two were lost. Soldiers were soon reduced to living on short rations.

The Japanese neutralized our offensive power at the start. Nine hours after Pearl Harbor, an enemy raid destroyed most of the heavy bombers and fighter planes [*December 8, 1941*]. Two days later Japanese planes wrecked the naval base at Cavite. Luckily, Admiral Thomas C. Hart's Asiatic "Fleet" of two cruisers, twenty-four patrol planes, the tender *Langley,* a squadron of destroyers, and many submarines had evacuated the base and gone south to help bring ten convoys of British reinforcements into Singapore. Later this fleet fought delaying actions in the Java Sea in defense of the Netherlands East Indies and almost every ship was sunk, but not before each had taken its count of an overwhelming enemy.

Bataan

Japanese troops first landed at Aparri and Vigan on the northern coast of Luzon three days after Pearl Harbor [*December 10, 1941*]; ten days later new landings were made at Davao on Mindanao Island, six hundred miles south of Manila. When Japan reinforced the troops in Luzon, by landings in Lamon Bay below Manila, and closed in on the city from north and south, General Douglas MacArthur executed defense plans drawn up several years before and withdrew all his forces westward into the rocky Bataan Peninsula, guarded at the tip by the island forts of Corregidor. Manila, declared an open city, was nevertheless bombed, and finally occupied by the Japanese [*January 2, 1942*].

On Bataan the Filipino-American forces at first made a stand in defense of the secondary naval base at Subic Bay. Enemy reinforcements compelled them to fall back southward to the main line of resistance across the center of the Peninsula. Here in foxholes they held their position from the middle of January until April, putting up a gallant defense which inspired Americans at home to resolve that the men of Bataan should not die in vain. During these months the main Japanese forces were busy with the conquest of Malaya, Singapore, Burma, and the Netherlands East Indies,

118

and the enemy troops in the Philippines were containing the Filipino-American force in Bataan. Once the Japanese had conquered Singapore and the Indies, they reinforced their units in Luzon for a drive in overwhelming strength under General Homma [*April 5, 1942*].

The defenders of Bataan were worn out by short rations and sickness. They lived on carabao, monkey, and rice, and were at last forced to eat their horses and mules. At least twenty thousand men were disabled by malaria. Their only air cover was provided by a few Curtiss P-40s flying from strips cut out of the jungle. Since they lacked not only food and planes, but tanks and heavy guns as well, their fate was inevitable. Lieutenant General (now General) Jonathan M. Wainwright, who assumed command [*March 17, 1942*] after General MacArthur was transferred to Australia, rejected the first Japanese demand for surrender [*March 22, 1942*]. But when the enemy penetrated and outflanked his lines with overpowering strength [*April 5-9, 1942*], there were no means to sustain the delaying action in Bataan. All troops left on Bataan to cover the withdrawal to Corregidor surrendered [*April 9, 1942*].

Corregidor

After overrunning Bataan, the Japanese mounted heavy guns in the mountains and directed a plunging fire at the forts of Corregidor. Planes and ships also bombed the beleaguered garrison. Nevertheless, crowded as it was with the survivors of Bataan, the tunnels in the rocks scarcely habitable, the main guns emplaced in the open without air protection, still Corregidor held out for almost another month.

Finally, opening their assault with a week of intensive bombardment by planes, ships, and artillery, the enemy swarmed across the narrow channel between Bataan and Corregidor and stormed the defenses at night. Corregidor and its three companion forts fell [*May 6, 1942*]. The Japanese terms were unconditional surrender. Soldiers, sailors, marines, and civilians, Filipino and American, became Japanese prisoners of war to the number of 11,574 on Corregidor; 36,853 had been captured on Bataan. The other islands also surrendered and were occupied by the enemy. The loss of the

Philippines was the sorriest defeat that this country ever suffered abroad, but as a delaying action the campaign was a success. Bataan and Corregidor, like Valley Forge, were triumphs of American courage: they promised that a war which began in defeat would end in victory.

Netherlands East Indies

As Japan's air and ground forces enveloped Southeast Asia, rolling up the British and American flanks in Malaya, Burma, and the Philippines, her land, sea, and air forces swept south through the Netherlands East Indies toward Australia and east across the Pacific Ocean toward the Hawaiian Islands. The Japanese caught the British, Americans, and Dutch off guard, or too poorly prepared to stop the onslaught, and hence did not need large forces to conquer an empire in the Pacific. Although the twenty-six divisions reportedly used in Japan's amphibious war outnumbered the Allied troops defending the Southwest Pacific, her victory was not due to superior numbers, but rather to speed, surprise, and the skill with which all arms were combined. Air power was basic, and the Japanese possessed it from the start in their "stationary island aircraft carriers" scattered through the Marianas and Carolines. To these bases they added others, extending their air power south and east. Under this air cover the Japanese Navy, divided into task groups, convoyed amphibious forces to conquer and occupy all the strategic islands of the western Pacific.

The Netherlands East Indies, scattered over more than fifteen hundred miles of water between Asia and Australia, and controlling the seas between these continents, offered the Japanese their richest prize. In Borneo, Sumatra, and Java, there was a wealth of oil, rubber, tin, quinine, hemp, and undeveloped iron and coal deposits, protected by a small colonial army of native troops, a miniature naval force, and a few planes bought from the United States. Only strong naval and air forces could have defended the Indies. The Japanese struck at them as soon as they established a base of operations at Davao, on Mindanao in the Philippines [*December 20, 1941*], whence they had access through the Celebes Sea to the Strait of Makassar running between Borneo

120

and Celebes Islands and leading to Java. In addition, they invaded Sumatra from nearby Malaya, cutting the Indies off from India in the north. From Truk in the Carolines they descended to New Guinea and the Solomons in order to close all waters in the south over which American reinforcements might come from Australia. Thus while the Indies were sealed off, the enemy was directing his main thrust at their heart, Java.

The Japanese made preliminary landings [*December 22, 1941*], after a heavy bombing, on the northwestern coast of Borneo in the British protectorate of Sarawak, neutralizing submarine and air bases which threatened Japanese convoys to Malaya. Enemy bombers based on the Philippines then began to raid Dutch Borneo and Celebes [*January 10, 1942*], where they transferred planes to cover the passage of troops through Makassar Strait into the Java Sea.

Java Sea Campaign

As the Japanese moved south through Molucca and Makassar Straits to conquer the Netherlands East Indies, Admiral Hart united with Admiral Helfrich of the Royal Netherlands Navy to stop the enemy with what American, Dutch, and Australian ships they could find. These weak forces fought a delaying action, attacking the Japanese four times with cruisers and destroyers, without air support except for a few Army bombers and fighters based on Java.

The Battle of Makassar Strait [*January 23, 1942*], an attack on a Japanese invasion convoy lying off the coast from Balikpapan, Borneo, was the first major sea battle between the Allied nations and Japan. Under cover of night, four old American destroyers ran three times at top speed through an enemy invasion fleet in a daring torpedo attack. The Japanese did not know what had hit them. How many ships were sunk by Lieutenant Commander (now Commander) Paul H. Talbot's flotilla no one could count in the black night. When all their torpedoes were spent, the destroyers left the blazing sea in safety. Dutch and American bombers pounded the convoy and added to its losses.

Though this convoy was stalled, nothing could stop the Japanese for long. Continuing eastward their forces landed

121

at Rabaul on New Britain [*January 23, 1942*] and at Bougainville in the Solomons [*January 29, 1942*]. They also seized new positions on the Borneo coast, captured the island of Amboina in the Banda Sea, and began to bomb Java [*January 30–February 4, 1942*]. Admiral Doorman led four cruisers and seven destroyers, Dutch and American, up through the Madoera Strait into the Java Sea [*February 4, 1942*] to destroy another enemy invasion fleet gathering at Balikpapan. Japanese bombers intercepted this force, hit but did not disable the U. S. cruiser *Houston* and crippled the *Marblehead*. The *Marblehead* repaired first to Java and then limped home across nine thousand miles of ocean. Admiral Doorman could do no more to save Sumatra from invasion.

When the enemy, having conquered Sumatra, Borneo, and Celebes, was ready to descend on Java, Admiral Hart relinquished his command [*February 11, 1942*] to Vice Admiral Helfrich of the Royal Netherlands Navy, who made ready for a last desperate stand. American ships left Soerabaja [*February 5, 1942*], the Dutch naval base which was now exposed to constant bombing, for Tjilatjap on the southern coast of Java. To this port also came ships from Darwin, Australia, where the airports, docks, warehouses, and almost every ship in the harbor were destroyed in a heavy enemy air raid [*February 18–19, 1942*]. The Japanese closed in on Java from the southeast, landed on Bali, and seized the airfield. Admiral Doorman attacked them in Bandoeng Strait, inflicting considerable damage, but lost a Dutch destroyer and suffered injuries to two of his cruisers and another destroyer [*February 19–20, 1942*].

Desperate but futile efforts were made to hold Java, the richest island of the Netherlands East Indies and the last Allied base in the southern Pacific short of Australia. Enemy bombers sank the U. S. tender *Langley* [*February 26, 1942*] as she tried to reach Java with reinforcements of fighter planes. Admiral Doorman's force suffered severely in its last vain thrust at superior invasion forces off Soerabaja. [*February 27, 1942*]. The Japanese sank two Dutch cruisers, two British and one Dutch destroyer, and disabled a British cruiser, the *Exeter*. The remaining ships were trapped in the Java Sea by Japanese naval or air patrols. Six warships,

122

including the *Exeter*, the American cruiser *Houston* and the destroyer *Pope*, headed for Soenda Strait. Only four American destroyers escaped through Bali Strait to Australia. As the Japanese landed on the northern coast of Java [*February 28, 1942*], ships at Tjilatjap evacuated the port hastily and steamed south for Australia. The American destroyers *Edsall* and *Pillsbury* never made port. Against overwhelming enemy strength and without air support these gallant vessels had fought in vain to hold the Java Sea, but the small Allied forces had first been split and then destroyed in detail.

Fall of the Indies

Japanese ground and air forces were not idle during the naval battles in the Java Sea. As the Dutch fired the oil wells of Borneo, the enemy seized Balikpapan to secure the Makassar Strait [*January 22, 1942*], and came down through the Molucca Passage into the Banda Sea, landing on Ceram and Amboina [*February 1, 1942*]. Daily bombing raids which gradually neutralized the naval base of Soerabaja and other key points in Java grew more intense after the Japanese seized a convenient airfield on the adjacent island of Bali [*February 18, 1942*]. Other forces landed on Timor and cut Java off from Australia. [*February 20, 1942*]. To the north, Japanese parachutists followed by seaborne troops invaded southern Sumatra [*February 14, 1942*] the day before Singapore surrendered, overran the rich oilfields of Palembang, and drove the Dutch back upon Java. Having reduced Allied air strength on this beleagured island to a dozen planes, the Japanese sent amphibious forces under strong naval and air escort down through the Makassar Strait to land at three points on the northern coast of Java [*February 28, 1942*]. They were quickly reinforced until the total invasion force exceeded one hundred thousand troops. With the surrender of Java [*March 9, 1942*], Tokyo announced the complete conquest of the Netherlands East Indies and the capture of ninety-eight thousand prisoners, of whom some five thousand were British, Australian, and American Australia lay open to invasion.

When General Douglas MacArthur reached Australia from the Philippines [*March 17, 1942*] to assume command of Allied defenses, the continent "down under" was being isolated by the Japanese sweep through the islands of the Southwest Pacific. Small amphibious forces of enemy marines, often unopposed, seized points in New Guinea and the So'omon Islands to prepare the way for the invasion of Australia. Japanese carrier-based bombers softened up [*January 3–20, 1942*] the defenses of Rabaul, on New Britain Island, which was conquered by a crushing defeat of the Australian garrison. On the same day [*January 23, 1942*] other enemy forces seized the centers of defense in the Solomons, Kavieng on New Ireland and Kieta on Bougainville. From these positions the Japanese struck west at New Guinea, bombing Madang, Lae, Salamaua, and Port Moresby, and even neutralizing Port Darwin on the northern coast of Australia [*February 19, 1942*]. Enemy troops seized Lae and Salamaua [*March 8, 1942*] under blanket air cover, driving the Australians back toward Port Moresby. The later capture of Guadalcanal and Tulagi marked the high tide of their conquests in the Southwest Pacific.

The timely arrival of American naval reinforcements halted the Japanese in this area and saved Australia. Supply lines to Australia, via Christmas, Canton, and the Fiji Islands, were established by American troops who landed, with the consent of the Free French, on New Caledonia and Espíritu Santo in the New Hebrides [*March 12, 1942*]. The decisive battles in the Coral Sea, first major victory in the war against Japan, stopped the advance of the enemy on Port Moresby and gave General MacArthur time to build up his forces for a counteroffensive.

III. GUAM, WAKE, AND MIDWAY

Two of the three American islands on the oceanic route from Hawaii to the Philippines fell to Japan. Guam, which the U. S. Congress had refused to fortify in 1939 for fear of provoking Japan, was an isolated outpost in the Marianas. Its garrison of some five hundred Americans made a brave stand, but without planes or heavy artillery they could not throw back the enemy descending upon them in force from nearby Rota [*December 11, 1941*].

Wake, thirteen hundred miles closer to Pearl Harbor, was defended for sixteen days by a battalion of Marines and one thousand civilian workmen, who survived repeated bombing and repulsed the initial attack by artillery fire at point-blank range. When the Navy radioed Major (now Lieutenant Colonel) James P. S. Devereux, to inquire what he needed, a message came back saying, among other things, "Send us more Japs." They came in force and overpowered the garrison [*December 23, 1941*]. This operation cost the invaders a cruiser, four destroyers, and a submarine, the heaviest toll ever paid by the Japanese in conquering so small an island.

The fall of Guam and Wake cut off the American army in the Philippines from seaborne reinforcements, and all naval and air forces were thrown back four thousand miles across the Pacific to Midway, which is only fifteen hundred miles from Pearl Harbor. But Midway held. In the days following Pearl Harbor, the garrison of U. S. Marines twice repulsed a Japanese task force which attacked them. The Marines waited for the enemy ships to come within very close range, then opened fire with their shore batteries and sank a cruiser and a destroyer. Midway was saved. Six months later bombers based there inflicted heavy damage on a second Japanese fleet invading these same waters.

IV. U.S. NAVY ON TACTICAL OFFENSIVE

Despite its heavy losses at Pearl Harbor, the U. S. Pacific Fleet was not immobilized. Following the decision made at Washington [*January 3, 1942*] by President Roosevelt and Prime Minister Churchill, to remain on the defensive in the Pacific until Hitler could be defeated in Europe, the U. S. Navy embarked on a vast holding operation with what ships it had. Any reinforcements of the Philippines or Netherlands East Indies would inevitably be too little and too late to save them. At best, we could delay the Japanese advance and halt it short of the crucial defense line running diagonally northeast from Australia to Pearl Harbor and thence north to the Aleutians. These Pacific outposts of the continental

125

United States must be held. To strengthen this line with bases, first for defense and later for offense, large supply fleets sailed to Australia under naval convoy.

Raids on Japanese Islands

While the Navy was on the strategic defensive, it nevertheless assumed a tactical offensive, raiding Japanese outposts to disperse their strength. Carriers and cruisers, grouped in task forces into which the Navy had divided its fleet, made swift jabs at the islands used by the enemy as "stationary aircraft carriers." The first raid [*January 31, 1942*] was a heavy bombardment of the Marshalls and Gilberts by a striking force of two carriers, one light and four heavy cruisers, and ten destroyers, under Vice Admiral (now Admiral) William F. Halsey, Jr. No vessels were lost, and enemy bases were damaged and weakened.

Other blows followed, each delivered swiftly by carrier task forces built around the *Enterprise, Yorktown,* and *Lexington,* with their escorts of cruisers and destroyers striking the enemy islands one after the other. Such a force under Vice Admiral Wilson Brown was intercepted by enemy planes [*February 20, 1942*] before it could surprise the Japanese at Rabaul in New Britain. The *Enterprise* led a group of ships under the command of Admiral Halsey in the bombardment of Wake and Marcus Islands [*February 24–March 4, 1942*]. The *Lexington* and *Yorktown* were spearheads of a force, again commanded by Admiral Brown, which raided the newly established enemy bases at Salamaua and Lae in New Guinea and sank several Japanese warships and transports [*March 10, 1942*].

The First Tokyo Raid

American morale was raised by a daring aerial raid on the main islands of Japan [*April 18, 1942*] foreshadowing the attacks which would be made by Superfortresses two years later. A task force under Admiral Halsey, which included two carriers, steamed to a position only eight hundred and fifty miles east of Tokyo. There sixteen regular B-25 Army land bombers took off from the *Hornet,* after a run of only eight hundred feet, to raid Japan. Colonel (now Lieutenant

126

General) James H. Doolittle, and his seventy-nine men flew close to the roof tops to avoid flak: at fifteen hundred feet they scattered sixteen tons of bombs and incendiaries on Tokyo, on the navy yard south of the city, and on other industrial cities. The Japanese were caught completely unawares. Until their gas was used up the planes flew on, crash-landing in China, except for one which came down in Siberia. Of the eighty crew members, sixty-four returned in safety with Chinese help. Three pilots were put to death by the Japanese in violation of the customs of modern war.

Battle of the Coral Sea

The first battle between Japanese and American carrier planes in the Coral Sea [*May 7–8, 1942*] was also, as Admiral King reported, "the first major engagement in naval history in which surface ships did not exchange a single shot." The action came about when Rear Admiral (now Vice Admiral) Frank J. Fletcher's task force, covering Australia, broke up the Japanese advance into New Guinea and the Solomon Islands [*May 3, 1942*]. The Japanese occupied Florida Island in the Solomons where, in the prologue to the battle, planes from the carrier *Yorktown* sank and damaged a number of enemy vessels in Tulagi harbor [*May 4, 1942*]. Then Admiral Fletcher's force joined American and Australian ships under Rear Admiral (now Vice Admiral) Aubrey W. Fitch; and their combined forces included two carriers, the *Yorktown* and *Lexington*, eight cruisers, and seventeen destroyers.

These vessels watched for a probable seaborne invasion of Port Moresby and sailed northward to intercept the enemy's concentration of ships. In the Coral Sea, American planes spotted and sank the carrier *Shoho* [*May 7, 1942*] and Japanese planes sank the destroyer *Sims* and a tanker [*May 8, 1942*]. Two enemy carriers were severely damaged the next morning. Japanese planes counterattacked the two American carriers, scoring hits with bombs or torpedoes on both. Fires caused by explosions on the *Lexington* so disabled her that she had to be sunk by torpedoes from her own destroyers.

Despite the loss of this 33,000-ton carrier, one of the four which were fighting in the Pacific, the U. S. Navy won the Battle of the Coral Sea. The loss of fifty-five American planes and 543 men was far less than enemy losses in aircraft and personnel. The attempt to cut the Australian supply line was checked and the Japanese withdrew their naval forces northward. The U. S. Navy prepared for action in the Central Pacific, where an enemy thrust at American bases and communications would, if successful, open the way to Australia. Risks had to be taken in defending the South Pacific which were unjustified in the Central Pacific.

18. TRAINING THE ARMED FORCES

While the United States Navy held the supply lines to Australia and performed the initial naval mission in 1942 of screening the coasts of America, the Army was reorganized, expanded, and trained for its own crucial mission of defeating all enemies. Only by bringing the war home to the Axis countries, on the ground and in the air, and breaking their will to resist by destroying their armed forces, could we defeat them completely. The strength of the Axis made it necessary for the United States to shoulder the heaviest burdens in this global war. Our allies had been a strong team when we joined them in 1917, but in 1941 the team was very weak. The United States would have to do more than in the last war, when they reinforced the French and British armies on the Western Front with two million infantry and artillery troops. The Air Force alone would demand two million men, and even larger Ground and Service forces would have to be mobilized, trained, and put into action on ten fighting fronts spread around the world. Above all, these needs had to be met quickly lest the enemy crash through a major front and win the war. Never before had the American people, a peace-loving people who had fought to secure their country and were now content to cultivate it, been called upon to do so much so quickly if they were to survive.

128

Reorganization

To accomplish the greatest military task in its history, the United States Army was reorganized for the three main jobs of training "a huge citizen army" for combat, developing a strong air arm, and providing supply. A study of the problem had been undertaken nearly a year before Pearl Harbor by a group of officers under Lieutenant General Joseph T. McNarney, later Deputy Chief of Staff. The Chief of Staff, General George C. Marshall, the Secretary of War, Henry L. Stimson, and President Roosevelt accepted their recommendations [*March 9, 1942*]. The Army was to operate in three great commands, all under the direction of the Chief of Staff: the Ground Forces, charged with training field armies, under Lieutenant General Lesley J. McNair; the Air Forces under Lieutenant General (now General of the Army) Henry H. Arnold; and the Service Forces under Lieutenant General (now General) Brehon B. Somervell, responsible for all functions of the Army not under other commands or directly under the General Staff. In the General Staff itself, an Operations Division, directed in turn by Major General (now Lieutenant General) Leonard T. Gerow, Major General (now General of the Army) Dwight D. Eisenhower, and Lieutenant General (now General) Thomas T. Handy, was organized for the strategic planning of war. The Operations Division prepared plans for the Joint and Combined Chiefs of Staff and maintained contact with every theater of war. In the overseas theaters of operations the commanding generals had full responsibility for executing strategic plans. The War Department in Washington remained the switchboard of all communications, and everything continued to be done in the name of the Chief of Staff, assuring a proper centralization of the war effort. Yet Ground, Air, and Service Forces, Operations Division, and the overseas theaters received sufficient authority to carry out their missions.

Training Ground Forces

The work of building an army fell to the Ground and Service Forces in the United States. The size of the job may be judged from the fact that in the defensive phase of the

129

war, from the middle of 1941 to the middle of 1943, the officer corps grew from 93,000 to 521,000 and the enlisted strength of the Army increased by five million men. Only 14,000 officers came from the Regular Army; 110,000 were added from the Reserves, 21,000 from the National Guard, 47,000 directly from civilian life, and most of the remainder from men selected from the ranks and trained in Officer Candidate Schools. The number of general officers increased in much smaller proportion, from 343 to 1,065, of whom 910 came from the Regular Army, all but 45 by temporary appointment to higher grade.

During the defensive phase of the war, in the two years following the summer of 1941, fifty new divisions were activated, in addition to the twenty-eight infantry, four armored, and two cavalry divisions with which we entered the war. To multiply units so fast, it was necessary to establish a cadre system. New divisions were built around units drawn from old divisions; some organizations were split several times to form the backbone of others. This method assured the efficient training of a rapidly growing army, but limited the number of units ready for early combat; for a division could not be quickly ripened until its cadre replacements were thoroughly seasoned.

Almost as many different types of skill and training went into making the average infantry division of fifteen thousand men as a civilian community of the same number would demand. Only eight thousand troops were schooled exclusively for fighting. All the others had to be prepared to move the combat troops and their weapons and to sustain them on the field of action. Transportation, equipment, and supply demanded the services of over 1,500 men; communications, nearly an equal number; administration, 700; repair and maintenance of equipment, 450; the preparation of food, 650; medical duties, 600; and a variety of other services occupied 1,600 men. All these troops were trained for combat, but nearly half of them were instructed in additional duties as well.

Each American citizen inducted into the Army normally had a year of training divided into four three-month periods, during which he became a soldier, not only a fighting man but one with special jobs to do in cooperation with others in closely knit organizations. During the first thirteen weeks of basic training at a replacement center he was taught the fundamental duties of a soldier. Less time was spent than in the last war on squad and parade-ground drill; of 572 hours of basic training, only twenty were to be devoted to close-order work. In the second phase the soldier became a member of a division to study the tactics of his particular arm of the service, using what he had learned in ever larger units as he was trained with a platoon, company, battalion, and finally a regiment. Units of all arms were combined in the third phase to work together as a regimental combat team. The last quarter of the year's training was devoted to divisional field exercises and corps maneuvers.

Beginning in March 1942, units selected for special combat operations rehearsed their assignments at the Desert Training Center, a Southwestern area of thirty thousand square miles resembling the sandy stretches of Africa; between May and September others went to the Amphibious Training Center for Pacific operations, or the Mountain Training Center at Camp Hale in Colorado where the men encountered all the difficulties of mountainous Italy. Other grounds for large-scale corps maneuvers were carefully selected and organized in Tennessee, Louisiana, and Oregon. "Battle indoctrination" prepared green troops to enter combat with seasoned enemies; under screens of live ammunition fire they learned to overcome such opposition as they would meet in action. The result of all this graduated and specialized training was to make skilled workers of American citizens, able in one year to face enemies who had been trained troops for many years. The American became a veteran in his first battle. He did not need to learn by the casualties of later battles what had been worked out by experience of trial and error in training. Because of this realistic preparation for combat, lives were saved and battles were seldom lost. The American infantry of the last war went into the trenches after two months or half a year of training; in this war the infantry was better prepared to fight, for the plan was normally carried out of giving him a full year of training before overseas duty.

131

The Air Forces

Many of the different arms required to win this war were developed almost from nothing. Among these, the United States Army Air Forces caught the public eye because of their spectacular expansion and deadly effectiveness all over the world. No other service grew so fast into an organization able to exploit the most complicated machinery of modern warfare. In nineteen years of peace only seven thousand pilots had been trained in aerial combat, and less than fifteen thousand men were skilled in the mechanics of repairing combat planes. Two years after Pearl Harbor, however, the Army Air Forces boasted over one hundred thousand pilots and half a million ground crew technicians, all graduates of an elaborate system of graded schools which taught more than a hundred different skills. At the School of Applied Tactics at Orlando, Florida, a postgraduate training ground which made use of all the lessons learned in combat, a complete air command flew bombers and fighters exactly as they must be operated overseas.

Not only was Air Forces training thorough; it was intensive and fast, so that Americans were ready to take to the sky against the enemy before our Ground Forces could assume the offensive. The engineering troops who built, operated, and defended airfields were a good example of Air Forces speed in training personnel. In 1939 the entire engineering strength of the Air Corps consisted of one officer and three enlisted men in the Aviation Section of General Headquarters. In June 1940, the 21st Engineer Regiment was transferred to the Air Forces and became the father of all the aviation engineer battalions. Twelve battalions were organized, besides the regiment, by the time of Pearl Harbor. Five months later, twenty were shipped to England, others to Panama, the Atlantic bases, and Hawaii. Exactly one year after Pearl Harbor, Air Forces engineers in England finished the first runways built in that theater entirely by Americans.

Service Forces

Another complex problem was that of providing for the range of professional and technical skills required by all the

132

tasks which fell to the Army Service Forces. Their work extended far beyond what was known in the last war as supply. Men and women of the Service Forces were doctors, dentists, nurses, chaplains, lawyers, bankers, postmasters, teachers, storekeepers, clerks, cooks, mechanics, and police for the whole Army. The largest branches of the Service Forces, each with one or more training centers, were the Medical, Signal, Engineer, Quartermaster, Finance, Transportation, Ordnance, Military Police, and Chemical Warfare divisions. Practically all service troops were trained for combat, though not for the specialized fighting which was the principal mission of Ground and Air Forces. Combat engineers or signal units, for example, had to be prepared to carry on their work under fire and to engage the enemy if necessary. In 1944 despite the magnitude of service and supply here at home, half the manpower assigned to the Service Forces was overseas.

For the 610 categories of work in the Army demanding specialized training, of which the larger number were service jobs, the American public schools provided an essential background of general skills. The additional training necessary to develop a soldier who would also be a mechanic or a cook was furnished by a wide variety of service schools. For professional work at a high level the Army drew heavily on the graduates of American colleges and professional schools. The fact that a majority of the citizens inducted into service had gone at least as far as high school in their civilian education, a few years beyond the grade school average of soldiers in the last war, added just so much to the military efficiency of the nation. It made possible an army which could work with machines and learn new jobs quickly.

The final result of all training, the objective of the entire Army, was the defeat of our enemies overseas. The Army Service Forces, together with the Navy, transported the Ground and Air Forces with all their equipment to the battle fronts and sustained them in action. It is impossible in this brief account of a whole world at war to describe the rear areas, communications, and supply which supported every fighting front, but it cannot be forgotten that for every soldier who fired a gun or flew a plane there had to be many more trained to back him up.

19. THE BATTLE OF PRODUCTION

For the United States the war was first of all a battle of production. With the largest industrial capacity of any nation in the world, American factories, mines, and shipyards, safely beyond the reach of enemy bombers, were expected to surpass the Axis and to equip not only our own fighting forces but also in part those of our allies. American management and labor, drawing upon rich natural resources and a highly developed technology, did not fail in their essential task. One year after Pearl Harbor the American production of war matériel was equal to the aggregate production of Germany, Italy, and Japan. Early in 1942, President Roosevelt asked for the manufacture of 60,000 planes and 45,000 tanks in one year; by the end of 1942, American factories had turned out 48,000 military planes and 56,000 tanks and self-propelled guns. This was only the beginning. After two years of war, with American production steadily increasing and German production starting to decline under the impact of heavy bombing, the United States achieved industrial supremacy both for itself and for its allies in the war against the Axis. No battle won on land, in the air, or at sea was a greater triumph than the victory of American supply, because it made possible every success in combat.

Since the United States was a greater industrial than military nation, stronger in supply than in armed forces, it fought a war of supply whose results were seen on all the battlegrounds of the world. Attacks both by land and sea were possible because thousands of new cargo vessels and transports were quickly built and fitted to cross the Atlantic and Pacific. Warships, planes, and weapons from assembly lines in America helped to slow down and finally stop the advance of the Axis everywhere. Even before many American troops were in combat, American supplies were arriving at all Allied fronts.

Offensive operations were delayed until enough mechani-
134

cal and explosive power had been accumulated to crush the enemy with the least cost in men. The Soviet Union was forced to mass its men against the German armies sweeping through its land, because it had no other choice. The United States and Great Britain, whose shores the enemy never stormed, were thrifty in the use of manpower, lavish in supply.

The Defense Program

Fortunately for the United States, in view of the sudden Japanese attack on Pearl Harbor, we did not enter the war entirely unprepared. Under the program launched in 1940, Congress had voted appropriations of sixty-four billion dollars for defense. This huge sum exceeded not only the direct cost of the last war, which was estimated at thirty-two billion, but even the entire national debt, which stood at forty billion in 1939. Before we entered this war, therefore, we were ready to spend twice as much as it took to win the last war. All this money, however, was not expended before Pearl Harbor. Only about one-sixth of the total appropriation had been used when war was declared, and of the amount spent nearly half had gone for new plants and equipment in the aircraft, munitions, shipbuilding, chemical, iron and steel, and machine tool industries.

The chief gains in war production during 1941 were made in ships, planes, and tanks. Most industries were still busy getting ready to make what would be required for war. Yet production increased steadily. In the month of Pearl Harbor two thousand planes were manufactured, equal to the entire production of 1939. The output of tanks which had not been manufactured at all before the war, had risen to several hundreds. From 131 new shipyards, added to the old, came a ship a day by the end of 1941. In this year nearly three times as many keels were laid for warships as in the previous year. The Garand rifle was just getting into production with a daily output of 250 in the summer of 1940; these rifles were being made at the rate of a thousand a day one year later.

As a result of the defense program we were far better prepared when Japan attacked us than when we entered the last war. In 1917 we had an army of 200,000 men, but in 1941 nearly that many troops were already in overseas garrisons, and our entire army numbered 1,800,000 men, partially trained and already housed in fifty cantonments. In 1917 we had fifty-five military planes; in 1941 the Army Air Forces included two hundred incomplete squadrons. We also had the largest navy in our history, another navy being built, and half as many seagoing cargo vessels on the ways as our whole merchant fleet numbered in 1917. We were not prepared for Pearl Harbor, nor for global war on ten different overseas fronts, but we were ready to defend the continental United States and strategic parts of the Western Hemisphere.

The defense program before Pearl Harbor was limited, chiefly because it operated as a supplement to our prosperous civilian peacetime economy. We prepared for war as we went to church, one day a week, and spent the other six days going about our private business. The Office of Production Management [*January 7, 1942*], set up under William S. Knudsen, had no power except to regulate Army and Navy purchases in competition with civilian production. A country which produced over three and a half million passenger automobiles in 1941, at a time when all other great industrial nations had long since given up making autos for planes and tanks, could not expect to be fully prepared to fight its enemies. Americans would not give up their cars for guns until peaceful fellow citizens were bombed and shot at.

Industrial Conversion

Despite our previous reluctance to abandon "business as usual," within one year of the Japanese attack on Pearl Harbor we were equaling the entire Axis in production for war. In 1942 we began to catch up with enemies who had a head start of ten years. President Roosevelt asked Congress [*January 6, 1942*] to devote half of our national production to the "war effort" and submitted a budget for fifty-six billion dollars to be spent in 1942–43.[1] For defense we had thus far spent only fifteen per cent of our national income; for war we must spend at least half of it. The President set high production goals: 60,000 planes in 1942, 125,000 in 1943;

[1] The fiscal year of the Federal Government runs from July 1 in one year to June 30 the next year.

45,000 tanks in 1942, 75,000 the next year; and most aston-
ishing of all, eight million deadweight tons of shipping in
1942, although little more than a million had been built
during the speed-up of 1941. "Only this all-out scale of production," declared the President, "will hasten the ultimate
all-out victory. Speed will count. Lost ground can always
be regained, lost time never. Speed will save lives, speed will
save this nation."

For speed and volume of production, over three-fifths of
all the prime war contracts were awarded to one hundred
large corporations. These giant concerns dealing in iron and
steel, automobiles, chemicals, and ships did the lion's share
of the work. But smaller business facilities were not neglected. Seventy thousand prime contracts and seven hundred thousand subcontracts were signed in 1942. Super-
vising this work was the War Production Board [*January
13, 1942*], established under Donald M. Nelson, with Charles
E. Wilson appointed in September as vice-chairman to take
charge of schedules. The automobile industry was converted
to the manufacture of tanks, planes, and ordnance during the
spring of 1942, when all automobile production was stopped
and machines were retooled for war. In anticipation of the
Japanese conquest of Malaya and the Indies, sources of the
American raw rubber supply, the sale of tires was banned
[*January 1, 1942*], and the armed forces were given priority
in using the national stockpile of 600,00 tons, less than
normal annual consumption; synthetic rubber plants using
oil and alcohol products were erected. Some fifteen billion
dollars of Government funds were poured into the expansion
of all kinds of manufacturing plants, leased to private concerns, a capital outlay of over three times as large as private-
investment in defense and one [*June, 1940–September,
1943*] which gave the Government a considerable interest in
American industry. Corporate profits were restricted by
higher taxation and rising costs to the point where earnings
of one thousand representative concerns in 1942, which had
increased to seven and a half billion dollars, were only about
five per cent of their sales and ten per cent of their net worth.

A crisis in industrial conversion came in the fall of 1942,
when production declined mainly because of the strategic

shift from defensive to offensive weapons. At the same time, Axis conquests had brought about shortages of certain raw materials; and inevitably complicated production schedules had caused some lines of goods to get ahead of others. The fact that we were making the shift to the attack was most encouraging, for it meant that American defenses were reasonably complete and that we were now able to carry the fight to enemies overseas. There were enough antiaircraft guns on hand to protect every town in America, and civilian defense was thoroughly organized against any possible bombing raids; but ships, planes, and tanks in vast quantities were needed to prepare for overseas operations. Production of these weapons jumped again with the institution of a system of priorities and salvage which eased and directed the flow of raw materials.

The Home Front

Supply of vital materials was assured by the rationing of competitive civilian goods [April 11, 1942] under the direction of the Office of Price Administration, with Leon Henderson and later Chester Bowles in charge of some six thousand local boards of voluntary supervisors. The primary purpose of this agency was to stabilize prices at the levels of March 1942, which were set as ceilings [April 28, 1942] by the General Maximum Price Regulation in order to prevent an inflationary rise in the cost of living. Although prices rose in 1942, ten per cent at the wholesale level and twenty-two per cent for farm products, they did not climb out of sight as in the last war. From the summer of 1939 to the end of 1942 it was estimated that the cost of living advanced twenty-one per cent; but in the period after Pearl Harbor, under price control and rationing, living costs increased only eight per cent. The high standard of living to which the American people were accustomed was nevertheless maintained even with the added burden of war production. In 1942, for example, eighty-one billion dollars were spent by civilians on food, clothing, rent and other necessities, an increase of six billion over the previous year. The national income after taxes, however, amounted to one hundred eight billion dollars, an excess of twenty-seven

138

billion, and this surplus of purchasing power over civilian goods and services available increased as the war went on. To some extent it was drained off by higher taxes and war bonds, which absorbed from one-tenth to one-fifth of the income of patriotic civilians, but it continued to threaten the economic stability of the country with an inflation of prices.

A tremendous increase in agricultural production, despite shortages of labor and machinery, was stimulated by rising food prices. Over five million acres, nearly equal to all the land cultivated in California, were added to the crop area of the country in 1942. The result was a gain of twelve per cent in our food supply, making possible the shipment of almost four billion pounds of Lend-Lease foods to Britain and Russia in 1942 without stinting Americans in any way. Indeed, the millions of men in the armed forces who were withdrawn from useful labor in production and distribution were better fed than any equally large class of people in the world, and civilians with increased purchasing power had more to eat than ever before. Although the British brought seven million new acres into production between 1939 and 1943, they remained dependent on American Lend-Lease for about one-tenth of their lean rations. This fraction was supplied with a great saving of shipping space by the dehydration of eggs, milk, and other products, a process that also helped to feed the people in countries liberated from the enemy. In everything needed to support as well as to protect human life, America became the "Arsenal of Democracy," not on a wasteful or lavish scale but with the strategic economy required to win the war.

Labor

All this production depended on labor. The demands of total war were well illustrated by a poster which showed three men, the farmer, the laborer, and the soldier, marching side by side to victory. Only such harmony and cooperative effort could win the war. But conditions on the battle front and the home front were entirely different, and it was not unnatural that the strict discipline, self-sacrifice, and exclusion of all thought of personal profit necessary in military life should be wanting in civilian life. Unlike Britain and Russia,

139

the United States had adopted a Selective, not a National, Service Act. It was believed that efficiency at home would be better served by voluntary patriotism than by bureaucratic regimentation, which would be intolerable without the morale and *esprit de corps* uniting soldiers in the face of danger where their lives depended on never letting the other fellow down.

Greater personal freedom rather than a higher standard of living distinguished civilian from military life. The American soldier was the best paid in the world. His basic weekly pay of $18.20, including an allowance for one dependent, was almost half the weekly average of $38.86 earned in factories in October 1942; and if to the soldier's money income were added the costs of feeding, clothing, and sheltering him, variously estimated at from twelve to eighteen hundred dollars a year, all of which a civilian had to provide for himself, military pay would be equal to or greater than civilian pay. The high wages earned in aircraft and shipbuilding plants, or in skilled machine trades, were not representative of the income of labor. Unless all civilians were to be deprived of their freedom, assigned to jobs by military order, and reduced to a uniform level of living, the monetary incentives of a peacetime economy remained the chief stimulus to maximum production.

On December 23, 1941, the leaders of eleven million workers, organized in labor unions, voluntarily gave up their legal right to strike. This pledge was conditional, however, because it was understood that nothing would be done to decrease union membership and that prices should not be allowed to rise out of proportion to wages. A National War Labor Board was established [*January 12, 1942*] under William H. Davis to cooperate with the Office of Price Administration in stabilizing wages and prices. The War Labor Board wrote maintenance of union membership clauses into many collective bargaining agreements. When C.I.O. (Congress of Industrial Organizations) steelworkers demanded an increased wage of one dollar a day because of increased prices, the War Labor Board granted a raise of forty-four cents under the so-called Little Steel formula which became the national wage policy. This decision was an attempt

140

to put "an end to the tragic race between wages and prices" by raising the former fifteen per cent [*October 3, 1942*] to catch up in cases of lag with an equal rise in the cost-of-living index since January 1941. By Executive Order of the President all wages and salaries under five thousand dollars were frozen, but Congress refused to adopt his other recommendation that all net incomes, after taxes, be limited to $25,000.

Although rising prices continued to provoke strikes, the record of American organized labor was better in this respect than in the last war; if threefold allowance be made for the larger American population, it was as good as the record of British labor. There were never as many strikes in the United States during any year of this war as there were in 1918 and 1937. No strikes were authorized by the American Federation of Labor or the Congress of Industrial Organizations. Aside from the coal strikes called four times in 1943 by the United Mine Workers under John L. Lewis, involving over four hundred thousand miners each time, the average number of days lost per worker in all strikes steadily declined during the war. In 1939 fifteen days were lost for every worker; in 1941, ten; in 1942, five; and in 1943, except for the coal strike, three days.

Despite all the exaggerated publicity which strikes received, a much more serious problem for management was the high rate of turnover and in some industries of absenteeism. The War Manpower Commission under Paul V. McNutt was assigned the task of overcoming labor shortages and adjusting the competitive demands of industry, agriculture, and Selective Service for manpower. When scarcity of labor developed in thirty-five industrial areas, the War Manpower Commission gave these centers priority, and required all labor to be hired through the United States Employment Exchanges [*December 5, 1942*]; in order to prevent one employer from robbing another, war plants were encouraged to train four million people in new skills.

The serious gap created in the supply of labor by the withdrawal of seven, and later of eleven, million men for the armed forces was filled by increasing the number of hours worked each week from an average of forty to forty-eight,

141

with overtime pay, and by employing women to replace men. Some four million women were added to the ranks of industrial labor in 1942 and 1943, making a total of nearly seventeen million women, as compared with thirty-four million men, in the battle of production. Unemployment, the plague of peacetime economy, was almost wiped out by war industry. When the defense program was adopted in 1940, there were seven million unemployed; four years later all but a million had been absorbed in an expansion of the labor force, bringing the total number fully employed to an all-time high of sixty-five million people.

Volume of Supply

The efforts of labor, combined with the directive skill of management, the rich natural resources of the United States, and the immense credits afforded by its people, won the battle of production. The credits, unfortunately, were debits, an increase of present spending power to be charged against the future. From June 1940 to the end of 1943 the United States actually spent one hundred fifty-three billion dollars for war purposes, nearly five times the cost of the last war. The national debt had risen, by June 1944, to a little over two hundred billion dollars, forty of which was pre-war debt. These figures indicate that the American people were borrowing against future income to pay for the war, financing it largely through loans rather than taxes.

The consumption of natural wealth in war production cannot yet be estimated, but it has been extraordinarily heavy in high-grade iron ore, zinc, copper, and accessible oil, vital industrial resources which cannot be replaced. The skill of management and the genius of invention have been apparent on every hand. Typical was Henry J. Kaiser who had built Boulder Dam but never a ship. By standardizing and prefabricating parts, he turned his shipyards into assembly plants, and cut the time for delivering a Liberty ship from nearly two hundred days to less than forty, so that a cargo vessel arrived in Australia fifty-one days after its keel had been laid in Portland, Oregon. The miracle worked in shipbuilding may be judged from the fact that the combined shipyards of the nation turned out a vessel a day in 1942; two,

142

and then three, ships a day in 1943; in the latter year merchant ships totaling nineteen million tons were launched and warships totaling two and a half million tons.

All records made in war production during 1942, which have been cited earlier, were surpassed in 1943. With full employment and expanded war plants the American people produced 29,500 tanks, over 22,000 motor carriages for self-propelled artillery, 47,000 scout and armored cars, 830,000 machine guns, 5,500,000 rifles and carbines, and 172,000 guns above 20mm. in caliber. During the first nine months of 1943, American shipyards delivered 1,429 merchant vessels of more than 15,000,000 tons. The production of heavy bombing planes reached a rate of one thousand a month in November 1943, and six months later, over eight thousand planes of all types were being turned out every thirty days. Never before had such overwhelming superiority in armament been achieved so quickly.

Mass production gave the United States the greatest air and tank forces in the world. In four years [*July 1, 1940– September 30, 1944*] our factories built 70,000 tanks and 232,403 airplanes. The aircraft were composed of the following types: 74,953 bombers, of which 25,000 were four-engined planes; 70,627 fighters; 54,642 trainers; 17,592 transports; and 10,785 planes for communications; 2,345 for naval reconnaissance; and 1,459 for special purposes.

Mighty as America was in war production, the contributions of the British Empire and the Soviet Union to the common cause were also great and indispensable in defeating the Axis. Russian figures have not yet been released, but anyone may guess at their staggering size by comparing the Lend-Lease totals of what the United States has sent Russia with the far greater need of her enormous armies in three years of warfare on fronts extending over a thousand miles. The British Empire had produced, from the beginning of the war in 1939 to the end of 1943, 90,000 aircraft; 83,000 tanks, armored guns, and gun-carriers; 1,000,000 vehicles; 115,000 heavy guns; and 5,500,000 machine guns, rifles, and pistols. In 1943, the United States and the British Empire together manufactured over fourteen planes every hour of the day and

143

night, a total of 127,000 aircraft. The combined production of the United Nations defeated the Axis in the battle of production.

20. THE BATTLE OF THE ATLANTIC

A month after Japan struck at Pearl Harbor, Nazi U-boats appeared off the eastern coast of the United States to renew the Battle of the Atlantic. A well timed attack threatened American shipping, without which the military power of this country was limited to its own shores, for while Japan drew our supply lines far out into the South Pacific, Germany tried to cut off the supply and reinforcements of our Allies in Europe. The submarine offensive was designed to destroy Lend-Lease supplies going to Britain, Russia, and the Middle East, and to defeat this country before it could arm and hit the enemy. The main attack of the Axis in the spring of 1942 was not in Europe but off the Atlantic coast of the United States, where U-boats proved far more deadly than in the last war. With a surface speed of twenty knots and a cruising range of twelve thousand miles, improved submarines lurked off American ports for three weeks at a time. U-boats made concentrated raids not only on coastal shipping but also on convoys crossing the Atlantic, entering the Mediterranean, and sailing the northern route to Murmansk in Russia.

American Coastal Shipping

The enemy undersea raids were most effective along the Atlantic coast. U-boats were continuously on patrol, concentrating first off Cape Hatteras, then Florida, and finally at the extremes, the Caribbean Sea and the St. Lawrence River. They attacked between dusk and dawn at high surface speed. At one time, they drove coastal oil tankers from the sea, and gasoline rationing went into effect in the seaboard states in May 1942. War goods piled up on East Coast docks, backed up at inland war plants, and on one occasion forty thousand military trucks stood at an eastern port waiting for ships. American defenses were overstrained because a one-ocean Navy was spread between the Atlantic and Pacific, coordination with Army Air Forces was new, and there was a lack of small craft, submarine chasers, destroyers, radio or sonic detectors, and of trained crews to operate them. In the first ten months of 1942 the newspapers reported the sinking of 201 American merchant ships, most of them from March through July, and a total loss of 498 Allied and neutral ships.

To defeat the U-boats the United States organized and manned sea frontiers along the Atlantic coast, in the Caribbean, and on the Gulf of Mexico, with new air and naval patrol bases for civilians as well as regular craft. All kinds of small boats were pressed into service, and the lights of coastal cities were dimmed, browned, or blacked out [May 14, 1942]. Finally the trans-Atlantic convoy system was operated close to our shores. From Florida to Maine, coastal ships herded together under guard of naval escorts, sailed only during daylight, and took refuge at night in ports or at anchorages protected by minefields. This adaptation of oceanic submarine defenses to home waters slowed up transportation but defeated the U-boats, and sinkings off the Atlantic coast declined sharply. As the U-boats moved south and north to easier hunting grounds of the Caribbean, the Gulf, and the St. Lawrence, the convoy system followed them [July 1, 1942]. Supplementing the convoys, a great force of Army, Navy, and civilian planes, together with small craft from the Navy and Coast Guard, scoured the seas for U-boats hiding in ambush. The submarines were driven out to sea, first to the coasts of South America, then to West Africa, and finally to the Cape of Good Hope. Coastal waters became safer in the middle of 1942, but the high seas remained dangerous. Throughout the year total shipping losses exceeded new shipbuilding.

Lend-Lease Convoys to Russia

The North Atlantic route to Murmansk and Archangel was the shortest to Russia but the most dangerous for cargo vessels, even in convoy, because the Nazi attacked them from a chain of air and U-boat bases around the north of Norway. Both merchant and warships were scarce because so many were needed to buoy up defenses in the Pacific and Middle East. As a result too little shipping was available for Russian supply, and too few warships could guard cargoes from Boston and Philadelphia, main ports for Russian Lend-Lease, on the perilous voyage to Murmansk.

The Nazis attacked these convoys with packs of U-boats northeast of Iceland, as they approached Norway, and with bombers from the North Cape to Murmansk. It was a running battle all the way. At one time 350 Nazi bombers swooped on a great convoy, and sank many ships before the raiders withdrew after losing forty planes. As the Arctic night turned into day during the spring and early summer, from March to July of 1942, the Murmansk-bound convoys suffered their worst losses. About one-fourth of all the ships from American and British ports which ran this gauntlet in 1942 went to the bottom. In addition two British cruisers and ten destroyers were sunk, and many other warships were put out of action for months by Nazi bombs.

Nevertheless, from the time Russia was attacked in 1941 to the end of 1942, nineteen Allied convoys made Murmansk or Archangel. After the number of escorting warships went as high as seventy-five for a single convoy, more and more supplies reached Russian battlefields. By the fall of 1942 new highways and railroads were made ready in Iran to handle traffic over the safer route from the Persian Gulf, and the bottleneck of Russian Lend-Lease supplies was broken in time to help equip the Red Army for its offensives after Stalingrad.

The Fight Against the U-Boat

For both Britain and the United States it was essential to win the Atlantic from Nazi submarines. "We British," said Churchill in Parliament [*June 8, 1943*], "must continue to place the anti-U-boat war first, because it is only by conquering the U-boat that we can live and act." The United States in turn could act with military power in Europe only after the Atlantic was made safe for convoys.

Early in 1943, when it was reported that the German rate of submarine building reached a peak of twenty U-boats a month, the Nazis were believed to have altogether four or five hundred in service. To destroy this fleet and the facilities for its replacement, British and American naval and air forces accelerated their work of destruction. Flying Fortresses did great damage to the German submarine yards at Vegesack in March, and heavy daylight raids were made on the concrete sub-pens at coastal bases in occupied France, but these bombings had little appreciable effect on U-boat operations. American shipyards, on the other hand, launched in May a growing fleet of destroyer escorts and escort carriers, the latter known as "baby flat-tops." Planes from these escort vessels followed convoys all the way across the Atlantic, pounced on U-boats before they could submerge, and broke up the under-sea wolf-packs.

The turning point in the protection of convoys came in May 1943 when thirty or more U-boats were sunk. In that month we wiped out the net increase in U-boats for the previous three months and were beginning to reduce the basic fleet itself. In May, June, and July an average of one submarine a day was sent to the bottom. In August, September, and October a total of sixty was sunk. Over two hundred U-boats were sunk in 1943; and from the beginning of the war to the middle of 1944, a total of more than five hundred was destroyed. Through the summer no Allied merchant ship was torpedoed in the North Atlantic; even the Mediterranean Sea was comparatively safe. Of some 2,500 vessels used in the invasion of Sicily, only eighty thousand tons were lost. By the middle of 1943 the Allies had three million more tons of shipping than at the start of the year.

The U-boats were offset by increased shipbuilding and the combined strength of Allied air and surface convoys. At last we had power enough to protect the growing fleet of supply vessels and to drive the packs of U-boats to cover. Destroyers, corvettes, and baby flat-top aircraft carriers did the work. Typical was the action which began with an attack by eight submarines on a large convoy in mid-Atlantic [*May 1-3, 1943*]. The escort fought them off; but for three days a gale slowed the convoy down and other submarines came in for the kill. As soon as the weather cleared, a pack of twenty-five made thirty torpedo attacks in three days and nights. Escort planes and corvettes sank four, probably six more, and dispersed the rest [*May 4-6, 1943*]. As escort carriers increased through the summer, they never let the under-water enemy get within fifteen miles of a convoy. In August

147

another battle with a pack of thirty U-boats went on for three days, but the enemy was kept out of torpedo range. The Atlantic Ocean, thanks to the convoy system, had again become Anglo-American waters, a good supply line from America to Britain.

In the two and a half years from Pearl Harbor to the invasion of Europe, the American and British navies escorted seven thousand ships across the Atlantic with the loss of only ten while under convoy. For American and British naval patrols the middle of the Atlantic was made the dividing line. Convoys, however, setting out from the United States with American naval escorts kept their guards, with British reinforcements, until they reached overseas ports. In addition to operating this convoy system, Admiral Royal E. Ingersoll, commanding the U. S. Atlantic Fleets, maintained a striking force to meet any heavy German units which might penetrate the western Atlantic.

Naval Actions, 1939–1941

Important naval actions marked the first two years of the war in the Atlantic Ocean and the Mediterranean Sea. The Royal Navy fought to control these waters against German surface raiders and the Italian Navy, and to neutralize the French warships left in African ports after the surrender of France.

The German pocket battleship, *Admiral Graf Spee,* a fast, heavily armored cruiser of 10,000 tons, with six 11-inch guns, designed to outshoot or outrace its opponents, was tracked down in the South Atlantic by two light and one heavy British cruisers and severely damaged in battle off the coast of Uruguay [*December 13, 1939*]. After making repairs in the neutral port of Montevideo, the German captain scuttled his ship rather than run the gauntlet of British cruisers lying offshore [*December 17, 1939*].

The British suffered a serious though temporary loss of naval power in the evacuation of Dunkirk when seventy destroyers of the Royal Navy were damaged and put out of action by German air power. The transfer of fifty over-age American destroyers to the British Navy more than restored the loss of ships at Dunkirk.

148

When France surrendered to Germany, Admiral Darlan assured Great Britain that the French fleet would not fall into Hitler's hands. But the British took no chances with French ships stationed in African ports. British naval forces destroyed or disabled most of the squadron at the French North African base of Oran after its commander had ignored an ultimatum to surrender [*July 3, 1940*]. The French squadron at Alexandria, Egypt, agreed to be neutralized. The British, supporting the Free French, disabled a French battleship at Dakar on the West African coast when General Charles de Gaulle vainly attempted to seize the port with Free French troops [*July 8, 1940*].

With the remainder of the French fleet bottled up at Toulon, the British undertook to contain the Italian Navy in the Mediterranean. Italian battleships and cruisers were damaged on three occasions [*November 11, 27, December 14, 1940*] by British torpedo planes raiding their bases in Sardinia, and at Taranto and Naples in Italy. Finally, the British caught two Italian squadrons off Cape Matapan [*March 28, 1941*]; naval gunfire and planes from the carrier *Formidable* damaged one battleship and sank three cruisers and two destroyers. After this engagement the Italian Navy remained in hiding.

The German battleship *Bismarck,* the most powerful warship afloat in 1941, with eight 15-inch guns and a heavily armored hull, designed with so many water-tight compartments as to be almost unsinkable, caused great alarm when she broke out into the Atlantic in the late spring of 1941. Intercepted by British vessels in the Denmark Strait between Iceland and Greenland, the *Bismarck* fired a salvo which sank the *Hood,* a lightly armored, much older ship of 37,000 tons [*May 24, 1941*]. After a chase back across the Atlantic toward the French coast, the *Bismarck* was first brought to bay by torpedoes from carrier planes, which slowed her down and wrecked her rudder, and was then sunk by aerial torpedoes, gunfire from two British battleships, the *Rodney* and *King George V,* and still more torpedoes from the cruisers *Sheffield* and *Dorsetshire* [*May 26–27, 1941*]. Other enemy air and naval actions during 1941 resulted in the crippling or sinking of four British battleships, three carriers, and

149

seven cruisers. Some of these losses occurred off Crete. The
damaged vessels were all repaired in American ports under
the Lend-Lease Act.

21. THE OLD WORLD GIVES THE NEW
TIME TO PREPARE

Americans were actually at war two years before they
could train and equip a large army, build the largest navy
and air force in the world, and join their allies in major
offensives against both Germany and Japan. The United
States began to arm for defense during the year and a half
of peace, between the fall of France and Pearl Harbor.
While Great Britain, Yugoslavia, Greece, and Russia kept
Hitler busy in Europe, Lend-Lease and Selective Service
were getting under way. Once we were in the war, our first
moves had to be defensive; even the campaigns in North
Africa and on Guadalcanal were relatively minor blows,
more defensive than offensive. Meanwhile our attempt to
check the enemy's advance on all fronts was immeasurably
strengthened by the long lines which the Red Army held in
eastern Europe. Here the Germans attacked with their greatest masses of manpower and matériel, taking ground at heavy
cost, only to lose it again to the indomitable Russian armies.

I. RUSSIAN COUNTEROFFENSIVE, 1941–42

In the first winter of the war in Russia, the Nazis went
into defensive positions. The German generals had wanted
to do this before snow fell and the vain drive on Moscow
extended their lines, but Hitler had refused to listen to them.
His first conflict with the army came to a head when he relieved Field Marshal Walther von Brauchitsch of supreme
command [December 21, 1941] and declared that henceforth
he would follow his own "intuition." He was no match for
"General Winter." Nazi troops in summer clothing perished.
Soviet guerrillas cut their supply and communications lines.
The bitter cold froze the lubricating oil and cracked the
cylinders of engines in tanks, planes, and trucks. Supply and
transport broke down over the vast distances which had been

150

overrun but not conquered. Nevertheless, the Nazis dug into Russia as if to stay. They began repairs on the great power plant at Dniepropetrovsk, reclaimed mines, distributed steam tractors through the Ukraine to speed production of food for their armies, and altered the railroad gauge for German rolling stock. Conscript Poles and prisoners of war were put to work building lines of defense in the rear. The Germans reversed the positions of the old Stalin Line west of the Dnieper and finished lines along the Bug and Oder rivers which had been started over a year before.

Estimates of Casualties

The Russians took the offensive because they thought that the Nazis were poorly prepared to weather the winter. They were also convinced that Nazi reserves had been exhausted by heavy casualties. On this score the Russians were mistaken. The rest of the world, like the Germans, wondered if it was not the Soviet Union which was exhausted. This idea was equally false. Moscow acknowledged total casualties of 2,122,000, and this figure may be accepted as a minimum. The Germans claimed that they counted 3,806,-000 Russian prisoners in their cages. Even if only half this number were military prisoners, the Red Army must be able to find trained reserves for its winter offensive among the eleven million available men of Russia. As for Axis losses, Moscow claimed that 3,500,000 were killed in the invasion. The Nazis, even after the winter was over, admitted the death of only 251,291. These figures were clearly absurd. They probably lost no less than 1,200 a day (the rate of loss at the height of the Battle of France) throughout the invasion of Russia. But such losses were partly offset by the annual German levy of 700,000 conscripts and the recruiting of Hungarian and Rumanian forces.

Red armies in the north, center, and south each undertook a winter campaign to relieve Leningrad, to free Moscow, and to raise the siege of Sevastopol. During the winter the Russians fought their way westward to regain a strip averaging 120 miles in width, but never penerated the enemy's main line of resistance. While the counteroffensive fell short of its chief objective, it proved that the great German offensive had also failed, for the Russian armies were so far from being destroyed that they could turn upon the invader in full force.

Support of Leningrad

The northern campaign to free Leningrad began with a two-pronged drive westward on either side of Lake Ilmen toward the enemy railroad center of Pskov [*December 15, 1941*]. The upper prong pierced the Spanish 11th Infantry Division, which Franco had sent to Hitler's aid, but failed to do more than create a deep salient. The southern prong advanced much farther and encircled three divisions of the German Sixteenth Army at Kholm and Staraya Russa which nevertheless maintained their hedgehog defenses through the winter with supplies from the air. Leningrad was not effectively relieved, but it was kept alive under siege by "The Road of Life" built across the ice of Lake Ladoga. Over this road in the long winter nights crawled columns of trucks loaded with food and munitions to arm the hard-pressed people of Leningrad.

Failing to raise the siege of Leningrad, the Red Army turned upon Finnish forces north of the city in an effort to regain control of the railway from Murmansk [*January 8, 1942*]. Through this northern port, British and American Lend-Lease tanks and planes were beginning to flow into Russia. The Finns held their grip on the strategic railroad, and all foreign imports continued to be routed via Soroka over the longer rail line from Archangel.

Moscow Breathes

On the central front the Red Army massed strong forces along a line 170 miles to free Moscow and the industries of Tula from the dangerous pincers which the enemy had thrust part way around the capital [*December 15, 1941*]. Both Nazi salients were wiped out. To the north the Russians took Klin and Kalinin, and struck west to cut the railway at Velikie Luki; to the south they reconquered the Tula area and created a bulge below Smolensk. In the center all attacks fell short of the enemy bastions of Rzhev and Vyazma. Likewise an attack on Smolensk from positions

152

above and below the city was unsuccessful. Farther south Timoshenko crossed the Donets River and drove a wedge into enemy lines below Kharkov. But nowhere during the winter did the Red Army penetrate the enemy's main line. All the Nazi strongpoints, Staraya Russa, Rzhev, Vyazma, Orel, Kursk, and Kharkov, held.

Defeat in the Crimea

The Russian winter offensive in the south was an elaborate operation to relieve Sevastopol, still besieged by Manstein [*December 29, 1941*]. The Russians made landings on the eastern and southern sides of the Kerch Peninsula, where the unsuspecting enemy had withdrawn most of his forces and resistance was light. Kerch and Feodosiya fell. Then a Russian force of fifty thousand landed north of Sevastopol at Eupatoria [*January 7, 1942*]. Manstein summoned reserves to defeat these forces, overwhelmed the enemy at Eupatoria [*January 10–13, 1942*], and then moved quickly eastward to take Feodosiya [*January 19–21, 1942*]. The Russians retired into the Kerch Peninsula, to be reinforced until their numbers reached two hundred thousand [*March 13–28, 1942*]. Even then their furious attacks were futile, and Manstein finally crushed them with tanks and planes [*May 7, 1942*], attacking along both coasts of the peninsula, piercing the front line, and encircling with combined arms units as far to the east as Kerch itself. The Russians trapped between Parpatsch and the northern coast fought desperately to break out [*May 11, 1942*]. Some divisions withdrew to make a stand on the heights before Kerch, but the city fell [*May 15, 1942*] because no adequate defense could be improvised. In this struggle the Nazis claimed to have annihilated nineteen divisions and seven armored brigades, and to have captured 150,000 prisoners.

Fall of Sevastopol

The German victory on the Kerch Peninsula left the Russians only one position in the Crimea, the great naval base of Sevastopol. It was said by the German press to be the "strongest single fortress of the world," not only because its rugged terrain was cut up into sharp hills and deep ra-

153

vines, but also because the Red Army had heavily strengthened its ancient defenses. There were nineteen modern forts, hewn out of rock, four levels deep, with 11-inch guns in battleship turrets, all protected by hundreds of pillboxes and thousands of land mines. A garrison of 125,000 soldiers and marines under General Petrov defended Sevastopol, and all but two hundred of the civilian population of 85,000 were evacuated. The Red Army proposed to endure siege, for if this toehold in the Crimea could be maintained, the Black Sea would remain Russian and the German right wing in Russia might be pinned down short of Rostov and the Caucasus.

Manstein attacked the outer fortification of the city [*June 2, 1942*] from the north and east with two hundred thousand troops while Richthofen's air fleet and heavy artillery attempted to pierce the defenses in a narrow sector in order to reach the interior forts quickly. After five days of intensive artillery preparation, however, the northern line anchored at Fort Maxim Gorki still held. Ten days later when its magazines blew up, Gorki fell and German infantry occupied the northern shore of the harbor which divides Sevastopol. Their enfilading fire assisted forces from the south in taking the hills of Inkerman east of the city [*June 28, 1942*]. Then a night landing was made on the southern shore and a pincers attack ended the siege with the capture of Fort Malakhoff. Sevastopol was occupied, but resistance did not cease. Finally, the seventy thousand troops, who had withdrawn south and east of the city to the Khersonese Peninsula, failed to find any ships for evacuation and were trapped into surrender [*July 2, 1942*].

The Germans succeeded at Sevastopol for two reaons. Their air fleet, jumping in waves from one front to another and flying continuously in support of ground troops, was greatly superior to the local Russian air force. Nazi planes made 25,000 sorties and dropped 125,000 heavy bombs. Above all, heavy artillery fired on the forts 30,000 tons of shell, fifty tons every hour, day and night, for twenty-five days. After this torrent of bombs and shells no steel or concrete could resist the massed assaults of infantry.

154

To forestall a Nazi summer offensive, Marshal Timoshenko attacked the enemy south of Kharkov with thirty-four divisions [*May 12, 1942*]. His plan was to draw off enemy reserves, spring a major drive farther south from Izyum, and recover the Dnieper Bend by a sweep on Dniepropetrovsk. His initial attack in the form of two wedges made great progress, but Kharkov did not fall, nor were enemy reserves committed to its defense.

Instead Bock surprised Timoshenko by a powerful counteroffensive which caught the main Russian forces at Izyum [*May 17, 1942*]. Nazi 88mm. batteries neutralized Russian tanks, and the Izyum hedgehog was encircled from the south. Armored spearheads surrounded the Russian forces west of the Donets. Timoshenko's advance elements were almost annihilated, and by his own admission he lost 70,000 men. The Germans claimed over 240,000 prisoners. The Russian army on the Kharkov front faced the enemy summer offensive with depleted forces, and Timoshenko was transferred to a new command.

This defeat did not undo the work of the Russian winter offensive. The Nazis could not start forward in 1942 where they had left off in 1941. They had lost men as well as ground, and Russian armies had killed more troops than "General Winter." The fighting in Russia never stopped for long, summer or winter; lines never stabilized. The Red armies had turned blitzkrieg into a war of attrition.

II. ROMMEL ADVANCES INTO EGYPT

The Germans had been halted in Russia, but they renewed their drive in the Middle East. Four times since 1940 the tide of war had swept back and forth across the Libyan sands, but this struggle for possession of Egypt and the Suez Canal came to a crisis in 1942. Through the spring months the British and German armies fought a battle of supply in Libya, and without American shipments Egypt might have been lost. In the course of two years, up to June 1942, the British Empire and the United States sent to the Middle East the bulk of their men and matériel: 950,000 men,

155

6,000 planes, nearly 5,000 guns, 4,500 tanks, 50,000 machine guns, and over 100,000 vehicles. These men and weapons were transported, not through the Mediterranean, but over ten thousand miles of water around Africa and up the Red Sea to Egypt or over a 9,000-mile air route from the United States via Brazil. Despite these great distances the British accumulated many more tanks and planes than the Axis could assemble in the Middle East.

Here, as elsewhere, the Axis had the advantage of short interior lines, but most of its supplies went to prepare a new offensive in Russia, and what could be spared for Africa had still to run the gauntlet of British planes from Malta. By continuous raids with a force of over six hundred planes the Luftwaffe tried to wipe out the garrison at Malta, and early in 1942 reduced its aerial strength to twelve fighter planes. British and American aircraft carriers, notably the *Wasp,* rushed in reinforcements, however, to keep the island a thorn in the side of the Axis. Malta was the key to the offensives launched in Libya by both the Germans and the British in 1942. The Germans aimed for Tobruk to gain a supply port free of interference from Malta, and the British sought to give the island air cover from Africa by advancing as far as Derna.

Rommel's Second Offensive

Rommel launched his offensive first by surprising the British with feints in the north and center of their Gazala defenses [*May 26–27, 1942*]. Then he enveloped the Bir Hacheim minefields, southern anchor of the line, and destroyed a brigade which deployed its superior tanks in detail [*May 31 1942*]. But Rommel advanced so far and so fast that the British surrounded him in a pocket which their troops named the "Cauldron." Here his situation was desperate, and minefields in the rear cut off retreat. Nevertheless, he broke open a corridor to the west for reinforcements and annihilated a brigade which tried to close the gap [*June 5–9, 1942*]. The British wasted their preponderance of tanks and artillery in scattered counterattacks, and the German threat to their communications finally compelled them to evacuate Bir Hacheim and withdraw from the Gazala line.

Then the British ran into a fatal ambush which robbed them of all their strength. On Black Saturday [*June 13, 1942*] in a decisive battle at Knightsbridge, Rommel lured British armor, concentrated for once, into the deadly fire of his massed 88mm. guns and destroyed all but sixty-five of three hundred tanks. This disaster hurled the British back into Egypt. British and American bombers covered the retreat and saved it from becoming a rout [*July 1, 1942*]. For fear of envelopment, however, the British could not stop short of El Alamein. Here they stood, only seventy-five miles from Alexandria, blocking a corridor which stretched for forty miles from the Mediterranean to the Qattara Depression. A South African division was left in Tobruk to hang on Rommel's extended supply lines, as in 1941, but the garrison of twenty-five thousand men surrendered to his sudden assault [*June 21, 1942*]. Altogether the British lost over eighty thousand troops in this campaign.

Stand at El Alamein

Rommel's men, however, were too short of water and supplies to break through at El Alamein. The timely arrival [*July 1–3, 1942*] of planes, tanks, and reinforcements at Suez helped the British to maintain defense in depth.

Several counterattacks [*July 14, 22, 27, 1942*] failed for want of coordination; and in August General Sir Harold R.L.G. Alexander replaced General Auchinleck in command of the Middle East, as General (now Field Marshal) Sir Bernard L. Montgomery took over General Ritchies' Eighth Army. Before the British forces could reorganize, Rommel renewed his offensive and penetrated twenty miles east of El Alamein. Here he ran into minefields and lost over half his tanks as he swung north to cut up the British rear. Since Rommel could not repair these losses, with long-range American Mitchell bombers taking increasingly heavy toll of his Mediterrnaean supply line, Egypt was safe. Hitler's main armies were committed to the invasion of southern Russia and the Caucasus at this time, and there was little to spare for the Afrika Korps. When the British forces were again recruited in October, Montgomery was to launch the attack which would drive the Germans out of Egypt and Libya to destruction in Tunisia.

Lend-Lease Wins the Battle of Supply

During the summer of 1942, while Rommel's forces still threatened El Alamein, the battle for Egypt was still a battle of supply. It was a race between Montgomery and Rommel to see who could gain superior power. The Axis had a head start with short supply routes from Italy into Africa, but all its supplies had to run the gauntlet of British and American bombers which took heavy toll of Axis shipping. Through the summer, the U. S. Ninth Air Force, based at Cairo, helped the British in raids against Axis supply routes.

America and Britain won the battle of supply. Bombers flew across the Atlantic. Fighter planes were shuttled across the South Atlantic by aircraft carriers, from whose decks they took off within range of the African coast and flew the rest of the way across the desert to Egypt. By October 23, when General Montgomery was ready for the final Battle of El Alamein, more than seven hundred twin-engnie bombers and one thousand fighters had reached Africa from the United States. With this air support the British Eighth Army blanketed Rommel's forces, cut off German supplies, and destroyed the Luftwaffe in Egypt.

The tanks which the Eighth Army needed, after losing most of its machines in Rommel's trap and falling back to El Alamein, came by sea, together with guns, munitions, and trucks. The voyage from the United States around the Cape of Good Hope took seventy days, and from England nearly as long. When one of the supply ships making this voyage was torpedoed, with fifty-one tanks and twenty-eight self-propelled guns aboard, an American armored division on maneuvers in the United States was stripped of tanks to replace those lost at sea. For the Battle of El Alamein, General Montgomery had nine hundred medium tanks, including over three hundred M-4 General Shermans. In addition, twenty-five thousand trucks and jeeps arrived for the supply services which were to follow in pursuit of Rommel to Tunisia; to cripple Nazi tanks, came ninety of the new American 105mm. self-propelled guns. With this armament, produced by American factories and shipped through Lend-Lease, the British won the Battle of El Alamein and saved the Middle East.

III. NAZI ADVANCE TO THE CAUCASUS, 1942

The Nazis renewed their long-expected offensive in Russia early in the summer of 1942 with an overwhelming superiority in tanks and planes built up through the winter. For this offensive 240 divisions of three million men were assembled, according to Stalin; in addition to 179 German divisions, there were 22 Rumanian, 14 Finnish, 13 Hungarian, and 10 Italian divisions, one from Spain, and another from Slovakia. It was a limited offensive, directed southeast toward the oil-fields of the Caucasus, and not as in 1941 to the annihilation of enemy forces along the entire front. Evidently the Germans were too weak or too wise to repeat the massive maneuvers of the invasion year. They had learned that the USSR, unlike Poland and France, could not be knocked out in six weeks, or even in six months, and they clearly did not plan another such attempt. The new plan, however, was no less grandiose. If they could penetrate southern Russia to the Volga and win the oil of the Caucasus, they could eventually cripple the Red Army, and be in position to strike at the Middle East or join hands with the Japanese in India. In either case, they would divide the British Empire, separating the eastern from the western half, cut off Russia and China from British and American supplies, and isolate the United States from its allies before its forces could reach any fighting front. Thus the hope that both Britain and Russia might be defeated in the Caucasus dictated Hitler's Napoleonic strategy.

Advance to Voronezh

Marshal Bock opened the summer offensive with a campaign on the Kharkov front, designed to cut the Moscow-Rostov railroad, separate the opposing armies of the center and south, and secure the line of the upper Don. His forces moved east 150 miles to Voronezh and threw the Russians into a general withdrawal [*June 10, 1942*]. The attack began with an envelopment of the bridgehead north of Kharkov,

159

and from this point the offensive spread along the whole Kharkov front. [*June 24, 1942*]. With air support, Nazi tanks drove fifty miles into the rear at Kupyansk and forced the Russians to retire from the upper Donets [*June 26, 1942*]. Then the main offensive became continuous north to Kursk. Three columns, each spearheaded by a tank division and covered by waves of dive bombers, plunged one hundred miles toward Voronezh [*June 28, 1942*]. The Red Army lacked reserves to fill the gaps and was pressed in retreat by overwhelming Nazi air fleets [*July 2, 1942*]. As German tanks crossed the Don at Voronezh, the infantry mopped up, taking more than eighty thousand prisoners [*July 7, 1942*].

This advance compelled the Russian forces left below in the Donets Bend to retreat to the Don. The Germans assumed a tactical defensive north to Bryansk, with the upper Don railroads in their hands, and shifted the offensive southeast. Ever since the fall of Sevastopol had secured their right flank along the Black Sea, they had been preparing this sweep to the Caucasus.

Penetration of the Caucasus

Three armies moved southeast through the Donbas, two on Stalingrad and another on Rostov and the Caucasus. Kleist's army captured Rostov on the Don [*July 25, 1942*] for the second time by outflanking the city from the north and using air power to crush fierce ground resistance. A tank thrust to Salsk [*July 31, 1942*] forced the Russians to retire south of the Don. The capture of Rostov and Salsk, cutting both railroads leading into this region, isolated the defenders of the Caucasus. Nazi armored divisions from Rostov circled north [*August 3, 1942*] to seize Voroshilovgrad in the Donbas, and turned south again to join other units on a swift drive into the Kuban, 120 miles below Rostov. The Red Army abandoned Krasnodar and all of the Kuban [*August 9, 1942*], evacuating troops through the Black Sea naval port of Novorossisk, and this base fell after a brief siege [*September 11, 1942*]. German efforts to deny the Russian Navy its last base at Tuapse, however, were frustrated by the defenses of west Caucasia.

160

Nazi forces plunged south into the Caucasian highlands to capture the Maikop oilfield [*August 8, 1942*]. They detoured roadblocks and ambushes on the military highways and caught the Russians in the rear of the strongpoints chosen for a defensive stand. But the higher they climbed into the Caucasian passes, at altitudes between five thousand and ten thousand feet, the more determined was Russian resistance. The Nazis slowly penetrated to Mozdok, sixty miles from the great Grozny oilfield, whose capture would have won them a quarter of all the Soviet's oil.

The fighting in the Caucasus Mountains was as savage as the country was rugged. The Nazis hurled their tanks in spearheads of one hundred to one hundred and fifty at each highland objective, but the Russians broke these attacks with self-propelling 76mm. antitank guns massed in regimental strength. Although the defenders of the Caucasus were isolated, the struggle at Stalingrad helped them to hold out because it absorbed enemy reserves and supplies. In the Caucasus no less than at Stalingrad, the Red Army fought to hold each strongpoint to the end. As winter came on, the enemy was finally halted at Ordzhonikidze [*November 10–19, 1942*], where the Georgian military highway runs through the mountains down to Tiflis and Iran. The invaders failed to capture the oil of Russia or to cut Russia off from the Lend-Lease supplies coming in through Iran.

Sweep to Stalingrad

Meanwhile the Nazis reached out across the Donbas to Stalingrad and the Volga River. The armies of Von Paulus and Schwedler made a concentric advance from the west to conquer the brown steppes between Voronezh and the Caucasus. As the Russians fell back northeastward on the Don, saving their tanks and planes, the Sixty-Second Army under General Chuikov fought stubborn delaying actions [*July 22, 1942*]. In the south, Schwedler's army reached the Don on a front of one hundred miles around Tsimlyansk where they were delayed by fleets of Red planes which destroyed bridges as fast as the Germans could build them. During this delay the Russians concentrated an army below Stalingrad to check

161

the Nazis swinging north upon the city from Kotelnikovski. The enemy flung his right arm eastward to Astrakhan, and the lower Volga was now within range of the Luftwaffe. Under constant bombing, beginning August 25, Stalingrad was reduced to ruins, but the Russians made strong defensive breastworks of their fallen homes and buildings.

In the north the German Sixth Army under General Von Paulus drove between two Red armies, advanced 125 miles in six days [*July 19–25, 1942*], and from three sides attacked the Don bridgehead at Kalach, west of Stalingrad. Resistance was so fierce that more than two weeks of continuous bombing by Richthofen's air fleet was required to take Kalach [*July 27, 1942*]. In this battle the Axis claimed the capture of 57,000 troops and one thousand tanks. Then Paulus turned north to Kletskaya where a Red army had launched a diversionary attack on his rear [*August 2, 1942*]. Another bitter battle ensued [*August 14, 1942*], carried on day and night, until Nazi tanks pushed a wedge between the defenders and all counterattacks failed.

Both Nazi armies were now across the Don and converging on Stalingrad forty miles away [*August 17, 1942*]. Bock mounted the assault in three great columns, as he had done the year before at Moscow, strongly supported by the Luftwaffe which was concentrated on this front. The northern column broke through [*August 23, 1942*] to the Volga River a few miles above Stalingrad, cut the city off from the north, and reduced its communications to one railroad beyond the river. By engaging this advance column, the main Russian forces which had retreated northeast of the Don saved the city from envelopment. Meanwhile the Nazi columns from Kalach and Kotelnikovski in the west and southwest drove the Russians steadily back on lines of tank traps and pillboxes prepared for the defense of Stalingrad [*August 31— September 14, 1942*]. But the "meat-grinder" of Chuikov's Sixty-Second Army gave General Yeremenko time to prepare the city for siege and to bring up sufficient reserves to hold it. When a Nazi tank column charged into Stalingrad and captured the height of Mamai Kurgan (Hill 102) [*September 14, 1942*], the 13th Guards Rifle Division of General Ro-

162

dimtsev, under cover of Soviet artillery across the Volga, stormed it in bloody and unsuccessful assaults. The siege of Stalingrad, an industrial center of some 600,000 people, was on. Stukas and artillery lashed at the city, but the defenders held. Here along the broad sandy ridge beside the Volga, Hitler was doomed to waste his forces as he had wasted them at Moscow.

PART FIVE

UNITED NATIONS TURN
THE TIDE

22. THE UNITED STATES HALTS JAPAN

In three years of naval war in the Pacific we passed, according to Admiral King, from the defensive to the offensive in four stages. Pearl Harbor threw us entirely on the defensive to protect our own shores and lines of communications. This initial phase [*December 7, 1941–May 8, 1942*] was marked by desperate engagements, such as the battles in Makassar Strait and the Java and Coral Seas, and the raids on the Marshalls, Gilberts, Tokyo, Salamaua, Lae, and Tulagi. In all of these operations our forces were either inferior to the enemy or gained superiority only by limiting their action to surprise raids.

The Battle of Midway [*June 3–6, 1942*] was a critical defensive-offensive operation in which the defeat of Japanese invasion forces gave us once more the balance of naval power that had been lost at Pearl Harbor and allowed us to seize the initiative from the enemy.

It was followed by a year of offensive defense [*August 7, 1942–August 6, 1943*], beginning with the landings at Guadalcanal and ending with the naval battles in the Kula and Vella Gulfs, during which our forces fought chiefly to defend their small gains, recruit their strength, and mount supply bases for the future offensive. In this phase, as at Midway, the enemy advance was definitely halted and his counter-attacks against our forward movements were defeated.

Finally, with the capture of Tarawa and Makin, we at last entered upon the fourth phase [*November 1943–1944*], a sweeping offensive by land, sea, and air, to penetrate the defenses of the Japanese Empire, reconquer the great islands lost to the enemy's lightning war in 1942, and to reach the China coast. Our naval superiority and well stocked advance bases in the Pacific gave us the power, as Admiral King said, "to attack the enemy at places of our own choosing."

I. THE BATTLE OF MIDWAY

The naval war in the Pacific changed from passive defensive to active defense with the Battle of Midway [*June 3–6, 1942*]. It was the first decisive defeat inflicted on the Japanese Navy in 350 years. Southwest of Midway Island in the Central Pacific, about fifteen hundred miles beyond Pearl Harbor, a Catalina flying patrol sighted a large enemy force. It proved to be part of a giant armada of at least eighty-eight ships, including four battleships and five carriers, with a convoy of fourteen transport and supply vessels, all divided into three groups, a striking force, a reserve, and a landing force. The strength and course of these fleets indicated that their mission was to conquer not only Midway but also bases in the Hawaiian Islands.

The foray into American waters, the greatest ever undertaken by the Japanese, found our naval forces deployed in the area between Midway and the Aleutian Islands. Orders went out to make ready all available ships but in these first months after Pearl Harbor we could muster only three carriers, including the *Yorktown,* which had been recalled from the Coral Sea and hastily repaired, seven heavy cruisers, one light cruiser, fourteen destroyers, and about twenty submarines. These vessels were divided into two task forces under Rear Admiral (now Admiral) Raymond A. Spruance and Rear Admiral (now Vice Admiral) Frank J. Fletcher.

Even before the Navy could get within striking range, Flying Fortresses from the Marine base at Midway bombed the enemy transports which had been first sighted [*June 3, 1942*]. Following the heavy bombers, came Catalinas fitted out with torpedoes which probably sank a transport in the first night torpedo attack in American naval history. Next morning over one hundred Japanese bombers and fighters struck at Midway in a raid which cost them forty planes and failed to destroy the base.

The enemy aircraft had come from a carrier group which was spotted two hundred miles northwest of Midway and

165

immediately attacked by twenty-six Army, Navy, and Marine torpedo planes and dive bombers. The Navy was still three hundred miles east and unable to provide fighter protection. The Midway planes dropped a thousand-pound bomb on a battleship, three more on a carrier which burst into flames and smoke, and sent one or two torpedoes into another carrier. This attack was delivered through such a heavy curtain of antiaircraft fire and Zero fighters, that only one of the six Navy planes and eight of Major Loften R. Henderson's sixteen Marine dive bombers returned to Midway.

As the American carriers came into range, swarms of planes flew to the attack and stung the enemy into retreat. The *Hornet's* Torpedo 8 Squadron of fifteen planes found four enemy carriers and went in without fighter protection to score a hit. Only one pilot survived. From the *Yorktown* and *Enterprise* twenty-six more torpedo planes, followed by dive bombers, put two enemy carriers out of action, damaged a third which was sunk later by submarine, and hit a battleship and cruiser. From their only undamaged carrier, the *Hiryu,* Japanese planes stopped the engines of the *Yorktown* and set her afire with three bombs and two torpedoes. The *Yorktown* was sent to the bottom by her own destroyers two days later, after an enemy submarine had hit the crippled ship twice with torpedoes [*June 6–7, 1942*]. Planes from the *Enterprise* avenged her loss by leaving the *Hiryu* in flames.

The American carrier-based planes won control of the air in the first day of battle, and the dive bombers developed by the Navy proved their power. On the second day of battle, Flying Fortresses from Hawaii joined with the carrier planes and those from Midway and helped bomb two battleships, three cruisers, a damaged cruiser, and a destroyer. The Japanese turned tail and ran for home in thick weather. Dive bombers from the *Hornet* and *Enterprise* found one group and hit four cruisers and a destroyer. The Navy pursued the enemy westward until shortage of fuel and losses in aircraft forced ships and planes back to Pearl Harbor.

Midway was another battle like the Coral Sea in which planes did all the fighting and warships did not exchange a single shot. The aerial victory was overwhelming. Losses suffered by the enemy were the heaviest of any sea-and-air battle in the war. Four carriers, the *Kaga, Akagi, Soryu* and *Hiryu*, the heavy cruiser *Mikuma,* and three destroyers were sunk; three battleships, three heavy cruisers, one light cruiser, and several destroyers were damaged; 275 aircraft were destroyed; and the enemy lost at least 4,800 men. American losses were relatively light: the carrier *Yorktown* of 19,900 tons; a destroyer, the *Hammann;* about 150 planes; and 307 men, chiefly from the Army and Navy air units. The battle of Midway removed any enemy threat to Hawaii and the West Coast from the Central Pacific, restored the balance of naval power in the Pacific which had been lost at Pearl Harbor, and confined the Japanese henceforth to home waters and to the South Pacific, except for their short stay in the Aleutians. The news was the best to reach Americans in 1942 and was to be equaled only by the British and American landings in North Africa and the Russian victory at Stalingrad.

Distance and Supply in the Pacific War

While Japan fought along interior lines radiating south from Tokyo for about three thousand miles, the United States defended the Southwest Pacific at the end of exterior lines stretching seven thousand miles from San Francisco. The war in the Pacific was therefore a problem in logistics, the science of planning military movements. To advance one mile on the road to Tokyo consumed not only days and nights of fighting but months of supplying. The first two years of the Pacific war were largely spent in establishing supply lines and bases from which the offensive could be launched against Japan.

The distance from American west coast ports to Australia is so great that convoys, sailing at the speed of the slowest ship, made the voyage out in seventeen to twenty-five days. A fighter plane, which flew at four hundred miles an hour within two hundred miles of its base, could not get into the combat range until it had first been ferried across the Pacific Ocean on a freighter making but fifteen miles an hour. From the speeded-up assembly lines in American factories, every plane of this type faced a month of inaction before it took off against the enemy. The same delay applied to all men and matériel, and was actually extended by the number of men and volume of supplies required to defend the Southwest Pacific. Every division of fifteen thousand ground troops sent into the Pacific combat theaters required thirty thousand service troops for supply and transport. One soldier on a transport needed eight tons of shipping space to reach the battlefront fully equipped and one ton of supplies every month after his arrival to keep him in action.

After the fall of the Philippines and the Netherlands East Indies the Allied forces were thrown back on Australia for their main base in the Pacific. Australia was not only farther from the United States than were England and Africa, the main bases in the Atlantic, but also much less convenient for military operations. Although the Australian continent is about as large as the United States, it has a population of only seven million, with little manufacturing and no oil, railroads of different gauge in each state, limited highways except on the southeast coast, and no large harbor except Sydney on the east coast. Through the middle of 1942 there was a desperate rush to protect its northern shore around Port Darwin from Japanese occupation, and to connect this outpost by rail and highway with the cities and ports of the southern and eastern coasts. From Australia northward to the combat zones in New Guinea and the Solomon Islands there was another stretch of more than a thousand miles. In these tropical areas, which lacked railroads, warehouses, or docks, advance bases had to be won from the enemy and converted into supply ports during 1942 and 1943.

II. GUADALCANAL AND BUNA

When the Japanese offensive against Australia was first thwarted in the Battle of the Coral Sea [*May 7–11, 1942*], the enemy did not retire from the Southwest Pacific. Having occupied most of New Guinea to flank Australia from the north, he developed air bases in the Solomon Islands which threatened American supply lines to the Australian continent. It was imperative for American forces, however weak, to protect both Australia and its supply lines; otherwise there would be no springboard closer than Pearl Harbor from which a counteroffensive could be mounted against Japan. The want of men and ships in the Pacific kept the United States on the strategic defensive through 1942. But tactically offensive measures were taken by American and Australian troops against the most advanced enemy positions in the Solomons and New Guinea. These operations became famous as the campaigns of Guadalcanal and Papua, long, hard battles in which Americans first defeated the Japanese in the tropical jungles of the Pacific.

Landings at Guadalcanal

Guadalcanal, an island eighty miles long and twenty-five miles wide, lay seven hundred miles south and east of the Japanese base at Rabaul. A thousand miles farther south, the American base at New Caledonia was threatened by an airfield which the enemy was building on Guadalcanal. To deny its use to the Japanese, amphibious task forces were quickly organized under Vice Admiral Robert L. Ghormley with headquarters at Auckland, New Zealand.

The 1st Marine Division, reinforced with elements of the 2nd and under the command of Major General (now General) Alexander A. Vandegrift, was assigned the task of taking and holding Guadalcanal and adjacent areas. Their landings [*August 7, 1942*] caught the Japanese by surprise, but the opposition on Florida, Tulagi, and other nearby islands to the north of Guadalcanal was vigorous and stubborn. On the larger island of Guadalcanal the Japanese fled without offering opposition. However, they would undoubtedly fight to regain the airfield which the Americans had captured. Our troops took up positions from which to defend their prize.

The Japanese began striking back with air power the first day and brought naval vessels into action the second night after the landings. The U. S. and Australian units screening our transports were surprised near Savo Island between Florida Island and Guadalcanal. The action was over in half an hour, costing us the cruisers *Canberra,* (Australian), *Quincy, Vincennes,* and *Astoria,* and badly damaging the *Chicago* and the destroyers *Talbot* and *Patterson.* Only the fact that the Japanese Navy retired north leaving us at

169

least temporary control of the waters between Guadalcanal and Florida, gave some assurance that we might hold what we had just gained.

The naval defeat began the contest to see whether we or the Japanese could build up the greater weight of reinforcements and supplies on Guadalcanal. The advantage of land-based aircraft was with the Japanese at first since their bases in Rabaul were closer than ours in New Caledonia. By holding the airfield on Guadalcanal, however, and completing it so that our aircraft might use it, we hoped to reverse that advantage. About ten days of strenuous labor by engineers made the field usable for small planes, and a fighter squadron was brought in. Japanese reinforcements had arrived—about a division were landed by the end of September. As these began to come in, they and those who had fled at our landing attempted to drive the Americans from positions about the airfield. But the Marines turned back every attack with extremely heavy Japanese casualties.

In the meantime, the Navy had taken partial revenge for its earlier defeat near Savo Island. Assisted by planes from Guadalcanal and Army bombers from more distant bases, aircraft from the carriers *Saratoga* and *Enterprise* badly damaged a Japanese carrier and several destroyes and made hits on another carrier, a battleship, several cruisers, and other vessels [*August 23–25, 1942*]. In the days that followed we in turn lost the carrier *Wasp* and five destroyers; while the Japanese lost the carrier *Ryujyo*. The "Tokyo Express," a Japanese destroyer ferry bringing reinforcements and supplies from Bougainville to Guadalcanal, now began to make nightly runs which threatened to build up a ground superiority that would overwhelm the Marines defending the airfield.

Battle for Henderson Field

To prevent the Japanese from gaining the advantage on the ground, elements of the Americal Division were sent in October to reinforce the Marines, and the rest of the division came in during the following two months. At the same time that these first reinforcements were nearing Guadalcanal, U. S. cruisers and destroyers under Rear Admiral Norman

Scott intercepted one of the Tokyo Express runs near Cape Esperance [*October 11, 1942*]. The accurate gunfire of the U. S. cruisers *Boise, Salt Lake City, Helena,* and *San Francisco* sank the carrier *Kinugasa* and four destroyers. As the airfield improved and more Navy, Army, and Marine planes arrived, Henderson Field, as we renamed the strip the Japanese had started, played a larger part in the battle. By the time the battle of Cape Esperance was fought we had air superiority over Guadalcanal. Vice Admiral (now Admiral) William F. Halsey, Jr., had succeeded to the command of the South Pacific [*October 18, 1942*]. But the Japanese continued running in their reinforcements and supplies by night, an additional division arriving in small groups after September. Ten days after the battle off the Cape, the Japanese believed again that they had enough strength on Guadalcanal to take the airfield. They launched a heavy attack with tanks and artillery on the Matanikau River position of the Marines [*October 21, 1942*]. Our lines held. On October 25, another large force made a surprise attack from the south against the Marine and Army lines in this sector. The next morning the rain softened our air strip, grounding our planes; Japanese bombers hit our positions and their cruisers shelled the area. That night the attack was renewed on both the south and west, and for a time threatened serious consequences, but the Japanese were turned back in the end with huge losses. While this land battle was in progress, planes from the carriers *Enterprise* and *Hornet* caught Japanese naval forces off Santa Cruz Island [*October 26, 1942*], put two Japanese carriers out of action, damaged two battleships and four cruisers, and sank two destroyers. We lost the *Hornet* to Japanese planes, but with Henderson Field still in our hands the Japanese Navy retreated to the north and did not again risk its carriers in the South Pacific.

Naval Battle of Guadalcanal

A little more than two weeks later the U. S. Navy scored a decisive victory in the battle for Guadalcanal. The engagement opened when a cruiser-destroyer force under Rear Admiral Daniel J. Callaghan intercepted the enemy [*November*

171

13–15, 1942]. His mission was to carry out a delaying action which would cover the attack of our battleship-carrier force under Rear Admiral (now Vice Admiral) Thomas C. Kinkaid. Admiral Callaghan's task force sunk or damaged several Japanese cruisers and destroyers, and at least one battleship. In the first fifteen minutes of gunfire we also suffered severely: seven cruisers and destroyers were badly damaged and two cruisers and two destroyers were sunk. Later, our battleship-carrier force became engaged. Planes from the *Enterprise* and from Henderson Field joined the battle to execute widespread destruction, helping to sink an enemy battleship and six transports. The battleships *Washington* and *South Dakota* destroyed another Japanese battleship and lesser vessels. These engagements cost us seven destroyers and two cruisers, and the lives of Admirals Scott and Callaghan. The Japanese lost at least two battleships, four cruisers, six destroyers, and a dozen transports. The Navy and land-based air units had carried out Admiral Halsey's orders to "hit hard, hit fast, hit often." Guadalcanal was saved.

This American victory, together with cruiser, submarine, and destroyer actions which followed, prevented the Japanese from landing heavy reinforcements on Guadalcanal and assured our own troops of sufficient strength to conquer the island.

Meanwhile action continued around Henderson Field. From the time of the first Japanese counterattacks in August, the Marines and later the Army units were continuously fighting a series of defensive battles, patrol actions, and limited objective attacks. Malaria, dysentery, and exhaustion wore down the men of the 1st Marine Division who got a well earned rest early in December when they were replaced by the Army's 25th Division. Elements of the 2nd Marine Division and the 147th Infantry had also come in, and Major General (now Lieutenant General) Alexander M. Patch replaced General Vandegrift in command. With the enlarged force, an improved airfield, and the naval victories, we were at last able to drive the Japanese army from Guadalcanal. Enemy reinforcements had now been cut down to those which could be run in by fast destroyers or submarines at night.

172

General Patch's forces began vigorous attacks upon the Japanese now entrenched on the high ground to the southwest and in the broken country between the airfield and Cape Esperance. In about a month, the Americans had cornered, killed, and captured all of the remaining Japanese troops [*February 9, 1943*].

Guadalcanal was ours; the threat to our supply line to Australia was lifted; and the Japanese drive farthest from their homeland had been checked and thrown back.

The Buna-Sanananda Campaign

While the fate of Guadalcanal was being decided, another long, hard battle was fought by American and Australian troops for the possession of southeastern New Guinea. Here the Japanese had landed about 11,000 men at Buna, Gona, and Sanananda, across the Owen Stanley Mountains toward Port Moresby, in a second attempt to strike at Australia. They were south of Ioribaiwa, only thirty miles from Port Moresby, when the Australian 6th Division stopped their advance. By the end of September the U. S. Fifth Air Force, attacking the Japanese route over the mountains, had cut the enemy's supply line. The Australians now threatened the Japanese front and flank. In an effort to keep his forces intact the enemy withdrew to skillfully planned fortifications in the coastal swamp at Buna and Sanananda.

When the remaining Japanese, reinforced by new troops, were settling into these coastal defenses, combat teams of the U. S. 32d Infantry Division arrived in New Guinea to support the Australians. The Americans came in mostly by air and attacked on the right flank, east and south of Buna, while the Australian 7th Division, replacing the 6th, formed the left flank and pushed toward Sanananda and Gona. The Japanese fought a stubborn defensive battle from a network of strongly built and well concealed bunkers.

The Buna front was almost a stalemate, despite hard fighting, until the arrival of the Australian 18th Infantry Brigade with light tanks. Then two weeks of tank and infantry assaults broke the Japanese resistance. After the fall of Buna [*January 2, 1943*], a regiment of the American 32d

Division and the Australian 18th Brigade moved to the Sanananada front, where the Japanese were even more firmly intrenched. The Australian 7th Division, assisted at first by a regiment of the 32d Division and later by a regiment of the 41st Division, had been attacking northward against the Japanese positions around Gona and Sanananda. The Australians had taken Gona, a comparatively weak flank position [*December 9, 1942*], but the Japanese perimeter at Sanananda, protected by blocks on the Soputa-Sanananda road, was still almost as strong as ever when the units from the Buna front arrived. The Australians, aided by the American regiments, finally smashed all resistance at Sanananda [*January 23, 1943*]. The success of the Allied infantry in the Papuan campaign could not have been achieved without the cooperation of the U. S. Fifth Air Force, which ferried supplies and reinforcements to the combat zone. The conquest of this southeastern tip of New Guinea started the Allies on the long road back to the Philippines and assured the safety of Australia.

III. REINFORCING CHINA, BURMA, AND INDIA

Japan had temporarily paralyzed Allied naval forces in the Pacific and enveloped all of Southeast Asia, threatening both India and China by the conquest of Burma. It was now essential for the United Nations to hold India and China bases where aerial and overland offensives could be prepared and launched for the reconquest of Burma and the liberation of Asia. Out of the strategic situation of India and China on the continental flank of Japan's expanded empire grew the CBI (China-Burma-India) Theater of Operations. Defense no less than offense depended on supply. In the Far East even more than in the South Pacific military strategy and operations were limited by this factor. Sea routes between the United Nations and CBI stretched over twelve thousand miles. The long voyage from home ports, such as Liverpool and New York, around Africa to Calcutta consumed both time and ships to far greater extent than in any other theater. During all of 1942 and most of 1943, therefore, CBI was primarily a theater of supply, its primary mission the

174

defense of India and the support of China in the war against Japan.

Burma Road

Overland transport into China rather than oceanic shipping to Burma and India proved to be the bottleneck of CBI supply. The Burma Road was China's life line to the outside world after Japan had occupied the coast and established a naval blockade in 1938. The distance by air from Lashio, the railhead in Burma fed by the port of Rangoon, to Kunming in Yünnan Province is 260 miles. Yet the country is so mountainous that the Road actually twists over seven hundred miles of hairpin curves and steep grades; part of it is fit only for one-way traffic, and none of it is over sixteen feet wide. The Chinese began to build it late in 1937 to circumvent the Japanese blockade. The Road was literally clawed out of the mountainsides by an army of workingmen numbering over a hundred thousand. The first traffic in 1939 brought supplies into China at the rate of 3,500 tons a month, rising to 12,000 tons monthly in 1941 with the introduction of American methods of maintenance, though a large proportion of the tonnage went for gasoline to fuel the trucks. From the middle of 1941 to the fall of Burma, which closed the Road, it was protected by the Flying Tigers, officially the American Volunteer Group under Brigadier General (now Major General) Claire L. Chennault. This small group, paid according to the number of Japanese planes they destroyed, and skilfully trained and directed in fighting against heavy odds, shot down 286 Japanese planes with the loss of only eight pilots.

The closing of the Burma Road, first by Japanese diplomatic pressure, then by the Japanese conquest of Burma, left China stranded for supplies. The only land routes into the country from India were pack-animal trails over the Himalaya Mountains, one from Darjeeling northeast to Lhasa in Tibet and thence east to Chungking, and another from Sadiya to Tali and Kunming. The trip into China over these trails took two months, and the country was so rugged that only light supplies such as medicines could be carried on the backs of porters. In this crisis Lieutenant General (now General) Joseph W. Stilwell, appointed the American com-

175

mander of CBI early in 1942, resorted to an air ferry over the Himalayas. The ferry system was pioneered by the U. S. Tenth Air Force under Major General (now Lieutenant General) Lewis H. Brereton and then transferred to the Air Transport Command in order to free the Tenth's bombers for raids on enemy targets in Burma. At first air traffic was limited because the planes consumed a large part of the gasoline they were trying to carry into China. The system grew steadily, however, and by the end of 1943 a greater tonnage was moving into China every month by air than had ever gone overland by the Burma Road. These supplies supported the operations in China of the U. S. Fourteenth Air Force, established early in 1943 under General Chennault to carry on the work of the Flying Tigers in defense of China.

Late in 1943 American engineers with the help of native labor began the building of a new branch road from Ledo in northern Assam to the Burma Road. They called it "The Road to Tokyo." To clear the way farther eastward, a limited campaign was launched in 1944 in northern Burma under the command of General Stilwell.

The Air Forces in CBI

Until the Burma campaign under General Stilwell, the most active military operation in CBI was the strategic bombing of Japanese targets in Burma and China by the U. S. Tenth and Fourteenth Air Forces. The Tenth flew from Indian bases with the threefold mission of defending India, protecting the "Hump Line" of the Air Transport Command into China, and attacking enemy supply in Burma and Thailand. It bombed 150 targets, including Rangoon, the Moulmein and Akyab docks, Lashio and Henzada storehouses, and the rail junctions of Rangoon, Mandalay, and Sagaing, almost denying the enemy use of rail lines in Burma.

The Fourteenth Air Force had the mission of cooperating with Chinese troops in central China against Japanese air and shipping lines. One wing was made up of American-trained Chinese pilots flying B-25s and P-40s. All supplies for the Fourteenth were drawn from the "Hump Line" over the Himalaya Mountains. To its fighter planes, long the backbone of the Fourteenth and once the entire force of the

Flying Tigers, were added medium and heavy bombers, which raided Hankow, Hong Kong, and the islands of Hainan and Formosa. In the first attack on Formosa, where the Japanese trans-shipped supplies for Burma and the Pacific, twenty-nine planes destroyed forty-two enemy craft and damaged twelve more without any American losses. Most important was the destruction of 274,939 tons of Japanese shipping off the South China coast during 1943. There air attacks forced the enemy to rely on barges for his coastal traffic and to employ his larger vessels on the open seas where American submarines were taking heavy toll.

IV. THE ALEUTIANS

Although Japanese task forces were turned back from Midway and Dutch Harbor, the northern ships proceeded to occupy Attu, Kiska, and Agattu in the foggy Aleutian Islands [*June 1942*]. This seizure of American territory on the Alaskan approaches to the United States alarmed the Pacific northwestern states. The occupied territory was strategically unimportant, however, except as a base for raiding Alaska and limiting American air and sea operations in the North Pacific. An immediate effort to recapture these islands was impossible so long as ships, planes, and troops were first needed for defense of the Central and South Pacific. Advanced airfields were set up on Adak and Amchitka [*August 31, 1942*] from which bombers constantly attacked Kiska and Attu [*January 1943*].

Attu

When enough troops and ships at last became available, an expedition was mounted against Attu, westernmost island in the Aleutians, bypassing Kiska. It was hoped that the capture of Attu would render Kiska untenable, and it did. U. S. forces landed in fog on northeastern Attu at two points, Holtz Bay in the north and Massacre Bay about five miles across the island to the south [*May 11, 1943*]. The American force consisted of elements of the 7th Infantry Division, reinforced by one battalion of the 4th Infantry and Alaska Scouts. Major General Eugene M. Landrum commanded the ground troops, supported by naval and air units.

177

The Japanese had bases at Chichagof Harbor and at Holtz Bay where they were completing a small airstrip. The enemy defended successive positions which were most of the time covered by the fog and snow of the mountains. The machine-gun posts and entrenchments dominated every pass. Dual-purpose antiaircraft guns and mortars were used effectively against the Americans. The Southern Force from Massacre Bay made extensive use of artillery, but the almost constant fog prevented our bombers from giving much aid to either group. Although it was May, the water-filled foxholes, the deep mud, the ice-cold surface water, the snow-covered mountainsides, and the bitter cold of the nights added exposure to exhaustion and caused many American casualties.

The two American forces moved toward each other, driving the Japanese into an ever-narrowing pocket about Chichagof Harbor. The Northern Force captured Hill X after sharp fighting and then occupied the Japanese camp near the end of the west arm of Holtz Bay. From here the Japanese positions on the ridge separating the two arms of the Bay were taken after a day and night of fighting. With the loss of the ridge the Japanese fell back toward Chichagof.

In the meantime, the Southern Force in Massacre Bay had been held up by Japanese occupying positions overlooking the valley. The advance of the Northern Force threatened to cut these Japanese off, and they were withdrawn to the north to help defend Massacre-Sarana (Clevesy) Pass, covering the southern approach to Chichagof. Against this gateway, flanked on both sides by high mountains, the Southern Force steadily pushed. The heights on either side were taken by frontal attacks and the force moved into Sarana Valley, from which another valley led to Chichagof. But the mountains on both sides had to be cleared of Japanese before the valley approach could be used. When these were taken, the movement on the valley floor followed. While the Northern Force was driving toward Holtz—Chichagof Pass, the Southern was attacking a high U-shaped and snow-covered mountain range, called the Fish Hook. With the capture of both of these objectives after battles at close quarters in which grenades were the chief weapons, both routes to Chichagof were open to the Americans. The Japanese were cornered, and the

178

Americans were prepared to move in for the kill. That night, May 28-29, those Japanese who were wounded and unable to walk committed suicide or were killed by their own countrymen. Shortly after midnight the remaining enemy force started a desperate attack up the valley which led from Chichagof toward the American artilley positions beyond Clevesy Pass. The suddenness and momentum of this suicidal attack completely disrupted the American units and overran our positions in the valley floor. The Japanese were prevented from capturing our artillery only by the hastily organized resistance of engineer and miscellaneous service units in front of the Clevesy Pass. We suffered heavy casualties but the Japanese were themselves wiped out in confused fighting which continued through the day and into the next. The few Japanese who were not killed by the Americans chose suicide rather than surrender. On May 30 only a few snipers remained to be hunted down, and we occupied Chichagof without opposition.

Kiska

The American capture of Attu isolated Kiska, 175 miles east, where the Japanese had developed their largest base in the Aleutians during the year that followed their first landing [*June 1942*]. From Adak and Amchitka our planes had raided Japanese installations on Kiska as often as weather permitted, and within twelve days of the capture of Attu a strip was built there for the operation of additional planes. During the first half of 1943 the U. S. Eleventh Air Force had dropped three million pounds of bombs on enemy positions in the Aleutians. Through June and July Kiska became the main target until it was ready for ground assault.

The strongest amphibious force ever mounted in the North Pacific made the attack. Units of the Western Defense Command, the 7th Infantry Division, and elements of the Royal Canadian Army, all under Major General Charles H. Corlett, descended on Kiska with a naval escort commanded by Vice Admiral Thomas C. Kinkaid. Troops landed at Quisling Cove on the northwest coast [*August 15, 1943*] and were followed the next day by forces landing at other points.

Swift probing of the enemy's camouflaged positions revealed that he had secretly evacuated all his garrison. Under cover of heavy mid-summer fogs the Japanese ships and submarines had been able to escape aerial interception, except for a few ships which were sunk or damaged by our bombers. The last Japanese may have fled Kiska but a day or two before the American landings. As late as July 22 our naval forces had encountered heavy fire from enemy shore batteries, and our planes met antiaircraft fire through August 13. No ground reconnaissance had been attempted lest its discovery inform the enemy of our intentions. The strong American forces landing on Kiska were prepared for a battle more difficult than Attu, and the well stocked caves in the hills proved that the enemy could have made a bitter last-ditch stand. Kiska was the first of their conquests which the Japanese abandoned without a fight.

With the occupation of Kiska the Americans had reclaimed all the Aleutians, and these islands became air bases for the bombing of the Kuriles on the northern approaches to Tokyo, 2,174 miles away. From every quarter of the compass American air power was expanding toward Japan: the Eleventh Air Force flew from the Aleutians; the Seventh was based in Hawaii; the Thirteenth in the Solomons; the Fifth in New Guinea; the Tenth in India; and the Fourteenth in China—six great air fleets which ringed the outer defenses of the Japanese Empire.

23. VICTORY IN AFRICA

The liberation of Africa was the first strategic victory won from Axis forces by British and American troops. They took the offensive in a joint operation, the British driving west from Egypt, the Americans and British landing in French North Africa and driving east, and both joining forces in Tunisia to squeeze the enemy out of Africa. These offensives, said Churchill [*November 10, 1942*], were "part of a single strategic and political conception" designed "to open a new front against Hitler and Hitlerism, to cleanse the shores of Africa from the stain of Nazi and Fascist tyranny, to open the Mediterranean to Allied sea power and air power and thus effect the liberation of the peoples of Europe."

Through the summer and fall of 1942 Rommel's forces stood checked at El Alamein. Their strength was greater on paper than in the field. There were twelve undersized divisions, including the Afrika Korps with the 15th and 21st Panzer and the 90th and 164th Motorized Divisions, and about six hundred tanks in two assemblies. The Axis starved the African front of men and matériel to feed the Russian front; but Britain and America diverted the bulk of their supplies available in Europe to the Middle East. Montgomery built up the British Eighth Army to ten divisions, five from Britain and five from the Empire, to full strength. Some fifty thousand men reached Egypt in American ships to replace those lost at Tobruk. British superiority in matériel grew with large shipments of tanks, trucks, and guns from America and with planes flown directly across the Atlantic. Over one thousand planes, more than five hundred medium tanks, and twenty thousand trucks had been sent from the United States under Lend-Lease in nineteen months. The Eighth Army had twice as many planes and tanks as the enemy, and strongest among the tanks were the U. S. General Shermans, with 5mm. guns. It was the quality of this equipment, as well as the quantity and the tactics of command, which won the Battle of El Alamein and drive the Nazis out of Egypt.

The Battle

Since the Axis line for thirty-five miles was a maze of strongpoints joined by wire and mines, the first and most difficult phase of the battle [*October 19–23, 1942*] was the clearance of forward areas by planes, artillery, infantry, and sappers. The RAF gained complete control of the air in a week by making seven hundred sorties a day. Axis air forces were grounded or destroyed. Then the 25-pounder concentrated the heaviest fire ever heard in the desert on enemy batteries and minefields [*October 23–24, 1942*]. In full moonlight four divisions of British infantry penetrated the northern sector for five miles under an artillery curtain, and sap-

181

pers cleared thousands of mines to open two tank lanes. Another attack like the first punched tankheads even deeper into enemy lines near the coast [*October 31–November 1, 1942*].

Rommel flew to the rescue of his forces: he concentrated his tanks in the north to stop what appeared to be the main British thrust, a move which left him no reserves to meet another attack; and then wasted his strength in counter-attacks which were foiled by the RAF [*October 28–November 1, 1942*]. British tank units, built around Shermans, carried out the second phase of the battle [*November 2–3, 1942.*] They split the Axis armor in the north, cut up the rear, and in a great two-day fight of tanks against tanks at El Aqqaqir destroyed 260 enemy machines. Rommel's second in command, General Stumme, was killed, and the commander of the Afrika Korps, General Thoma, was captured, together with 8,000 German prisoners. Altogether it was estimated that the Axis lost 500 tanks, 1,000 guns, and 59,000 men, killed, wounded, and captured, of which 34,000 were Germans, 25,000 Italians. Of the total German and Italian casualties, 30,000 were prisoners of war. After two long years of war in the African desert, the British Eighth Army had won the last decisive battle.

Rommel's Retreat

Rommel withdrew the remnants of his army rapidly to El Agheila, 860 miles west, destroying supplies, and delaying the British pursuit by strewing mines behind him [*November 13, 1942*]. From El Agheila he retreated all the way to Tunisia without fighting. The British followed, covering thirty miles a day along the coastal road, and in rapid succession took the old battlegrounds of Mersa Matruh, Sidi Barrani, Tobruk, Derna, El Meckili, and Bengasi until they faced Rommel at El Agheila [*November 8–27, 1942*]. But they failed to catch Rommel's force because heavy rains and minefields slowed down their supply train of 110,000 trucks.

From December to February, however, the British advanced 1,400 miles west from El Alamein. They converted Tripoli into a port through which flowed 2,800 tons of supplies every day. West of Tripoli General Montgomery, with

182

only an armored division and brigade, kept at Rommel's heels. The remainder of Montgomery's troops were busy building up supply dumps along the westward routes of march. Fighting French troops under General Leclerc made a heroic march across the Sahara from Lake Tchad to join the British Eighth Army south of Tripoli. But none of these forces caught Rommel. His retreat was a military masterpiece of speed and economy, for his men withdrew faster than planes and tanks could advance.

II. ANGLO-AMERICAN LANDINGS IN NORTH AFRICA

The Allied offensive to drive the Axis out of Africa, which began with the Battle of El Alamein, was first contemplated by President Roosevelt and Prime Minister Churchill when they met in Washington in the dark days following Pearl Harbor. It was calculated that enough troops and supplies could be sent across the Atlantic for a small offensive in Africa by late 1942, or a larger offensive against Hitler-held Europe by the middle of 1943. The Joint Chiefs of Staff decided to strike at the earlier date in North Africa, where the Axis was weakest. In Morocco, Algeria, and Tunis were French Colonial forces whose help in driving the Axis out of Africa we might gain. From African bases we might jump to Sicily, freeing Britain's life line to India and opening a way for invasion of Italy and Southern France. Lieutenant General (now General of the Army) Dwight D. Eisenhower, appointed to command the operation, prepared his plans for Operation Torch in London during 1942.

The day the British Eighth Army started to drive west from El Alamein [*October 24, 1942*], a great troop convoy put to sea from American ports, and in the next twenty-four hours two more convoys left British ports, all bound for North Africa. Thus the offensive began from east and west, on land in Egypt and at sea five thousand miles across the Atlantic Ocean. Three convoys of seven hundred ships converged west of Gibraltar and went into French North Africa. Within six months this Anglo-American army, joining the British Eighth Army, would crush half a million enemy troops and liberate Africa.

Three major landings were made on the African coast, two

on the Mediterranean and one on the Atlantic [*November 8, 1942*]. At Algiers the invasion met little opposition; at Oran, Vichy French troops capitulated after two days; at Casablanca, the Vichy French Navy fought bitterly for five days. French resistance ceased [*November 12, 1942*] when Admiral Darlan, the Vichy deputy Chief of State who had broken with Pétain, reached an agreement with General Eisenhower and ordered the French in Africa to cooperate with the Allies. By winter fifty thousand French colonial troops were ready to fight under General Henri Giraud in support of Allied forces. Meanwhile other landings were made at Agadir, Mogador, Port Lyautey, and close to Tunisia at Philippeville and Bone.

These landings caught the Axis by surprise, but Nazi troops soon poured southward to hold the Mediterranean coasts of Europe and Africa. They swept into unoccupied France [*November 27, 1942*] and found three-quarters of the French Navy scuttled when they reached Toulon [*November 11, 1942*]. They took the island of Corsica, hitherto occupied by the Italians, seized the Tunisian ports of Bizerte and Tunis, and rushed troops into Tunisia by plane at the rate of a thousand a day. The Luftwaffe covered these reinforcements from interior bases in Sicily and Sardinia, but the British Navy sank about one-third of all enemy naval convoys.

The Allies had not been able to seize Tunisia by landing there, first because they lacked enough ships and aircraft carriers to penetrate the central Mediterranean, and second because they had to keep large forces in the rear for supply and for protection against a possible enemy thrust through Spain and Spanish Morocco. Yet General Eisenhower ordered advance guards overland into Tunisia in an effort to keep the enemy from occupying it [*November 11, 1942*]. There was hardly more than a division in Algiers, and troops pushing eastward moved over bad roads, without good communications or airfields, leaving their main bases five hundred miles behind them [*November 15, 1942*]. The enemy was waiting for them at Mateur, having seized the mountain approaches to Tunisia [*December 1–28, 1942*]. He proved too strong to be brushed aside, and the Tunisian front was stabilized for the cold, rainy winter on a line running north and south of Medjez-el-Bab. Both sides raced to build up strength for the inevitable Battle of Tunisia. It was not to be won, as the Allies had hoped, by beating the enemy to the draw.

III. CASABLANCA CONFERENCE: UNCONDITIONAL SURRENDER

The American troops who had landed in North Africa were surprised to be reviewed by their Commander in Chief, President Roosevelt, at Casablanca. He had come to foreign soil for the first time since the deployment of American forces all over the world, to confer with the British Prime Minister on the prosecution of the war and the requirements for victory [*January 14–26, 1943*]. Churchill and Roosevelt had met before in Washington and on the Atlantic, but this was the first prolonged conference of the two Allied leaders with their Combined Chiefs of Staff. Premier Stalin of the USSR and Generalissimo Chiang Kai-shek of China, both unable to attend, were kept informed of the discussions. General Charles de Gaulle, commanding the Fighting French, and General Henri Giraud, High Commissioner of French Africa, were brought together at Casablanca to unite their countrymen in opposition to Hitler.

In these discussions and negotiations the United Nations began to pass from the paper declaration which they had signed a year before in Washington to an actual union whose strength would be put forth on the battlefields of the world. The tide was turning in the war against the Axis from defense to offense, defeat to victory, by the time of the Casablanca Conference. The strategic initiative had been snatched from the enemy at Guadalcanal, in New Guinea, at El Alamein, Stalingrad, and in Tunisia.

Victories at these enemy outposts pointed to future penetration of the main lines of enemy resistance in Europe and Asia. The leaders meeting at Casablanca planned operations with the principal aim according to the communiqué, of drawing "as much weight as possible off the Russian armies by engaging the enemy as heavily as possible at the best selected points." The conference was not only occupied with strategy against Germany. "The entire field of the war was surveyed

185

theater by theater throughout the world, and all resources were marshalled for a more intense prosecution of the war by sea, land and air."

The most immediate task was to finish the Tunisian campaign and destroy the enemy in Africa. The next offensive move was to be the invasion and conquest of Sicily, where we could extend our control over the Mediterranean and knock Italy out of the war. Steps were also taken to assist China and widen the range of offensive action in the Pacific. The Combined Chiefs of Staff drew up a schedule for simultaneous blows against the Japanese during the summer of 1943 in the Southwest and South Pacific, and approved plans to eliminate the Japanese from the Aleutians in the North Pacific.

The ultimate object of this strategy, stated President Roosevelt, was the "unconditional surrender" of the Axis Powers. He borrowed the phrase from General Ulysses S. Grant, who had used it in a letter to the Confederate commander of Forts Henry and Donelson demanding their capitulation in the American Civil War. In the last war President Wilson had called for "force to the utmost" and declared that there could be no peace without absolute victory. Now President Roosevelt asserted that there would be no appeasement, no negotiation, no end to the war short of complete victory, unconditional surrender of the enemy. The Casablanca Conference was the first meeting of the United Nations which set these terms for peace.

IV. BATTLE OF TUNISIA

The Tunisian campaign was the first in which American troops joined the British to defeat the Nazis. It fell into four phases. First came the landings in Africa and the vain rush to beat the enemy to Tunisia [*November 8–December 28, 1942*]. Then followed the winter scramble by both sides to recruit their forces and capture the best tactical jump-off positions for battle in the spring [*January 1–February 10, 1943*]. The third phase was marked by a strong German raid which threatened the American base at Tebessa but was concluded by the plunge of the British Eighth Army around the Mareth Line [*February 11–April 13, 1943*]. Finally

186

came the offensive in which the Allied Eighteenth Army Group worked like a machine to compress the enemy in the Tunisian cylinder until he was at last destroyed [*April 14–May 13, 1943*].

Rommel's Raid

Through the winter the Nazis stabbed at the Allied lines in the west, first with a force of one armored and four infantry divisions under General Arnim and then with panzer divisions from the Afrika Korps. These troops launched five attacks which kept the Tunisian corridor open for Rommel's retreat but failed to break the Allied lines.

The strongest Nazi offensive, indeed their last in Africa, was a raid by the veteran 21st Panzer Division against green American units dispersed at the end of long supply lines in front of Gafsa. German armor swept through the Faïd Pass to Sbeitla, Gafsa, and Feriana in a three-pronged thrust which overran the Kasserine Pass [*February 14, 1943*]. Almost half the tanks of the 1st Armored Division were lost in fierce fighting, and the Americans fell back to escape encirclement from the south. The Allied position in central Tunisia was in danger. To check the enemy breakthrough, the 9th and 34th Infantry Divisions sped to the front from Oran, and artillery of the 9th rushed forward on a forced march of 770 miles in three days. British units contained the enemy's northern flank, and all the Allied bombers took the sky [*February 22, 1943*]. This concentration of force stopped Rommel short of Thala and drove him back through the Kasserine Pass [*February 25, 1943*]. He withdrew under the protection of artillery and minefields. American troops recaptured Sbeitla [*March 1, 1943*], Gafsa and El Guettar [*March 17, 1943*], and advanced to Maknassy to threaten the rear of the Mareth Line [*March 22, 1943*]. "The troops that come out of this campaign," observed General Eisenhower, "are going to be battle-wise and tactically efficient."

Allied Reorganization

For the great offensive in Tunisia the Allied forces were combined in the 18th Army Group [*February 4, 1943*] under General (now Field Marshal) Sir Harold R. Alexander, with General Eisenhower in supreme command of all forces— military, naval, and air. The 18th Army Group embraced the British First Army under General Anderson, the Eighth under General Montgomery, the French XIX Corps, under General Alphonse Juin, and the U. S. II Corps of four divisions, first commanded by Major General (now Lieutenant General) Lloyd R. Fredendall, then by Lieutenant General (now General) George S. Patton, Jr., and later by Lieutenant General (now General) Omar N. Bradley. Air Chief Marshal Sir Arthur Tedder took charge of all air forces. to give ground troops the close tactical support he had developed in Libya, and Admiral (now Admiral of the Fleet) Sir Andrew Cunningham commanded the Mediterranean Fleet. Thus there was unity of Allied command from start to finish of the Tunisian offensive.

Altogether a total of 500,000 troops had been landed in North Africa, but many of these men were operating railroads, guarding the rear, and providing supply. Opposed to the Allies were General Arnim, with an estimated 92,000 troops in the north, and Marshal Rommel with about 75,000 of his Afrika Korps in the Mareth Line to the south. The enemy intended to fight a delaying action while he improved the defenses of southern Europe, and if it were possible, of course, he wanted to hold his African bridgehead. The Allied forces planned to destroy the enemy in Africa by reducing his Tunisian perimeter, first by punching it in from the south and then by squeezing it from the west.

Battle of the Mareth Line

The British Eighth Army had caught up with Rommel's forces after they retired into the fortified hills of the old French Mareth Line [*February 18, 1943*]. A panzer jab at Montgomery's right cost Rommel fifty tanks [*March 6, 1943*], and he was recalled to Germany, ostensibly on sick leave [*March 15, 1943*]. With the Americans at Maknassy and the French south of them around Ksar Rhilane, to hang on Axis communications and divide their reserves, Montgomery broke the Mareth Line. After heavy artillery preparation [*March 21–22, 1943*], the 50th Division bridged an

188

antitank ditch under murderous machine-gun fire and got tanks across the water-logged Wadi Zigzaou, but recoiled from the counterattacks of two panzer divisions. Pinning the enemy in front, Montgomery turned the Mareth Line by a left hook delivered with all his reserves. On this flank Freyberg's New Zealand Division penetrated minefields and breached the Roman Wall, and the 4th Indian Division circled the enemy's rear through the Matmata Hills. American armor closed in from Maknassy. To escape this trap, the Germans switched troops from front to flank [*March 26, 1943*], and the British 51st Division plunged through the weakened Mareth Line [*March 27, 1943*]. As the Nazis abandoned the Mareth sector, they maintained their western flank with minefields, and British armor pressed them along the coast to Gabes [*March 29, 1943*]. In ten days the Eighth Army took eight thousand prisoners.

To cut off the enemy's retreat, the U. S. 1st Armored Division pushed east from El Guettar, ran into defiladed tank fire, and closed on the enemy flank after engineers cleared mines to provide wider approaches [*April 2, 1943*]. In a surprise night attack [*April 6, 1943*] the 4th Indian Division broke the new enemy line at Wadi-el-Akharit with another left hook, and the Afrika Korps withdrew still farther north toward Enfidaville, losing 9,500 prisoners [*April 12, 1943*]. As the British moved north to occupy Sfax and Sousse, patrols met advance guards of U. S. II Corps on the Gabes road and linked up the Allied lines [*April 8, 1943*]. Henceforth the British Eighth Army could be supplied from North African ports, and troops could be shuttled back and forth along the entire Tunisian front. The U. S. 34th Infantry Division and British 6th Armored Division combined to capture Fondouk Pass [*April 12, 1943*], leading to the German flank, but occupied Kairouan too late to catch the enemy by a breakthrough to the sea. The Afrika Korps fell back on Arnim's reinforcements and established a perimeter defense of northern Tunisia along a front of 122 miles.

To Bizerte and Tunis

For the final reduction of the Axis perimeter General Alexander shifted his attack from the narrow bottleneck at the south to the broad western side, where British, American, and French troops could maneuver in unison. Three divisions of the Eighth Army were transferred to the First Army with such secrecy that the enemy still kept his reserves in the south to check the Eighth. U. S. II Corps of 100,000 men under General Bradley moved 150 miles north, passing through the British First Army and crossing a dense traffic in supplies, to the Beja road which ran to Bizerte [April 16, 1943]. After this reorganization the British Eighth Army opened the final offensive with a show of force which succeeded and enabled them to pin the enemy in the south and take Enfidaville [April 20, 1943].

The British First Army launched the main drive toward Tunis [April 21, 1943] on two flanks from Medjez-el-Bab, and made slow progress against enemy tanks until stopped before Djebel-bou-Aoukaz, a hill 2,200 feet high which dominated the route of advance. Three savage attacks under air and artillery cover finally won the crest, but the position was isolated by enemy counterattacks [April 27–30, 1943]. The French XIX Corps had the greatest success in the south, taking the highest mountain, Djebel-el-Zaghouan, and punching in the flanks at Pont-du-Fahs.

The Allies moved eastward on Bizerte and Tunis with constant air support through the parallel valleys of Melah, Djoumine, and Medjerda. But the going was tough and slow because the enemy held the hills. U. S. II Corps, made up of the 1st Armored and the 1st, 9th, and 34th Infantry Divisions, joined the attack with an advance of five miles from Djebel Abiod [April 23–25, 1943]. The corps advanced in two groups, a northern wing astride the road from Sedjenane and a southern wing along the Beja road, both converging on Mateur. Hill after hill was stormed or flanked in bitter fighting. Key positions often changed hands several times before the German defenders were forced to fall back. The heaviest fighting on the corps front took place around Jefna (Jaffna) and Sidi Nsir on the road to Mateur and in the hills south and east of the Tine (Mousetrap) [April 26–27, 1943].

The crux of the American attack was at Djebel Tahent, Hill 609 [April 28–29, 1943], the enemy's main position covering Mateur. The storming of two supporting heights prom-

190

ised to envelop it, but terrific mortar fire swept the Americans from a line half-way up the rocky sides of 609. An attack launched the next day [May 1, 1943] captured this hill fortress, and our troops took full possession after one day's fighting. Meanwhile, the 9th Division had outflanked Jefna on the north, and the Germans had to abandon the hills that made up the Jefna position [May 3, 1943]. The Americans captured Mateur and came within thirteen miles of Bizerte, north of Lake Achkel, as the enemy began to move south on Tunis where he could find refuge at Cape Bon. This withdrawal made it easier for U. S. II Corps to move up the Ferryville road and to send units south to cooperate with the British in squeezing the 15th Panzer Division out of Tebourba [May 4–8, 1943].

The British First Army renewed its drive on Tunis [May 5, 1943] along a front of ten miles, with tanks in the center, and infantry on the flanks, covered by 1,200 sorties of the Twelfth Air Force. Massicault was taken [May 6, 1943], and tanks broke through enemy lines to surprise German soldiers sitting in the cafés of Tunis. With the occupation of this port [May 7, 1943] the Axis forces in Tunisia were cut in two.

The same day the U. S. II Corps occupied Ferryville, a motorized battalion reached Bizerte [May 7, 1943], and next day U. S. armored units cleared the streets of snipers, crossed the ship channel and captured enemy rear guards. The Americans, together with the French Moroccan Corps under General Giraud, had trapped about 25,000 Nazi troops in northern Tunisia. The enemy was now confused and disorganized. His perimeter defense had been flattened in the north at Bizerte, cut in the center at Tunis, and pressed in from the south by the advancing French and British. British motor patrols from Tunis raced along the base of the Cape Bon peninsula [May 11, 1943] and joined the Eighth Army to prevent the enemy from carrying out Hitler's order to "fight to the last cartridge." With no place left to make a last stand, the Nazis surrendered.

In the Battle of Tunisia fifteen enemy divisions were destroyed. Prisoners, including fourteen German and four Italian generals, numbered 267,000. When General Arnim was

191

captured [*May 12, 1943*], Italian units in the south—last to hold out—surrendered. Enemy losses in matériel ran to 250 tanks, over 2,330 aircraft, and 232 ships. Allied casualties in the Tunisian campaign were less than 70,000. The Americans lost 2,184 killed, 9,437 wounded, and 6,937 missing, a total of 18,558. For the four American divisions of II Corps who fought there, Tunisia was a school of battle; they landed in Africa green and entered Bizerte seven months later veterans.

The air forces under Marshal Tedder, which had answered every call of ground troops in Tunisia for reconnaissace and bombardment, now launched a furious aerial assault upon the Italian islands off the Tunisian coast [*May 30–June 8, 1943*]. A severe naval and air bombardment demoralized the Italian garrison of 11,150 on Pantelleria [*June 11, 1943*], and they surrendered without resistance. Lampedusa also fell after one day of continuous bombardment [*June 12, 1943*]. Linosa and Lampione, small adjacent islands were taken over with little difficulty [*June 13, 1943*]. The capture of these islands completed the conquest of North Africa and gave Allied sea power more effective control of the Mediterranean. The Middle East was at last safe and Africa had been liberated from the Axis.

24. THE RED ARMY ON THE OFFENSIVE

I. BATTLE OF STALINGRAD

The high-water mark of the German invasion of Russia, outside the Caucasus, was Stalingrad. The siege and relief of this city proved to be a turning point of the war. Here the Nazis lost the momentum of their advance, never to regain it. Here the Red Army first changed from strategic defense to offense all along the front south of Leningrad. The Red Army had thus far demonstrated its mastery of defense in depth; now it was to gain superiority on the offensive.

Stalingrad was the Russian Detroit. It lies forty miles east of the Don Bend and straggles twenty miles along

192

the western bank of the Volga River. The Nazis had approached this city of tank and tractor factories in a pincers movement from northwest and southwest and penetrated its outskirts in a three-pronged assault. If Stalingrad fell to the invaders, they would be able to circle north on Moscow or swing south to the Caspian Sea and cut off the oil of the Caucasus. Even if they went no farther than Stalingrad, they could choke communications on the Volga and seize its rich freight.

"The occupation of Stalingrad," boasted Hitler, "will become a gigantic success . . . no human being will push us away from that spot." The conqueror "cuts off thirty million tons of traffic, including nine million tons of oil. There flows the entire wheat gathered from the Ukraine and Kuban, and manganese ore. I wanted to take it." [*November 8, 1942*] This was the strategy of the hungry Nazi.

The Nazi Siege

For sixty-six days [*September 14–November 19, 1942*] the German Sixth Army of twenty-two divisions under General von Paulus smashed at Stalingrad with everything it had —Stukas, howitzers, tanks, mortars, and men. Not since Madrid in the Spanish Civil War had a great city become a battlefield. Nazi infantry actually conquered most of Stalingrad in the course of two months' relentless fighting, and occupied four miles along the western bank of the Volga around the Barricade Factory. But they never swept the Russians entirely out of the city or across the Volga River.

The Sixty-second Army of sixteen divisions under General Chuikov, ordered to hold Stalingrad while the great counteroffensive was prepared, fought for every street and factory, defended the strongpoints made by the walls, rubble, and craters of shattered buildings, and died by the thousands in the ravines leading down to the Volga. There they caught the enemy with enfilading fire from batteries mounted across the river. When Stukas destroyed the bridges by which the garrison was supplied, a bridge one mile long was laid under water and used at night unseen by the Luftwaffe. The defenders of Stalingrad were finally driven back into the high bluff along the Volga. There in a maze of dugouts, underground forts, and firing posts, only one hundred to one thousand yards from the river, they held fast. Each mile of the sixteen-mile barrier was covered by a division, and among these units were six of the finest in the Red Army. The 70th Division of ten thousand men under General Ivan Ludnikov had eight hundred survivors. The heaviest bombardment of the war reduced Stalingrad to a mass of girders, broken walls, and iron bedsteads, but its garrison survived. Despite its capture, the city never gave up.

When the Red Army came to drive the Nazis out, it found them as difficult to exterminate as rats. There was little fighting in the open streets, and no barricades were built, but the ruins of every building had to be stormed. At night the Russians secretly dug foxholes and trenches to approach a strongpoint. Then, without any artillery preparations, small shock squads of six to eight men, each armed with ten grenades, a tommy gun and a dagger, surprised the enemy post. These assault detachments were supported by reinforcements heavily armed with machine guns, mortars, pickaxes, and explosives, and by reserves who broke up counterattacks. The defenders scaled the upper stories of buildings to reach firing points against the enemy outside, set up gun posts on the corners to ward off counterattacks, forced the Germans indoors, and drove them down to the cellars to be killed. "Throw a grenade and follow in"—those were the tactics. In this way they stormed in twenty-six hours the six-storied "L-Shaped House," which sprawled over two city blocks and gave the Germans domination of the Volga. The surprise, speed, and daring of Indian raids, added to systematic planning, characterized the Russian tactics to clear the ruins of their great city.

Russian Counteroffensive in the Donbas

But the main blows to liberate Stalingrad were struck from far outside the city. They took the form of an offensive, mounted in two months by Marshal Zhukov, to trap the Nazis in Stalingrad and drive other enemy armies back to the Donets. The first mission of some half million troops was to isolate the enemy at Stalingrad by cutting his two railroads from Rostov and Kharkov. A double envelopment was

194

planned in the German style, although the Russians called it a hammer and sickle, to trap the Nazi Sixth Army in an area of fifty square miles. The first blow was struck from the north through Serafimovich by three tank and two cavalry corps, and next came a thrust from the south by two tank and one cavalry corps. These forces possessed overwhelming fire power. For the first time since the Battle of Moscow all the weapons that the Russians could muster, including three thousand planes and four thousand tanks which had come by Lend-Lease from America and Britain, were hurled into battle.

In the north they destroyed three divisions of Italian and Hungarian infantry in a swift advance southwest across the Don [*November 19–24, 1942*] to cut the Rostov railroad at Oblivskaya. General Rodin's I Tank Corps raced sixty-two miles to take the Don bridgehead of Kalach forty miles west of Stalingrad. Tolbukhin penetrated the northernmost defenses of the enemy corridor stretching from the Don to the Volga. The Nazi left flank was enveloped. From the southeast Rokossovsky and Malinovsky struck at the Novorossisk railroad, shutting the last door by which the enemy could retreat [*November 20–27, 1942*].

The German Sixth Army was trapped by the closing of the pincers west of Kalach when Red tanks met at Marinovka [*November 23, 1942*]. Until it was too late to break out of this trap, the enemy did not guess the strength of the encircling Russians. The Nazi garrison consisted of twenty-two divisions, ten German, six Italian, and the remainder from the Balkans, a total of between 300,000 and 400,000 men. General von Paulus organized these troops in a hedgehog defense, and reduced his perimeter under pressure until its boundaries north and south were only twenty miles apart [*December 12, 1942*]. Because the railroads had been cut, the garrison was supplied daily by air fleets of four hundred to five hundred Ju-52 transports, which the Russians shot down by the score.

To the relief of the Sixth Army came a force of 120,000 troops under General Manstein [*December 12–24, 1942*], organized in two tank, two cavalry, and four infantry divisions. They swept up the Kalmuk steppes from Kotelnikov-

195

ski, 110 miles southwest, and ran into a Red Army under General Malinovsky which recaptured the city [*December 29, 1942*] and hurled them back two hundred miles toward Rostov. Caught in the Stalingrad sack, von Paulus counter-attacked on all sides [*December 12–31, 1942*] with losses mounting up to 100,000. His fate was sealed by the defeat of Manstein's relief forces.

Paulus refused the Russian demand for surrender because Hitler had ordered him to resist to the last man [*January 8–9, 1943*]. So Rokossovsky annihilated his army. The ring of iron and fire around Stalingrad was drawn ever tighter, with the main attack from the west, enfilade fire from north and south, and savage fighting by Chuikov's army inside the city [*January 10–February 2, 1943*]. The Nazi field forces were driven back on Stalingrad as the Russians had been in August. After twelve days the Germans lost their last means of supply, the airfields, and relief planes disappeared from the sky. Then Soviet troops from the west smashed to the Volga and split the enemy forces in half.

The end came when General Paulus, recently promoted by Hitler to Field Marshal, was captured in what had been the business district of southern Stalingrad. The Axis lost 330,000 men. They were beaten, one of the captured generals said, "by hunger, cold, and lack of ammunition." The Red Army which beat them claimed the capture of more than 200,000 troops, 60,000 trucks, 6,700 guns, and 1,500 tanks in the greatest defeat ever administered to a German field army. It was the turn of the tide in the Russian war: henceforth the Nazis were pushed steadily west until they were driven from the Soviet Union.

II. THE WINTER CAMPAIGN, 1942–43

Clearing the Donbas

When the Russians first encircled Stalingrad, they also mounted two other offensives south and north of the city to clear the Don basin. It was probably to cover the withdrawal of his troops from the Caucasus and the Don menaced by these offensives, that Hitler ordered the Sixth Army to stand at Stalingrad. Maslenikov pressed the Germans as they retired from the northern Caucasus toward Rostov [*December 13, 1942–January 17, 1943*] and with the cooperation of Malinovsky's army forced them to evacuate Rostov and fall back toward Taganrog [*February 15, 1943*]. Although the Nazis had to abandon the Caucasus entirely, they retired in good order and with few losses. At the Black Sea base of Novorossisk they managed to retain a bridgehead to protect their southern flank in the Crimea and to close the Sea of Azov.

Meanwhile, northwest of Stalingrad on the middle Don, two armies under Vatutin and Golikov drove southwest to cut the railroads below Voronezh [*December 20, 1942*]. Loss of these lines would trap the enemy in the Don Bend. Under heavy artillery fire and tank attacks, Manstein withdrew rapidly from the Don to the Donets [*January 18, 1943*]. The Russians claimed 56,000 prisoners in this advance of 150 miles.

Farther north on the Don, a pincers movement of Vasilevsky [*January 16–28, 1943*], encircled the lagging Axis infantry at Voronezh and captured 27,000 prisoners. The aim of this drive was to catch the enemy in the upper Don and free the main railroad from Rostov to Moscow. The Russian advance in February gathered such momentum that the Germans could not even defend a second railroad through Belgorod and Kursk, as they had planned, but were compelled to abandon Kursk, Belgorod, and Kharkov. In this campaign along the Voronezh front, Moscow estimated that the enemy lost almost as many men as at Stalingrad. The Red Army reclaimed both the Don and Donets Rivers, with two main railroads to Moscow, and recovered all the territory which the Nazis had taken in 1942.

Capture of the Rzhev Salient

Another offensive north of Moscow, planned by Zhukov to divert enemy strength from Stalingrad, wiped out the dangerous Rzhev salient that had threatened the capital since 1941. Hitler had said that the Germans would feel the loss of Rzhev as much as the destruction of half of Berlin. Rzhev was one of the most strongly defended salients in the main line of German defenses. It contained hedgehogs bristling with tank traps, minefields, and gun emplacements, arranged for mutual support and stocked to hold out, even if surrounded, until reinforcements came. Gaps between hedgehogs were held by infantry, a division to every nine miles, and armored divisions formed a mobile reserve.

In the initial assault on Rzhev [*November 25, 1942*], tanks surprised the enemy by crossing the Volga over a bridge, like that at Stalingrad, secretly laid eighteen inches under water. While attacks proceeded on the whole front, the main effort was directed toward Velikie Luki, rear supply base on a railroad feeding Rzhev. The Germans were surrounded [*January 1, 1943*], but broke out in desperate counterattacks [*January 15–16, 1943*]; and as they withdrew west they left the area more devastated than any earth scorched by Russians. After nearly a year and a half of persistent attacks the Red Army had finally recaptured a salient of 160 miles covering Rzhev, Velikie Luki, and Vyazma [*March 12, 1943*]. It was a strategic victory as great as Stalingrad because it opened the road to Smolensk.

Second Winter Counteroffensive

The Russians also opened a corridor to Leningrad, which had been under siege since 1941 and was supplied only across Lake Ladoga. Artillery preparation on a ten-mile front, covered by two hundred guns every mile, demoralized the enemy. The Leningrad garrison attacked eastward to join Voroshilov's troops advancing west [*January 18, 1943*]. Although German artillery still controlled the corridor, the relief of Leningrad was begun.

In the south the Russians pressed forward to liberate the mines, factories, and wheatfields of the Ukraine, but were driven back by a limited German counteroffensive. "General Winter" deserted the Russians. An early thaw bogged down supply wagons at a time when troops were still widely dispersed as a result of the rapid winter advance. The Germans finished the general withdrawal begun in December and reinforced their troops with several armored divisions [*February 17, 1943*]. When Vatutin attempted to encircle Stalino from the northeast, Manstein simultaneously started a pincers movement with superior forces to annihilate Vatutin's army

198

[*March 2, 1943*]. The Russians withdrew safely across the Donets, losing only their rear guards, but since the Nazis outnumbered the Russians three to one, they circled north to recapture Kharkov. Bad weather stopped all fighting and lines were stabilized, as each side prepared for summer offensives.

Since taking the initiative at Stalingrad, the Russians had advanced 435 miles west on several fronts, and recovered 185,000 square miles of territory. In this winter campaign Moscow claimed the death of 850,000 and the capture of 343,000 Axis soldiers. The Red Army made its gains partly because it was willing to accept heavy losses and had the reserves to survive them. Russian success was also due to new tactics. To penetrate the Nazi system of defense in depth, they combined all arms, with air officers at infantry head-quarters to direct Stormovik planes in close tactical support of ground troops; they massed heavy artillery to fire at short range over open sights; and they consolidated tank brigades into armored corps which swept the flanks of hedge-hog defenses. New weapons were important too. There was "Katusha," the rocket gun, and the low-flying armored Stormovik, the plane which the Germans called "Black Death." Essentially it was the union of fire and movement and men that overcame the enemy.

Although the Germans retreated to prepared lines in good order, their first-line fighting strength in Russia was permanently depleted. They had 211 divisions along the Eastern Front in 1942, besides their satellite forces, but after the winter campaign 188 divisions were left. These losses would be repaired and a new Sixth Army would take the field; but none of the new divisions would ever prove equal to the old. No longer were there veteran strategic reserves to sustain a new offensive or to avert further retreat. Attrition foreshadowed the defeat of the Nazis in Russia.

III. THE CONTINUOUS OFFENSIVE, 1943

By the summer of 1943 the Axis strength in Russia reached 218 divisions of 4,500,000 men. Stalin announced that almost as many Russians—4,200,000—had been killed in two years of war. But the Soviet Union had recruited and trained an army still larger than any the enemy could put in the field. Both Germany and the USSR opened limited offensives on the upper Don front north of Kharkov which quickly proved decisive. Here their lines took the form of a letter "S" upside down, the Nazis holding the upper loop east of Orel and the Russians the lower bend west of Kursk. Each aimed at wiping out the other's salient in order to shorten lines and secure the main railroad running north through Russian Kursk and German Orel. As their lines were interlocked, so were their offensives.

Kursk–Orel Battles

Russian reconnaissance spotted every enemy move to cut off the Kursk wedge. Since the Nazis could spare only thirty-nine divisions for pressing in the Russian flanks from Orel and Belgorod, they attacked on narrow two-mile fronts with concentrated armor [July 5, 1943]. For spearheads they used two or three hundred Tigers, a 60-ton Mark VI tank; and to cripple Soviet armor, they massed Ferdinands, self-propelled 70-ton tank destroyers firing an 88mm. gun. Through gaps in the southern neck of the Russian salient, Tigers raced twenty miles into the enemy rear. A gigantic tank battle developed [July 7, 1943]; losses were estimated at over one thousand machines for each side. The Russians knocked out Tigers and Ferdinands alike at five hundred yards with massed artillery fire and mobile antitank, reserves. With superior air power and almost equal numbers of troops, the Red Army doggedly maintained the flanks of its salient, absorbed the enemy tank punches without giving much ground, and crippled the Nazi armor.

Once the Nazis had committed their reserves above Belgorod, three Soviet armies in the north attacked fifty German divisions with concentric blows on the Orel salient [July 12, 1943]. Konev pushed south rapidly, but the main attack was directly on the enemy front. Rokossovsky hammered it with the greatest artillery preparation of any war. He fired 2,950 guns on every mile of his 19-mile front, a barrage ten times heavier than at Verdun. A path was blasted open for tanks to advance slowly but steadily about two miles a day, until they outflanked Orel from the south, captured the city,

200

and ironed out the Nazi salient of one hundred miles [*August 5, 1943*]. Each day of the advance both tanks and planes were heavily engaged. This was the severest fighting that the Germans had ever encountered. It was a battle of attrition which the Russians were prepared to repeat on every front until they exhausted or annihilated the Nazi armies. The Red Army had snatched the offensive from the Nazis within a week of the attack on Kursk. Their first summer offensive at Orel was the beginning of a continuous offensive which would be interrupted only for reorganization and supply.

Nazi Retreat to the Dnieper

The German command decided to withdraw to positions west of the Desna and south along the Dnieper River. The strategic position in Russia alone was enough to make retreat the order of the day. Moreover, the fall of Mussolini, the approach of British and American armies through Sicily, and the raids of Tito's guerrillas in Yugoslavia created an imperative need for reserves to strengthen the Italian and Balkan walls of Fortress Europe. For three years the Germans had mounted their Russian offensives with diminishing strength, but this was the first to fail. Now they must shift to defense and rely on new levies of troops, inadequately trained to withstand the fierce Russian fighting.

The Red Army did not wait for the Germans to retreat. At no time were German armies allowed to disengage themselves, to withdraw without losses, or to take up strategic positions more favorable for defense. The strength of their forces deteriorated as they shortened their lines. The Russians unleashed drives along the whole front south of Leningrad, spacing them hundreds of miles apart in order to exhaust Nazi armor and prevent reserves from being combined on any front.

Because the Nazis thought the enemy had engaged all his force to take Orel, they were surprised by a simultaneous attack on the Kharkov front. They lost the city to a threat of double envelopment, the familiar Nazi maneuver which had become the Red Army's hammer and sickle. The envelopment of Kharkov began with a Russian breakthrough of

201

fifteen to thirty-seven miles north of the city. Soviet tanks, with air and artillery support, served as a battering ram and the infantry was able to smash through enemy defenses [*August 4, 1943*]. When German tanks covered one gap, the Russians broke through again farther west where the enemy had no reserves [*August 7, 1943*]. Then the attack shifted quickly to Chuguev, twenty-five miles southeast of Kharkov [*August 7, 1943*]. Soon there was fighting in the suburbs of Kharkov, and the Nazis evacuated the city [*August 12, 1943*]. In three columns the Red Army pressed them back nearly two hundred miles to the Dnieper [*August 22, 1943*]. For the first time Red tanks out-maneuvered Nazi tanks to prove that blitzkrieg could oppose blitzkrieg.

Meanwhile, far to the south at Taganrog in the Donbas, Tolbukhin encircled seven enemy divisions with tanks and Kuban Cossack cavalry [*August 18, 1943*]. Although the Nazis fought their way out, Taganrog fell, and after it, Mariupol [*August 30, 1943*]. The Russians swung north, recaptured the industrial city of Stalino, seventy miles away, and advanced west almost to the Dnieper. Malinovsky moved forward with another army to a position in front of Dniepropetrovsk [*October 5, 1943*].

North of Kharkov on the Kursk front, Vatutin's army advanced rapidly westward, took Konotop [*August 26, 1943*], trapped four divisions south of Chernigov, and reached the Desna River above Kiev and the Dnieper below in a pincers formation [*September 25, 1943*]. Parachute troops cleared the intervening area of enemy units at the price of heavy losses. A bridgehead was established across the Dnieper south of Kiev [*October 5, 1943*].

Below Moscow, Rokossovsky struck west to take Bryansk [*September 17, 1943*], and Sokolovsky drove still farther forward to reoccupy the great German base at Smolensk [*September 25, 1943*]. Both cities were important rail junctions and supply bases lying west of the Desna River, the line to which the Germans planned to retreat. The Russians took these points by switching the attack from one front to another as Nazi reserves vainly tried to stem the tide. They failed because they needed to be everywhere at once, for the Red armies were strong on all fronts.

In this summer offensive, during the six weeks after the fall of Kharkov, the Red Army liberated an area seven hundred miles long and as much as 180 miles wide. It became imperative for the Germans to make a stand on the Dnieper if they hoped to keep any part of their Russian conquests.

Third Winter Offensive

The Red Army did not stop. It prepared a winter offensive by throwing bridgeheads across the Dnieper. There were secondary attacks on the whole front south of Velikie Luki, but the main efforts were directed against Gomel, Kiev, and the Dnieper Bend. The strategy of the Russian winter offensive was dictated by the weak points in the German line of defense. West of Gomel, on the central front, lay the Pripet Marshes, which would split retiring German armies north and south and cover the Russian flanks as they advanced upon the divided enemy. The key to the southern front was Kiev, the rail junction from which the main roads ran into the Dnieper Bend. Here the Nazis might be trapped, if Kiev fell, and the rich bread-basket of the Ukraine would again be Russia's.

Heavy artillery fire opened operations along the entire front [*October 7, 1943*]. Strong German counterattacks failed to prevent Russian reserves from making a bridgehead south of Gomel. To the bridgehead already secured below Kiev, another was added above the city. The most intense fighting occurred in the Dnieper Bend [*October 17, 1943*], where the Nazis tried to hold their easternmost salient. Konev threatened to trap these troops as he crossed below Kremenchug, but Manstein stopped him with tanks in force, supported by over one thousand planes [*October 7, 1943*]. Malinovsky crossed the Dnieper on both sides of Dniepropetrovsk and forced the enemy to abandon the city [*October 25, 1943*]. Tolbukhin met desperate house-to-house fighting in Melitopol, southern anchor of the Nazi line, and took the city by envelopment from the north [*November 6, 1943*]. The Nazis evacuated the Donbas and fell back one hundred miles to the southwestern curve of the lower Dnieper, where they clung to bridgeheads at Nikopol and Kherson.

The Germans were driven out of Gomel by Rokossovsky's surprise pincers movement [*November 11, 1943*]. First a strong attack from the Loev bridgehead cut one of the two railroads supplying the city at Rechitsa [*November 22, 1943*]; then with a secret concentration of tanks far to the north, he raced into the enemy rear on a front of thirty-eight miles and threatened the other railroad [*November 25, 1943*]. The large Nazi garrison escaped, despite furious Russian attacks, but all the enemy forces were now divided by the Pripet Marshes.

Recapture of Kiev

In the Ukraine, meanwhile, Vatutin's overwhelming forces occupied Kiev [*November 6, 1943*] after Manstein saved his troops from envelopment in the North. A Russian attempt to swing south into the Dnieper Bend was repulsed at Fastov [*November 7, 1943*]. But other forces fanned westward and took the rail junctions of Zhitomir and Korosten [*November 12, 17, 1943*]. A strong Nazi counteroffensive from the west and south drove them out, and Red troops in Zhitomir barely escaped encirclement. Nazi artillery and planes reduced so many strongpoints west of Kiev that all the Russian gains here were imperiled [*December 6–11, 1943*]. With heavy reinforcements, however, the Red Army recaptured Zhitomir and Korosten, and hurled the Germans back almost to Poland. One wing of the advancing Russians swung southeast to embarrass the Nazis in the Dnieper Bend.

Here, when Konev's army penetrated to the rail junction of Zhnamenka [*December 9, 1943*], the Germans retired from the river between Cherkassy and Kremenchug. To hold the exposed northern shoulder of Krivoi Rog, the Nazis brought up reserves from the south, and consequently the bridgehead at Kherson had to be evacuated [*December 20, 1943*] in the face of Tolbukhin's persistent attacks. The Nazis still clung to Nikopol, but they were dangerously extended at this easternmost point, and the flanks of the Dnieper salient were liable to collapse.

Isolation of the Crimea

When the Germans withdrew to the Dnieper, they left
204

strong forces in the east to control the Black Sea by holding the Kuban and Crimea. Through most of 1943 the Russians mounted raids and local offensives to clear this region. Kleist's perimeter defense of the Kuban was gradually reduced, and finally he evacuated his troops to the Crimea [October 8–9, 1943]. The Caucasus Mountains and Kuban River valley were at last liberated. By withdrawing to the Dnieper the Nazis left their troops in the Crimea without any overland communications with the main forces. The Red Army seized the Perekop Isthmus in the northwest, but their landings in the southeast succeeded only in establishing in December a beachhead north of Kerch.

During 1943 the Axis armies had been driven west all along the line south of Velikie Luki, except in the Crimea, and their positions in the Dnieper Bend became extremely precarious. Here 750,000 troops under Manstein risked being trapped if the main railroad from Warsaw to Odessa should be cut. Military safety depended on a retreat for the sake of shortening their lines by hundreds of miles and gaining badly needed reserves. But for political reasons Hitler insisted that they hold the Dnieper Bend and keep the Russians from encroaching on his satellite states in the Balkans.

PART SIX

BREAKING THE AXIS

25. THE UNITED NATIONS FIND STRENGTH IN COALITION

In 1943 the United States, Great Britain, the Soviet Union, and China, the leading United Nations, became united in fact as well as in name. Their statesmen, generals, and admirals traveled the long roads which led to cooperation in military strategy and diplomatic policy. Milestones on this road to a union of strength were the conferences held at Casablanca, Quebec, Moscow, Cairo, and Teheran. Representatives of the United States and Great Britain met, together with the Free French, at Casablanca; at Quebec and Cairo, China joined in the conference. The Soviet Union took part at Moscow and Teheran.

The coming together of the United Nations in these conferences assured the defeat of the Axis with the greatest speed and efficiency, and produced sufficient harmony among them to promise a durable peace as well as a quick victory. The hopes of the Axis that their enemies would fall out and make peace separately for national or class advantage were all disappointed. It was fortunate for the United Nations that they lived up to their name and achieved a diplomatic triumph which made possible the military or naval victories to come, for only by coalition could the Axis be defeated. The United States was the strongest power industrially and in the air; Great Britain and America were superior on the sea. But the Soviet Union was strongest on land, and China, facing Japan, was a bulwark of Asia. No nation could win this global war alone. A coalition of the United Nations, with a common strategy, pooled resources, and fundamental agreement on what the fight was for, was needed to break the Axis.

I. THE QUEBEC MEETING AND COMBINED STATEGY

Military strategy, especially in the Far East, was the chief business of the conference at Quebec [*August 11–24, 1943*],

206

where President Roosevelt and Prime Minister Churchill met with their staffs for the sixth time; and Cordell Hull, Anthony Eden, and T. V. Soong, foreign ministers of the United States, Great Britain, and China, came together for the first time. Three decisions were made at Quebec which affected the European theater of war. The leaders resolved to hasten the invasion of Italy because of the collapse of Mussolini and the uncertain peace overtures of his successor, Marshal Badoglio. Next they agreed to draw the Soviet Union, which was not represented at the meetings at Casablanca and Quebec, into full concert with the Allied powers. Finally, the French Committee of National Liberation, headed by General Charles de Gaulle, was recognized as the representative of Free French people who were fighting the Axis.

It was, however, the defeat of Japan by aid to China which engaged the most attention at the Quebec Conference. T. V. Soong spoke for Generalissimo Chiang Kai-shek, so that in reality an Anglo-American-Chinese strategic conference was elaborating the plans made by the Combined Chiefs of Staff in May 1943. China-Burma-India came of age as a military theater at Quebec. Supreme military command of Southeast Asia was vested in Admiral Lord Louis Mountbatten, whose leadership of combined Commando operations in England indicated repetition on a large scale in Burma; Brigadier General (now Lieut. General) Albert C. Wedemeyer of the U. S. Army was appointed his Deputy Chief of Staff; Lieutenant General (now General) Joseph W. Stilwell remained in command of all Chinese and American ground forces in CBI; Major General (now Lieutenant General) George E. Stratemeyer became senior air commander; and Major General (now Lieutenant General) Raymond A. Wheeler the principal administrative officer with supervision of supply in CBI. The conference approved plans for an offensive early in 1944 against the Japanese in northern Burma to facilitate the supply of China. The war in the Far East was to be waged with increasing force and without any relaxation of the war in Europe: this was the answer of combined strategy at Quebec to those people in the United States and China who still argued that Japan and not Germany was the chief enemy of the United Nations.

The meetings at Casablanca and Quebec were primarily Anglo-American councils of war to plan offensives against Germany and Italy in the Mediterranean and against Japan in Asia. At Moscow [*October 19–30, 1943*] the foreign secretaries of the United States, Great Britain, and the Soviet Union reached an agreement on problems of both war and peace. To hasten the end of the war, military advisers of the Chiefs of Staff discussed preliminary plans for a joint offensive in Europe. These plans were to be perfected and approved later in the year at Teheran. The distinguishing work of the Moscow Conference, however was the definition of common policies guaranteeing a democratic peace.

Looking toward this end, two declarations were adopted on the treatment of Italy and Austria, setting forth a program that might be applied to all of Europe as it was released from Nazi domination. Austria, "the first free country to fall a victim of Hitlerite aggression" in 1938, was promised freedom and independence. The United Nations gave the Austrian people an incentive to break loose from Hitler by the assurance that their responsibility for fighting on his side would be diminished by what they did to free themselves. Austria and the other small countries of Central Europe were to be encouraged by their independence "to find that political economic security which is the only basis for lasting peace."

The democratic aims which inspired the United Nations in their war against the Axis were stated in the declaration on Italy. "Allied policy," it proclaimed, "must be based upon the fundamental principle that Fascism and all its evil influences and emanations shall be utterly destroyed." Italy, like Austria and presumably the other nations of Europe, was "to be given every opportunity to establish governmental and other institutions based upon democratic principles." The distinct emphasis upon "other institutions" besides government indicated that Democracy was not to be limited as in the last peace to political arrangements; Fascism was to be rooted out of the life and culture of European peoples.

To insure more than a formal Democracy, the declaration specifically provided in the case of Italy that the Democratic

208

Bill of Rights should be introduced, with freedom of speech, religion, press, assembly, and political association; and that all Fascist institutions should be suppressed, Fascist elements removed from office, and Fascist chiefs who were "war criminals" should be "arrested and handed over to justice." Until Allied armies could drive the Germans out of Italy, the question of putting these principles into operation was left to the Combined Chiefs of Staff. But consultative machinery to deal with problems of policy was established in the form of an Advisory Council on Italian Affairs and a European Advisory Commission, composed of civilian representatives from the United States, Great Britain, and the Soviet Union.

China joined these nations, through its Ambassador at Moscow, in the Declaration of Four Nations on General Security, the most far-reaching agreement of the Moscow Conference on both peace and war. The United States, Great Britain, China, and the Soviet Union would prosecute the war until the Axis Powers "laid down their arms on the basis of unconditional surrender." To insure "a rapid and orderly transition from war to peace," and to guarantee "international peace and security with the least diversion of the world's human and economic resources for armaments," the four leading United Nations pledged their cooperation in peace as in war. They would act together in disarming their enemies and enforcing upon them terms of peace; against the hostile actions of their enemies the United Nations would maintain a common front.

Among themselves the United States, Great Britain, the Soviet Union, and China promised to establish as soon as possible "a general international organization, based on the principle of the sovereign equality of all peace-loving states, and open to membership of all such states, large and small, for the maintenance of international peace and security." Until order and law prevailed in the world these four nations would consult with others and act "on behalf of the community of nations." Once the war was ended, however, they promised not to use military force in the territories of other states except for general security, and then only after joint consultation. They would seek, moreover, to reach an agree-

209

ment with the United States for "the regulation of armaments in the post-war period."

The practical effect of these solemn written pledges by the four Great Powers fighting the Axis was to assure some kind of international organization, open to "all peace-loving states" for the security of world-wide peace. This security was to be won by defeating and disarming the Axis nations and regulating the armaments of all nations. Collaboration for peace was to grow out of union for war, but it was not to be limited as in war to the strongest nations; military alliance for victory in war was to give birth to an association of all nations for security in peace. This was the fundamental principle to which Great Britain, the Soviet Union, China, and the United States subscribed.

American Indorsement

In view of what happened after the last war, when the American Senate refused to let the United States enter the League of Nations, there was considerable doubt at home and abroad whether this country would stand by the Moscow Declaration after the war was over or revert to a position of isolation and extreme nationalism. Such doubt was answered for the present by the immediate action of the American Congress. The House of Representatives had adopted the Fulbright Resolution [September 21, 1943] by a vote of 360 to 29, in favor of American participation in "the creation of appropriate international machinery with power adequate to establish and maintain a just and lasting peace." The United States Senate adopted the language of the Moscow Conference in passing the Connally Resolution [November 5, 1943], 85 to 5, in favor of international organization. It resolved that "the United States, acting through its constitutional processes, join with free and sovereign nations in the establishment and maintenance of international authority with power to prevent aggression and to preserve the peace of the world." Although these resolutions do not have the force of treaties and would not bind future Congresses, their influence might be as great as that of traditional world agreements. They did constitute an indorsement of the Moscow Declaration by the American people.

Out of the Moscow Conference came a statement on atrocities, signed by President Roosevelt, Prime Minister Churchill, and Premier Stalin, who warned "the recoiling Hitlerites" against "monstrous crimes" committed in desperation as they retreated from the Soviet Union, France, and Italy. All German soldiers and all Nazis responsible for such atrocities would be returned to the countries "in which their abominable deeds were done, in order that they may be judged and punished according to the laws of these liberated countries and of free governments which will be erected therein." "German criminals" whose offenses were not localized within a single foreign country would be punished by joint decision of the Allied Governments. But those who had massacred people in Poland, France, Belgium, the Netherlands, Norway, Russia, and Crete would be "judged on the spot by the peoples whom they have outraged."

In language as stern and righteous as the Old Testament the enemy was warned against cruel treatment of the people of occupied Europe: "Let those who have hitherto not imbued their hands with innocent blood beware lest they join the ranks of the guilty, for most assuredly the three Allied Powers will pursue them to the uttermost ends of the earth and will deliver them to their accusers in order that justice may be done." This admonition of justice to come was designed to obtain mercy for those who had so far survived Fascism.

III. BLUEPRINTS FOR VICTORY: CAIRO, TEHERAN, DUMBARTON OAKS, AND YALTA

The Moscow Conference had been chiefly concerned with guarantees of peace for the whole world; the first meeting of Generalissimo Chiang Kai-shek with President Roosevelt and Prime Minister Churchill, at Cairo, Egypt, was devoted to terms of peace for the Far East [*November 22–26, 1943*]. It was agreed that the war in the Pacific was being fought to "restrain and punish the aggression of Japan." The United States, Great Britain, and China declared that they coveted "no gain for themselves and [had] no thought of territorial

211

expansion." But Japan was to "be stripped of all the islands in the Pacific which she has seized or occupied since the beginning of the first World War, in 1914," and of all territory "stolen from the Chinese" since the first war against China in 1894. Land which had once been Chinese, including Manchuria and Formosa, was to be restored to China. Japan was to "be expelled from all other territories which she has taken by violence and greed." Among these, Korea was "in due course [to] become free and independent." The United States, Great Britain, and China pledged that they would carry on the war against Japan until the enemy was brought to "unconditional surrender." These territorial terms for Asia were specific; nothing so definite had been announced for Europe. However, the fate of all the Axis Powers had been declared, at Casablanca, Moscow, and Cairo, to be unconditional surrender.

After Cairo came a conference at Teheran, in Iran (Persia) [*November 26–December 2, 1943*], which had been arranged during the sessions at Moscow. It was the first face-to-face meeting of Stalin with either Roosevelt or Churchill. Out of the discussions of their military staffs came "complete agreement as to the scope and timing of the operations to be undertaken from the east, west and south" in 1944 "for the destruction of the German forces." Churchill and Roosevelt agreed to Stalin's demand for a second front against Germany in Western Europe, British and American invasion to be mounted as one part of a gigantic pincers on German-held Europe, the other arm of which would be a Russian drive from the east through Poland to Berlin. The diplomatic advisers of Roosevelt, Churchill, and Stalin also agreed "to make a peace which will command the goodwill of the overwhelming mass of the peoples of the world and banish the scourge and terror of war for many generations." Thus the strategy of war and the goals of peace were shaped in coalition at Teheran by the United States, Great Britain, and the Soviet Union. These were the blueprints of victory.

The Dumbarton Oaks Plan

Representatives of the United States, the United Kingdom, the Soviet Union, and China, meeting at Dumbarton

212

Oaks in Washington, D. C., agreed [*October 9, 1944*] that an international organization should be established by the United Nations whose purposes should be:

1. To maintain international peace and security, to take effective collective measures for the prevention and removal of threats to the peace and the suppression of acts of aggression and other breaches of the peace, and to bring about by peaceful means adjustment or settlement of international disputes which may lead to a breach of the peace;

2. To develop friendly relations among nations and to take other appropriate measures to strengthen universal peace;

3. To achieve international cooperation in the solution of international economic, social and other humanitarian problems; and

4. To afford a center for harmonizing the actions of nations in the achievement of these common ends.

A charter embodying the principles of the Dumbarton Oaks plan was to be drawn up at a future conference of the United Nations.

The Yalta Conference

On February 12, 1945, announcement was made of the conclusion of an eight-day conference between Churchill, Roosevelt and Stalin at Yalta on the Crimean Peninsula. Final plans for the military defeat of Germany were laid. Agreement was reached on policies and plans for enforcing the unconditional surrender terms. Separate zones of occupation were agreed upon. The inflexible purpose of the three principal Powers to destroy German militarism and the Nazi Party was restated. Swift justice was promised for Axis war criminals. A commission was to be set up to determine the extent and methods of compensating damage caused by Germany to the Allied countries. Announcement was made calling for a conference at San Francisco on April 25 to draw up a charter for a United Nations Security organization on the foundations of the Dumbarton Oaks plan. Other agreements were made concerning the control of liberated areas and Poland.

213

26. LIBERATION OF ITALY

Following the victory in Tunisia, Allied forces prepared for two months [*May 15–July 9, 1943*] to invade and conquer Sicily, Operation Husky. They aimed, as Churchill said, at "Axis-held Europe's soft underbelly along the Mediterranean" and to knock Italy out of the war. Sicily was defended by about ten Italian and three German divisions, including the 15th Panzer and the Hermann Goering Panzer Divisions, and these troops would be reinforced under attack.

General Eisenhower in supreme command assigned the mission of invading Sicily to the Allied 15th Army Group, under General Sir Harold Alexander. This group consisted of the British Eighth and the American Seventh Armies. The Seventh, commanded by Lieutenant General (now General) George S. Patton, Jr., was composed of the 1st, 3d, 9th, and 45th Infantry Divisions, the 82d Airborne, and 2d Armored Divisions. These troops were veterans of Tunisia except for the 45th, which came directly from the United States. The Eighth Army, commanded by General Sir Bernard Montgomery, was composed of four British infantry divisions, two brigades, and an airborne division. In addition, a Canadian infantry division was brought in to keep liaison between British and American armies.

Strategy of Landings

The final plan of attack called for the Americans, sailing from North Africa to land on the south central coast of Sicily, mop up the western half of the island, and swing east along the northern coast to Mount Etna, where the British would join them after landing on the southeast and advancing up the eastern coast. Then the Allied armies would trap the enemy in the northeastern corner of Sicily, cutting off any escape to Italy through the Strait of Messina. British and American airborne infantry, equal to a division in strength, were to land in rear areas and seize enemy airfields. Unfortunately, these troops were dropped thirty to fifty miles from their objectives [*July 9–10, 1943*]; they succeeded in interfering with enemy communications but failed to capture the airfields.

The night of D-day a huge armada of 3,266 vessels carried 160.000 men with 1,008 guns and 600 tanks from Africa to Sicily [*July 10, 1943*]. The American troops, seasick in choppy waters, landed under cover of naval artillery and secured beachheads at Licata, Gela, and Scoglitti [*July 11, 1943*]. Next day around Gela one hundred Nazi tanks, spearheads of a counterattack on three sides, threatened to drive the Americans into the sea. An artillery barrage knocked out many tanks and the stout resistance of the 1st Infantry Division repulsed the entire counterattack. East of Gela the 45th Division captured and held the Biscari airfield after a day of bitter fighting [*July 14, 1943*]. This defeat cost the enemy eighty planes and control of the skies over Sicily.

The British landed from Cape Passero to Syracuse [*July 10, 1943*], on the eastern end of a 100-mile front, quickly overcame resistance on the beachhead, and occupied the port of Syracuse [*July 12, 1943*]. Then they advanced north along the coast beyond Augusta, slowing down as they approached Catania. For artillery support the infantry relied on naval fire from ships along the coast. The Canadians fanned westward to link with the Americans at Ragusa.

American Advance

Opposition to the Americans declined after their push north to Canicatti, for the Germans realized that they did not have strength enough to defend the whole island and that the Italians no longer had heart for the fight. Hence the enemy held the British on his left and fell back toward Mount Etna in the northeast from his right and center, leaving only one division to cover his withdrawal. This was the strategy the Germans had adopted in Tunisia. Their aim was to delay and contain the Allies in Sicily and thus prevent attacks elsewhere in the Mediterranean.

The American forces moved with surprising speed over difficult country with few roads. Infantry and tanks pushed west to take Agrigento [*July 22, 1943*], then raced north across Sicily to seize the port of Palermo [*July 30, 1943*]. The 2d Armored and 3d Infantry Divisions covered seventy-two miles in two days. Then, spearheaded by the 45th Division, they fanned east along the northern coastal road to the enemy's main line of resistance, which ran southeast from a point just west of San Stefano di Camastra to Troina.

Meanwhile the 1st Infantry Division and the Canadians advanced over the hills of central Sicily to capture Nicosia and Agira [*July 29, 1943*]. Here the mountins rose to five thousand feet, and the ridge of Troina lay behind a valley in which the enemy had demolished the road and built numerous blocks. Across this valley and up the slopes the 1st Infantry Division attacked Troina in the bitterest assaults of the Sicilian campaign [*July 29–August 5, 1943*]. Bombing by A-36s and B-25s and heavy shelling by massed artillery in support of an envelopment from the south compelled the enemy to withdraw. At the same time, the British outflanked Catania on the eastern coast with the capture of Paterno. The Axis center broke at Adrano and enemy forces fell back into a triangle whose apex was Messina.

Nazis Retreat

The German withdrawal was hastened by a new strategy which contributed to the subsequent surrender of Italy. Hitler and Mussolini had been told by their generals at Verona [*July 19, 1943*] that because the Italian peninsula could not easily be defended against Allied naval power, the Axis must evacuate Italy to the Po Valley, where a defense in depth could be erected for the industrial north. The enemy forces were therefore ordered to withdraw from Sicily [*August 1, 1943*] as soon as ships and artillery could be prepared to cover the crossing of the Strait of Messina.

Toward this point American and British forces pressed from the west and south, across minefields, over roadblocks, and through mountain gaps where the cliffs had tumbled down under artillery fire. Twice an American force, helped by the Navy, made landings in the enemy rear along the northern coast. The first time, the German line was cracked in a surprise assault [*August 8, 1943*] by the units which landed at Torrenova and captured San Agata di Militello [*August 11–12, 1943*]. Another amphibious assault in battalion strength was made around Cape Orlando to cut the

216

enemy off from his communications south to Randazzo, but the heoric landing force faced an enemy which held dominating positions in the surrounding hills [*August 12, 1943*]. Our troops suffered heavy losses until the rest of the regiment drove through to its support at Brolo. Meanwhile American units pressing northeast from the interior captured the keypoint of Randazzo [*August 13, 1943*].

It was now a race to trap the Nazi before they could evacuate all their forces. Combat teams leapfrogged one another along three routes to Messina. Our air and naval forces constantly harassed the enemy's attempt to escape across the narrow four-mile Strait of Messina. However, the German air umbrella and intense fire from coastal batteries and antiaircraft guns made possible the evacuation of some 88,000 troops in scores of ferry boats and barges. Among the troops successfully evacuated were elements of the Hermann Goering Panzer Division which later fought tenaciously in Italy. When the American 3d Infantry Division reached Messina, followed quickly by British units, the enemy had departed into Italy, leaving behind him stores of matériel [*August 7–16, 1943*].

Sicily was conquered in thirty-eight days. About 100,000 prisoners were taken and 12,000 of the enemy were killed or wounded. Among the weapons captured or destroyed were 267 planes and 188 tanks. Allied casualties were some 25,000, of which American losses ran to 7,400. The conquest of Sicily hastened the collapse of Italy and made the Mediterranean Sea more secure for Allied convoys. Italy lay open to invasion.

II. SURRENDER OF ITALY

Italy was first of the Fascist nations to capitulate. Weary of war, after three years and three months during which Britain with the help of American supplies had conquered her whole African empire, Italy surrendered unconditionally [*September 3, 1943*]. The armistice was signed secretly by Marshal Pietro Badoglio, named by the King to replace Mussolini [*July 25, 1943*], and a week later official announcement came from General Eisenhower. The announcement was delayed in order to prevent the Nazis from taking over Italian defenses before Allied troops could enter through the Gulf of Salerno.

Military Results

The Germans were not to be caught off guard. Of sixty-two divisions in the Italian Army, only nine—in Corsica and Sardinia—were left free to surrender to the Allies. Ten divisions in the Balkans gave up their arms to Yugoslav guerrillas [*September 10, 1943*]. The Germans disarmed forty-three Italian divisions on garrison duty in Italy, France, and the Balkans. They also established themselves strongly as far south as Naples, with lighter forces to the end of the Italian peninsula, seized the naval ports of Genoa and Spezia, and rescued Mussolini from confinement in Abruzzi Province in a daring raid by parachutists who spirited him away to his German overlord.

The Italian Army was out of the war, but the chief military gain to the Allies was the acquisition of the Italian Navy. Although the Nazis sank one battleship and seized ten cruisers, ten destroyers, and many submarines, the bulk of the Navy, following Badoglio's orders, sailed into Allied ports [*September 10–12, 1943*]. Among the vessels which arrived at Malta were six battleships, eight cruisers, twenty-seven destroyers, and nineteen submarines. No longer were Allied warships contained within the Mediterranean Sea by the passive threat of the Italian fleet; additional vessels could now be sent to patrol Indian and Pacific waters against Japan.

Why Italy Surrendered

The surrender of Italy resulted from war weariness inside the country and Allied military pressure outside. The attempt to detach Italy from the Axis was decided upon [*May 11, 1943*] by President Roosevelt and Prime Minister Churchill in the conference at Washington following the conquest of Tunisia. Roosevelt urged the Italian people [*June 11, 1943*] to overthrow Mussolini and the Fascists, and to expel the Nazis, promising them that they would be free to choose their own government, provided it was not Fascist; Churchill threatened the Italians with ruin if they did not abandon

218

Mussolini and surrender [*June 30, 1943*]. When Allied troops swept into Sicily and Allied bombers struck at Italian ports and communications, crowds in the northern cities shouted for peace.

The growing unrest of the people threatened rebellion until a palace plot forestalled it by ousting Mussolini. He had appealed to Hitler for protection against the Allies [*July 19, 1943*], but at a military conference Hitler persuaded him to defend only the industrial heart of the country, in the north along the Po River [*July 24, 1943*]. When Mussolini presented this plan to the Fascist Grand Council, he was denounced by Count Dino Grandi and voted down by nineteen of the twenty-five councillors. King Victor Emmanuel appointed Marshal Badoglio to take the lealership of the Government. After twenty-one years of dictatorship, Mussolini was thrown out.

The fall of Mussolini surprised Hitler, but his General Staff realized that Italy would get out of the war. They prepared for this event by ordering the evacuation of Sicily and the reinforcement of Nazi units in Italy so that they could take over the country [*July 29–August 5, 1943*]. When Mussolini fell, Allied bombers stopped raiding Italian cities to give Marshal Badoglio "breathing space" in which to make peace. When the Nazis took advantage of the respite to move into Italy, the aerial offensive was resumed [*August 1, 1943*].

Political Stalemate in Italy

Badoglio, like the King, was almost a prisoner of the Nazi troops in Italy. He could not easily deliver the country to the Allies, whose bombers flew overhead but whose troops were still in Sicily. To make matters worse, he pursued an undemocratic policy which failed to give the people who wanted peace any voice in the government. He tried to get rid of Fascism by dissolving the party and incorporating its militia into the Army, but he indicted none of the Fascist leaders. At the same time he endeavored to suppress popular agitation by declaring martial law and putting a ban on all political meetings. [*July 26–30, 1943*].

Strikes broke out in Genoa, Turin, and Milan [*August 3–19, 1943*]. Workers demanded an immediate change from war to peace production in all factories, the revocation of martial law, and the release of political prisoners. Badoglio compromised. He abolished the ban on labor unions by suppressing the Fascist employers' corporations [*August 10, 1943*], and arranged an armistice under which labor agreed to call off general strikes [*September 2, 1943*] and he promised to seek peace with the Allies. The rising of the Italian people in the north hastened the surrender made inevitable by the military victory in Sicily.

Yet Italy surrendered too late to gain peace. The Nazis occupied the country and deprived all soldiers of their arms. Italy was not to be free of war until the Allied armies drove out the Nazi intruders.

III. INVASION OF ITALY: OPERATION AVALANCHE

After Sicily came Italy. With the fall of Mussolini the Allies hastened preparations to invade Italy before the country could be taken over by quislings or occupied completely by the Germans. The separation of Italy from the Axis was the goal of Allied strategy in the Mediterranean, from the landings in North Africa to the conquest of Sicily, because it would knock the weakest Axis partner out of the war, dispose of the Italian Navy, open the whole Mediterranean Sea to Allied shipping, weaken Nazi control of the Balkans, and furnish southern bases for an Allied aerial offensive against German-held Europe. To attain these objectives the Allied Fifteenth Army Group under General Alexander planned to invade Italy at three points. The first landings were to be made by the British Eighth Army at Reggio di Calabria and Taranto to prevent the Germans from establishing themselves firmly in southern Italy and to give the Allies control over the Adriatic ports. The major assault was to be in the Gulf of Salerno where the Fifth Army would attempt to establish a firm base for future operations to cut off German troops withdrawing to the north in front of the Eighth Army, and to seize Naples. The Eighth Army, after clearing southern Italy, would swing north to drive up the eastern half of the peninsula parallel with the Fifth Army on the west.

Two divisions of the British Eighth Army, commanded by General Montgomery, crossed from Messina to Reggio di

Calabria at the toe of Italy [*September 3, 1943*] under cover of four battleships and the concentrated fire of four hundred guns lined up on the Sicilian shore. With this support the British advanced up the Calabrian coast, meeting little opposition. The British 1st Airborne Division occupied the naval base of Taranto [*September 9, 1943*] after the surrender of Italy, struck northward to Bari and closed the Adriatic Sea.

Landings at Salerno

The Fifth Army, commanded by Lieutenant General Mark W. Clark, was chosen to make the principal assault on the Italian mainland. British and American units organized into two corps were to land in the Gulf of Salerno, advance inland to secure a firm beachhead some twenty-six miles wide and ten miles deep, then wheel to the north for a drive through the mountains to capture Naples and the communication center of Benevento. Salerno was chosen, among other reasons, because it was the northernmost point at which fighter planes based on Sicily, some two hundred miles south, could provide an air umbrella. A speedy junction between the Fifth Army and the British Eighth Army might result in trapping enemy forces south of Naples.

Convoys bearing the invasion forces put out from ports in Africa and Sicily [*September 8, 1943*]. As the armada approached Salerno, General Eisenhower made the startling announcement that Italy had signed an armistice. Although some of the men then felt that the invasion might prove to be another "dry run," there were definite indications that the landings would be heavily opposed. An enemy reconnaissance plane had discovered the convoys off Salerno [*September 8, 1943*], and by the time the ships were at anchor waiting for H-hour, the Germans were on the alert. They had disarmed nearly all of the Italian units manning the coastal defenses and were now compelled to dispose their forces thinly in order to guard the long coast line.

No naval bombardment had been planned to soften the shore defenses, partly because it was hoped that surprise might be achieved. When our first assault waves hit the beaches at 0330 on September 9, they were met by heavy fire

221

from machine guns, 88mms. and mortars. In the British sector a last-minute naval preparation was fired, but the initial American landings were made without such support.

In the British X Corps zone north of the Sele River, resistance was especially bitter and the two assault divisions suffered heavy casualties in their advance toward the Montecorvino airfield and Battipaglia. Rangers and Commandos, attached to the X Corps, landed on the army left flank and quickly secured key mountain passes leading to the city of Salerno and the plain east of the gulf. Their success in holding these passes during the following critical week was an important factor in defending the beachhead against furious German counterattacks. In the center of the X Corps zone, the British pushed advance units of an infantry division into Battipaglia [September 12, 1943]; but the Germans counterattacked. threw back our assault, and kept possession of that important rail and highway junction.

South of the Sele U. S. VI Corps landed on beaches near the ancient Greek temples of Paestum, with the 36th Infantry Division, reinforced, in the lead [September 9, 1943]. Here the 16th Panzer Division had been in position two weeks before the landings. Most of the assault waves broke through the barrier of wire, mines, and fire from automatic weapons and reached the coastal highway by dawn. From daylight until afternoon the panzers tried to disrupt the landing by attacking the beachhead with small groups of tanks, but our artillery, naval gunfire, dive bombers, and infantry defeated these efforts [September 10, 1943]. Soon our troops were pushing out rapidly to the south and east to enlarge the beachhead, and two combat teams of the 45th Infantry Division were unloading to reinforce the 36th Division.

Failure of German Counterattacks

Expansion of the beachhead continued against steadily mounting enemy resistance. The Germans now had the 16th, 26th, and Hermann Goering Panzer Divisions, the 15th and 29th Panzer Grenadier Divisions, and elements of the 3d Panzer Grenadier Division in the Salerno area. These units launched counterattacks [September 11, 1943] with increasing intensity during the next two days. On the Fifth Army's left, the British repelled every German attempt to drive them into the sea but could not completely close the gap between the Sele River and their main body. Here the American 45th Division became involved in a seesaw struggle for a tobacco factory east of Persano, a keypoint north of the river.

German counterattacks increased in fury [*September 12–13, 1943*]. Our troops had to fall back, and for a time the German drive threatened to force a wedge through to the beaches. All available units were thrown into the defense; the 36th Division on the south and the 45th Division on the north established a firm line. Tank-destroyer, artillery, and naval fire crashed unceasingly upon the Germans and our Air Forces bombed and strafed their communications and positions. At the peak of the Nazi counterattack all the Allied air forces, including heavy bombers, threw their weight into the battle. In one day the Northwest African Air Force flew 1,888 sorties over the beachhead. Thirty-six B-25 bombers endeavored to cut off the 16th Panzer Division by cratering the key highways. Africa-based B-17s and B-26s hit road junctions to break up enemy divisions descending on the beachhead. Saturation raids were made on the Nazi airfields at Foggia. By September 15 the counterattacks had spent their force. Three days later the enemy began to withdraw toward the north, with both Fifth and Eighth Armies in pursuit. We had won the Battle of Salerno and our line stretched across Italy to Bari.

Capture of Naples and Foggia

With quick, heavy blows the Fifth Army punched back the German right wing, taking Oliveto [*September 23, 1943*], and Nocera [*September 27, 1943*], and drove the enemy from the mountains shielding Naples. The Nazis retired north through the city, shooting civilian snipers, demolishing the port, destroying the water supply, mining buildings, and removing everything on wheels [*October 1, 1943*]. The Fifth Army occupied Naples [*October 7, 1943*], aided by a civilian uprising, and pushed on to the new enemy defenses along the steep northern banks of the Volturno River.

223

Total American losses thus far, including the Salerno casualties, were 511 killed, 5,428 wounded, and 2,367 missing.

Meanwhile the British Eighth Army captured the great airfields of Foggia [*September 27, 1943*] and moved north to Termoli on the Adriatic coast. This advance threatened the enemy line westward along the Volturno. By an amphibious assault [*October 1, 1943*], Commandos in the enemy rear attempted to cut behind Termoli. The Nazis counterattacked against the landing force [*October 6–7, 1943*], and with reinforcements from the 16th Panzer Division, struck at the British lines until their own tanks were whittled down. Then the Eighth Army broke through [*October 9–10, 1943*], with the help of enfilading fire from destroyers on the coast, and made contact with their Commandos. Since the advance was bound to be slow along the steep Adriatic coast, where mountains came down to the sea, the main drive was shifted to the interior along the Apennine Mountains. Here the British moved forward slowly [*October 9–15, 1943*] to a line extending from Larino west to Campobasso, where they were abreast of the Americans on their left.

Crossing the Volturno

After Fifth Army engineers reclaimed the port of Naples, supplies and ammunition poured in for the coming battle at the Volturno. The attack began with heavy artillery fire and an amphibious sally [*October 12–13, 1943*] by X Corps against the enemy rear on the Tyrrhenian coast. From the coast to the Calore River, bridgeheads were established across the Volturno [*October 14, 1943*]. Capua, in the center, changed hands several times in tank and infantry engagements [*October 13–14, 1943*]. Within two days the enemy was compelled to withdraw from his delaying positions north of the Volturno under pressure which had forced both flanks back three miles.

After crossing the Volturno the Fifth Army met several stubborn rearguards covering the German withdrawal to positions already partly prepared in the mountains at the head of the Volturno Valley. Every bridge and culvert had been blown by the enemy; bypasses were mined, and demolitions were defended by small enemy units. There were sev-

224

eral sharp engagements but no great battles until the Fifth Army struck the Winter Line early in November. By this time the fall rains had flooded the valleys and turned secondary roads into quagmires. From one side of Italy to the other, Allied troops had to overcome difficult problems of supply as well as enemy opposition.

Fighting Through the Winter Line

The Winter Line was a series of positions in depth located in extremely rough mountains. On the far west was the Garigliano River. In the center were the highest peaks of the Apennines. East of this principal range the Sangro River marked the main German position in front of the Eighth Army.

Patrols of the Eighth Army reached and crossed the Sangro River on November 8. The army then consolidated its bridgeheads in preparation for crossing the Moro River and attacking Orsogna and Ortona. On December 5 it reached the Moro, crossed four days later, and assaulted Ortona. This city fell at the end of the month after two weeks of street fighting [December 27, 1943]. In November, General Clark's troops had made preliminary attempts to break the Winter Line and now paused to bring up supplies and to relieve the battle-weary 3d and 34th Divisions by elements of the II Corps. The assault was unleashed by the X and II Corps against the Camino hills [December 1–2, 1943]. After clearing these mountain fortresses of enemy troops [December 9, 1943], the X Corps rested while the II and VI Corps continued the struggle. Troops of liberated Italy entered the battle against the Germans on December 6. At the same time the 36th Division, under command of the II Corps, attacked San Pietro in a bloody battle that ended successfully after nine days of fighting. In the mountains farther north, the 45th Division could make little progress.

There were few changes in our lines during the rest of December. The French Expeditionary Corps, commanded by General Alphonse Juin, began to relieve the VI Corps in January. Then the II Corps resumed its drive and by mid-January had broken through the Winter Line in a drive that carried the main German defenses south of Rome—the Gustav Line.

The rest of the winter the Allies were stalemated along the Gustav Line. Terrain and weather gave the Nazis every advantage in fighting a long delaying action to hold the Allies south of Rome. However, continuing the Italian campaign was important in Allied strategy because this campaign weakened other enemy fronts, robbing them of twenty divisions. Italy was a secondary theater with the primary mission of consuming enemy strength while the Russians pushed forward in the east and preparations were made in England for the invasion of Europe from the west.

IV. THE GUSTAV LINE AND ANZIO

In the first three months of 1944, the Fifth Army tried twice to break through the strong enemy defenses and capture Rome. One attempt was to turn the Gustav Line by a landing fifty miles north at Anzio on the Tyrrhenian coast. The other was to cut through the line beyond Cassino. Neither operation was wholly successful; but each tested American, British. and French troops with the toughest prolonged fighting they had met in the Mediterranean theater.

The Gustav Line

Cassino was a key position in the Gustav Line. The town and its dominating hills barred the entrance into the Liri River Valley—the road to Rome. Another road to Rome runs along the Tyrrhenian coast, following roughly the old Appian Way. General Alexander planned the Gustav Line operation to clear each of these highways. The main effort was thrown against the German positions protecting the highway in the Liri Valley.

Rome was the objective of the Gustav Line campaign, and the Liri Valley was the most logical avenue of approach. This valley is flanked on both the north and the south by huge mountain masses and is bounded on the west by the Garigliano, Gari, and Rapido Rivers. Minefields and wire guarded the rivers on each side. Steel "crabs," portable pillboxes,

226

were staggered in depth in the mountains and across the Liri Valley west of the Rapido. Reinforced concrete pillboxes, often built in stone houses and on mountain sides, were all but impregnable positions.

The 15th Army Group's strategy for the January offensive called for the British X Corps on the Fifth Army's left to force a crossing of the Garigliano River with two divisions, establish a bridgehead, then wheel north to cross the Liri River. These maneuvers were planned to force the Germans to fall back from the Rapido line south of Cassino. In two more attacks on successive nights, one division of the X Corps was to cross the Garigliano near its junction with the Gari River, and the 36th Division was to make a frontal assault on Sant' Angelo. The next day, the VI Corps was to land at Anzio in the enemy's rear to cut his lines of communication south of Rome. Following the Rapido assault, the 34th Division and the French Corps would cross the Rapido north of Cassino, then turn south to outflank the town. The enemy was already off balance because of several shifts of his forces; it was hoped that these moves would compel him to withdraw north of Rome.

The assault by the X Corps was successful at first. Within four days [*January 17–12, 1944*] the British gained a substantial bridgehead west of the Garigliano, but they could not break through to the Liri River. The 36th Division, crossing the Rapido River, met enemy opposition so intense that our troops fell back to their original positions [*January 20–23, 1944*] after suffering very heavy casualties. At the end of January the 34th Division crossed successfully and breached the north end of the Gustav Line. [*January 29–31, 1944*]. The French Corps at the same time paralleled this advance and captured several key hills east of Mount Cairo, the snow-capped peak which dominates the entire Cassino area.

Struggle for Cassino

The battle for Cassino itself began when the 34th Division and a combat team of the 36th Division drove on the town from the north [*February 1, 1944*]. Our troops fought

227

their way into the north edge of town and in twelve days had captured several hills north and northwest of Hill 516, on which stood the venerable Benedictine Monastery. A handful of our troops actually reached the walls of the monastery but were compelled to withdraw by German reinforcements.

The New Zealand Corps, formed initially by bringing together the 2d New Zealand Division and the 4th Indian Division, joined the Fifth Army and began to relieve the II Corps early in February. On the day that the New Zealand Corps took over the battle a heavy bombing raid partially destroyed the Monastery [*February 15, 1944*]. The 2d New Zealand Division then captured about one-third of Cassino, but the 4th Indian Division could no no more than hold its positions. The drive to complete the conquest of Cassino was postponed until March, when another bombing raid by about five hundred planes again blasted the Cassino stronghold. When the New Zealanders attacked after extremely heavy artillery concentrations, they found that the bombing had cratered the roads and blocked the streets with debris. Tanks, therefore, could not be used effectively. The German 1st Parachute Division fought viciously under direct orders from Hitler to hold at all costs. Indian troops captured Castle Hill (Hill 193), Hill 165, and Hangman's Hill (Hill 435) just below the Monastery [*March 15–20, 1944*]. But the Monastery held out, as did isolated strong points in Cassino. The New Zealand Corps called off the battle again [*March 23, 1944*], and General Alexander waited until May to resume the drive. These failures along the Gustav Line prevented the Fifth Army from connecting with the Anzio beachhead.

Anzio Beachhead

To turn the Gustav Line and to facilitate the capture of Rome, a landing had been made by two divisions, and the U.S. 3d Infantry Division, on the west coast at Nettuno and Anzio [*January 22, 1944*]. These resort villages are on a flat beach thirty-six miles south of Rome, fifty miles north of Cassino, and only twenty miles west of the enemy's lines of communication between these points. The violent attack on Cassino preoccupied the Germans and enabled British and American units of the Fifth Army to surprise them by the flank assault on Anzio. Very little resistance was encountered at first as patrols advanced through Aprilla toward Campolene [*January 25, 1944*], sixteen miles below Rome, and inland to only seven miles from the Appian Way at Cisterna [*February 2, 1944*]. Against growing enemy resistance the Allies supplied and reinforced the beachhead, British units and the American 45th Division arriving to hold the position. The Nazis soon hemmed in the beachhead with elements of six divisions, including Fascist Italians, under General Mackensen. They swept the low-lying Allied positions with enfiladed batteries, and fired on supply vessels, using 170mm. guns posted in the mountains inland. The enemy rear was beyond range of Allied guns, and the beachhead was so narrow and crowded that almost any enemy bomb or shell found a target, and German artillery raked it day and night. American soldiers on the beachhead walked with the "Anzio gait," hugging walls and crouching along on bent knees, but the work of supply never stopped [*February 3–9, 1944*]. Strong Nazi counterattacks by tank-and-infantry teams chopped at the northern British flank until Aprilia fell. There the enemy was halted by British tanks [*February 16–17, 1944*], an American sidesweep coming westward from Cisterna, the concentrated fire of naval vessels on his flanks, and the whole Air Forces over his lines.

After fruitless counterattacks the Allies organized a perimeter defense of the beachhead. This was actually a triangle with its base running nineteen miles along the coast and its apex inland about two miles southwest of Cisterna. Over this area both sides were harassed by constant shelling, some bombing, and frequent raids. A final Nazi attack on the American sector was repelled [*March 2, 1944*]. The Anzio beachhead stood, a thorn in the enemy's side, engaging his tactical reserves. But it had failed either to turn his defenses in the south around Cassino or to open a breakthrough north to Rome. The Allies had not enough ships or men in the Italian theater to develop and extend the beachhead.

229

27. AMERICAN ADVANCE IN THE PACIFIC

On the other side of the world from Italy, in the tropical jungles of the Southwest Pacific, the fighting was as tough as in the mountains around Cassino. And progress on the road to Tokyo seemed at times as slow and difficult as on the road to Rome.

Operations in the South Pacific during 1942 had been confined to Guadalcanal and Buna because of limited resources. As Allied strength in this area grew through the winter of 1942-43, the commanding officers of the Central, South, and Southwest Pacific met in Washington [*March 1943*] to make plans for an offensive which would roll up the Japanese outposts. After the reduction and mopping up of Guadalcanal and Buna early in 1943, there was a period of apparent stalemate, during which American forces and supplies were accumulated in the Pacific to penetrate the outer defenses of the Japanese Empire. The larger part of all American military and naval forces overseas in the middle of 1943 were stationed in the Pacific. They were divided between two theaters, with most of the land forces in the Southwest Pacific under General Douglas MacArthur, and most of the naval forces in the Central Pacific under Admiral Chester W. Nimitz. In each theater a great amphibious offensive was launched by all arms combined against the Pacific islands held by the Japanese.

I. CLIMBING THE SOLOMONS–NEW GUINEA LADDER

The amphibious forces advancing up the Solomons–New Guinea ladder were not engaged, as the press put it, in "island-hopping." The oceanic highway to Tokyo was too long a road for the Americans to take every island which the Japanese had occupied. "We have been moving," said Admiral Nimitz, "not from island to island, but, from one area to another to get naval bases. In effect, we have simply been expanding our sea-power control westward in order to enable us to get on."

The key Japanese base in the Southwest Pacific, covering sea routes north to the Philippines, which General MacArthur was pledged to reconquer, was the port of Rabaul in the northeastern corner of New Britain Island. It supported and was protected by numerous airfields and naval patrol bases which the enemy had established around the Bismarck Archipelago off the northeast shore of New Guinea, the Admiralty Islands, New Ireland, and the Solomons. To reach Rabaul by air and outflank it by land, a two-pronged offensive was mounted by Allied forces. On land, American and Australian troops under General MacArthur, supplied in part by the U.S. Fifth Air Force under Lieutenant General George C. Kenney, advanced up the eastern coast of New Guinea. At the same time, American troops, with the support of the task forces under Admiral Halsey's South Pacific command, took island after island in the Solomons. As they climbed the Solomons–New Guinea ladder toward Rabaul, the U.S. Fifth Air Force from Australia and New Guinea combined with the Thirteenth Air Force from New Caledonia and Guadalcanal to pound Rabaul to pieces. Air and naval forces together covered all landings and intercepted Japanese supply and warships in the waters of the Southwest Pacific. ranging in 1944 as far north as Java, Borneo, and the Palau and Truk island groups.

New Georgia Campaign

The advance in the Solomons started from Guadalcanal, where fighter planes were based on Henderson Field, and proceeded first toward enemy air bases about two hundred miles north, at Munda on New Georgia Island and near the Vila River on Kolombangara Island. The Japanese concentrated so much air power at these fields in the northern Solomons that our air and naval bombardments were unable permanently to destroy them [*January 23–24, 1943, March 5–6, 1943, May 12–13, 1943*]. American amphibious forces landed in the Russell Islands group to provide an air strip for fighter planes sixty miles northwest of Guadalcanal [*February 21, 1943*]. As preparations were made for the invasion of New Georgia, the Japanese put up furious opposition in the air. Over Guadalcanal, in one of the greatest engagements of the Southwest Pacific [*June 16, 1943*], 107 enemy craft were shot down by Army, Navy, and Marine Corps pilots who lost only six planes.

231

The U. S. 43rd Infantry Division moved to Rendova Island, off Munda, while Marines landed at Viru Harbor [*June 30, 1943*]. Covered by fighter planes, which shot down over a hundred Japanese craft, both forces quickly overcame the enemy garrisons. [*July 2–3, 1943*]. From the landings which followed on New Georgia, at Rice Anchorage, and elsewhere, troops of the XIV Corps (the 37th, 24th, and 25th Infantry Divisions) converged on the enemy air base at Munda [*August 5, 1943*]. It fell after six weeks of hard fighting during which some 350 Japanese planes were destroyed with a loss of 93 American planes. The enemy held out at Bairoko Harbor, eight miles north, for another three weeks [*August 25, 1943*].

The Japanese airbase at Vila on Kolombangara was neutralized as soon as Seabees had rebuilt the Munda air strip for American operation [*August 15, 1943*]. Kolombangara was finally bypassed with the landing of Army, Marine and New Zealand forces on Vella Lavella Island [*August 15, 1943*] fourteen miles northwest, and was brought under artillery fire from Arundel, occupied somewhat later [*August 27, 1943*]. The Japanese lost heavily in both ships and men as they made attempts first to reinforce and then to evacuate New Georgia and Kolombangara. In the close naval battles of Kula Gulf [*July 6, 13, 1943*] and Vella Gulf, in August, American cruisers and destroyers sank three enemy destroyers and a cruiser, and damaged another force, but lost the cruiser *Helena*, the destroyer *Gwin*, and suffered damage to three other cruisers [*August 6, 1943*]. Baanga and Arundel Islands were occupied by elements of the 25th and 43rd Infantry Divisions [*September 22, 1943*]. There were also destroyer actions off Vella Gulf, Vella Lavella and Kolombangara, with a total of nine Japanese warships sunk [*October 6, 1943*].

Bougainville Campaign

The conquest of the northern Solomons centered on Bougainville Island, which was approached by landing just to the south of it at Mono and Stirling in the Treasury Islands [*October 26–27, 1943*]. While the main forces under Lieutenant General (now General) Alexander A. Vandergrift

232

landed on the west coast of Bougainville at Empress Augusta Bay [*November 1, 1943*], a battalion of Marine Raiders made a feint against Japanese positions on Choiseul Island. A large enemy force of cruisers and destroyers tried to break up this advance to Bougainville but were dispersed with considerable damage by an American force under Rear Admiral A. S. Merrill [*November 2, 1943*]. The 148th Infantry of the U.S. 37th Division reinforced the Marines at Empress Augusta Bay [*November 8, 1943*], and additional troops landed during the next two months at the base established on Cape Torokina. Though the enemy was too strong to be destroyed in combat, land-based bombers neutralized his airfields in the Buka-Bonis area of northern Bougainville, and American cruisers and destroyers shelled his coastal positions.

Instead of slugging it out with the Japanese on Bougainville as in the slow and costly operation on Guadalcanal, the American command took advantage of its naval and air superiority to contain the enemy garrisons on Bougainville and cut their supply lines to Rabaul by occupying the Green Islands just north of the Solomons [*February 14, 1944*]. This jump forward isolated all the Japanese forces left in the Solomons, at Bougainville, Choiseul, Shortland, and Buka Islands. They did not cease resistance, but they were no longer strategically effective as fighting troops. The Solomons were at last completely dominated by American air and naval power.

New Guinea Campaign

On the other side of the Solomons-New Guinea ladder, American, Australian, and New Zealand troops of General MacArthur's command moved north from one strategic point to the next with the goal of outflanking and isolating the main Japanese base at Rabaul. Progress in New Guinea was slower than in the Solomons, because the country was larger and more rugged, with jungle swamps along the coast and unmapped mountains inland, and in this difficult terrain the enemy held all strategic positions in force. The chief burden of the fighting in New Guinea was borne by the Australian 7th and 9th and the American 32d and 41st Divisions, paratroopers were frequently used as assault battalions

233

to cut off enemy positions in the mountains. and the U.S. Fifth Air Force often acted as a service of supply to remote outposts. American units were organized in the Sixth Army under Lieutenant General Walter Krueger. All these Allied forces in the Southwest Pacific were nearly equal in numbers and strength to the Allied armies in Italy, proof of the importance and difficulty of their operations.

After the enemy lost his southernmost outposts at Buna and Sanananda [*January 19, 1943*], he did not give up New Guinea. From Rabaul he sent reinforcements to his garrisons at Lae and Salamaua. These convoys were heavily attacked by Allied bombers [*January 6-9. 1943*]. In the Battle of the Bismarck Sea [*March 1–3, 1943*] it was estimated that eighteen enemy ships with fifteen thousand troops aboard were sunk by Flying Fortresses and Liberators which trailed and bombed them for three days. The Japanese increased their air strength from Rabaul to Salamaua until it was reported that they had twice as many planes in this area as the Fifth Air Force. Flights of a hundred or more bombers struck Allied supply depots at Port Moresby, Oro and Milne Bay in New Guinea, and at Port Darwin in Australia [*March 15, April 12, 14, May 2, 1943*]. The U.S. Fifth and Thirteenth Air Forces, aided by planes from naval carrier forces, hit back and wore down the enemy air strength centered at Rabaul, in a relentless offensive that lasted through the winter and spring of 1943.

From Salamaua to Madang

The advance on Rabaul by land had begun simultaneously in the Solomons and New Guinea, so that the enemy had his hands too full to deal with both offensives adequately. In surprise landings we gained without opposition air strips on the Woodlark and Trobriand Islands [*June 30, 1943*], which lie between the Solomons and New Guinea. From their main base at Salamaua, however, the Japanese had crept toward the strategic center of lower New Guinea in the Bulolo Valley. Here they were turned back by the Australian 6th Division which was flown into the jungle. After nine months these troops had pushed the enemy back from Wau to the coast. The base at Salamaua was now

234

flanked by Americans landing to the south at Nassau Bay and by Australian reinforcements put ashore at Tambu Bay [*June 29, 30, 1943*]. After hard fighting overland, reminiscent of Buna, Salamaua was invested by combined artillery and occupied by American and Australian troops [*September 11, 1943*].

Airborne and amphibious units of the Australian 9th Division jumped across the Gulf of Huon to capture Lae [*September 16, 1943*], which was then converted like Salamaua into a forward air and naval base. Allied amphibious forces moved by sea to take the next objective, Finschhafen [*October 2, 1943*], at the eastern end of the Huon Peninsula. The Japanese spread inland from these coastal points, and only after three months of bitter fighting through the mountain jungles were they driven out of Huon. Large numbers were caught in the Markham River Valley between the 9th Australians pushing up the coast from Lae and the 7th Australians driving down the valley [*September 16, 1943*]. American paratroopers and Australian artillery, dropped on Nadzab in the rear of the enemy, drove north under air cover to clear the Markham and Ramu valleys and to corner the Japanese in the foothills of the Finisterre Range before Madang. Here the enemy made a prolonged and stubborn stand. In order to encircle the Japanese, units of the U. S. 32d Division landed without losses at Saidor [*January 2, 1944*], fifty-five miles below Madang, and met Australian troops who had pushed up the coast from Finschhafen and Sio [*February 13, 1944*]. This junction of Allied forces completed the conquest of the Huon Peninsula and, with the occupation of Umboi Island [*February 12, 1944*], covered the flank of American troops who had moved into western New Britain.

Neutralization of Rabaul

The invasion of New Britain was the climax of the drive up the Solomons-New Guinea ladder, for at the eastern end of this island was Rabaul, chief enemy base in the Southwest Pacific. While Army and Navy bombers pounded Rabaul in daily raids, the approach overland was made by landings about 280 miles west, first at Arawe and then at Cape

235

Gloucester, giving American forces contol of western New Britain [*December 15, 1943*].

The invasion of Arawe by units of the U. S. Sixth Army was preceded by a bombardment of 350 tons of bombs, and within five days after their landing the Americans cleared the enemy out of Arawe Peninsula. The 1st Marine Division under Major General William H. Rupertus, veterans of Guadalcanal, landed at points east and west of Cape Gloucester [*December 26, 1943*], after Allied bombers prepared the way with thirteen hundred tons of high explosives, and squeezed the enemy out of the Cape in four days. The Marines drove east to Borgen Bay, captured Hill 660 [*January 14, 1944*] in a battle lasting ten days, and joined the infantry driving inland from Arawe to complete the conquest of western New Britain [*February 24, 1944*]. Marines jumped up the northern coast by landing at Talasea [*March 6, 1944*], 110 miles above Cape Gloucester, and drove eastward on Rabaul to Cape Hoskins.

Amphibious hops across the islands of the Admiralty and St. Matthias groups, the northern ring of the Bismarck Sea, finished the neutralization of Rabaul by cutting it off from Truk, eight hundred miles north, the main Japanese base in the Central Pacific and connecting link with the Southwest Pacific. The first landing in the Admiralty group [*February 29, 1944*] was made by elements of the U. S. 1st Cavalry Division, dismounted, at Los Negros Island. With the capture of Larengau on Manus Island [*March 18, 1944*] the Admiralty group fell into American hands. Air strips on these islands endangered the supply line of some fifty thousand Japanese stranded in Rabaul and New Britain.

II. NAVAL SUPERIORITY

Backing up the American advance in the Pacific, and the landings in North Africa, Sicily, and Italy, was the strength of the United States Navy, without which the Army could never have crossed the Atlantic and Pacific to engage the enemy. It was not enough for the Navy to be able to defeat the Japanese battle fleet and German submarines; in the Pacific our naval forces had also to mount amphibious attacks, sweep the enemy from the skies, and conquer the

236

island defenses of the Japanese Empire. We needed the strongest navy in the world to defeat the Japanese fleet. While we knew it ranked third at the outbreak of hostilities, we had to reckon with new ships built in secret and the distant bases won by amphibious blitzkrieg. To overwhelm Japan, therefore, the United States needed one fleet, the largest, in the Pacific; we needed other fleets just as large to patrol the seaways which led to American troops and bases scattered all over the world.

To meet its world-wide responsibilities, the United States Navy became the strongest in the world. In three years, from 1940 to 1943, it developed the greatest power ever seen in combination on the sea and in the air. American naval strength increased from 1,076 to 4,167 ships, besides 80,000 landing craft, and from 383 to 613 warships. Planes multiplied from 1,744 to 18,269, and in 1944 approached a total of 37,000 for the Navy alone. One fleet grew into several, and in addition developed a large air force. The personnel required to man these ships and planes, with all their shore stations, expanded in the two years between Pearl Habor and 1944 from less than half a million officers and men, including the Marine Corps and Coast Guard, to three million. By the middle of 1944 it was estimated that American naval strength was many times that of Japan and three times that of Great Britain.

These increases were all the more remarkable because they continued despite the losses inevitable in war. Up to the last quarter of 1943 enough ships were sunk or transferred to other uses to make up a small navy of half a million tons. Fifty-nine warships were lost: two battleships, four large aircraft carriers, nine cruisers, thirty-two destroyers, and twelve submarines. In addition, one hundred twenty-nine warships were assigned to other nations or converted to non-combat duty. These losses were small compared to what Japan lost during the first year after Pearl Harbor: two battleships, seven carriers (five of them the largest in the world), three cruisers, and a considerable number of destroyers and submarines which could only be guessed at. Thus the American Navy became superior to the Japanese in 1943, chiefly by new construction, and with this superiority was able to take the offensive and destroy the enemy forces in combat.

Not only did the United States become the mightiest sea and air power in the world, but its program of construction exceeded all other nations in speed as well as in size. The Government collaborated with industry in expanding shipyards and building new ones. The time required for completing a ship from laying the keel to launching it was progressively diminished. Before Pearl Harbor an aircraft carrier took nearly three years to build, but in 1943 little more than one year. Destroyers whose construction formerly required over a year were turned out in less than half a year. This gain was the work of management and labor in the shipyards, where the number of men and women who built and repaired naval vessels increased from less than half a million to over a million between Pearl Harbor and July 1943. These men and women in overalls gave the men in uniform the ships and arms to fight at sea. Their achievement is illustrated by the fact that they delivered five vessels to the Navy in June 1940; two years later, in a single month, they produced twelve hundred vessels.

Priority went to different classes of ships at different times according to changes in our strategic needs. The crises of the war at sea are reflected in the order of preferred vessels, from battleships to aircraft carriers and baby flat-tops in 1942, to destroyer escorts and cruisers in 1943, and to landing craft in 1944. When five of the eight old battleships at Pearl Harbor were sunk or disabled, only two of ten new battleships, the *North Carolina* and *Washington,* were in service. Immediate priority was given to other capital ships with the result that in the next two years seven more were launched, the *South Dakota* of 35,000 tons, the *Indiana, Massachusetts,* and *Alabama* and the largest battleships of 52,000 tons, the *Iowa, New Jersey,* and *Missouri.* Three more of these giants, the *Wisconsin, Illinois,* and *Kentucky,* were soon to join the others, giving the Navy a total of twenty-five battleships.

When four of the seven aircraft carriers with which we entered the war were lost in the Pacific, leaving only the *Saratoga, Enterprise,* and *Ranger* afloat in the fall of 1942, the construction of carriers was speeded up. Twenty big carriers, of the 27,000-ton *Essex* class, were finished in 1943; nine light cruisers were converted into 10,000-ton carriers of the *Independence* class; and other carriers, the 10,000-ton *Breton* and 9,000-ton *Casablanca* classes, were built. By the end of 1943 more than fifty aircraft carriers joined the forces in the Pacific. Their completion months ahead of schedule enabled the Navy to advance its timetable of operations and launch an offensive which resulted in the conquest of the Gilbert, Marshall, Caroline, and Marianas Islands long before it was thought possible to deliver such crippling blows to Japan.

The most significant accomplishment in building carriers during 1942 was the production of the baby flat-tops which drove the German U-boats to cover in the Atlantic. The first escort carrier was the *Long Island*, converted early in 1941 from a merchant ship and commissioned in 1942. The success of this improvisation promised all convoys the air cover necessary to win the Battle of the Atlantic. C-3 (cargo) hulls and oilers were quickly transformed into small combat carriers. Besides serving as anti-submarine escorts for our supply lines, they were used to deliver planes to distant shores where and when they were sorely needed, and they also added their air strength to the striking force of the larger carriers.

The Navy did not limit its expansion to ships. It developed its own air arm with land-based as well as carrier-based planes. The world's largest flying boat, the Martin *Mars*, entered service in 1944 on the seventy thousand miles of scheduled flights operated by the Naval Air Transport Service. The Grumman *Wildcat* fighter was followed by the *Hellcat* and the Chance-Vought *Corsair*, superior in speed, armor, and fire power to any Japanese planes. The Douglas *Dauntless*, a dive bomber which worked great destruction in the Pacific, was improved on by the Curtiss *Helldiver*. The Grumman *Avenger*, a versatile torpedo bomber which first went into action at the Battle of Midway, became the mainstay of the aerial attack in the Pacific.

The United States Pacific Fleet was so heavily reinforced early in 1943 that it could be divided into task fleets, and these fleets into task forces, each like a military combat team with variable strength adapted to special missions. Admiral Chester W. Nimitz remained in command of all naval forces in the Pacific, but delegated several task fleets to operations in different parts of these waters. Early in 1944, Admiral William F. Halsey, Jr., commanded the Third Fleet, and Admiral Raymond A. Spruance the Fifth Fleet. These were the same fleet at different times, operating in the Pacific, all ships identical. In the Southwest Pacific was the Seventh Fleet under Vice Admiral Thomas C. Kinkaid, and around the Aleutians the Ninth Fleet under Vice Admiral Frank J. Fletcher.

In other waters, too, there were American fleets in 1944. Two patrolled the Atlantic: the Fourth in the South Atlantic under Vice Admiral (now Admiral) Jonas H. Ingram, and the Tenth in the North under Vice Admiral Royal E. Ingersoll. The Twelfth Fleet sailed European waters with Admiral Harold R. Stark; the Eighth was in the Mediterranean with Vice Admiral Henry K. Hewitt. The naval power of the United States circled the world.

The construction and assignment of new aircraft carriers to the Pacific gave the Navy command of the air against Japan in 1944. Altogether there were nearly one hundred carriers, large and small, with over one thousand planes, in the Pacific task forces. Most of them operated under Vice Admiral Marc A. Mitscher as Task Force 58 (or 38, depending on whether Halsey or Spruance was in command) screened by battleships, cruisers, and destroyers, with the whole Pacific for their hunting ground. Overwhelming naval superiority such as this threatened not only the Japanese Navy, if it could be brought to battle, but Japan itself.

III. THE CENTRAL PACIFIC

With increasing naval and air-power, the American forces in the Central Pacific launched a drive to reach the coast of China and win island bases for air fleets to strike directly at Japan. The offensive began with an invasion of the outer defenses of the Japanese Empire in the far-flung Gilbert, Marshall, Caroline, and Marianas Islands. All forces combined their strength in operations by land, sea, and air, the

240

scale of which had never before been witnessed in the world's history.

Makin and Tarawa: Operation Galvanic

The first islands to be conquered were Makin and Tarawa in the Gilberts 2,500 miles southwest of Pearl Harbor. On November 20–24, while the Tarawa garrison was under Marine attack, the 27th Infantry Division Task Force under Major General Ralph C. Smith overwhelmed a small garrison of three hundred Japanese infantry in stout defenses on Makin, enemy seaplane base a hundred miles north of Tarawa. The American casualties were 253. Two battalions of the 165th Infantry, the New York "Fighting Irish," with all their artillery and some tanks, established themselves nearly two miles west of the strongly held area, providing fire support for the later attack of the remaining battalion. Pillboxes were cleaned out in two days and the enemy, disorganized from the start and fortified with *sake*, dissipated their remaining strength in a suicidal night counterattack. A single battalion mopped up. Apamama Island was also occupied by the 27th Division.

Tarawa was a different story. It was conquered only by the unflinching bravery of our soldiers in one of the bloodiest assaults in American history. The coral island of Betio in the Tarawa Atoll, three miles long and one mile wide, was defended by three thousand Japanese Imperial Marines. Concrete bunkers impervious to naval and aerial fire had been prepared there by fifteen hundred labor troops. The blockhouses had outer walls ten feet thick of sand and coral and were roofed with iron rails laid on palm logs more than a foot in diameter, all of which protected concrete emplacements five feet thick. These amazing forts could not be shattered even by the one thousand tons of bombs which the Seventh Air Force rained down. They had to be taken by direct infantry assault with grenades, flamethrowers, and bangalore torpedoes hurled through the eye slits and gunports. At both ends of the island, moreover, were batteries of six-inch and eight-inch guns brought from Singapore. Never before had a little tropical island been converted into such a mighty fortress.

241

The attack began with a night bombardment by naval vessels and carrier planes which covered the island with smoke and flame. When it seemed as if no human being could be left alive in this inferno, the 2d Marine Division under Major General Julian C. Smith stormed ashore [*November 21, 1943*]. The first three waves landed at high tide and gripped the beach under intense machine-gun fire from enemy bunkers. Three beachheads 150 feet deep were secured. The fourth and fifth waves grounded five hundred yards off shore on reefs exposed by high wind and a falling tide. Marines jumped into water up to their necks and waded ashore, suffering severe losses from a rain of machine-gun bullets.

That night in bright moonlight, while the beach parties barely held their ground against snipers, we landed tanks and reinforcements At dawn the enemy flanked the Marines on a nearby beach and caught them in an enfilade fire. Cruisers, destroyers, and dive bombers rooted the Japanese out. Then began the systematic reduction of enemy pillboxes with TNT charges, flamethrowers, and torpedoes. By noon of the next day the Japanese were confined to the western end of the island, and that night they made a suicide charge. The last snipers were killed on the fourth day of the assault. Tarawa had cost the Marines 913 killed and missing, and 2,037 wounded.

Kwajalein: Operation Flintlock

The next American blow in the Central Pacific fell northwest of the Gilberts on the Marshall Islands, which extend over six hundred miles of water and screen the island of Truk, key Japanese naval base. The invading force by-passed the strong eastern garrisons at Jaluit and Wotje, and sprang a tactical surprise on the enemy northwest at Kwajalein. This atoll is 2,415 miles southwest of Pearl Harbor and 1,046 miles east of Truk. It is formed by low sandy islands which enclose a lagoon eighty miles long. The chief islands are Kwajalein, Roi, and Namur, among which the enemy divided a force of about eight thousand men to guard his airfields. Heavy bombing crippled these airfields before the invasion [*January 21–29, 1944*] and on the eve of attack a great naval task force under Vice Admiral Richmond K. Turner shelled and bombed the Kwajalein atoll for two days and nights with 14,500 tons of high explosives [*January 30–February 1, 1944*]. The fire preparation was more thorough than at Tarawa; it cut Kwajalein up into a maze of craters.

The 7th Infantry Division, commanded by Major General Charles H. Corlett, landed on undefended islands which outflanked Kwajalein, emplaced artillery, and next day landed on Kwajalein itself with tanks [*February 1, 1944*]. It was occupied yard by yard with the aid of air and naval fire and additional flank landings [*February 3–6, 1944*]. The same tactics carried out by the 4th Marine Division under Major General Harry Schmidt took Roi and Namur [*February 1–3, 1944*]. Concrete pillboxes were reduced by bazookas and flamethrowers. Throughout this operation, which was essentially a mopping-up job, naval and air forces covered the troops with concentrated fire. Total American casualties were 1,516, of whom 286 were killed, while the enemy lost 8,122 killed and 264 captured. From Kwajalein a naval task force carried the 22d Marine and 106th Infantry Regiments 340 miles west to capture the enemy air base of Engebi [*February 17–19, 1944*] in the Eniwetok Atoll with casualties of five hundred.

So overwhelming was American air and sea power that the naval task force, with several battleships and aircraft carriers, proceeded east into the heart of enemy waters. Hundreds of planes attacked the great Japanese base at Truk and destroyed 201 planes and 23 ships with a loss of only 17 planes [*February 16, 1944*]. Although this daring raid did not catch the Japanese fleet, which had deserted Truk, it upset the Nipponese so much that Premier Tojo took over the duties of Army Chief of Staff himself, while the Navy Minister, Admiral Shimada, was made Navy Chief of Staff [*February 21, 1944*]. The U. S. fleet, continuing its sweep westward next struck at the enemy base of Saipan [*February 21, 1944*] in the Marianas Islands, fifteen hundred miles south of Tokyo. Here 135 Japanese planes were destroyed, one ship was sunk, and ten others damaged. The American Navy sailed with impunity through waters over three thousand miles west of Pearl Harbor. Enemy bases in the Marshall and Carolines, outer perimeter of the Pacific defense of the Japanese Empire, were either captured as at Kwajalein, left to starve as at Jaluit, or rendered useless as at Truk. This daring American victory proved that the offensive in the Central Pacific was under way.

IV. BURMA: OPERATION CAPITAL

It was nearly two years after the fall of Burma before Allied forces could undertake a major offensive to pry loose the Japanese grip on the northern country into which the Ledo Road was being built for the supply of China. This long delay was due to the weakness of the Allies in CBI and the slow rate at which supplies were accumulated in mountain jungles halfway around the world. Ground operations here were limited from May to October by the monsoon, and throughout the year by the relative lack of supply. Hence the Allies first took the offensive in Burma with small forces of airborne troops.

Airborne Invasion

British airborne infantry organized by Major General Orde C. Wingate first invaded the jungles of northern Burma in March 1943 and operated for several weeks behind enemy lines. They were supplied entirely by air as they struck at Japanese communications without ever being caught by the enemy in force. The success of Wingate's Raiders in disorganizing the Japanese rear [*August 11–24, 1943*] inspired the Allied leaders at the Quebec Conference to develop this method of penetrating Burma.

General Arnold ordered Colonel Philip G. Cochran and Lieutenant Colonel (now Colonel) John R. Alison to organize and train the First Air Commando Force of the United States Army Air Forces. They chose their glider pilots from volunteers, insisted that every airplane pilot should also be his own mechanic, and in December 1943 transferred their limited force secretly to India, where two bases on opposite sides of the country were turned over by the Royal Air Force, one for gliders, another for light planes. There the force was organized in several sections, to fly B-25 Mitchell bombers, P-51 Mustang fighters, lightplanes, gliders, C-47

244

Skytrain transports, and UC-64 supply planes. To the original personnel were added a photographic reconnaissance detachment and a company of engineers. Tactically the whole force was to act in support of other units, especially of Wingate's Indian Raiders and Merrill's Marauders, carving air strips out of the jungle, flying planes from them, and bringing in supplies and reinforcements. Strategically their operations were designed to weaken the Japanese rear in the Chin Hills and northern Burma.

Two landing sites were picked in this region 160 miles behind enemy lines and dubbed "Piccadilly" and "Broadway" in token of their British and American visitors. The invasion began at night when twenty-six transport planes with thirty-seven gliders in tow landed more than five hundred men in the Broadway jungle [*March 5, 1944*]. All thought of using Piccadilly was abandoned when photographic reconnaissance showed at the last minute that it had been mined by the enemy. Engineers improved Broadway and prepared another jungle strip, Chowringhee, and to these fields in the next six nights were brought thousands of men, 250 tons of supplies, bulldozers, and 1,183 Missouri mules. When the enemy discovered and attacked Broadway a week later, he was repulsed by airborne reinforcements. General Wingate was killed in a plane crash [*March 13, 1944*], and his command passed to Major General W. D. A. Lentaigne [*March 25, 1944*]. Through the spring of 1944 these airborne troops in the Burmese jungles—Merrill's Marauders and Wingate's Raiders—lived up to their names in supporting larger operations by British and American ground troops on the thousand mile front between India and Burma.

Arakan Campaign

At the southern end of this front the Japanese forces covering the forward port of Akyab launched a tactical offensive [*February 4, 1944*], while still on the strategic defense, against British troops assembling for a drive south. The Japanese penetrated the Mayu Mountains and enveloped the British 7th Indian Division [*February 7-20, 1944*], which maintained a hedgehog defense until the 5th Indian Division succeeded in opening communications with it by

245

pushing south on both sides of the Mayu range and capturing Kyauktaw [*February 25, 1944*]. The British attack was renewed with tanks and artillery, despite the hilly jungle swamps, and carried as far as Buthedaung. [*April 6, 1944*]. As the enemy counterattacked above the Kaladan Valley, Buthedaung was evacuated [*May 6, 1944*]. The Japanese and British then transferred the contest northwards to the Manipur front. The 5th Indian Division, with all its mountain batteries and mules, was moved to this sector in sixty hours by American transport planes of Brigadier General William D. Old's Troop Carrier Command.

Manipur Campaign

After preparations which consumed the winter of 1943-44, the Japanese made their main strike in Burma at the center of the Allied front, in the Manipur sector [*March 13, 1944*], in an effort to cut the Assam-Bengal railroad. This railroad, running parallel to the Burmese border about one hundred miles west of the frontier, was the supply line of Chinese-American forces along the Ledo Road in northern Burma. It gave strategic importance to little Manipur, a native state in India about the size of New Jersey, with a village capital at Imphal.

Three Japanese divisions converged upon Imphal and cut off the British 17th Indian Division of British IV Corps, covering the southern approach at Tiddim [*March 30, 1944*]. This division broke through the enemy lines and retired northward to support the 23d, also of IV Corps, which was hard pressed by another Japanese column cutting the highway from Tiddim to Imphal at Bishenpur. The defense of this area was crucial, because it was the eastern end of a supply trail to Silchar on the Bengal-Assam railroad. Sixty miles north the railroad itself was threatened by an enemy force surrounding Kohima.

When another Japanese column penetrated the hills to within twenty-five miles of Imphal, the British awoke to the fact that these enemy columns, which had been mistaken for patrols, were actually enclosing Imphal on three sides in force. A cordon defense of the Imphal Plain was improvised by the 17th and 23d Divisions. Counterattacks

246

northeast pushed the Japanese back toward Ukhrul [*April 20, 1944*], undoing their advance of a month past; and troops to the south around Bishenpur stopped the enemy at a narrow mountain pass. The British III Corps, defending the railroad farther north at Dimapur, reinforced by the 5th Division from the Arakan sector, punched a hole in the enemy lines around Kohima and temporarily relieved the encircled garrison. [*April 19, 1944*]. But in the month that remained before the monsoon started late in May, the British were unable to raise the siege of Imphal, and supplies were brought in by air as the Japanese closed the road west to Silchar.

Around Kohima, farther north, the III Corps drove the enemy back upon the town and secured the Bengal-Assam railroad with communications to the junction at Dimapur [*April 25–28, 1944*]. The Japanese dug into the town of Kohima and made it the "Cassino" of Burma [*May 11–15, 1944*]. Here they were worn down by constant assault. After two months of bitter fighting, which went on during the monsoon, Anglo-Indian troops recaptured Kohima and raised the siege of the Imphal Plain [*June 30, 1944*]. It was estimated that thirteen thousand Japanese were killed in this campaign. The fighting in Manipur had a character all its own, combining mountain and jungle warfare, and could be compared only to New Guinea.

Ledo Road Campaign

The most successful campaign in Burma during the spring of 1944 was fought in the north by Chinese and American troops under General Stilwell. To cover the construction of the Ledo Road, as it was extended southward into enemy country, a Chinese corps of two divisions, trained in India by Americans and equipped on Lend-Lease, pushed up the Hukawng Valley and captured Taihpa Ga [*February 1, 1944*]. American troops, under Brigadier General (now Major General) Frank Merrill, on one side of the valley and Chinese on the other caught the Japanese between them and pushed them back through Maingkwan and Walawbum with enemy losses of four thousand men [*March 4, 1944*]. In their advance up the Hukawng Valley the Chinese and American forces penetrated the jungle about a mile a day for forty

247

miles. Their progress seemed slow, but it was rapid enough to prevent the building of the Ledo Road from keeping pace with it.

The Allies moved southward into the Mogaung Valley and pushed the Japanese back toward the old Burma Road. Their objective was Myitkyina, chief enemy air base and railhead of the only line in Burma. Three columns, composed of Chinese and Indian troops with American reinforcements, advanced up parallel valleys against the Japanese 18th Division, victors at Singapore, supported by 150mm. artillery who stood their ground doggedly. In the enemy rear Wingate's Raiders, roving in small parties and avoiding pitched battles, destroyed the supply dumps south of Mogaung.

When the Chinese advance was slowed down after reaching Wakaung [*April 5, 1944*], Merrill's Marauders moved secretly across country in three columns, keeping liaison by radio, being supplied by air, and advancing along jungle trails about five miles a day [*April 27, 1944*]. They crossed a mountain range eight thousand feet high and seized the Myitkyina airfield [*May 17, 1944*], where glider-borne Chinese and American engineers were landed. An attack was launched against Myitkyina from the rear [*May 19, 1944*], as the Chinese pressed slowly forward in front through the Mogaung Valley. In July, Mogaung and then Myitkyina fell under the pressure of these converging forces.

The next objective was Bhamo, farther south, where the road from Ledo, 250 miles away, was to connect with the old Burma Road. While the Chinese were engaged in the reduction of Myitkyina, another corps of the Chinese Twentieth Army Group opened a drive eighty miles to the east along the Salween River, supported by the U.S. Fourteenth Air Force [*May 10–15, 1944*]. They crossed the Salween, bypassed a Japanese division, and threatened to advance astride the Burma Road to Bhamo. In the mountains their progress was slow because small Japanese machine-gun nests commanding the passes could hold up whole divisions.

Allied military operations in Burma, to sum up, assured the completion of the Ledo Road and promised to increase supply to China with the liberation of the Burma Road. Chungking still depended on India but looked forward to

248

Burma as its main base. Whether Burma could be reconquered before the American forces in the Central Pacific
reached the South China coast was a question for the future
to answer.

28. RESTORATION OF THE SOVIET UNION

The great Soviet offensive which started rolling on the
Kursk-Orel front in the summer of 1943 did not stop until
the following spring when the Nazi invaders were driven
completely out of southern Russia. The success of this offensive was due primarily to Russian arms, but they received
powerful assistance from the United States and Great Britain.

British and American Aid

Most helpful was the tremendous quantity of American
Lend-Lease supplies which reached Russia during 1943.
Shipments were doubled over 1942 and losses in transit from
enemy bombers and U-boats fell from twelve to one per cent.
From October 1941 to January 1944, a total of 7,800 planes,
of which 3,000 flew all the way, 4,700 tanks and tank destroyers, 170,000 trucks, six million pairs of military boots,
over 200,000 field telephones and 700,000 miles of telephone
wire, 177,00 tons of explosives, 740,000 tons of aviation
gasoline, 1,350,000 tons of steel, and 2,250,000 tons of food
were exported from the United States to the Soviet Union.
Russia also received a few entire industrial plants removed
from American factories and put to work in the Soviet Union,
such as the equipment for an oil refinery and all the machinery for a tire factory, capable of turning out a million
truck tires a year. The total value of all these Lend-Lease
supplies amounted to about four and a quarter billion dollars. When added to the much larger production of the Soviet
Union for its own forces, Lend-Lease matériel gave the Red
armies greater mobility, better communications, and for the
first time during the war, command of the air.

The United States and Great Britain contributed to Russian success not only in supply but also in actual combat.
When their offensive in the Mediterranean drove Italy out

of the war, Germany took five to twenty divisions from the Russian front to replace Italian troops who had surrendered and to build up the defensive forces in Western Europe. The majority of German troops who stepped into the breach left by the Italians came from Occupied France. Their places in turn were filled by reserves from Germany, and thus the Nazis had fewer reserves at home to reinforce the Russian front, where manpower was at a premium.

Even more helpful to the Russians than this tapping of German manpower was the great aerial offensive of British and American bombers in 1943 and 1944. It sapped Nazi morale and reduced the capacity of German industries trying to supply both the Russian and Italian fronts. Above all, by drawing the bulk of Nazi fighter planes from east to west, the bombers from Britain gave the Red air forces command of the air in Russia.

Railroad Strategy of the Red Offensive

Red ground troops, with close tactical air support, engaged by far the larger part of the German armies. To drive the Nazis out of the Soviet Union the Russians struck at railroads and strongpoints on their main lines of resistance. The two generally coincided. From north to south the strongpoints of Staraya Russa, Vitebsk, Mogilev, Zhlobin, Korosten, Zhitomir, Kiev, Smela, Krivoi Rog, and Nikolaev were all railway junctions. While the public watched the war in Russia to see who won and lost the great cities, Moscow, Leningrad, Kharkov, Kiev, and Odessa, or the great rivers, the Don, Donets, Dnieper, Bug and Dniester the high commands of both armies fought for railroads. These lines were necessary for supply and communications over the vast distances of Russia, and the lateral connections between them, running north and south, were vital to the quick transfer of reserves for attack or defense on a threatened front.

The network of Russian railroads was therefore the skeleton of every campaign. The northern or Leningrad front of the Germans was fed by the railroad from Warsaw through Vilna, Dvinsk, Ostrov, and Luga to Leningrad. Another line from Warsaw led to the central Moscow front through Minsk, Orsha, and Smolensk, with a southern branch through Gomel and Bryansk to Kaluga. The southern front was divided into two sectors, the upper Don and Dnieper, and the lower bends of these long rivers. The first depended on the railroad from Warsaw through Lublin, Kowel, Sarny, and Kiev to Konotop and Kursk; the second upon southern branches from Kowel and Kiev to Smela, Dniepropetrovsk, and the Crimea, and upon a trunk line from Berlin to Breslau, Krakow, Lwow, Tarnopol, Zhmerinka, and Odessa. The Russian summer offensive in 1943 robbed the enemy of many lateral rail connections north and south, and the winter offensive in 1944 cut the great trunk lines from Germany and Poland into southern Russia.

Retreat Beyond the Dnieper

The Russian offensive moved swiftly and stabbed at one front and another with a speed and weight calculated to bleed Nazi manpower into rapid exhaustion. The cost of defense to the enemy was high—perhaps 200,000 casualties in each of the worst months. No Nazi armies were lost as at Stalingrad, and none were encircled except at Korsun. Yet the power of the Russian drives may be judged from the estimate that 320 divisions were massed against the 250 Axis divisions struggling to retain their conquests.

The Germans had resolved, in a high command conference during the summer of 1943, to withdraw only as far as the Dnieper River. But the relentless Russian drives made them retreat from the Dnieper across the Dniester in southern Russia, back into Poland on the central front, and almost to the Baltic states below Leningrad. It was not a strategic withdrawal, nor was it voluntary. The Nazis wasted forces, exhausted reserves, lost vital railway arteries, and in the south, where the fighting was heaviest, never succeeded in maintaining a defensive line of prepared positions. There was no rout of the German armies: they retreated in good order. Nevertheless it was always retreat, and no counteroffensives lasted beyond six weeks or permanently regained any Russian soil.

Central Front

The central front was least active in the Russian winter

251

offensive of 1943-44, but sprang to life in the following summer, when the Red armies first drove in its flanks at the extreme north and south. After these sectors were cleared, it became strategically possible to take the enemy in the center on either side of the Pripet Marshes. In preparation for the summer drives to come, General Rokossovsky captured the rail junction of Mozry on the lateral line from Nevel to Korosten and drove forward to positions north of the Pripet Marshes, threatening Zhlobin and Mogilev [*January 12, 1944*]. Farther north, Siberian soldiers of the First Baltic Army. led by Cossack and ski troops, outflanked the Nazi strongpoint of Vitebsk and cut off its rail supply in the rear [*January 2, 1944*]. The Germans maintained their central front intact through the winter, though under constant pressure, and Russian forces were shifted north and south for the principal drives in those sectors.

Relief of Leningrad

Leningrad, besieged by German and Finnish troops, for two and a half years, survived an ordeal of intermittent shelling by 12- and 16-inch guns which shattered public buildings, wounded fifteen thousand people, and killed five thousand. Private dwellings had no water, no heat, no electric light. The scarcity of food was worse than daily bombardment, for malnutrition caused more deaths than shells or bombs. The civilians of Leningrad fought, like those of London, by never stopping their daily work.

The siege was raised in the winter of 1944 by an offensive which drove the Germans southward to a line between Pskov and Lake Ilmen [*January 15, 1944*]. Heavy artillery blasted the fortified German lines [*February 20, 1944*] with two and a half million shells in four days. Two Red armies, reported to have an overwhelming strength of forty infantry and twenty armored divisions, went into action on a front of sixty-six miles against an enemy force estimated at twenty-three infantry and four tank divisions.

The advance was slow, averaging four miles a day at the start, for Nazi rear guards fought stubbornly at every village, mined the swamps, cut roadblocks out of the forest, and defended them with combat teams of tanks and armored in-

252

fantry. A mild winter made it impossible for the Russians to cross the swamps, and infantry dragged the artillery along. Soviet guerrillas worked havoc in the enemy rear and derailed or blew up thirty-seven Nazi supply trains. As the Russians advanced, they captured 150 of the 12-inch guns with which the Nazis had bombarded Leningrad.

There were two offensives, one southward from Leningrad, another westward from the Volkhov River. The latter drive outflanked Novgorod and the former cleared the railroad to Moscow [*January 20, 1944*]. These two drives joined in a front northwest of Chudovo to trap the Nazis retreating toward Estonia [*February 1, 1944*]. Luga fell to Red ski troops [*February 13, 1944*]. Staraya Russa, chief Nazi strongpoint in the north, was encircled and captured [*February 17, 1944*]. The Germans withdrew on a front of three hundred miles to a line running from the Gulf of Finland south to Pskov, east to Lake Ilmen, and halfway south to Velikie Luki [*February 21, 1944*]. Moscow claimed that the enemy lost ninety thousand men in this retreat. Leningrad breathed again, its vital war factories resumed production, and the Russian command began preparations for the breakthrough which was to reclaim the Baltic states in the summer.

Fanning Out from Kiev

Most of the fighting in Russia during the winter of 1943-44 took place in the south, where the Dnieper Bend and the Ukraine were entirely reclaimed. The Nazi invaders were driven out of the USSR and back upon the borders of Poland and Rumania. For six weeks at the end of 1943, however, the German army around Kiev counterattacked in force and reconquered much territory. The Red Army had recovered these losses ten days after launching its winter offensive in this area.

In a spectacular breakthrough on a front of 185 miles, the First Ukrainian Army commanded by Marshal Vatutin drove west of Kiev [*December 29, 1943*], sweeping twenty-two Nazi divisions before it, captured the rail junctions of Korosten and Zhitomir, eighty miles beyond, and advanced to the old Polish border, along the railroad running from Kiev to Warsaw. This line was cut at Sarny and the enemy was thrown back against the Pripet Marshes [*January 12, 1944*], which divided his forces and broke the continuity of his front. The left flank of Vatutin's forces thrust southward toward Zhmerinka, junction of the Lwow-Odessa railroad, the only trunk line left to the Nazis in southern Russia. The Russians knew that if it fell, the German armies far to the east in the Dnieper Bend might be trapped. In February, however, heavy Nazi counterattacks in support of Zhmerinka stopped the Red Army on this front for over a month.

Encirclement at Korsun

As the Germans withdrew westward on the strategic defensive, they often assumed a tactical offensive to slow up the Russian advance. Southwest of Kiev, for example, fifteen Nazi divisions pushed back toward the city as far as Zhaskov in an effort to stem the Russian thrust to Zhmerinka and protect the forces in the Dnieper Bend [*January 11–30, 1944*]. Against this counteroffensive two Red armies undertook one of the most complicated operations of the war and demonstrated their superiority in the strategy of maneuver—secret of the rapid Russian advances.

The First and Second Ukrainian Armies, commanded by Vatutin and Konev, encircled the German Eighth Army which held the upper Dnieper on a front of fifty miles above Cherkassy and east of Korsun. Each Russian army, consisting of twelve to fifteen motorized divisions, converged on the other [*January 24–February 3, 1944*] and advanced about fifty miles in four days through the enemy rear to complete the circle. They caught the Germans by surprise because they had opened their maneuvers with tactical feints away from the Eighth Army.

The operation was complicated by the necessity of cutting off and containing not only the encircled Eighth Army but also Manstein's forces advancing northeast on Kiev. Vatutin rendered the latter powerless by swinging his troops westward to stand back to back against the troops of Konev, and face the Germans. As soon as Manstein discovered the trap, he supplied the encircled Eighth Army by air and hurled his forces east to break the circle [*February 4–19, 1944*]. Rear echelons and service units escaped, among them over two thousand wounded who were evacuated by plane, but the Red armies succeeded in destroying or capturing ten enemy divisions west of Korsun [*February 17, 1944*]. The Nazis lost 52,000 killed and 11,000 prisoners. This defeat broke the German grip on the upper Dnieper as Stalingrad had dislodged them from the Volga, and they retreated sixty miles across the Ukraine.

Clearing the Dnieper Bend

Three Soviet armies joined in powerful drives to clear the Dnieper Bend and liberate the Ukraine. The Third Ukrainian Army under General Malinovsky pried the Nazis loose from the lower Dnieper by breaking through their defenses [*February 8, 1944*] on a front of one hundred miles and capturing Nikopol, the city which produced one-fifth of the world's manganese. With Nikopol gone, the iron-ore city of Krivoi Rog to the northeast was open to attack. It surrendered [*February 22, 1944*] to a concentric advance which the Germans failed to check when they committed their reserves too hastily on one flank.

Farther south, above Nikolaev, a new German Sixth Army, recruited to replace the one lost at Stalingrad was routed by a hammer-and-sickle maneuver which exposed Nikolaev [*March 6–16, 1944*]. Nikolaev fell, together with Kherson on the lower Dnieper [*March 13, 1944*], to a pincers attack by infantry and tanks supported by Black Sea naval units. The Nazis withdrew [*March 28, 1944*] hastily southwest to the great port of Odessa, which was captured by assault [*April 10, 1944*], after a brief siege, with Nazi losses reported at 26,000 killed and 11,000 prisoners. Most of the German forces had beaten their way out of the Dnieper Bend, but not without paying for their escape.

Clearing the Ukraine

Meanwhile, after sustaining Nazi counterattacks beyond Kiev, the First and Second Ukrainian Armies, commanded by Zhukov and Konev, resumed their offensives to drive the Germans out of the Ukraine. Konev's forces struck southwest toward Rumania, overwhelmed fourteen enemy divisions, captured their air bases at Uman, and crossed the middle

Bug [*March 15, 1944*]. They rolled on sixty miles to the Dniester [*March 19, 1944*], the old Rumanian border, forced a crossing at Mogilev into Bessarabia, and advanced to the Pruth [*March 26, 1944*]. The arrival of Russians at the Pruth marked their recovery for the first time of what Marshal Stalin hailed as the "Soviet state frontier." In a year and a half they had come nine hundred miles from Stalingrad and reconquered all but sixty thousand square miles of their pre-1939 territory.

Zhukov's First Ukrainian Army mounted an offensive on a front of one hundred miles west of Kiev and drove toward Poland. The offensive opened with the usual overpowering massed artillery barrages, which destroyed enemy batteries and strongpoints [*March 7, 1944*]. Zhukov's forces swept southwest forty miles in three days to cut the Lwow-Odessa railroad between Tarnopol and Proskurov [*March 17–22, 1944*]. The rail junctions of Vinnitsa and Zhmerinka, key strongpoints of the western Ukraine, were captured [*March 30, 1944*] and held against heavy enemy counterattacks. The advance continued southward to the rail junction of Cernauti, fifteen miles from the Tatar Pass through the Carpathian Mountains into Hungary and Czechoslovakia. Marshal Zhukov claimed that in his swift advance he had routed twenty-four Axis divisions. As his forces entered old Poland and Rumania, the Ukraine was at last entirely free. [*April 2, 1944*].

Restoration of the Crimea

The Nazis had retreated to the Dnieper but kept German and Rumanian troops in the Crimea hanging on the Russian flank and controlling the Black Sea. Cut off when Malinovsky took Nikolaev, they were later destroyed by Soviet forces [*March 28, 1944*]. From the Kerch bridgehead two Red armies under Tolbukhin and Yeremenko fought their way westward for two weeks and finally swept forward forty miles in a day to isolate the Rumanian garrison at Sevastopol [*April 15, 1944*]. The demoralized enemy lost 37,000 prisoners, it was reported, including one German and two Rumanian divisions.

Sevastopol, the naval fortress captured by the Nazis in

256

1942 after a siege of over six months, was liberated by the
Russians [*May 10, 1944*] in one month. The fall of the base
came three days after Tolbukhin's Fourth Ukrainian Army
united with Yeremenko's Maritime Army and stormed the
fortified defenses in the Yaila Mountains. The innermost belt
of iron-and-concrete gun bastions was smashed by tanks and
infantry supported by massed artillery and air power.

During this campaign, the Russian Black Sea Fleet intercepted enemy efforts to evacuate troops. A total of 191 vessels, including 69 transports, was sunk. With the fall of
Sevastopol the Red Army claimed that 50,000 troops had
been killed in the Crimea and 61,000 had surrendered.

Results of the Winter Offensive

In the winter campaigns of 1944 the Red Army raised the
siege of Leningrad, pushed the Nazis back to the Pripet
Marshes in the center, and swept them out of southern Russia into Poland and Rumania. These drives restored most of
the USSR to the Soviet peoples. Now Red armies were in a
position to free the Baltic states, Poland, and the Balkans,
and to drive the Nazis back where they came from. The
enemy had lost the power to mount a sustained offensive
after Stalingrad and the later drives in the winter of 1943.
In 1944 his defensive power was slowly sapped. It was estimated that he had lost eight divisions at Korsun and the
fighting strength of at least another ten in his retreat from
the Dnieper Bend. What reserves he had left, he would need
in France and Italy to oppose the British and Americans.
The United Nations were ready to crush him in the nut-
cracker made at Teheran where Churchill, Roosevelt, and
Stalin planned the final blows to fall in 1944 from east and
west, north and south.

257

PART SEVEN

TRIUMPH OF THE UNITED
NATIONS

The spring of 1944 brought a period of mounting tension
and secrecy to Europe. No one outside the Allied High Command knew exactly where or when the great American and
British offensive against Germany would be launched from
the west. But the whole world had been told in the winter
months following the Teheran Conference that some time in
1944 the United Nations would strike Hitler-held Europe
from all directions. The first blows were delivered from the
south in Italy by the veteran Fifth and Eighth Armies,
which captured Rome and pursued the disorganized Nazis
north to the Arno River. Next came the American and British
landings in Normandy, prepared by a powerful air offensive
against Germany and followed by two Russian offensives
from the east, the first to knock Finland out of the war and
the second a major drive to the Baltic Sea and deep into
Poland. The great offensive to crush Germany was well under
way by the summer of 1944. Never before had strategy been
applied on such a grand scale to liberate all Europe by
a continental pincers attack with the combined force of
millions of armed men. With these armies and this strategy,
the United Nations were able to crush Fascism in Europe
and to defeat its strongest protagonist, the Germany of
Adolf Hitler.

The development of a strategy of coalition for the defeat
of Germany began in the spring of 1943 when the Combined
Chiefs of Staff drew up plans for the Anglo-American invasion of France. These plans, which even designated the landing beaches, were approved in August 1943, at the Quebec
Conference by President Roosevelt and Prime Minister
Churchill. At Teheran, in December, they discussed the projected invasion with Premier Stalin, and agreed to mount it
at the end of May or the beginning of June 1944, when

all the Russian armies would also take the offensive again in the east.

Following the Teheran Conference, changes were made in the Anglo-American command to prepare for the great drive in the west. General (now General of the Army) Dwight D. Eisenhower was transferred from the Mediterranean to become Supreme Allied Commander in Western Europe, with Lieutenant General Walter B. Smith, Chief of Staff; Air Chief Marshal Sir Arthur Tedder, Deputy Supreme Commander; Field Marshal Sir Bernard L. Montgomery, commanding all ground forces; General Omar N. Bradley, commanding American ground troops; Air Chief Marshal Trafford L. Leigh-Mallory, in charge of all Allied Expeditionary Air Forces; Lieutenant General (now General) Carl Spaatz of U. S. Strategic Bomber Forces, and Air Chief Marshal Sir Arthur T. Harris, of British Strategic Bombers; Admiral Sir Bertram Ramsey, in command of Allied Naval Forces, with Vice Admiral Alan G. Kirk commanding U. S. naval units participating in the invasion; and Lieutenant General John C. H. Lee in charge of American supply in England and the European rear areas.

The Mediterranean Theater was likewise reorganized. General (now Field Marshal) Sir Henry Maitland Wilson took supreme command, uniting the eastern and western Mediterranean, with Lieutenant General (now General) Jacob L. Devers as his American deputy. General (now Field Marshal) Sir Harold Alexander commanded the Allied Central Mediterranean Forces in Italy, which were made up of the British Eighth Army under Lieutenant General Sir Oliver Leese, succeeding Marshal Montgomery, and the British-American Fifth Army under Lieutenant General (now General) Mark W. Clark. Lieutenant Geneal Ira C. Eaker took command of the Allied Air Forces in the Mediterranean, with Air Marshal Sir John C. Slessor as deputy, Major General (now Lieutenant General) Nathan F. Twining, commanding the U. S. Fifteenth Air Force, and Major General John K. Cannon, the Twelfth Air Force. Admiral Sir Andrew Cunningham remained in command of all Mediterranean naval forces, and Vice Admiral Henry K. Hewitt of the American naval forces.

29. AIR OFFENSIVE AGAINST GERMANY

In two and a half years of war, from Pearl Harbor to the middle of May 1944, the United States Army Air Forces dealt severe blows to the Axis. During this period they dropped 468,391 tons of bombs on enemy targets all over the world and destroyed 20,174 enemy planes—16,510 in aerial combat and 3,664 on the ground. In the course of these activities they lost in action a total of 6,154 planes— 5,718 in the air, 236 on the ground, and 200 noncombat craft. Of their operations, on all fronts, the strategic bombing of Germany and German-occupied Europe was the most destructive and the longest offensive ever carried out from the air against an enemy. It was the greatest demonstration of modern air power. For two years, from the spring of 1942 through the summer of 1944, British and American bombers brought the war home to German soil. Long before Europe could be invaded by land, the roof of the Continent was torn off, and from a "second front" in the skies the bombs rained down on enemy cities, industries, and communications. The air attack was a necessary preparation for the invasion of Europe by land.

Although strategic bombing worked terrible destruction in Germany and inflicted many more casualties on the civilian population than any other country suffered, terror was not its object. The area bombing of the Royal Air Force at night and later the daylight precision bombing of the U. S. Army Air Forces were both directed primarily at military targets. First came the submarine pens on the French coast and the shipyards in Germany, because the U-boats threatened to starve Britain and isolate the United States; next the factories which produced planes, ball bearings, synthetic oil, and critical war matériel, for these were the sources of Nazi strength in the air; and finally the Luftwaffe, which took the air to defend the ground from which it drew its power. This order of strategic bombing was followed by tactical bombing of the railroads and rolling stock of enemy supply lines, over which resistance to our invasions of Italy and France was mobilized; then bombers hit the rear areas and coastal defenses of the Nazi armies which faced our troops.

260

Although there were many other targets, such as the robot-bomb installations on the coasts opposite England, the industries of the Rhineland, and the ports on the Baltic Sea, they were accessory to the main order of strategic and tactical targets. In the course of this aerial offensive, planned scientifically and executed with growing ferocity, British and American fliers exhausted the enemy air forces, destroyed a large part of the Nazi war industries, and softened up Hitler-held Europe for the smashing assaults of American, British, and Russian ground troops.

Begun by British Bombers

The air offensive was started by the British under Air Chief Marshal Sir Arthur Harris before the United States entered the war. Only by air could the British then attack Germany directly. From the beginning of 1941 Blenheim bombers raided enemy shipping despite heavy losses, in an effort to deny the Germans the use of coastal waters. With the Nazi invasion of Russia the British policy of bombing was directed to any target whose destruction would help the Soviet Union. British bomber strength became sufficient in the summer of 1941 to send three hundred planes over Germany [*August 14, 1941*], and toward the end of the year, four hundred in a concentrated raid on Berlin [*November 7, 1941*].

In the first phase of Allied bombing [*July 1941–February 1942*], during which the Royal Air Force cooperated with the Russian ground forces, night raids were made on German rail junctions and war plants to disrupt enemy supply. Berlin and Lübeck were the most distant targets; Aachen, Münster, and Cologne in the Rhineland were most frequently raided.

The second phase, beginning in February 1942, was concentrated on German supplies at their source, the steel works of Essen, Düsseldorf, and Cologne, with night raids over Germany and day raids on the factories of northern France and Belgium. A Nazi invasion fleet preparing at Lübeck for a descent on Leningrad was broken up in a heavy raid [*March 28, 1942*] typical of those which continued to help Soviet Russia.

As the Nazis improved their antiaircraft defenses, a new

261

tactic was tried in a blow against the Renault auto and tank works near Paris [*March 3, 1942*]. Bombers were massed for a quick run over a single target in order to saturate ground defenses. This concentration of offensive power proved so effective that it became the pattern of all strategic bombing. In the heaviest raid on Cologne [*May 30, 1942*], one thousand planes made a saturation attack, dropping three thousand tons of bombs in ninety minutes, at the rate of one every six seconds. Neutral observers estimated that twenty thousand people were killed and the chemical and machine-tool industries seriously dislocated. The next night over one thousand planes bombed the Krupp works at Essen. British losses in these swift, heavy raids fell from ten to four per cent, and the damage suffered by the enemy increased in far greater proportion. Such raids, said Churchill, were "a herald of what Germany will receive city by city from now on."

Reinforced by Americans

The British bombed chiefly at night; the Americans joined them in the summer of 1942 to start bombing by day. On their first independent mission [*August 17, 1942*], twelve Flying Fortresses went more than fifty miles into France, dropped eighteen tons of bombs on the railway yards at Rouen, and returned to their base in safety. The raid was the experimental beginning of daylight precision bombing introduced by the armored Forts, with their numerous guns, cannon and pin-pointing bombsights. The U. S. VIII Bomber Command, first under Lieutenant General (now General) Carl Spaatz and later under Lieutenant General Ira C. Eaker, built up its forces during 1942 and 1943 at seventy-seven bases in England, Scotland, and Wales. The average base grew until in 1944 it housed over two thousand men with all the gasoline, parts, and munitions necessary to keep a bomber group of forty-eight to seventy-two Forts or Liberators in operation. The development of the Britain-based Eighth Air Force was interrupted during the winter of 1942-43 by the transfer of air strength from Britain to the Mediterranean to cover the invasion of North Africa and the Battle of Tunisia. To these ground operations the U. S. Eighth and Ninth Air Forces contributed most of the air power, and heavy American bombing of enemy-occupied Europe was consequently delayed until the middle of 1943.

By that time Britain had become primarily a base for air power, with over one thousand heavy American bombers. When the U. S. Eighth Air Force and the Ninth as its tactical and fighter escort were recruited to full strength, they prepared to carry out the task assigned them at the Casablanca Conference, to destroy the German war industries. One year after their first experimental raid on Rouen, the American Air Forces in Britain were strong enough to strike three blows at German industries, each carried out by more than three hundred Flying Fortresses. Two groups dropped 573 tons of bombs on Schweinfurt, center of Nazi ball-bearing production, and fought their way home to England; a third group hit fighter-plane factories in Regensburg with 298 tons of bombs and flew south across the Alps and the Mediterranean on the first shuttle to American bases in North Africa [August 17, 1942]. A week later they bombed Bordeaux on their way back to England.

In their first year of bombing Europe, American planes flew 124 missions from British bases, dropped 16,977 tons of bombs on enemy targets, destroyed 2,050 Nazi fighter planes, and lost 472 bombers with 4,481 men, including the missing and captured. Except for the large number of enemy fighters destroyed, these operations probably did not accomplish more than one-fifth of what the RAF was able to achieve with its greater bomb capacity and heavier night raids. In its first year of operations, for example, the U. S. Eighth Air Force dropped about 15,000 tons of bombs on enemy-occupied Europe, while the RAF dropped 136,000 tons.

In 1942, during the experimental phase of their operations, American bombers had concentrated on submarine bases and nearby targets in occupied France. By the summer of 1943 they were ready to penetrate deep into Germany. The Flying Fortress proved to be not only an efficient daylight bomber, despite its limited capacity compared to Liberators and British Lancasters, but it was also a much better fighter than any other heavy bomber. The unexpected fighting strength of the Flying Fortress contributed to the great tactical surprises achieved by our air forces.

The success of American daylight precision bombing persuaded the Combined Chiefs of Staff, meeting at Casablanca, to order a joint British and American air offensive against Germany. Their mission was "the progressive destruction and dislocation of the German military, industrial, and economic system and the undermining of the morale of the German people to the point where their capacity for armed resistance is fatally weakened." In the language of the fliers, Germany was to be "softened up" for invasion. Until an invasion could be mounted, an attempt was to be made to knock Germany out of the war by air power.

British and American bombers were to alternate, the RAF with area bombing at night and the U. S. AAF with target bombing by day, in a round-the-clock schedule. In this division of labor the RAF struck at the German cities to destroy their resources and morale, while the U. S. Eighth Air Force aimed its bombs at key factories in German war industry. The offensive began in the summer of 1943 with night flights of eight hundred British planes, followed by day flights of three hundred American bombers.

As summer weather enabled the Allied offensive to increase in power, the Nazi aircraft industry shifted its production from bombers to fighters, a sure sign that in the air Germany was being forced back from offensive to defensive. To forestall these aerial reinforcements the U. S. VIII Bomber Command in July attacked Focke-Wulf factories which were estimated to produce sixty-five per cent of the Nazi fighters. The airplane tire factories at Huls and ball-bearing plants at Schweinfurt were also heavily bombed. Flights over such vital areas sharply increased American losses. On their anniversary raids over Schweinfurt and Regensburg, the Eighth Air Force lost more planes in one day [*August 17, 1943*] than it had lost in the first six months of its flights over Europe. The air war threatened to become a war of attrition, but the Allies were bound to win it. One thousand four-engined heavy bombers alone came every month from American factories.

While planes based in England attacked the Axis day and

264

night from the west, Liberators of the U. S. Ninth and Twelfth Air Forces in North Africa hit targets all over Italy, the Messerschmitt factories near Vienna [*August 13, 1943*], and the Ploesti oilfields in Rumania [*August 1, 1943*]. The last mission was notable for the low-level bombing run of 162 Libya-based B-24s which flew a round trip of 2,400 miles. In the month of September, which saw the greatest air fights in Europe since the Battle of Britain, the U. S. Eighth Air Force alone dropped 8,190 tons of bombs, more than double the tonnage of any previous month.

To oppose the mounting British and American attack, the Nazis increased their concentrations of antiaircraft batteries and fighter squadrons in Germany. During the first half of 1943 they doubled the number of single-engine fighters in a vain effort to neutralize American daylight raiders. The necessity of defending their own country and its vital war plants robbed the Germans of air superiority on the Russian and Italian fronts. By the middle of 1943 it was estimated that the Nazis had 39,000 antiaircraft guns and over half their fighter-plane strength on the western air front. Perhaps a million men operated the guns, searchlights, and barrage balloons on the ground, and at least one in every ten civilians was busy all or part of the time with air-raid defense and rescue work.

Defensive tactics varied as the Germans experimented with novel means to break up the growing assault of Allied bombers. Nazi fighter-bombers, powered with twin engines, waited beyond the range of the bombers' guns and harried them with rockets. Messerschmitt 109s and Focke-Wulf 190s pounced upon any bomber which dropped out of formation.

Although the average loss of Flying Fortresses did not exceed four per cent of the planes engaged, they required fighter protection to avoid high casualties on some missions and to make smooth, uninterrupted bombing runs. Lightnings, Thunderbolts, and Mustangs by the hundreds escorted them, giving Allied bombers better protection than the Luftwaffe had ever furnished its own planes and targets. The American fighters often registered a four-to-one score against the Nazi rocket-carriers. Nothing the enemy did could stop the Allied bombers: through flak, fighters, aerial bombs, and rockets, the Fortresses, Liberators, and Lancasters flew relentlessly on to bomb their targets. Some of the Amercian planes. dubbed by their crews *Memphis Belle, Bat Outa Hell, The Sweater Girl,* and *Flak-Happy,* became as famous in the sky as warships of old on the seas.

From the first sorties flown by our Air Forces to the beginning of 1944, British and American bombers had dropped 330,000 tons of bombs on Germany alone; to this total the U. S. Eighth Air Force contributed 50,000 tons during 1943. On 64,000 sorties they lost almost one thousand heavy bombers and claimed the destruction of 4,100 Nazi planes. From the Mediterranean Theater, during 1943, the Northwest Africa Strategic Air Force and the U. S. Fifteenth Air Force dropped 74.000 tons of bombs on Axis targets in Africa, Sicily, Italy, the Balkans, and Germany. Still the German armies fought on.

By the early winter of 1944, however, it had become clear that, despite the weight of the Allied aerial attack, Germany could not be crushed by air power alone. It had sustained staggering damage but never more than could be repaired. The greatest weakness of the bombing attack was that the destruction of German war industry was temporary, not permanent; and while total production steadily declined, it was not stopped.

Reduction of German Air Power

Through the winter of 1943-44 Allied planes sought to destroy German air power so that the troops invading Europe would meet only the enemy ground forces. The German fighter planes were the quarry of every mission. "We realized," said General Arnold [*May 18, 1944*], "that we had to get them in the factories, in the modification centers, the depots, the flying fields and in the air." General Arnold estimated that after six months of heavy raids the combat strength of the Luftwaffe was undiminished. All its reserves were gone, however, and three-fourths of the enemy plane production was thought to be destroyed.

The winter campaign against the German aircraft industry began [*January 11, 1944*] with daylight raids on Oschersleben, Brunswick, Halberstadt, and other industrial centers at

266

a cost of fifty-nine American bombers. Despite this heavy loss, the attacks continued through the next six weeks [*January 11–February 22, 1944*] with the percentage of losses among bombers engaged dropping to 2.2. The decline in casualties was explained by three facts. First, the Luftwaffe suffered from cumulative strain, because of the alternating British and American raids night and day. As an example of the Germans' inability to sustain around-the-clock defenses, a night raid on Leipzig [*February 20, 1944*] cost the British seventy-nine aircraft. The next day, when Americans attacked, all but twenty-one bombers returned safely. Sometimes the ratio was reversed, the Americans losing more than the British; but the Germans, on 24-hour alert, suffered twice as much as either of them. Another factor in decreasing American losses was the marksmanship of our gunners, which was good to begin with and improved with practice. Most important, however, was the tremendous strength of each American mission, with fighters escorting bombers. American air power had been reinforced to a point where on any mission, eight hundred bombers could range over Europe in broad daylight with seven hundred fighters.

The climax of the winter campaign came in February, during a spell of clear weather called "Blitz Week," [*February 20–25, 1944*] when the Britain-based Eighth and the Italy-based Fifteenth Air Forces combined in a heavy assault on the Nazi aircraft factories at Leipzig, Brunswick, Hanover, Stuttgart, Schweinfurt, Regensburg, and other cities. Against factories producing two-thirds of the German fighter planes, the Americans made 3,800 bomber and 4,300 fighter sorties in one week, cutting enemy production in half for at least the next month. Nazi losses in the air were also heavy. During the whole month of February it was estimated that nine hundred enemy fighters were shot down on raids which cost 250 American bombers.

Berlin was a special target because of its importance as an industrial city, and the enemy defended it heavily with fighter planes. The RAF had started the aerial Battle of Berlin [*November 18, 1943–February 15, 1944*], dropping over twenty thousand tons of bombs on the city, destroying or damaging 326 factories, and losing nearly five hundred

267

bombers. The Americans took over the attack on Berlin in March 1944, with nine heavy daylight raids in which they shot down 524 planes and lost 242 bombers. These raids were made in great force. On one mission, for example [*March 8, 1944*], over two thousand American planes, divided between bombers and fighters, dropped 350,000 incendiary and 10,-000 demolition bombs. In the course of six raids it was estimated that seventy-four vital German war plants were damaged or destroyed. Berlin became a ruined city when nearly half of its central area was burned out.

The first phase of the strategic bombing of Germany [*February 20–March 9, 1944*] ended with the intensive operations from Blitz Week through the March raids on Berlin. During these two weeks the U. S. Eighth and Fifteenth Air Forces, comprising eighty thousand flying men, the equivalent of eight mechanized divisions, penetrated deep into enemy country. They dropped over seventeen thousand tons of bombs on industrial targets, shot down a thousand enemy planes, losing 414 bombers, 121 fighters, and more than four thousand men, probably half of whom parachuted to earth and were taken prisoners. They bombed single-engine fighter factories at Leipzig, Oschersleben, Regensburg, and Steyr; twin-engine fighter factories at Brunswick, Gotha, and Furth; bomber plants in Bernburg, Rostock, and Halberstadt; and ball-bearing shops at Schweinfurt and Stuttgart. It was believed that German fighter production had been cut, at least temporarily, by two-thirds since the beginning of 1944, and the output of bombers by one-third.

Pre-Invasion Assault

The fury of the Allied strategic bombing of Europe increased during April and May in preparation for the invasion of France. During April, British and American planes broke all bombing records, dropping 81,000 tons of incendiaries and high explosives on German-held Europe. The U. S. Eighth and Fifteenth Air Forces, carrying over half this weight of bombs, destroyed 1,282 enemy planes, and lost 537 bombers. In May, when the British and Americans together pounded enemy supply with 118,000 tons of bombs, the Americans dropped 63,000 tons and destroyed 1,200 German planes.

268

losing 481 bombers and 235 fighters. There was a growing contrast between the large number of Nazi planes shot down and the declining number of American aircraft which were lost. Fighters escorting our bombers reported that in May they were meeting only half the force of enemy fighters encountered in the winter months. It was evident that the strength of the Luftwaffe had been seriously reduced.

Tactical Preparation for the Invasion

Besides the strategic bombing to reduce air power and weaken industries in Germany, it was necessary to undertake tactical bombing in preparation for the invasion, to destroy enemy lines of communication and supply in the assault area. To assist the light and medium bombers of the U. S. Eighth Air Force in this work, the Ninth Air Force was transferred from the Mediterranean to British bases. These two air forces, the Eighth under Lieutenant General James H. Doolittle and the Ninth under Lieutenant General Lewis H. Brereton, started the tactical bombing of railroads and bridges from Germany into France during April. Thirty-four railways yards were wrecked.

The first full phase of tactical bombing, beginning a month before D-day, was directed against the bridges across the Seine River from Paris northwest to the English Channel. This phase of the attack was the special mission of the Ninth Air Force, which used Marauders, Havocs, and Thunderbolts to knock out twenty-three of the largest bridges in thirty-five days. Without these crossings the Seine was a barrier dividing northern France and seriously delaying the reinforcement of German troops west of the river.

Bombing in the second phase was aimed at the bridges and choke points in the gap between Paris and Orléans, and particularly at the bridges across the Loire River, which were all destroyed by the middle of June. The Eighth Air Force joined the Ninth in this work, and all heavy bombers were pressed into service. Even Mustang and Lightning fighters were fitted out with thousand-pound bombs. They bombed and strafed traffic on the roads in the seventy-mile corridor between the Seine and Loire, isolating Normandy and Brittany from the rest of France.

The third phase began with D-day and belongs with the story of the Allied landings in Normandy. The invasion had been prepared by both strategic and tactical bombing: the former spread confusion and destruction through the German zone of the interior and neutralized German air power, while the latter upset enemy supply lines into France, choked up traffic in the French theater of operations, and sealed off Normandy and Brittany for assault.

30. THE RUSSIAN OFFENSIVES

During the spring of 1944, the Russians prepared to mount stronger offensives than ever before, regrouping armies, extending railroads, and bringing up to the Eastern Front vast quantities of supplies and munitions. According to reports, Germany and her satellites had over 270 divisions holding this front, of which 200 were German, 28 Rumanian, 20 Hungarian, and 15 Finnish, all grouped in nine armies. Ready to engage them were Soviet forces of more than 300 divisions, grouped in ten armies from the Gulf of Finland to the Black Sea.

Knocking Finland Out of the War

The Russians began their summer operations with a campaign on the Leningrad front to knock Finland out of the war. Throughout the war six German and fifteen Finnish divisions in this sector had maintained a tenacious grip on the coveted territory of Karelia, only twenty miles above Leningrad. The Russians, attacking in great force with overpowering artillery [June 10, 1944], drove the Finns back along the northern shore of the Gulf of Finland to the old Mannerheim Line. This line, no longer as strong as in 1940, was quickly penetrated [June 18, 1944]. With the capture of Viipuri (Viborg) [June 20, 1944], some twenty-five miles beyond, however, the Russians came to a region of marshes and lakes easily defended by the Finns, who threw back a Soviet amphibious expedition across Viipuri Bay [July 1–7, 1944].

Meanwhile, the Russians launched another drive to the

270

east [*June 21, 1944*], in the Aunus Isthmus, and swept forward more than 150 miles between Lakes Ladoga and Onega. Still another drive farther north freed the ship canal from Leningrad to the White Sea. These two offensives met with stubborn Finnish resistance but made far greater progress than the one in Karelia.

Under steady pressure from the Russian forces, Finland finally slipped out of the German noose and concluded an armistice with the Soviet Union and Great Britain. The Finns had rejected Russian peace terms in the spring of 1944 [*March 8, April 19, 1944*]. By summer they were isolated and weak. The United States had broken off diplomatic relations with Finland [*June 30, 1944*] because she had "entered into a hard and fast military partnership with Nazi Germany." Germany could no longer give Finland any military support. Hence the Finns finally made an armistice [*September 4, 1944*] that guaranteed their political independence. Fighting broke out [*September 23, 1944*] between German and Finnish troops over the failure of the Germans to evacuate Finnish territory.

Strategy and Tactics

The three Russian drives against Finland were minor operations in the major offensives which the Red armies launched against Germany along the entire Eastern Front of 1,300 miles from the Gulf of Finland to the Black Sea. Even these vast offensives were but part of the concentric blows struck by the United States, Great Britain, and the Soviet Union. Before the Russians went into action in the summer of 1944, American and British armies had opened a second front in France and extended the third front, established ten months before in Italy. The drive to carry the war to German territory began on three sides of Hitler-held Europe. Victory on every one of these sides was necessary to liberate Europe.

The long Russian front was divided into four theaters, from which the Red armies launched four major offensives in the summer of 1944. The Baltic front extended from the Gulf of Finland south to Vitebsk, where it joined two White Russian fronts, separated by the Pripet Marshes but converging on Poland; in the far south the Rumanian front ran west of the Dniester River to the Black Sea.

It was on the southern (White Russian) front that the Red Army had advanced farthest towards Poland and Rumania in the late winter and early spring of 1944. Here across the flat, open country below the Pripet Marshes the Germans evidently expected them to open their summer offensive. All through the spring German planes bombed supply and communication lines in the south of Russia and massed their reserves to meet the expected attack. The Russians surprised the Germans by striking in the north, and then it was nearly three weeks before Axis reserves could be brought north to stem the Russian drive. Meanwhile the Red Army had broken down the enemy's defenses.

Then, with the flexibility which had characterized earlier Russian offensives, the Red armies went into action against the now vulnerable southern front. Their strategic policy was literally to follow the line of least resistance, and their ability to shift the attack wherever the enemy was weakest arose from their great superiority in men and matériel. With overwhelming strength in artillery and tactical bombing planes, the Russians laid down rolling barrages of shells and bombs to open every offensive. They had learned in 1943 the telling effect of massive fire power, and used it in 1944 to blast enemy strongpoints.

By summer the Red armies were so completely mechanized they advanced with the same speed which the Germans had displayed when they introduced blitzkrieg to the world. More remarkable was the fact that although their advance averaged a mile an hour, day and night, in the first nine days of the summer offensives, their supply kept pace with the lengthening lines. Such speed was due in part to 300,000 American Lend-Lease trucks which kept rolling forward with the tanks and mechanized artillery.

The tactics with which the Russians drove west on all fronts took two forms. In one, a pincers movement, two armies converged on a strongpoint. The other was a more elaborate movement in which each army advanced in three elements. The first made a frontal assault on a strongpoint; the second outflanked and encircled the strongpoint; and the

272

third took advantage of the second's advance and pressed forward as rapidly as possible, either to outflank another enemy position or to cut off the retreat of forces falling back from the first point of attack. Thus each army was in effect a hammer, a sickle, and a scythe, pounding and cutting the enemy to pieces. The Germans gave ground to avoid an encirclement comparable to the one they suffered at Stalingrad; but they fell back so slowly, hanging on to most positions as long as they could and leaving behind heavy-footed infantry for rear guards, that as a result many divisions were cut up, captured, or destroyed.

Drive to the Baltic

The Russian summer offensives opened as two Red armies joined in a pincers attack on Vitebsk [*June 22, 1944*], the hinge of the Baltic and northern White Russian fronts, which was held by five German divisions. The city was outflanked by the Russians, who broke through the fortified zone in the south and repulsed two German reserve divisions rushed forward to prevent encirclement of the city. As the larger part of the German garrison evacuated Vitebsk [*June 24, 1944*], the Russians caught them in the rear at the Dvina River, and after a battle lasting two days [*June 26–27, 1944*] reported that 20,000 enemy troops were killed and 10,000 captured.

The Russian attack now swung north against the Baltic front in an effort to trap the thirty divisions which the Germans were believed to have in the former states of Lithuania, Latvia, and Estonia. To perform this mission, three Red armies took up the offensive, one after the other, from south to north on the Baltic front. The First Baltic Army, having outflanked Vitebsk on the north, crossed the Berezina River under German counterattacks, bypassed and captured the strongpoint of Polotsk [*July 4, 1944*], guarding the Baltic front, and turned northwest towards Dvinsk and Riga, advancing at the rate of three miles a day. They slowed down, however, as they entered a difficult country of lakes and swamps and met strong German reinforcements.

Then the Second Baltic Army launched an offensive [*July 11, 1944*] farther north into Latvia. It finally reached the

273

Baltic Sea west of Riga [*August 1, 1944*] and threatened to cut off the enemy forces to the north, but sustained German counterattacks reopened a narrow corridor near the coast. Here the Germans were hard-pressed by the Third Baltic Army, which swung into action last, broke through enemy defenses below Pskov, captured this strongpoint, and pushed into Estonia [*July 22, 1944*]. Throughout the Baltic there was hard, confused fighting. Although the German forces in this theater were not entirely isolated, they were divided into two groups by the Russian thrust toward Riga, and their bases in East Prussia were dangerously exposed by the advance of other Red armies farther south.

Drive to East Prussia and Warsaw

While the Russians on the Baltic front were drawing their nets around the enemy, three Red armies on the north White Russian front rolled into action from Vitebsk south to the Pripet Marshes and drove forward through Poland [*June 22, 23, 25, 1944*]. East Prussia was the goal of one army, the northernmost or Third White Russian under General Ivan D. Chernyakovsky; Warsaw, the capital of Poland, was the objective of the other two. All three armies cooperated at the start of the summer offensive in outflanking the strongpoints on the main railroad leading to Warsaw—Orsha, Borisov, and Minsk [*June 27, July 1, 3, 1944*]. In addition, elements of each army swung left or right to the army alongside. to envelop the remaining strongpoints on the White Russian front. Vitebsk, Mogilev, and Bobruisk fell in turn during the first ten days of the summer advance [*June 26, 28, July 1, 1944*].

The Russians won the initial phase of this offensive at two decisive points. Chernyakovsky's northern forces, after outflanking Vitebsk, swept south and broke through the German defenses [*July 1, 1944*] on a front of sixty miles above Borisov and Minsk, compelling the enemy to evacuate these cities. The Germans east of Minsk fell back, hoping to catch the advancing Russians on the flank. Instead they were caught and badly cut up by the other White Russian armies. one pounding their front, another their rear [*July 1–6, 1944*]. Because the southernmost of these armies, the First White

274

Russian under Marshal Konstantin Rokossovsky, was largely motorized, it had been able to sweep forward forty miles in two days [*June 25-26, 1944*] at the start of the offensive, and after the battle near Minsk it drove west to capture Baranovichi [*July 8, 1944*] and upset the enemy on his second line of defense.

In the second phase of the summer campaign the Germans brought up reserves [*July 4-5, 1944*] from the inactive front below the Pripet Marshes to reinforce the line from Vilna through Baranovichi to Pinsk. But the center of this line had been cut by Rokossovsky's earlier drive, and the northern anchor at Vilna fell to Chernyakovsky's army [*July 13, 1944*], as it advanced from Minsk toward East Prussia. While Rokossovsky cleaned up pockets of the enemy in the Pripet Marshes, the Germans fell back to the last line of resistance on White Russian soil [*July 14-18, 1944*], from the Bug River north through Bialystok and Grodno to Kaunas. This line crumbled as had the other two, because of the swift Russian advance upon both ends. Grodno fell in the north [*July 16, 1944*], outflanked by Chernyakovsky, and in the south Rokossovsky swept forward to the Bug above Brest-Litovsk [*July 18, 1944*]. Stiff resistance at this point slowed down his advance on Warsaw.

All the German forces on the Polish front covering Warsaw were menaced by a new offensive, the third major drive of the summer, from the front south of the Pripet Marshes. Shortly after the Germans withdrew their reserves from this area, evacuating Kowel, two Russian armies under Marshal Ivan S. Konev leaped to the attack on a front of one hundred miles, crossed the Bug River, and drove northwest toward the Vistula below Warsaw [*July 14, 1944*]. They split the German forces in the south of Poland by encircling Lwow and capturing Lublin [*July 25, 1944*]. In the face of this threat to turn their entire right flank north of the Bug, the Germans fell back on Warsaw and East Prussia. Rokossovsky took Brest-Litovsk [*July 28, 1944*] and advanced to the north of Warsaw, bringing the suburbs of the city under fire of his artillery. At the same time [*August 17, 1944*] Chernyakovsky arrived at the borders of East Prussia. Konev's armies in the south had meanwhile diverged, one turning southwest to capture two thousand oil wells in Polish Galicia [*August 7, 1944*] the other moving west and almost reaching Krakow after it had shattered the German defenses on the Vistula River [*August 4, 1944*]. This breakthrough was the last great advance of the Russians in Poland for the remaining three weeks of August. All along the line from East Prussia through Warsaw to the Krakow front the Germans, reinforced by reserves from within Germany, launched strong counterattacks.

In the first month of the summer offensive on the Eastern front [*June 22–July 23, 1944*] six Russian armies had moved toward the Baltic Sea and into Poland an average distance of two hundred miles. During this advance Moscow reported that 381,410 enemy soldiers were killed on the Baltic, White Russian, and Polish fronts. On the White Russian and Polish fronts alone, military prisoners numbered 150,231 Germans, including twenty-two generals. Estimates of the number of enemy divisions destroyed during the first ten days of the offensive ranged from fifteen to twenty-two, and many additional units were cut up in the weeks that followed. During the first month of the offensive the Russians reported the capture of 631 aircraft, 2,635 tanks and self-propelled guns, 8,602 field guns, and 57,152 trucks.

Of such losses, and of all the earlier casualties which the Germans suffered during three years of war in Russia, Prime Minister Churchill said [*August 2, 1944*]: "It is the Russian Army that has done the main work of tearing the guts out of the German Army. In the air and on the ocean and seas we can maintain ourselves, but there was no force in the world which could have been called into being except after several more years that would have been able to maul and break the German Army and subject it to such terrible slaughter and manhandling as has fallen upon the Germans by the Russian Soviet armies."

Collapse of the Balkans

The drives at the northern end of the Russian line had not yet stirred the southernmost front, from the Carpathian Mountains to the Black Sea, into activity. The signal for the launching of a new Russian offensive on this front came

276

as the advance on other fronts lost momentum through enemy resistance and inevitable delays in moving forward supplies. While the northern armies repulsed German counterattacks [*August 13–19, 1944*] in the Baltic, along the borders of East Prussia, and in front of Warsaw and Krakow, two Red armies under Generals Malinovsky and Tolbukhin took the offensive [*August 20, 1944*] around Jassy and farther east in Bessarabia. Their objective was to knock Rumania out of the war.

Jassy fell to a pincers movement which encircled twelve enemy divisions [*August 25, 1944*]. Then the Russians broke through Rumanian defenses and reached the Danube River on a front of eighty-five miles, capturing Constanza, the Black Sea port at the mouth of the Danube [*August 29, 1944*]. They claimed that 205,000 Axis troops were killed or captured in the first week of the breakthrough [*August 20–26, 1944*]. This blow compelled Rumania, long a reluctant partner of Germany, to change sides overnight. Young King Michael ousted Marshal Antonescu, the Prime Minister [*August 23, 1944*], and ordered the Rumanians to turn upon the Nazis and above all, to fight Hungary in order to regain Transylvania.

The collapse of Rumania, with Russian forces rushing through the Galati Gap [*August 30–31, 1944*] to seize the Ploesti oil fields and occupy Bucharest, turned the whole eastern front of the Axis, which had been anchored on the Black Sea, and threatened to cut off fifteen German divisions in the Balkans. The capture of Ploesti, the last natural source of oil left to Germany, was no longer of great strategic importance, because the Mediterranean Allied Air Forces, according to General Eaker, had destroyed three-quarters of its production in a year of bombing raids from Africa and Italy.

As Russian forces swept through Rumania to the southern frontier, the adjoining country of Bulgaria showed signs of deserting the Axis camp. Yet the Bulgars were content to declare their "neutrality" and rejected the Russian demand that they enter the war against Germany, a necessity if the German troops stationed in the lower Balkans were to be captured. Impatient of delay, Russia declared war on Bulgaria

[*September 5, 1944*], and the Bulgars at once turned upon Hitler and joined the war against him.

The Russian penetration of the Balkans deprived Hitler of all his allies except Hungary and opened the southern flank of Germany to the threat of invasion through Hungary, Austria, and Czechoslavakia. Russian forces in Rumania pushed west to the Iron Gate leading into Yugoslavia, where for more than a year the Partisan guerrillas under Marshal Tito had been holding down 125,000 Axis troops. With troops in Greece and the Ægean Islands, Germany could only try to retain control of escape routes through Yugoslavia, parts of which had always been in a state of siege. As the Russians moved toward a junction with Tito's guerrillas, the liberation of the entire Balkan Peninsula was in sight.

31. STRATEGIC ADVANCE TOWARD JAPAN

The American offensive in the Central Pacific entered a new stage in the summer of 1944 with the conquest of Saipan and Tinian, and the reconquest of Guam. These islands, belonging to the Marianas group, were strong Japanese bases about fifteen hundred air miles south of Tokyo and east of the Philippines. With the penetration of the southern Marianas, American naval forces entered the inner-oceanic defenses of Japan and won possession of advanced air and naval bases for carrying the offensive forward both to the Philippines and Japan. The Japanese were thrown back on the strategic and tactical defensive everywhere, except in China and Burma, by the overwhelming superiority of the American power in the Pacific. The U. S. Navy, now five times stronger than the Japanese, could challenge them with planes and ships even in the far Pacific. The attack on Saipan was such a challenge; it led to the First Battle of the Philippine Sea, which cost the Japanese their best naval air pilots and much of their carrier strength.

First Battle of the Philippine Sea

The U. S. naval task forces which arrived off Saipan were large enough to engage the entire Japanese Navy if it chose

278

to give battle. Admiral Raymond A. Spruance was in top command, with carrier fleets operating under Admirals Mitscher, Clark, Ragsdale and Connolly. Admiral Turner commanded the amphibious forces. Planes from the carriers bombed Saipan, Tinian, and Guam, in the southern Marianas, for several days [*June 11–14, 1944*]. Japanese planes from an approaching fleet counterattacked, and a great aerial battle ensued [*June 19, 1944*] in which the enemy lost 402 aircraft and the Americans 27. Three of our ships, one battleship and two carriers, were slightly damaged. The Japanese carriers were apparently stripped of their planes in the greatest aerial victory at sea, and ships of Admiral Spruance's command chased them halfway to the Philippines [*June 20, 1944*]. American planes located the escaping fleet and, by admission of the Japanese after the war, sank three carriers and two tankers; in addition, they damaged three carriers, one battleship, three cruisers, three destroyers and another tanker. The enemy ships, fleeing westward in the darkness, left the Americans in undisputed control of the waters around the Marianas. The First Battle of the Philippine Sea, like the Battles of the Coral Sea and Midway, was fought entirely by carrier planes, and although the warships were the objects of attack, they did not exchange shots.

I. BATTLE OF SAIPAN: OPERATION FORAGER

Before the naval battle, transports had arrived with the invasion forces which were to land on the lower west coast of Saipan [*June 15, 1944*]. These forces consisted of the 2nd and 4th Marine Divisions under Lieutenant General Holland M. Smith, and the 27th Infantry Division under Major General Ralph C. Smith, with the former in command. Troops stormed ashore after dawn in the face of artillery and mortar fire so strong that it was necessary to call on planes and warships for additional support. By noon, however, the Marines had secured two shallow beachheads, each two miles long, north and south of Charan-Kanoa. In the next two days they repulsed strong enemy tank attacks and swung north almost to Garapan. The 27th Division wheeled south to capture the Aslito air strip [*June 19, 1944*], which Seabees at once prepared for the use of our own planes.

Although Saipan is a small island only seventeen miles long, the two Japanese divisions holding the northern half had the advantage of a mountain range in the center, fifteen hundred feet high and honeycombed with caves. There they posted mortar and machine-gun batteries for their main line of resistance. The American troops could not penetrate this line immediately by frontal assaults. With the help of air, naval, and artillery fire, they first had to clean out the caves, in which the Japanese burrowed so deep that nothing but a direct hit could destroy their positions. For eighteen days [*June 19–July 6, 1944*] the enemy troops resisted desperately until they were driven back to a pocket four miles from the northern end of Saipan. Then the Japanese made a strong but suicidal counterattack [*July 7, 1944*] which penetrated the American artillery line before it was checked. All the higher enemy officers fell in this assault, among them Vice Admiral Chuichi Nagumo, who had commanded a Japanese task force in the attack on Pearl Harbor. This final charge ended organized resistance [*July 9, 1944*].

The bitterness of the fighting for Saipan is reflected in the total of 15,053 American casualties, of whom 2,359 were killed, 11, 481 wounded, and 1,213 missing. The number of Japanese buried was 19,793. Over one thousand military prisoners were captured, more than in any previous battle with the Japanese. The loss of Saipan was so great a shock to Japan that the entire Cabinet of General Tojo resigned; at the same time, drastic changes were made in the Army and Navy high command for the better defense of Asia and the home islands [*July 19, 1944*].

Following the conquest of Saipan, the 2nd and 4th Marine Divisions under Major General Harry Schmidt, with Rear Admiral Harry W. Hill commanding the escort ships, invaded and won the smaller island of Tinian [*July 23, 1944*] which lies about two or three miles south of Saipan. The enemy put up little resistance as the Marines landed, covered by artillery on Saipan, but opposed them with tanks as they pushed inland to capture two air strips and storm the town of Tinian [*July 25, 1944*]. When the last remnants of the enemy were bottled up at Lalo Point in the south after nine days of fighting, all resistance ceased [*August 1, 1944*].

American casualties were relatively light: 195 killed, 1,526 wounded, and 24 missing. Japanese dead were counted at 5,745.

II. RECONQUEST OF GUAM

The reconquest of Guam, which had been seized by the Japanese the day after Pearl Harbor, was prepared by intensive air and naval bombardment. For seventeen days [*July 3–20, 1944*] carrier planes from the forces under Admiral Spruance pounded the island and, in addition, destroyed the garrison at Rota, which lies halfway between Saipan and Guam. For a week before the landings, battleships and cruisers bombarded the western coast of Guam.

The landing forces consisted of the 3rd Marine Division and the 1st Provisional Marine Brigade under Major General (now Lieutenant General) Roy S. Geiger, reinforced by elements of the 77th Infantry Division under Major General Andrew D. Bruce. They went ashore [*July 20, 1944*], meeting little resistance, on either side of Port Apra and within two days cut off the Orote Peninsula in the west. The enemy lost two thousand men in night counterattacks. Then the Americans drove across Guam to the eastern coast and reduced enemy opposition where it was strongest, in the mountainous north, by capturing Mount Barrigada [*August 3, 1944*]. Organized resistance came to an end after twenty days of fighting in which 14,067 Japanese were killed and the Americans suffered casualties of 1,226 killed, 5,765 wounded, and 329 missing.

The Japanese contested every yard of ground and died rather than surrender. In the Central Pacific, from the invasion of the Gilberts late in 1943 to the conquest of Guam ten months later, Admiral Nimitz reported [*August 13, 1944*] that 52,323 Japanese were killed. Only 3,022 were taken prisoners. The number of Americans who died was 5,903.

On July 19, 1945, the Navy announced that 13,932 Japanese had been killed on Tinian, Guam, and Saipan Islands since the islands were secured.

III. APPROACH TO THE PHILIPPINES

In the Southwest Pacific, General MacArthur's American

and Australian forces were making rapid strides on the long road toward the Philippine Islands. By the Spring of 1944 two Japanese armies had been neutralized and isolated in Bougainville, New Ireland, and New Britain by Allied advances up the Solomons-New Guinea ladder. A third Japanese army of some sixty-thousand still held the northern coast of New Guinea from Madang to the Moluccas. General MacArthur was now prepared to engage this army, whose defeat would give the Allies complete control of the island.

While American and Australian troops faced the enemy just before Madang, an amphibious expedition was prepared in the Admiralty Islands to land behind the enemy and cut his one line of communications, which ran along the coast because the interior of New Guinea was impassable jungle. Since the U. S. Navy controlled the sea, the enemy's only escape from envelopment would be flight into the mountains and jungles where there was hardly enough food to sustain the scanty native population and nothing to support a large army.

The U. S. 41st Division, escorted by a powerful American fleet, with carrier planes destroying one hundred enemy aircraft and pounding their airfields [*April 21, 1944*], secured beachheads on a front of 175 miles along the north New Guinea coast. The landings were made [*April 22, 1944*] almost unopposed, at Tanahmerah Bay, Hollandia, and Aitape, and within four days all three airfields were in American hands. An Australian division, which landed near Madang, advanced eighty miles up the coast toward Wewak and Aitape in the course of a month and finally occupied Hansa Bay [*June 15, 1944*], capturing vast stores of enemy supplies. Meanwhile, the 41st Division mounted an amphibious expedition from Hollandia, captured less than a month before, and jumped 125 miles farther west to land at Sarmi [*May 17, 1944*] against little opposition. Then they crossed over to the island of Wakde off the New Guinea coast [*May 21, 1944*], and took an enemy airfield, killing 835 Japanese. This action marked the strategic end of the New Guinea campaign, begun at Buna in the fall of 1942, for the entire northern coast and its waters were now dominated by Allied troops, planes, and ships.

The Allied forces did not pause. With naval and air cover the 41st Division and the 34th Infantry Regiment of the 24th Division sailed two hundred miles west from Wakde and lanked on Biak [*May 27, 1944*], largest of the Dutch Schouten Islands, about nine hundred miles southeast of the Philippines. As they pushed inland to capture Mokmer, the first of three airfields which were their objectives, they ran into fierce Japanese resistance. The first tank engagement in the Southwest Pacific took place when Shermans repulsed enemy counterattacks [*May 29, 1944*] spearheaded by medium tanks. Allied troops poured into the beachhead and also landed on Owi and Wundi [*June 2,1944*], small islands to the south of Biak, in order to secure an air strip. Japanese attempts to reinforce their troops were frustrated when Mitchell bombers sank four enemy destroyers [*June 8, 1944*]. American forces finally captured the Mokmer airfield by outflanking it from the north, two columns advancing up the coast and another along an inland ridge [*June 17, 1944*]. Once the enemy was driven from Mokmer, the other two air strips fell into American hands and all organized resistance came to an end [*June 20, 1944*]. In another two weeks the Americans mopped up remnants of the enemy: altogether 3,268 Japanese were killed and fifteen taken prisoner on Biak.

About one hundred miles west of Biak lay Noemfoor Island, the next objective. For three weeks it was pounded by American bombers of the Far Eastern Air Force under Lieutenant General George C. Kenney. A merger [*June 25, 1944*] of the Fifth Air Force, which had operated in Australia and New Guinea, and the Thirteenth, from the Solomons and New Britain, had made a force strong enough to send 150 heavy bombers on a single mission. In a record assault [*July 1, 1944*] for the Southwest Pacific they dropped 230 tons of bombs on the enemy air base at Noemfoor. The 158th Regimental Combat Team landed the next day. Reinforced by paratroops of the 503rd Parachute Infantry Regiment they seized an air strip within three hours and captured the last airfield three days later, killing or capturing 871 of the enemy [*July 6, 1944*].

The Japanese Eighteenth Army, which had been isolated around Wewak in British New Guinea, attempted to break through the American lines east of Aitape [*July 11, 1944*]. When their frontal attack across the Driniumor River failed, they tried in vain to outflank the Americans [*July 18–23, 1944*]. Allied planes blasted their rear [*July 28, 1944*], while cruisers and destroyers came inshore to shell their positions. Then the Americans crossed the Driniumor below Aitape [*July 31, 1944*], and drove east along the coast, turned south to cut the enemy lines from Wewak, and finally split his forces into three groups [*August 2, 1944*]. It was estimated that the Japanese suffered eighteen thousand casualties before their effort to break out of encirclement was defeated.

In eleven weeks General MacArthur's forces had advanced well over eight hundred miles. By concentrating overwhelming power in ships, planes, and men in assaults on ports and airfields essential for enemy supply the Allies had cut the Japanese in New Guinea into isolated segments which would rot in the jungle. We had devised a technique for rapid penetration of Japanese defenses and were making giant strides toward the Philippines, now only eight hundred miles away. And the Philippines flank the China Sea, the life line between Tokyo and the stolen empire of the East Indies.

IV. THE ATTACK ON JAPANESE SUPPLY AND INDUSTRY

Destruction from the air of Japanese war plants and shipyards began a year after the aerial offensive against Germany was under way [*June 15, 1944*]. The delay in the strategic bombing of Japan resulted from the concentration of American air power over Europe and the lack of bases in Asia close to Japan. Outer Pacific defenses of the Japanese Empire, in New Britain, the Marshall, Caroline, and Marianas Islands had been blasted by U. S. Navy carrier planes through late 1943 and early 1944. Yet the Japanese homeland had seen American bombers only once, on Doolittle's famous raid of April 18, 1942.

For two and a half years after Pearl Harbor the greatest
284

damage to Japanese supply had been inflicted by American submarines. The "silent service," which operates in complete secrecy, penetrated the home waters of Japan and even took pictures of the mountain top of Fujiyama through their periscopes as they went about the stealthy business of cutting interior enemy supply lines. By September 1943, the late Frank Knox, Secretary of the Navy, estimated that Japan had lost one-third of her prewar merchant shipping, a total of more than 2,500,000 tons. By the summer of 1944, American submarines had sunk a total of 687 Japanese vessels and damaged 115. In the most successful months they destroyed 130,000 tons. The Japanese were forced to convoy supply vessels even off their own coasts, and with the increasing loss of tankers and large vessels, they began to use barges and smaller boats along the China coast. This reduction of ocean traffic, the only result our submarines could achieve in their war of attrition, did not, however, lessen Japanese war production.

The destruction of supply at its sources was the mission of a new U. S. Army Air Force, the Twentieth, which had been secretly organized and equipped with giant new bombers, B-29 Superfortresses. Under direct command of General Arnold in Washington, the Twentieth was the first global air force in history, an aerial battle fleet with bases in Asia, which could make any continent its theater of operations. The B-29, developed since 1939 from the B-17 and now put into mass production, had the greatest striking range of any bomber in the world. Able to fly round trips of thirty-six hundred miles, it was peculiarly suited to the specialized mission of bombing Japan from remote Chinese bases. Through the winter and spring of 1943-44 several hundred thousand Chinese laborers built airfields for the B-29. Supplies, gasoline, bombs, and planes were flown in over the difficult Himalaya Hump from India. The Superfortress was half again as big as the Flying Fortress, with a wing span of half a city block, a speed of over three hundred miles an hour, heavy armor and guns, and a potential bomb load greater over comparable ranges than the British Lancaster's eight tons.

The first force of these planes to strike at Japan came out

285

of the west on a night raid [*June 15–16, 1944*] and hurled their bombs down on the Yawata steel works, located in Kyushu, the southernmost of Japan's main islands. Four planes were lost, two in accidents, one to antiaircraft fire, and another for unknown reasons. Three weeks went by before the second raid [*July 7–8, 1944*], suggesting the difficulties of supplying Chinese air bases. Then the B-29s returned to Japan, bombing the Yawata steel works again, and the naval base at Sasebo. On this night raid there were no losses.

The range of bombing operations extended to Japanese war industries situated on the Asiatic mainland. B-29s struck targets at Anshan in Manchuria, and Tangku, the port for Tientsin in occupied China. This was the first daylight raid by Superfortresses, and two planes were lost [*July 29, 1944*]. On their fourth operation [*August 11, 1944*], two forces of B-29s, one flying from a Chinese base, the other from Southeast Asia, bombed widely separated Japanese industrial targets with incendiaries. They struck the Nagasaki area of Kyushu in the north, and in the south the large Pladju oil refinery at Palembang, Sumatra. Three planes failed to return; another came down in friendly territory. These four operations were the experimental beginning of the strategic bombing offensive against Japanese war industries all over Asia, a growing offensive carried on by mightier war planes than Germany had ever seen.

32. THE FIRST BLOWS IN ITALY

In the great offensive against Germany, it was logical for the Allies to strike their first blows from Italy, where British and American armies had fought hard all through the winter of 1944. Italy was never a "side show." The Mediterranean was the only European theater in which American and British troops engaged the enemy before the spring of 1944. Here some fifteen or more Allied divisions pinned down an enemy force estimated at twenty-five divisions, of which five contained the Allied beachhead at Anzio and twelve the southern front. The fighting in Italy was as tough as anywhere else in the world, for it fell largely to the infantry,

slugging their way through fortified enemy lines and storming or bypassing snow-topped mountains. Allied progress in
southern Italy had been slow because the mountainous terrain protected the enemy and made his delaying actions
count heavily.

The Spring Drive

After the assaults on Cassino failed and the Anzio beachhead troops were checked in the winter and early spring of
1944, the Allied forces regrouped for their part in the summer offensive [*March 26, 1944*]. The Fifth Army, including
the U. S. 85th, 88th, and 36th Infantry Divisions, transferred to the west coast along the Tyrrhenian Sea, the Anzio
garrison was reinforced, and the British Eighth Army, with
French and Polish units, came over from the Adriatic to
take the place of the Fifth around Cassino. With their forces
concentrated in the west and center, the Allies could exert
the strongest pressure toward Rome.

Marshal Albert Kesselring also regrouped his divisions in
preparation for the expected Allied offensive. His defenses
consisted of two mountain barriers, strongly fortified: the
Gustav Line along the Garigliano and Rapido rivers, with
Cassino as the main bastion; and behind it the so-called
Hitler Line from Terracina to Aquino. The Germans flooded
the Pontine Marshes [*May 3, 1944*] which lay between the
Allied forces on the Anzio and Cassino fronts; and British
fliers, to protect their flank on the Adriatic Sea, blasted the
dam of the Pescara River [*May 5, 1944*]. The Mediterranean Allied Air Force, flying 21,000 sorties through the
month of April, wrecked all the enemy railroad yards below Florence.

After heavy artillery and aerial preparation, the Eighth
and Fifth Armies launched a spring drive to destroy the
Nazi forces in Italy and to liberate Rome. [*May 11, 1944*].
Their plan, similar to the Anzio-Cassino pincers of the winter campaign, was to drive the enemy back against the Anzio
beachhead, from which the reinforced garrison would break
out to trap him below Rome. In the first week of fighting,
the Allied forces broke the Gustav Line and advanced twelve
miles to the Hitler Line. French troops under General Al-

phonse Juin pressed forward south [*May 14–16, 1944*] of the Liri River to Mount d'Oro and struck southwest to capture Mount Chiavica. Polish troops, commanded by General Wladyslaw Anders, cut in behind the mountain towering over Cassino and joined British spearheads in the encirclement of the town [*May 17, 1944*]. Cassino was captured, with fifteen hundred prisoners.

On the coast the Americans pushed forward from the Minturno along the Gulf of Gaeta. They captured Formio [*May 18, 1944*], and drove the Germans back over fifteen miles to Terracina, which fell [*May 24, 1944*] after a battle lasting three days. In the first two weeks of the offensive U. S. II Corps of the Fifth Army, comprising the 85th and 88th Divisions, the first all-Selective-Service outfits to fight in Europe, advanced sixty miles. They turned the enemy's right wing, and compelled him to abandon his mountain strongholds in the interior.

Liberation of Rome

The Fifth Army opened the roads to Rome, the Appian Way and the Casilina Way, as it fought up the Tyrrhenian coast from Terracina to join the troops on the Anzio beachhead, commanded by Major General (now Lieutenant General) Lucian K. Truscott, Jr., and crack the Nazi defenses in the Alban Hills. The Anzio garrison opened a drive on all sides of its perimeter while the Americans approached from the south [*May 23, 1944*]. There was bloody fighting at Cisterna, the strongpoint from which the German Fourteenth Army under General Mackensen had contained the beachhead. Cisterna was taken only after seven counterattacks made by Nazi tanks were repelled. Over one thousand American field guns had laid down a deadly fire on Cisterna. With its fall the Anzio and southern forces joined hands near Borgo Grappa, south of Cisterna [*May 25, 1944*].

The German Tenth Army, withdrawing from the southern front, might now be cut off if the two strongpoints covering its escape, Velletri and Valmontone, could be taken quickly. The Fourteenth Army, falling back from Cisterna, clung to these positions, reinforced by the phoenix-like Hermann Goering Division which had been routed in Tunisia, Sicily,

288

and at Salerno. Although a direct attack on Velletri failed [*May 31, 1944*], the town was nearly encircled when American infantry cut it off from Valmontone and stormed Mount Peschio to the north. Fighting down this mountain and up Faete, both extinct volcanoes about three thousand feet high, the Americans broke through the German defenses and captured Velletri and Valmontone [*June 2, 1944*]. Although the enemy had not been cut off, the roads to Rome lay open. On the 275th day of the Italian campaign, the Fifth Army advanced twenty-two miles and captured the Eternal City, first Axis capital to fall [*June 4, 1944*].

Rome was yielded, its historic monuments saved by the speed of the Allied advance, as the Nazis retreated north without fighting for the city. They had suffered sixty thousand casualties since the Allied offensive began; over twenty thousand prisoners were taken and five divisions were badly cut up. Field Marshal Kesselring's Tenth and Fourteenth Armies, objective of the Battle of Italy, were not entirely destroyed, but they were in headlong retreat after incurring heavy losses. "One of Kesselring's two armies," said General Clark, "will never fight again." The Americans did not stop to celebrate their triumphal entry into Rome. All through a winter of grim fighting at Cassino and Anzio they had struggled to reach this city. Now they were in hot pursuit of the stubborn enemy.

Allied Advance to the Arno

Not since their retreat in the last days at Tunisia had the Nazis forces fallen back in such haste. Yet this time they maintained good order, fought persistent delaying actions, mined all the roads heavily, and reached the Gothic Line. This natural defensive barrier ran across Italy from Pisa to Rimini along the heights above the Arno River, about 150 miles north of Rome. During all of June and July the Allied forces fought their way to the Arno, delayed by lengthening supply lines and dogged enemy resistance. The Germans lost heavily in supplies, weapons, and transport as they fell back under continuous attack by Allied planes. The Mediterranean Allied Air Force flew 50,800 sorties during the month of June, destroying 480 Axis planes and losing 374.

289

In its advances from Rome to the Arno, the Fifth Army made the most rapid progress along the Tyrrhenian coast to Leghorn and Pisa. At the outset they pressed forward at the rate of seven miles a day. But the roads were so thickly strewn with mines and demolitions were so thorough that the troops avoided them and traveled through the hills for greater speed. Meanwhile, a French amphibious force landed on the island of Elba and captured a German garrison of 1,800 men [*June 17–19, 1944*]. The Fifth Army advanced to Cecina [*July 2, 1944*], where enemy resistance stiffened. American and French troops occupied Siena [*July 3, 1944*]. Then they pushed beyond Volterra, the mountain town guarding Leghorn fifteen miles away, and ran into the hardest fight since the breakthrough below Rome [*July 9, 1944*]. Leghorn was a seaport strongly defended by the Germans. The Americans captured the city [*July 19, 1944*] by outflanking it on the east and laying down heavy artillery fire from the surrounding heights. The day Leghorn fell, Polish troops on the Adriatic coast captured Ancona. These two seaports improved Allied supply when the heavy demolitions of the Germans were repaired three weeks later. As the enemy drew back from Leghorn across the Arno [*July 23, 1944*], American patrols fought their way into the southern part of Pisa, where a long duel [*July 31–September 2, 1944*] ensued between American and German heavy artillery, the latter commanding the city from the northern banks of the Arno.

While the Fifth Army was moving forward one hundred miles along the Tyrrhenian coast [*June 5–18, 1944*], the Polish Corps on the Adriatic coast advanced fifty miles. The British Eighth Army in the center had the hardest time of all. Their advance was retarded by strong enemy positions in the hills of Umbria and Tuscany [*June 19, 1944*]. After capturing Perugia, ninety miles north of Rome, the British found the last third of the distance to Florence the slowest. They made repeated attacks [*June 28–July 3, 1944*] to pass both sides of Lake Trasimeno and finally broke through into Arezzo [*July 16, 1944*], the fall of which opened the way to Florence. The Germans gave up this city reluctantly [*July 29, 1944*], defending it from hills to the south, in the streets, and across the Arno, where they left only one bridge standing. After British patrols entered Florence [*August 4, 1944*], the Eighth Army came up in force to outflank pockets of resistance in the northern half of the city [*August 10, 1944*]. The Germans fell back here, as from Pisa, to the Gothic Line.

33. THE GREAT INVASION: OPERATION OVERLORD

The great invasion of Western Europe, planned to liberate France, Belgium, and Holland, and finally to drive the Nazis back into Germany, came late in the spring of 1944. It was the supreme test of the combined arms of the United States and the British Empire, the largest and most dangerous military operation ever undertaken by their forces. Hitler boasted that all Europe was a Fascist fortress. His engineers claimed that the Atlantic coast was an impregnable wall, the beaches mined, the cliffs girded with artillery, and every landing place covered by batteries of guns emplaced in concrete fortifications.

In the face of defenses so formidable, millions of people throughout the world held their breath in fear or hope as the time for invasion approached. They remembered the last time an assault was made on this fortified coast, by a force of five thousand Canadian and British troops raiding Dieppe [*August 19, 1942*], when a few hours of fighting cost them 3,350 casualties. Since then, nearly two years before, British and American troops had made four successful landings in the Mediterranean, on the coasts of North Africa and Sicily, at the beaches of Salerno and Anzio, each assault a perilous one but a triumph of training, supply, command, and courage. Nowhere in the Mediterranean, however, did the Nazis have such strong defenses as they had prepared along the Atlantic coast of Europe. Behind these defenses, from the Netherlands to the south of France, waited sixty or more enemy divisions, ready to concentrate against the Allied armies, which could land only a few regiments at a time, and drive them back into the sea.

Strong as the Nazis appeared, they proved to be too weak to repulse the great invasion. Their ground forces were divided among three fronts, the largest number fighting against

291

Russia, a smaller group trying to hold Italy and the Balkans, and the rest standing guard over all of Western Europe. Everywhere they had lost control of the air and coastal waters. A year of strategic bombing had crippled the war industries of Germany and worn down the Luftwaffe. Two months of tactical bombing destroyed main railroads and bridges in the west of Europe and hindered the concentration of enemy forces against the invading armies.

Massed in the British Isles were two million or more troops from the Empire and the United States, all well trained and equipped. To supply them, over sixteen million tons of matériel were shipped from the United States to Britain in the year preceding the invasion, twice the total tonnage received by American forces in France during the last war. If the Allies could seize a beachhead in Western Europe, they would eventually overwhelm the enemy with superior numbers and fire power. The exact date for D-day no one knew except Allied high command, but everybody realized that upon the success of the invasion depended the defeat of Fascism in Europe.

Massing the Troops Overseas

In 1944 the United States was ready to enter what Secretary Stimson called [*June 1, 1944*] "the period of decisive action." For America it was the third year of war; for Germany, the fifth. Troops were now massed abroad in sufficient force, and with enough equipment, to hit the Nazis hard in Europe. There were 5,223,000 Americans stationed abroad or at sea; of this number, over 3,500,000 were soldiers, the rest sailors or marines, representing almost half the total manpower in each service. Protected supply lines to these forces, on duty in every continent and ocean of the world, stretched over 56,000 miles of land and water. In the United States, preparing to go overseas, the Army had 1,300,000 men, the Navy, 900,000. The maximum fighting force of the United States at last was marshalled to engage the enemy.

This vast force had been deployed in three phases according to a pattern designed by the Joint Chiefs of Staff in Washington. They planned the over-all size of the American Army, determined the equipment it required, and allocated the shipping necessary to take men and supplies overseas. These plans were drawn up and continually revised to meet changing strategic needs. But there were three goals of grand strategy which never changed throughout the war, and they shaped the three phases in which the fighting power of the United States was deployed overseas. It was necessary first to hold the enemy, then to drive him back from the offensive to the defensive, and finally to take the offensive and defeat him.

In the first phase, extending through 1942, men and supplies were hurriedly transported overseas to "plug the line" of defense which had to be held if the Axis was to be prevented from overrunning the Middle East and the Pacific. Supply lines were established to Australia and Africa, bases developed in the Pacific and Middle East, and the hard-pressed fronts in these theaters were reinforced.

In the second phase, extending roughly from late in 1942 through most of 1943, ground and air forces crossed the Atlantic and Pacific to crack the enemy's outer defenses. The Germans were driven back to Italy from Africa and Sicily, and Italy was knocked out of the war. The Japanese defenses were penetrated in the Solomon, Gilbert, and Marshall Islands. While combat divisions went abroad and into battle in both these phases, the bulk of the ground troops remained in the United States to finish their training. Hence the majority of men going overseas in 1942 and early in 1943 belonged to the Army Air and Service Forces, which stationed nearly half their personnel abroad. It was their mission to prepare the way for ground troops and to launch the offensive from the air. By the middle of 1943 almost one and a half million Americans were engaged in these tasks overseas.

They were joined in the following twelve months by two million men, the majority of whom were ground troops, prepared to enter the final phase of decisive battle in Europe. Through the winter and spring of 1944, great convoys of troops and supplies crossed the Atlantic to British ports. In May, when preparations for the invasion of France reached the climax, the Army Service Forces moved nearly four mil-

293

lion tons of cargo overseas, twice the total shipped abroad during the same month of the preceding year. To mount the invasion of Europe, American factories and shipyards speeded up their production through the winter and spring of 1944. In November 1943, landing craft were given top priority, but their construction lagged behind schedule until an all-out effort in the last two months before D-day met the need for tens of thousands of ships to launch the invasion. Heavy artillery for follow-up fire power was given priority in April and production of such weapons increased rapidly as American troops landed in France.

The American divisions in England, including some which had arrived in 1942 and others which had not arrived until 1944, rehearsed the invasion for months, first in the interior of the country and then along the coasts. They learned the hundreds of special tasks involved in an assault on a hostile, fortified coast. They perfected their communications, supply, and battle tactics, made "dry runs" and "wet runs," the latter in full cooperation with British and American naval forces, each man thinking it was the actual invasion. In the course of all these maneuvers the troops assigned to the invasion acquired confidence in themselves, their outfits, and their weapons. When they moved at last into the staging areas for embarkation, their morale was invincible.

I. ALLIED LANDINGS IN NORMANDY

D-day came on Tuesday, June 6, 1944. Allied battleships and cruisers opened fire on the northern coast of Normandy, at 0630. H-hour was at 0730. The landing of troops, originally scheduled for Monday, had been postponed at the last moment, because the worst June gales in forty years swept over the Channel. Thousands of ships loaded with men and guns waited in English ports for General Eisenhower's order to start the invasion. Before the great armada of landing ships reached the French coast in the early morning darkness of D-day, the enemy was under furious attack. From midnight the tactical air forces swept down on his defenses with a tornado of bombs, and thousands of airborne troops landed behind his lines.

294

Air Operations

Over eleven thousand Allied aircraft of all types covered the invading armies. From D-day to D plus 4 [*June 6–10, 1944*] they flew 32,500 sorties and dropped 27,000 tons of bombs. Enemy fighter planes offered little resistance, for the prolonged aerial offensive against Germany had almost driven them from the skies. In the first forty-eight hours of the invasion the Allied air forces shot down 176 enemy planes and lost 289, mostly to antiaircraft fire. Tactical bombing which preceded D-day undermined the enemy's coastal defenses and destroyed railroads and bridges across the Seine, making it difficult for the Germans to move troops and supplies in northern France. Not until D-day, however, was the Normandy coast singled out for the heaviest bombing. Consequently, the enemy, unable to guess where or at how many scattered points the Allied forces would land, suffered a tactical surprise.

On the eve of D-day, at midnight, one thousand British heavy bombers began to pound the French coast. At daylight an equal force of American bombers took over this mission. Half an hour before the landings, American medium and dive bombers concentrated on the Normandy coast. Because of stormy weather, which reduced the ceiling to one thousand feet, the Marauders went in "on the deck" and struck their targets from only nine hundred feet.

The skies were clouded with planes all the way from England to inland France. As the landing boats crossed the Channel in the dark hours of D-day, swarms of P-38 Lightnings covered them, and P-47 Thunderbolts flew ahead to strafe the beaches. In France medium and light bombers struck at railroads, motor roads, and supply dumps as far east as the Paris–Orléans gap between the rivers Seine and Loire. These aerial operations, intricately contrived and precisely executed, assured the Allied assault forces of good air cover.

The first troops to land in Normandy [*June 6, 1944*] were airborne. They crossed the enemy coast six minutes after midnight and parachuted to earth ten minutes later. In four hours the U. S. IX Troop Carrier Command, cooperating with the RAF, landed three divisions behind the German coastal defenses. Mosquito bombers had first neutralized inland antiaircraft batteries; then Pathfinder planes had marked the drop zones with flares. Paratroopers followed, seizing fields and setting up their own antiaircraft guns. Finally came the transport planes and gliders with airborne infantry. It was the largest and most efficient airborne operation in five years of war. The Allied forces landed exactly as planned and plane losses ran to less than three per cent of those suffered by the Germans in Crete.

The primary mission of these airborne units was to disorganize the enemy rear and establish the east and west sides of a perimeter to be formed by ground troops when they landed at the beachheads. In these tasks they were successful and soon made contact with the assault forces driving forward from the beaches to meet them. Landing nine miles inland near Caen, the British 6th Airborne Division seized the bridges across the Orne River and became the advance guard of the British Second Army on the eastern flank of the Allied beachheads. The American 82d and 101st Airborne Divisions covered the central (Omaha) and western (Utah) beachheads established by the American First Army. The 82d, dropped near Ste. Mère Église to protect the right flank, assisted the landing of the 4th Infantry Division by overwhelming German batteries which enfiladed the causeways over marshes which had to be crossed by these troops. The 101st was dropped farther east and later joined in linking at Carentan the central and western beachheads, divided by the Vire River.

Winning the Beachheads

The Allied armies crossed the English Chanel in an immense fleet of some four thousand boats. They were convoyed by eight hundred warships, two-thirds of them British, divided into two task forces. Mine sweepers cleared enemy coastal waters and marked out channels with buoys for the landing craft to follow. Over one hundred German submarines and flotillas of "E" torpedo boats were waiting in the Bay of Biscay, but none penetrated the Allied naval escort which sealed off one hundred miles of water across

296

the English Channel. At 0630, while more than one thousand American bombers were hurling down explosives on the Normandy coast, the naval bombardment began. Battleships, the American *Texas, Arkansas,* and *Nevada,* the British *Warspite, Nelson,* and *Rodney,* added their heavy fire to the barrage laid down for half an hour by cruisers and destroyers running close inshore. From midnight the air forces had dropped over ten thousand tons of bombs, and the warships fired over two thousand tons of shells. Behind this screen of fire the landing craft swarmed toward the beaches. As troops waded and climbed ashore, at 0730, both planes and warships shifted their fire to targets picked out by the assault forces.

The invaders landed on five beaches along a sixty-mile stretch of the Cotentin Peninsula, from east of Caen toward Montebourg in the west [*June 6, 1944*]. The British Second Army, landing in the eastern sector of the Allied beachhead, met little opposition at first. On the right the Canadian 3d Division penetrated seven miles inland and captured Bayeux [*June 7, 1944*] to cut the lateral road running east to Caen. On the left the British 6th Airborne Division reinforced by glider-borne tanks, clung to the bridges until the Germans swept them back. Marshal Rommel sent the 21st Panzer Division against them in an effort to roll up the Allied beachhead. Falling back from Caen, which was cut off from the beaches by an enemy roadblock at Douvres, the advance British elements joined their 7th Armored and 50th Infantry Divisions to halt the German tanks between Caen and Bayeux. In the course of four days [*June 7–11, 1944*] with assistance from the Canadians and the support of cruisers offshore and planes overhead, the Second Army drove inland as far as Tilly and joined its beachheads.

The American First Army established the central and western beachheads [*June 6, 1944*] on either side of the Vire River. To the west, on Utah Beach, VII Corps under Major General (now Lieutenant General) J. Lawton Collins, with the 4th Infantry Division in the vanguard, encountered light resistance and pushed inland over the marshes toward Carentan to make contact with the 82d Airborne Division. The fiercest struggle of the invasion was on the eastern side of the Vire River at the central beachhead. Here on Omaha Beach the V Corps under Major General (now Lieutenant General) Leonard T. Gerow stormed ashore with the 1st and 29th Infantry Divisions in the lead. Mines and underwater obstacles wrecked many landing craft. The troops who got ashore could advance only one hundred yards in several hours, for enemy batteries on the cliffs, secure from small naval guns, made a death trap of the beach until they were wiped out by bombers and a rain of shells from battleships offshore. The remaining elements of the 1st and 29th Divisions got ashore in the afternoon and seized the beachhead from a reinforced enemy division. "Only by guts, valor and extreme bravery," observed General Bradley, "were we able to make the landing a success."

From their beachheads on either side of the Vire River, the U. S. V and VII Corps fought inland along the marshes, captured Isigny, and after a battle lasting four days [*June 8–12, 1944*], joined their lines on high ground at Carentan. The 101st Airborne Division entered the town under a smoke screen and with strong artillery support. The capture of Carentan cut one of the two railroads running across Normandy to the port of Cherbourg and provided dry ground on which local air strips were soon established. Although a few fighter planes flying from an emergency field had participated in the battle the third day after invasion, it was not until D plus 9 that the fighters had enough local strips to operate in large numbers.

The joining of the Allied beachheads for eighty miles along the Normandy coast, and the penetration to a depth of twenty miles at Bayeux, the southernmost point, marked the end of the first two phases of the invasion. The landings were everywhere successful, although bitterly contested, and in the first five days of the invasion sixteen Allied divisions stormed ashore to meet the fourteen enemy divisions concentrated under General Rommel. Pushing inland and fanning out along the coast, they established a beachhead for the steady flow of men and supplies into the combat area.

Stormy weather twice interrupted the race to build up the Allied forces, even suspending seaborne reinforcements at one time. Not until they won the deepwater port of Cherbourg, first major objective of the invasion, did the Allies hope to get enough troops and supplies ashore to overwhelm the enemy. Yet, when the weather was clear, they continued to land men so rapidly on the beaches, averaging 37,500 a day and reaching a total strength of one million by D plus 20, that the fourteen enemy divisions opposing them at first could not long hold their ground. From the Russians came full recognition of the victorious start of the Allied invasion. "The history of wars," said Marshal Stalin [*June 13, 1944*], "does not know any such undertaking so broad in conception and so grandiose in its scale and so masterly in execution."

The Robot-Bomb Attack

Shortly after Allied forces landed in Normandy, the Nazis attacked southern England [*June 15, 1944*] with a "secret weapon" by which Hitler hoped to demoralize the civilian population and to postpone defeat. It was the robot or "buzz bomb." A miniature plane, with a wingspread of sixteen feet, jet-propelled, it was gyroscopically balanced, guided by a magnetic compass, and flew a level course. When its fuel was gone, the plane plunged to earth with a ton of high explosives. Because of great flying speed, four hundred miles an hour, only the newest planes, Tempests, Spitfires, and Mustangs, could overtake it. Most of the robots were launched in salvos from heavily camouflaged ramps along the Channel coast above Calais. Since it was impossible to aim the robots at a specific military target, a large city like London was their only effective destination.

This aerial barrage lasted for eighty days [*June 15–September 1, 1944*]. At its height, on cloudy days in June and July, the Nazis fired two hundred robots every twenty-four hours, but the bombs generally came spasmodically, day or night. At first casualties ran high: up to the beginning of September, 5,479 people were killed, chiefly in London, and 15,934 were wounded. A million people, one-fourth of whom were mothers with children, were evacuated from London to avoid higher casualties. The greatest damage was done to buildings. Windows were shattered at a considerable distance by the blast of the bombs, and flying glass cut many people. A large number of schools and hospitals were destroyed and altogether over a million homes suffered damage; the majority of them were in London.

The British were well prepared for this second Battle of London, so much more terrifying in its way than the experience of 1940 because the mechanical bombs struck at random, without human control, and destroyed everything in the immediate radius of their blast. Over a year before the attack began, British secret agents had reported to the Combined Chiefs of Staff that the Nazis were experimenting with a mysterious weapon, which was soon discovered by aerial reconnaissance [*May 1943*] to be some sort of rocket or flying bomb. When the Nazis built one hundred concrete launching stations along the French coast [*November 1943*], Allied planes completely destroyed them during a winter of intensive bombing. So great was the ruin that in March 1944, the Nazis set to work, building entirely new ramps, simpler, better camouflaged, with hidden storage depots. On these and previous sites, Allied bombers dropped a total of 100,000 tons of bombs, losing nearly 450 aircraft in the heavy flak which was encountered on their low bombing runs.

When, nevertheless, the robot attack began, the British improvised new air-raid defenses to meet it. The barrage balloons guarding London, increased to two thousand and fitted with extra cables, brought down almost fifteen per cent of the bombs reaching the outskirts of the city. In two days of mid-July over one thousand antiaircraft guns were moved from London and set up along the coast, where a clear view over the sea enabled the gunners finally to shoot down nearly three-quarters of the bombs flying over their stations. Twenty American antiaircraft batteries joined the British "shooting gallery" with 350 guns. Fighter pilots, both British and American, aided by radio-telephone spotters during the day and guided by a twenty-cent range finder at night, shot down nineteen hundred bombs. These combined defenses became so effective that nine out of every ten robots fired late in August 1944 were stopped and only one reached London. Altogether, about 8,000 V-1s (Vengeance Weapon One) were launched, of which 2,300 exploded in the English capital, where most of the fatal casualties occurred.

On September 8, 1944, the day after it was officially announced that the last V-1 robot bomb fell in England, the Germans introduced a new type of "vengeance weapon," the V-2. This was a stratosphere rocket with a warhead of about the same weight as the V-1 and a body 45 feet in length. Fired at an almost vertical position from bases on the Continent, these rockets reached tremendous altitudes and came to earth at a speed greater than that of sound. Their deep penetration before detonation limited the area of blast, but they were almost as deadly as the V-1. A total of 1,050 V-2 rockets reached England between September 8, 1944 and April 25, 1945, killing 2,754 persons and seriously injuring 6,523. Unlike the V-1 weapon, there was no immediate defense against the V-2 rocket. Its speed rendered all forms of fighter plane and antiaircraft interception impossible. The V-2 did not affect the course of the war, but it pointed to frightening developments in the future.

II. THE BATTLE OF NORMANDY

The battle for Normandy opened with a swift American drive to secure the port of Cherbourg. The Cotentin Peninsula, at the northern end of which the port is situated, extends northward into the English Channel at almost a right angle to the mainland of France. In the third phase of the invasion, the U.S. VII Corps cut the peninsula in half [*June 18, 1944*], isolating Cherbourg, by a sweep to the coast opposite their beachhead. In the fourth phase, Cherbourg was captured [*June 27, 1944*].

Against light resistance the 82d Airborne and 9th Infantry Divisions pressed westward to the sea, each moving over a secondary road through rolling country covered with apple orchards. One column advanced from St. Jacques, cleaning out snipers, and reached the coast at Carteret, the other column moving from St. Sauveur with tanks, cut the last road to Cherbourg and fanned south and west along the coast to Portbail [*June 18, 1944*], establishing a corridor seven miles wide which extended from coast to coast. The U.S. VII Corps swung north to reduce the four enemy divisions believed to be cut off in the Cherbourg area and to win the port.

Capture of Cherbourg

On the left, troops advanced toward Cap de la Hague [*June 19–20, 1944*] to seal off all evacuation points; others, on the right, moved north on Pointe de Barfleur, and in the center a column swung north directly on Cherbourg. Montebourg, an enemy strongpoint on the right-rear, which had held out under persistent attacks for ten days [*June 9–19, 1944*] was bypassed. In the face of the American advance, the Germans withdrew into the strong fortifications of Cherbourg [*June 21, 1944*], protected on its overland approaches by a semicircle of wooded ridges studded with such forts as Montagne du Roule, which extended several stories underground and was armed with heavy guns. Although the enemy had no chance of escape by land, he was apparently resolved to endure a siege which would delay the conquest of Normandy by denying the Allies a port to reinforce and supply their armies.

The U.S. 4th, 9th, and 79th Infantry Divisions under General Collins launched the direct attack on Cherbourg [*June 22, 1944*]. After a concentration of one thousand bombers and a half-hour of artillery preparation, the infantry advanced under a rolling barrage. They overran some forts, bypassed others, and next day entered the outskirts of Cherbourg from the southeast. The enemy was putting up his strongest resistance inside the city. In the street fighting that followed, the infantry reduced pillboxes and machine-gun nests, while the forts above the city were subjected to the fire of heavy artillery, battleships, and medium bombers diving in waves on their targets. Fort du Roule was captured by our assault troops, then lost to an enemy counterattack at night, and finally recaptured the next day [*June 25, 1944*]. On the left flank, troops advanced two miles north, bypassing the fort at Octeville, and turned east on the Cherbourg naval base, which surrendered while street fighting still went on in the city. On the right, troops bypassed the Maupertus airfield and swung west into the heart of Cherbourg. The German garrison surrendered [*June 27,*

1944] to infantry after the Air Force had dropped 8,200 tons of bombs on the area in one week. Organized resistance on the peninsula did not end, however, until the last enemy pockets on Cap de la Hague were cleaned up. Altogether some forty thousand prisoners had been taken by the Allied forces since D-day [*July 4, 1944*]; the majority were captured at Cherbourg.

The ruined port of Cherbourg was an example, like Naples and Leghorn, of the excellence of German demolitions. What the Nazis could not hold, they destroyed. The harbor and wharves were heavily mined, all the cranes blown up, and the breakwaters damaged; as a result, American engineers could not reclaim Cherbourg until August. During all this time, despite the lack of a natural deepwater harbor and in the teeth of strong offshore gales, Allied reinforcements and supplies streamed into Normandy through an artificial port.

Within the first two weeks of the invasion Allied naval engineers had established two artificial harbors in the Baie de la Seine with a total capacity larger than the port of Cherbourg. One of these harbors, in the exposed water of the American beachhead near St. Laurent-sur-Mer, was practically destroyed by a gale which blew across the bay for three days [*June 19–22, 1944*]; but the other harbor, near the British beachhead of Arromanches, weathered the storm. Each harbor consisted of an outer roadstead, where ocean-going vessels anchored in the lee of a floating breakwater, and an inner roadstead, where a fixed breakwater of submerged concrete caissons protected the piers at which smaller craft unloaded. More than sixty blockships—over 300,000 tons of shipping—had been scuttled offshore to make a temporary breakwater three days after the invasion began. Then 150 concrete caissons were flooded and sunk 1,500 yards from the beaches to secure a permanent breakwater, and seaward of these caissons were anchored steel floats to serve as an additional buffer against tides and storms. Over the calm waters inside the caissons some ten miles of steel piers ran to shore, carrying all the tanks, trucks, guns, munitions, and men racing to build up the Allied forces.

Such a miracle of engineering was not hastily improvised. It had been conceived in London in June 1943, and through the following winter hundreds of caissons, floats, and piers had been secretly built in British shipyards. Instead of opening the invasion by storming a strongly fortified French port, at a terrible cost in lives, the Allied navies towed their own port facilities across the Channel and set them up in the Baie de la Seine.

Through this harbor one million British and American troops had landed in Normandy by the time the port of Cherbourg was captured [*June 26, 1944*]. In the weeks that followed they were supplied with more than enough equipment, landed at the artificial port, to compensate for the loss of 3,000 planes, 900 tanks, 1,750 trucks, 1,500 mortars, 2,400 automatic rifles, and 83,000 miles of field wire, between D-day and the end of August. Never before had such large armies, with all the heavy guns, tanks, and motorized equipment of modern war, invaded a hostile country without seizing large ports. The amazing rate at which stores were accumulated in Normandy was a triumph of supply.

Americans were prepared for the cost of invasion to be high. During the first two weeks of fighting in Normandy [*June 6–20, 1944*] Allied casualties were 40,549; and of these three-fifths were Americans, since Americans had struggled for the central beachhead and made the drive on Cherbourg. The total figures, issued by General Bradley's headquarters, showed that 3,082 Americans were killed, 13,121 wounded, and 7,959 missing.

Fall of Caen

In the next phase of the invasion the British Second Army, under Lieutenant General Sir Miles C. Dempsey, tried twice to break out of Normandy at the eastern end of the Allied beachheads, where Caen was the hinge of the enemy lines. Had they succeeded here in turning the enemy right flank, they would have divided the German Seventh Army in Normany from the Fifteenth Army guarding the northern Channel ports and robot-bomb platforms along the Flanders coast. To avoid such a strategic catastrophe, threatening to force retreat on both the main German armies in France, the enemy concentrated the main weight of his armor and reserves throughout the Battle of Normandy against the British around

304

Caen. The Second Army captured this inland port, then pinned the enemy down and consumed his tanks and men under the relentless pressure of almost continuous battle.

The British opened their attack on Caen [*June 25, 1944*] without waiting for the Americans to finish the reduction of Cherbourg. As the Second Army crossed the Odon River [*June 28, 1944*] in a flanking movement southward, it ran into the strongest opposition which the enemy had thus far put up in Normandy. In three days and nights German tanks made twenty-four counterattacks, but always in detail and never in sufficient force to throw the British back. Worn down by the loss of over two hundred tanks, the enemy could carry out only feeble sallies in which two companies of infantry and ten or twenty tanks took part.

Because they were short of reinforcements, the Germans wasted their mobile reserves of armor in small units. So great was the damage which Allied bombing had inflicted on their transport in France that a division required two weeks to reach the Normandy front from Holland, detouring as far east as Alsace-Lorraine. Allied fighter planes denied the enemy the use of roads by day, and bombers worked havoc on his railway yards at night.

After the British were halted at the Odon, they shifted to the north to attack Caen. The new drive began with a concentration of heavy bombers, tactics which became characteristic of the Allied offensive in Normandy. RAF planes pounded the Caen area [*July 7, 1944*] with 2,300 tons of bombs, and cruisers offshore joined in the heavy artillery in laying down a barrage of fire. Then the Canadians drove east down the Bayeux road and the British south along the Caen Canal, converging on the town and compelling the enemy to withdraw across the Orne River into the southern end of Caen [*July 9, 1944*]. Here the Germans clung to the east bank of the river and sustained their flanks with persistent counterattacks.

The British made a second attempt to break out of Normandy ten days later when they resumed the offensive and struck southeast above Caen against the enemy line along the Orne. The attack was launched by 2,200 planes dropping 7,000 tons of bombs, followed by 600 B-24s with 500 tons, a concentration of explosives so heavy that the enemy was dazed. The Second Army, with tanks massed in the center and infantry on both flanks, pushed forward from their bridgehead on the east bank of the Orne, cleared the enemy from Caen, swept four miles beyond, and took 1,250 prisoners, all in a hard day's fighting. Heavy rains had turned the land into a sea of mud. Then the tanks ran into a barrier of antitank guns, supported by light and heavy artillery in great depth, and the drive bogged down in the center [*July 19, 1944*]. The British fought on, pushing their infantry forward on the flanks; and although they failed to achieve a breakthrough, they wore down the enemy reserves. It was estimated that the Germans had by now brought a total of 300,000 troops, from twenty to twenty-five divisions, into Normandy. Their casualties since D-day, reported General Montgomery [*July 19, 1944*], had reached 156,000, of which 60,000 were prisoners of war. To this toll Americans contributed their share in the heavy fighting which went on in the central and western sectors of Normandy.

Capture of St. Lô

The British were pinning down enemy strength around the Caen hinge, in the fifth phase of the invasion; in the next, the Allied offensive was transferred to the American center. Here the First Army attempted to divide the German forces in Normandy by piercing their lines at St. Lô. This offensive developed with the expansion southward of the American corridor across the Cotentin Peninsula. The movement threatened to outflank St. Lô by a drive down the coast beyond La Haye du Puits.

In the first stage [*July 1–3, 1944*], following the capture of Cherbourg, the American First Army pivoted south and built up a new front from which to conquer Normandy. The VIII and XIX Corps, landing to hold and reinforce the Cotentin corridor, opened the offensive on a 35-mile front from east of Carentan to the west coast of the peninsula. The VIII Corps on the right, advancing in heavy rains, drove south [*July 3, 1944*] against the junction town of La Haye du Puits and soon captured the surrounding hills. After a bitter but inconclusive struggle for thirty-six hours in Haye, the town was enveloped from east and west [*July 6, 1944*] by columns which had succeeded in getting to the road below it. Three days later all resistance was crushed.

On the left, southeast of Carentan, the XIX Corps, meanwhile, attacked toward St. Lô [*July 7, 1944*], crossing the Vire River under an artillery barrage, and closing in on the town from the north. The V Corps captured Hill 192 [*July 11, 1944*] commanding the road from St. Lô to Bayeux. While the Americans in the center fought without pause to reduce the enemy defenses around St. Lô, the troops on the right moved down the Coutances road [*July 16, 1944*] from La Haye to Lessay and Périers in an advance which threatened to outflank St. Lô. This vital railroad center was finally captured [*July 18, 1944*] after two weeks of bloody fighting, by the 29th Division. The fall of St. Lô unhinged the entire western flank of the German line and unlocked the gateway to the south and east through which the Americans, with freedom to maneuver, broke out of Normandy.

Up to this point the battle for Normandy had been a savage fight. The country was broken up into hedgerows, from three to five feet high, covered by dense thickets which afforded natural protection to enemy snipers, machine-gun and mortar posts. At every critical point the enemy had set up a maze of defenses, often extending over four hundred yards in depth. The hedgerows, according to a Virginia infantryman, were "horse-high, bull-strong, and hog-tight." Artillery could not reduce them. The infantry had to outflank each field and work slowly forward, taking hedgerow after hedgerow with heavy casualties.

During this period [*June 20–July 20, 1944*], from the assault on Cherbourg to the capture of St. Lô, American losses mounted higher than in the earlier phases of the invasion. In one month, 7,944 Americans were killed, and 39,549 wounded. But the Allies drove the enemy halfway out of Normandy and won a bridgehead large enough to serve as a springboard for a great plunge by American tanks.

The American Breakthrough

The battle for Normandy was won, in the seventh phase of the Allied invasion, by armored divisions of the American

307

Third Army which broke through the German left flank at Avranches, burst into Brittany, swung northeast on the Seine, and outflanked Paris from the south. This spectacular demonstration of the speed and power of American armor could be compared only to the German breakthrough of 1940 in France. The strategic consequences of the two drives were of equal importance, for while the German dash to the Channel divided the British and French forces, the American breakthrough led to the separation of two German armies, and their withdrawal into Germany. The Nazi thrust had led to the downfall of France; the Allied success opened the way to her liberation.

The decisive turn of events was not the work of the American Third Army alone. Their breakthrough was the spark which touched off the explosion; but three other Allied armies turned the initial breakthrough into complete disaster for the enemy. Two other Allied armies cooperated with the Third to crush the German Seventh Army in Normandy. The enemy left flank was enveloped by the American First Army, while his right was pinned down by the British Second. The latter, at the Caen hinge, acted as a pivot upon which the Americans wheeled around the enemy rear.

The last phase of the Allied offensive in Normandy opened with assaults [*July 25, 1944*] on both flanks of the German Seventh Army. After heavy air and artillery preparation, the British attacked the enemy's right flank before dawn on a four-mile front astride the Caen-Falaise road. Some ground was won, but part of it was soon lost again under a strong enemy counterattack, for on this flank the Germans were reported to have massed six panzer divisions. To hold them there was the mission of the British.

Against the German left flank, bolstered at the start by only two panzer divisions, the American First Army mounted the main attack on a six-mile front from St. Lô to Périers. Before the assault, 1,575 heavy bombers of the Eighth Air Force flew in low and during one hour unloaded 3,400 tons of bombs; 1,000 medium and light bombers of the Ninth Air Force followed, dropping 1,000 tons of bombs. The hedgerows and ditches of the *bocage* country were blasted away. Then, under a rolling artillery barrage, the 1st, 4th, 9th, and

30th Infantry Divisions surged forward two miles [*July 26, 1944*] and pressed south toward Coutances against the German flank anchored on the coast.

Inland, American armor suddenly entered the battle from the east. Four divisions of tanks sliced like a knife west and south through the enemy lines. The 4th Armored Division struck west and captured Coutances [*July 28, 1944*], cutting the enemy coastal line, then swung southeast and joined the 1st Infantry, 2d Armored, and 4th Infantry Divisions to envelop large numbers of the enemy in retreat [*July 29, 1944*]. Finding the German rear badly disorganized, the 4th Armored broke through its defenses near St.-Denis-le-Gast and raced twelve miles south to Avranches, where Normandy and Brittany meet [*July 30, 1944*]. The 6th Armored Division swept down the coast as far as Granville and the 1st Infantry Division came up to Brécy [*July 31, 1944*], east of Avranches, expanding the breakthrough salient.

The American tanks, striking like forked lightning, first at the enemy flank, then deep into his rear, sent the Germans reeling back. As they patched their lines with reinforcements from the Caen front, the British attacked southward [*July 31, 1944*] and cut the lateral road to Avranches. The Germans improvised counterattacks on the American salient and recaptured some minor points, but failed to halt the motorized infantry in its onward rush to consolidate the positions staked out by tanks. In eight days of continuous fighting the Americans had advanced thirty-five miles, captured 18,587 prisoners, disrupted five enemy divisions, and turned the entire German left flank.

As American armor poured through the funnel at Avranches to exploit its breakthrough, the Battle of Normandy became the Battle for France. The American Third Army under Lieutenant General (now General) George S. Patton, Jr., whose identity as commander of armored forces the Germans had guessed, did not pause after Normandy was won. Columns of Third Army tanks, moving swiftly and secretly, debouched from Normandy and headed for three objectives. After capturing Rennes they overran Brittany to secure deepwater ports which the Allies needed, in addition to Cherbourg, for the supply of their immense forces of over a million men.

309

From Le Mans, east to Rennes, tank colunms circled north towards the Seine to catch the German Seventh Army withdrawing from Normandy, and still other colunms swept east on Paris to cut enemy communications. Spearhead of the Third Army's eastward drive was the XX Corps under Lieutenant General Walton H. Walker.

Overrunning Brittany

At Avranches, the exit from Normandy, the 6th Armored Division fought its way southeast through increasing German resistance to Pontorson [*August 1, 1944*]. The capture of this point gave the Americans a wide corridor into Brittany, where there was almost no resistance until they reached the fortified ports of St. Malo, Brest, Lorient, and St. Nazaire. The speed of the armored sweep west to the Brittany coast was slowed only by mines and occasional demolitions. From Pontorson, the tanks raced south forty miles in one day [*August 2, 1944*] down the road to Rennes, capital of Brittany, and moved in three colunms 125 miles west across the peninsula to Brest in six days. All Brittany was then cut off from the rest of France by tanks which drove ninety miles south across the base of the peninsula to Nantes on the Loire River [*August 10, 1944*].

Large elements of four German divisions garrisoned the principal ports of Brittany, besieged by American infantry with the support of heavy artillery. St. Malo on the north coast was the first to surrender [*August 17, 1944*], but in Brest and Lorient, the enemy's strong fortifications made it difficult to dislodge his stubborn garrison. Coordinated assaults by air, land, and naval forces [*August 26–28, 1944*], as at Brest, drove the enemy deeper into his forts. The beleaguered Germans in Brittany were left far behind by the tide of battle rushing east from Normandy.

The Falaise–Argentan Pocket

The German Seventh Army, instead of withdrawing from Normandy when the Americans broke through their lines to Avranches, tried to cut the corridor [*August 3, 1944*] which American infantry had expanded over twenty miles from Avranches to Mortain and Domfront. Four panzer

310

divisions counterattacked [*August 7, 1944*] at the north end of the corridor and penetrated the American lines for three miles. Although they forced our advance units to evacuate Domfront and Mortain, they failed to break through to the sea. The American 3d Armored Division rushed to meet this counterattack and destroyed over one hundred German tanks with the support of dive bombers and antitank artillery. For four days [*August 7–11, 1944*] German armor wasted its strength vainly in furious jabs at the American lines, for even if it had reached the sea, it would have been enveloped by the American First Army pressing east. When the enemy counterattacks were spent, the Americans secured their corridor by the recapture of Mortain and Domfront [*August 13–15, 1944*].

Eastward between Falaise and Argentan the enemy now found himself caught in an exposed salient under pressure from elements of three Allied armies. The American First Army had continued to push east out of Normandy toward Vire, central bastion of the German line, and in cooperation with the Third Army it had swung south and east on a fifty-five-mile front deep into France as far as Alençon and Le Mans, enveloping the German left flank [*August 9–11, 1944*]. On the right flank, the British Second Army continued its offensive [*August 8–14, 1944*] southeast toward Falaise, which fell to Canadian units [*August 16, 1944*]. Polish and Canadian troops fanned out to Trun [*August 18, 1944*] and met American tanks driving north from Argentan to seal the pocket. Six enemy divisions, besides elements of two more, were trapped. When the encircling Allied forces penetrated and sewed up the pocket during the next four days [*August 19–23, 1944*] they captured 25,000 prisoners, a considerable portion of what was left of the German Seventh Army. In the earlier stages of the offensive, the American First Army had captured 76,000 prisoners, the Third Army 31,500 and together they had buried 20,942 enemy dead. The Battle of Normandy was over, and the Germans were in full retreat.

Throughout the battle the American and British air forces had given Allied ground troops close tactical support. In addition, they had continued to wear down Nazi airpower

311

over both France and Germany. During the first seventy days of the invasion the Allied air forces destroyed 2,990 enemy planes in aerial combat, 651 on the ground, and lost 2,959 planes.

III. ADVANCE TO THE GERMAN FRONTIER

The Second Battle of France, like the First in 1940, was more a pursuit than a battle. In 1944, however, it was the Germans' turn to retreat before an overwhelming mass of troops armed with superior fire power and supported by planes and tanks in overwhelming strength. Even if the enemy had been able to stand his ground on any of the defense lines which he had held for four years in France during the last war, his forces would have been exposed to the flanking movement developed with the Allied invasion of the south of France.

Allied Landings in Southern France: Operation Anvil

Here on the coast between Toulon and Cannes the American Seventh Army under Lieutenant General Alexander M. Patch, as well as French units, landed against light opposition [*August 15, 1944*] and penetrated 140 miles inland in eight days. The amphibious expedition of more than 1,500 ships, including two American and seven British aircraft carriers and a total of 641 American craft, was mounted in Corsica and Italy. From the Fifth Army in this theater were taken veterans of Sicily, Salerno, and Anzio, the U.S. 3d, 36th, and 45th Divisions which made up the VI Corps under Lieutenant General Lucian K. Truscott, Jr., to spearhead the new invasion. Their objective, according to the order of General (now Field Marshal) Sir Henry Maitland Wilson, commanding the Allied forces in the Mediterranean, was "to drive out the Germans [from the south of France] and join up with the Allied armies advancing from Normandy."

The landings were prepared by four days of heavy bombing. On D-day strong naval forces joined the tactical bombers for two and a half hours in laying down a concentration of fire on the coast. The 1st Airborne Task Force, composed of British, French, and American units, was the vanguard of the invasion. British and American troops were dropped in-

312

land near Le Muy on the right flank of the projected beachheads; on the left near Bormes, a French force came in with armor. They established roadblocks which were never needed, for the enemy did not send reinforcements. The German Nineteenth Army was holding the south of France with very weak forces; only two divisions defended one hundred miles of coast from Toulon to Nice. On the fifteen-mile beach front where the Seventh Army landed it encountered two enemy regiments, half of whose personnel were Czech conscripts and Polish prisoners of war, who soon surrendered. Within three days after the landings [*August 18, 1944*], the Seventh Army, together with the French Forces of the Interior, which rose from the Underground, captured over ten thousand prisoners.

Advance to the Belfort Gap

The main resistance met by the Seventh Army, as it fanned westward towards the Rhône valley, was at the naval base of Toulon and at the port of Marseille. The latter although farther west, was taken first [*August 23, 1944*], but not before the Germans had carried out their customary demolitions, wrecking the docks and warehouses and scuttling ships in the entrance to the port. French infantry and tanks moved swiftly on Marseille and captured it after sealing off routes of escape. French forces also captured Toulon [*August 26, 1944*], enveloping it from the north and west, and penetrating to the southern forts after a week of bitter street fighting. With the end of organized resistance in these two cities [*August 28, 1944*] seven thousand more Germans were prisoners.

Meanwhile the Americans drove rapidly north through the Durance Valley and reached the Rhône above Montélimar, one hundred miles from the sea. There they trapped one panzer division and elements of two other German divisions. This enemy force of some fifteen thousand men tried in vain to break through the American roadblocks [*August 25—26, 1944*], but most of them were killed or captured. Farther east, the Americans advanced along the main railroad to Grenoble, whence they drove northwest to Lyon, the indus-

313

trial city which commands the railroads and communications of southern France.

North from the Mediterranean coast, the Seventh Army pressed toward the Italian frontier. Here they were greatly aided by the Maquis, the French Forces of the Interior; for in these forested mountains bordering Italy and Switzerland, the Underground had trained its armies in the years of the Nazi captivity. Prisoners of war taken by the Allies in the first two weeks of the invasion were reported at fifty thousand.

The Seventh Army swept north and east from Lyon, swinging around the Swiss border toward the Belfort Gap between the Vosges and the Jura Mountains. In September 1944, it was pushing toward Alsace and the Rhine and had taken its place at the southern end of the Allied line, ready for the Battle of Germany.

Liberation of Paris

While the Seventh Army was overrunning the south of France, in the north the Third swept around Paris in a drive to turn the left flank of the German Fifteenth Army. From Le Mans, where American armor concentrated, columns of tanks raced north and east towards the Seine on an arc of seventy miles [August *14–20, 1944*]. They reached the river on two sides of Paris, at Mantes thirty-five miles northwest of the city and at a point the same distance southeast, near Fontainebleau.

Upon the approach of these armored spearheads, the people of Paris rose against their Nazi masters [*August 19, 1944*]. Orders from Underground leaders brought fifty thousand armed members of the French Forces of the Interior, together with the unarmed populace, into the streets. They liberated large parts of Paris in four days of fighting. The French 2d Armored Division, veterans of Tunisa commanded by General Jacques-Philippe Leclerc, came to the aid of the patriots, entering Paris from the south and west [*August 24, 1944*] with American units following them. To these forces the German garrison of ten thousand surrendered [*August 25, 1944*]; but sniping, particularly by Frenchmen

314

who had collaborated with the Nazis, continued for several days.

After four years in captivity, Paris was free, the first capital of the United Nations to be reconquered from the Nazis, General Charles de Gaulle entered the city [*August 26, 1944*], to become President four days later of the French Provisional Government which was established in cooperation with leaders of the Underground movement. General Eisenhower reviewed the Allied soldiers, French, American, and British who marched under the Arc de Triomphe. Then our troops moved out of the city toward the Marne in pursuit of the enemy.

Allied Advance Toward Germany

As armored columns of the American Third Army crossed the Seine River at Mantes and near Fontainebleau [*August 21, 1944*] they enveloped Paris and turned the left flank of the German Fifteenth Army, now in full retreat from the Flanders coast. At the same time the British Second and American First Armies swung northeast toward the Seine and Belgium. On the left of this advance, Canadian units drove some elements of the enemy into a pocket below Le Havre and Rouen [*August 22, 1944*]. The British Second Army crossed the Seine between Rouen and Paris [*August 26, 1944*], at Vernon and Louviers, and swept forward thirty-four miles towards the Somme River [*August 29, 1944*]. On the right, west of Paris, the American First Army cleaned up enemy rear guards on the south bank of the Seine and pushed beyond Laon to a point only thirty miles short of the Belgian border [*August 26, 1944*]. Still farther east, on the extreme right of an Allied front which now stretched nearly two hundred miles across northern France, the American Third Army continued to set the pace of advance for all the armies. From Paris, armored spearheads of the Third reached the Marne River [*August 27–28, 1944*], drove through Château-Thierry, swept twenty-two miles beyond to take Soissons, and closed in on Reims. Smashing through the Argonne Forest, the Third Army captured Verdun [*August 3, 1944*] and pressed on toward Metz and the German Saar. On the Channel coast, the Canadians took Dieppe [*September 1, 1944*] and sealed off the Germans in the port of Le Havre, while the British Second Army, after an advance of sixty miles in two days, captured Amiens [*August 31, 1944*], crossed the Somme, took Arras, and pushed towards Lille. On their right, in what was now the center of the Allied line, the American First Army stormed Sedan and reached the Belgian frontier [*August 31, 1944*].

By the end of August the Allied offensive in France was five days ahead of schedule, General Eisenhower announced. The Germans had lost 400,000 men, of whom half were captured. General Eisenhower reported that five panzer divisions had been destroyed, six more badly mauled; twenty infantry divisions had been eliminated, and twelve others disorganized. Total American casualties in France, killed, wounded and captured, were 112,673. This swift, overpowering offensive in France demonstrated the complete maturity of the American armies.

Americans and Allies, united in command and in purpose to destroy Nazi power, were defeating the greatest military force that the world had ever known. In the east the massive strength of Russia was marshalled from the Baltic and East Prussia to the Balkans; on the west, Allied armies drove toward the Rhine and the Ruhr. As Allied troops crossed the western frontier of Germany, their Supreme Commander, General Dwight D. Eisenhower, issued a proclamation to the German people [*September 28, 1944*]: "We come as conquerors, but not as oppressors . . . We shall overthrow the Nazi rule, dissolve the Nazi party and abolish the cruel, oppressive and discriminatory laws and institutions which the party has created. We shall eradicate that German militarism which has so often disrupted the peace of the world."

34. VICTORY IN THE WEST

The Battle Over Ports

The success of the Allied invasion of France and the destruction of the greater part of the German Seventh Army compelled a German retreat to the Siegfried Line. With the sweep across France Allied supply problems were multiplied and ports became important objectives. Ports evacuated by the Germans were blocked and harbor installations thoroughly demolished. The stiffest delaying action was fought by the Germans in the north to deny the Allies use of the cross-Channel ports. Holland was stubbornly defended. A considerable number of German troops were left in French Atlantic ports with orders to fight to the last. They were supplied by plane or submarine, but in some cases possessed stores of food and munitions sufficient to last for many months. These units were doomed to ultimate death or capture, but as long as they held out, the Allies were unable to use these ports. According to German estimates, Allied supply and transport difficulties would become critical by the time the battle line reached the German frontier.

German-held ports included Bordeaux, St. Nazaire, Lorient, and Dunkirk. The use of Marseille and Toulon was delayed after their capture by demolitions and by German garrisons on nearby islands. After the capture of Antwerp, its use was prevented by German garrisons holding out in the area surrounding the Scheldt River mouth. German garrisons on the Channel Islands were by-passed and remained there until the final surrender. About 130,000 German troops garrisoned these by-passed ports and areas. The Allies were forced to divert military personnel and supplies in order to contain them.

Other ports came into Allied hands as a result of heavy fighting. The Canadian forces captured Dieppe [*September 1, 1944*], scene of their heavy losses in 1942. Elements of the British Second Army entered Antwerp [*September 4, 1944*] after a brilliant advance. The Canadian First Army cut off Calais and captured Ostend [*September 6, 1944*]. Two days later the same army carried the port of Le Havre by storm. After four days of bitter fighting the Canadian First Army captured Boulogne [*September 18, 1944*] together with 10,000 German prisoners. Brest fell to the U.S. Ninth Army with 36,000 prisoners [*September 19, 1944*]. German resistance in the Cape Gris Nez sector ended [*Sep-*

317

tember 30, 1944] with the capture of Calais and 7,000 German prisoners by the Canadian First Army.

While the Allied armies were making slow progress in driving the Germans out of Metz and other areas of Alsace, plans were developed to outflank the Siegfried Line in the north. The Allied Supreme Command had a choice in September 1944. It could concentrate Allied military power on opening the port of Antwerp, or it could play for bigger stakes and attempt to outflank the Siegfried Line at Cleve, its northern hinge. If this operation were successful, it would prevent a German stand in the West and might conceivably lead to a collapse of the Third Reich in the autumn of 1944.

Allied Airborne Landings at Eindhoven and Arnhem

Four days after the first units of the U.S. First Army crossed the Reich frontier some forty miles northwest of Trier, glider and paratroops of the First Allied Airborne Army, commanded by Lieutenant General Lewis H. Brereton, landed [*September 15, 1944*] at Eindhoven and Arnhem. Organized in Britain [*August 10, 1944*], the First Allied Airborne Army consisted of the British 1st and the U.S. 82d and 101st Airborne Divisions.

The 82d and 101st Divisions were to capture the bridges over the Maas (Meuse) and Waal Rivers. The British 1st Division was landed farther north at Arnhem. It was to secure the crossing of the Lek River guarding the approaches to Cleve. The British Second Army driving northward was to join up with the airborne units to consolidate and expand the breakthrough.

The landing of the Allied airborne troops took place almost according to plan, but the German high command reacted so violently to this threat against the northern flank that the progress of the British Second Army was not up to schedule. Contact was made with the American forces at Eindhoven, and the British advance reached Nijmegen [*September 19, 1944*]. German pressure on the Allied supply and reinforcement corridor to Nijmegen prevented further advances. After a week of heroic resistance in their isolated pocket at Arnhem, the remnants of the British 1st Airborne Division, about 1,800 men, were evacuated to the British lines across the Lek River [*September 25, 1944*].

Capture of Aachen

The first penetration of the German frontier in the West was made [*September 11, 1944*] by units of the U.S. First Army. When the Allied airborne thrust at Cleve failed, the U.S. First Army was fighting in the outskirts of the Siegfried Line approaching Aachen. Sustained fighting led to the penetration of the outer defenses of this city [*October 5, 1944*]. With the capture of Crucifix Hill [*October 8, 1944*], the American encirclement of Aachen was almost complete. Demands for the unconditional surrender of the city were made [*October 10, 1944*] but refused by the Germans. The American ring around Aachen was completed [*October 16, 1944*], and after heavy bombardment by artillery and repeated air strikes, troops of the First Army captured the city in bitter street fighting [*October 21, 1944*].

Aachen was the first large German city to fall into Allied hands. Its prewar population of 160,000 had been reduced to about 8,000 through evacuation. Almost totally destroyed as a consequence of the futile German resistance, Aachen was a warning to the rest of the German nation. Later on many German cities decided to avoid similar destruction by surrender.

The Nazi government made an effort to popularize the tenacious defense of Aachen. It ordered German citizens not to leave their posts until ordered to do so by Wehrmacht officers. By decree of the Führer [*October 18, 1944*], all German males between the ages of sixteen and sixty not already in the military service were to join a German Home Army, the *Deutsche Wehrmacht Volkssturm,* under direct command of SS Chief and Minister of the Interior Heinrich Himmler.

Clearing the Port of Antwerp

It was accounted a prize of great value when the port of

Antwerp fell into Allied hands almost undamaged. If the Germans had simultaneously withdrawn from the territory surrounding the mouth of the Scheldt River, the magnificent harbor installations and railroad connections of the port would have gone far toward solving Allied supply problems. However, a strong German garrison defended the islands of Walcheren and South Beveland. German batteries on both banks of the Scheldt denied Allied transports entrance into the river mouth. The German 64th Infantry Division held a line along the Leopold Canal on the south bank of the Scheldt.

The task of opening the port of Antwerp fell to the Canadian First Army, the British Second Army and Commando units. It proved to be a difficult and costly operation. Advances were made in this sector only after hard fighting and heavy losses. A crossing was made of the Leopold Canal by Canadian troops [*October 6, 1944*], but prompt German counterattacks limited their gains. Landings were made by British and Canadian forces on the south bank of the Scheldt estuary near Breskens [*October 8–9, 1944*], but German artillery fire prevented exploitation of the gains made.

Operations by the British Second Army led to the capture of Hertogenbosch [*October 24, 1944*], and Breda [*October 29, 1944*]. Attacks by RAF bombers carrying 6-ton bombs cut the dikes around Walcheren Island and flooded a number of German battery positions, but some long-range German guns were still in operation on that island when the final attacks were driven home. Canadian troops cut the causeway from the mainland to South Beveland [*October 10, 1944*], and German resistance on that island ended [*October 30, 1944*]. British Commando units landed on Walcheren Island at West Kapelle and Flushing [*November 1, 1944*], and after three days of fighting killed or captured the German garrison. The estuary of the Scheldt was finally free for the entrance of Allied transports [*November 3, 1944*].

Hardly had the port of Antwerp been freed and put to use when the Germans began to attack it with V-1 bombs. Despite these attacks which caused heavy losses, hundreds of thousands of tons of military goods flowed through this port to Allied armies on the German frontier.

Rundstedt's Ardennes Offensive

While the Allied armies were preparing for their main attacks on the German frontier defenses and fighting their way forward in Alsace, the German high command decided to use their last strong reserve in a bold bid to break through the Ardennes, to isolate the British armies in the north, to take Liège and possibly Antwerp. Well equipped and trained *Volksgrenadier* divisions and panzer units were assembled under the cover of cloudy weather to augment German forces and to assault the thinly held Allied lines in the Ardennes area. An estimated force of 25 German divisions was concentrated for the attack whose code name was "Operation Greif." There had been no serious German counterattack since the ill-fated effort to block the Allied advance at Mortain in Normandy [*August 3–7, 1944*]. In preparation for their own coming offensive, Allied leaders accepted the "legitimate risk" involved in holding the Ardennes area with limited forces. German preparations for the attack were well concealed. A period of bad flying weather restricted Allied air reconnaissance, and the German assault came as a surprise.

The general area chosen for the German attack was that of the 12th Army Group (Bradley), consisting of the U.S. First, Third, and Ninth Armies. The point of the assault fell in the area of the VIII Corps (commanded by Major General Troy H. Middleton) of the U.S. First Army.

The German drive was heralded by a sudden assault on Allied airfields by the carefully husbanded remnants of the Luftwaffe. After a short but heavy artillery preparation beginning at 0500 hours, an estimated force of 24 German divisions comprising the Fifth and Sixth Panzer Armies supported by the Seventh Army advanced through the heavily wooded but well roaded area of the Ardennes [*December 16, 1944*]. For two days news about the German offensive was limited, but the announcement that the Germans had reached to within six miles of Stavelot [*December 18, 1944*] gave

321

some indication of the weight and speed of the German advance.

By the third day of the German offensive [*December 19, 1944*], the situation in the Ardennes had taken so critical a turn that Allied command arrangements had to be altered. Because the rapid German advance threatened to cut Allied command communications, Field Marshal Montgomery commanding the 21st Army Group was placed in temporary command of the U. S. First and Ninth Armies. Allied reinforcements were hurriedly sent to the endangered area. Among these was the U. S. 101st Airborne Division, temporarily commanded by Brigadier General (now Major General) Anthony C. McAuliffe in the absence of the division commander. The 101st Airborne Division was ordered to the area around Bastogne and was destined to make an epic defense of that position.

The 101st Airborne Division had barely taken up a position at Bastogne when the German advance cut the road to Neufchâteau [*December 20–21, 1944*], isolating Bastogne. As the German advance continued with paratroops dropping behind the American lines to disrupt our communications, SHAEF issued a General Order [*December 22, 1944*] calling upon every man in the Allied armies to rise to new heights of courage and resolution and thus turn the Germans' greatest gamble into their greatest defeat. The counterattack of the U. S. Third Army made some progress but met heavy resistance between Arlon and Bastogne. The German advance westward reached its greatest penetration [*December 24–25, 1944*] when Celles was captured. At this stage the enemy was approaching the important communications centers of Dinant and Namur. The Germans had driven forward more than fifty miles. If unchecked their advance threatened to cross the Meuse River.

But the enemy never got beyond Celles. In fact they lost that position to an Allied counterattack [*December 26, 1944*]. Repeated German attacks failed to widen the bulge either on the northern or southern shoulder. Meantime, in the south the advance of the U. S. Third Army continued, and the Germans were unable to reduce the tough pocket of the 101st Airborne Division at Bastogne. To a German re-

322

quest for the surrender of the encircled garrison [*December 22, 1944*], General McAuliffe replied: "Aw, nuts"—which has gone down in history as "Nuts!"

The first relief units of the U. S. Third Army to enter the lines of the 101st Airborne Division at Bastogne [*December 26, 1944*] at 1650 hours were three tanks of Company C, 37th Tank Battalion of the 4th Armored Division. These were followed by others and by infantry units. By the end of December Allied strength in the Bulge area was so great that all German hopes of continuing the offensive ended. Rundstedt's offensive was over and the Battle of the Bulge began.

The Battle of the Bulge

Rundstedt's surprise offensive in the Ardennes was a showy operation. It made the headlines and caused more concern in the British and American homelands than it did at SHAEF. The Allied high command, in possession of more information than it could release to the public, knew that the Germans were throwing in their last reserves. General Eisenhower was reported to have said jokingly to General Bradley: "Brad, you've always wanted a German counterattack—now you've got it."

Though certain American divisions were badly cut up in the first days of the offensive, the Allied armies in that area were competent and veteran fighters. They did not panic when the Germans unexpectedly rolled over their positions. The German advance and the time required to pinch out the Bulge probably set back the ultimate collapse of the Third Reich by thirty days. However, it made that collapse all the more inevitable by using up the last German reserves in the West.

Allied efforts to reduce the Ardennes Bulge began before the German offensive had spent its force. The U. S. Third Army had been attacking from the south for many days. Apparently the Germans interpreted the check at Celles and the failure to take Bastogne as an indication that the salient could not be held. They defended their southern and northern flanks firmly but withdrew under heavy pressure from the tip of the salient, losing Rochefort [*December 30,*

1944]. This stage of the fighting was accompanied by another outbreak of German air activity, and the Allied command announced that 125 German planes were downed in air battles on January 1, 1945.

The 21st Army Group launched a strong offensive on the northern flank of the Bulge [*January 3, 1945*]. Advances were made in heavy fighting along the line from Malmédy to Marche. Rain turning to snow, and ice hampered operations. The temperature fell on this front to zero on January 8. Fighting continued despite the weather and small Allied gains progressively reduced the German holdings in the salient. Laroche fell to units of the British 51st and U. S. 84th Divisions [*January 10, 1945*]. Houffalize was captured [*January 16, 1945*]. Further advances of the U. S. First Army led to the capture of the important road junction of St.Vith [*January 23, 1945*]. The Ardennes salient was practically reduced [*January 28, 1945*] when American troops crossed the Belgian-German frontier in this sector.

As a measure to divert Allied strength elsewhere while the German withdrawal in the north was taking place, the German armies in northern Alsace launched a series of attacks against the U. S. Seventh Army near Reipertsweiler [*January 19–20, 1945*]. A local American withdrawal to the Moder River was made during the following two days. A sector of northern Alsace remained in enemy hands until the Allied offensive to clear the Saar and the Palatinate began.

An Allied offensive by the 6th Army Group, commanded by Lieutenant General (now General) Jacob L. Devers, was launched on the line St. Amarin–Cernay–Mulhouse in southern Alsace [*January 20, 1945*] aimed at reducing the last German foothold west of the Rhine. Colmar was entered by troops of the French First Army [*February 2, 1945*]. A concentric advance on Rouffach [*February 5, 1945*] cut off a considerable number of German troops. A general German withdrawal from southern Alsace to the east bank of the Rhine was completed [*February 9, 1945*].

The inability of the German armies to hold the Ardennes salient foreshadowed the Allied crossing of the Saar and the loss of the Palatinate. It showed that German reserves were

324

lacking to meet the two-front assault which came with the great Red Army offensive in January on the Eastern Front. The bitter fighting of the Battle of the Bulge had its effect on German morale. The Allied armies had demonstrated their moral and material superiority over the German troops. From this time on the German military situation in the West deteriorated rapidly. The Allied threat to the Cologne Plain, which probably was one of the German considerations in launching their offensive, could no longer be staved off.

II. THE BATTLES OF GERMANY

Order of Battle of the Allied Armies in Western Europe

As the Allied armies in the West poised for the final battles of Germany, the Supreme Allied Commander was Army General Dwight D. Eisenhower, USA. His deputy was Air Chief Marshal Sir Arthur Tedder, RAF, and his chief of staff was Lieutenant General Walter Bedell Smith, USA. Air Chief Marshal Sir Arthur Harris, RAF, was head of the Bomber Command of the RAF, and General Carl Spaatz was commander of the U. S. Strategic Air Forces in Europe.

Allied armies were grouped from north to south as follows:

21st Army Group, Field Marshal Sir Bernard L. Montgomery
    Canadian First Army, Lieutenant General H. D. G. Crerar
    British Second Army, Lieutenant General Sir Miles C. Dempsey

12th Army Group, General Omar N. Bradley
    U. S. Ninth Army, Lieutenant General William H. Simpson
    U. S. First Army, Lieutenant General Courtney H. Hodges
    U. S. Third Army, Lieutenant General George S. Patton.
    U. S. Fifteenth Army, Lieutenant General L. T. Gerow

6th Army Group, General Jacob L. Devers
    U. S. Seventh Army, Lieutenant General Alexander M. Patch
    French First Army, General Jean de Lattre de Tassigny

The First Allied Airborne Army was commanded by Lieutenant General Lewis H. Brereton, the U. S. Eighth Air

Force by Lieutenant General James H. Doolittle, and the U. S. Ninth Air Force by Lieutenant General Hoyt S. Vandenberg.

Breaking into the Cologne Plain

With the defeat of their Ardennes offensive, the Germans were no longer able to forestall an Allied breakthrough into the Cologne Plain. Advances in the Roer sector were held up for some time by threat of flood waters controlled by the Roer dams, but this threat was removed when troops of the U. S. First Army captured the main Roer dam at Schammenauel [February 10, 1945]. The 21st Army Group began an offensive in the north [February 9, 1945] which led to the capture of Cleve [February 12, 1945] and Goch [February 21, 1945]. Farther south, the U. S. Third Army crossed the Saar River near Saarburg [February 22, 1945], and the following day [February 23, 1945] the U. S. Ninth Army crossed the Roer River. Three days later [February 26, 1945] troops of the U. S. First Army crossed the Roer River near Nideggen. Germany's river barriers were beginning to collapse. General Eisenhower announced [February 24, 1945] that the mission of the new offensive was to destroy the German forces west of the Rhine.

Under heavy pressure from three allied armies the Germans withdrew from München-Gladbach, Venlo, and Roermond [March 1–2, 1945]. Allied troops were now approaching the Rhine opposite Düsseldorf. Cologne, the first great German city to fall into Allied hands, was captured by troops of the U. S. First Army [March 5–6, 1945]. German troops withdrew across the Rhine destroying the Cologne bridges or retreated southward to Bonn.

On the following day there occurred one of the great "breaks" of the war. Elements of the U. S. 9th Armored Division, after entering Rheinbach with little opposition, pushed forward its patrols to Remagen [March 7, 1945] on the Rhine. Finding the Ludendorff Bridge intact but wired for demolition, an American patrol raced over the bridge ten minutes before the charges were set to explode. The capture of the Remagen bridge intact was an exploit of great daring and initiative. Tanks were poured across and infantry units

326

followed. In the words of Lieutenant General Walter Bedell Smith: "While the bridge lasted, it was worth its weight in gold." Several divisions were hastily sent across the Rhine and soon established a firm bridgehead. Repeated attacks by German aircraft and shelling by long range artillery weakened the bridge which had been damaged as it was captured. It collapsed [*March 17, 1945*] after several days of use by our forces.

Clearing the Saar and the Palatinate

With the Remagen bridgehead established, the center of gravity of the Allied attack shifted to the Saar and the Palatinate. It was part of the overall Allied plan to clear this area before launching our armies across the Rhine for the final battles of Germany.

The territory of the Saar and the Palatinate lying between the Moselle, the Saar, and the Rhine Rivers, was one of the richest German industrial districts. Its capture was entrusted to the U. S. Third and Seventh Armies, and the French First Army. Operations began [*February 19, 1945*] in the Eifel area between Prüm and the Moselle River. This area had to be captured before the assault on the Moselle–Saar–Rhine triangle could begin.

In steady fighting [*February 19–March 11, 1945*] enemy troops were cleared from most of the Eifel area, and a strong position established along the Rhine in the north. The north bank of the Moselle River was occupied from a point near Coblenz to Cochem.

While these preliminary battles were being fought by the U. S. Third Army in the north, the U. S. Seventh Army was attacking from the south in the direction of Forbach, which was captured [*March 5, 1945*]. The Allied plan was to cut off the enemy's line of retreat across the Rhine by a concentric attack from north and south. The U. S. Third Army crossed the Moselle [*March 15, 1945*], while the Seventh Army was battling for possession of Hagenau and Saarbrücken. Rapid advances were made in the north as Coblenz fell to the Third Army [*March 16, 1945*]. By-passing Mainz, the Third Army swept forward to Worms [*March 20, 1945*] and Ludwigshafen [*March 21, 1945*]. The Seventh

Army captured Zweibrücken [*March 20, 1945*] and Pirmasens [*March 22, 1945*]. From this time on, the reduction of the German pocket west of the Rhine was extremely rapid. The last German forces withdrew east of the Rhine [*March 25, 1945*]. The Saar and the Palatinate together with many thousands of German prisoners were now in Allied hands. The stage was set for the crossing of the Rhine in force.

Passage of the Rhine

With the end of the campaign in the Saar and the Palatinate the German armies in the West were defending a line about 450 miles long running along the Rhine River from Switzerland to the North Sea. To man this line the Germans had an estimated force of 70 understrength divisions. By March 23, 1945, when the initial stages of the Rhine operation began, the Remagen bridgehead had been extended to a depth of about 8 miles and a length of 25 miles. It constituted a strong sally port from which to exploit Allied crossings to the north or south.

As the Allied armies lined up from north to south, the 21st Army Group held a front of about 95 miles from Holland to the neighborhood of Cologne. The 12th Army Group held a front of about 110 miles long from Cologne to the Neckar River. The 6th Army Group front extended southward from the Neckar.

The Rhine crossing found the Allied armies in the West at the peak of their military strength. Their capacity to fight an "engineering war" was fully demonstrated during this gigantic operation. Allied air forces had driven the Luftwaffe to the ground. Strategic bombers had done their work so well that few remunerative targets remained in the Reich. With the preparations of the 21st Army Group in the north further developed than that of the American forces in the south, the Germans probably expected the major Allied crossings of the Rhine to take place in the north. But by March 23, 1945, the Allied armies were, in fact, prepared to cross the Rhine all along the front. Allied air strikes and smoke screens covered the operation and seven armies almost simultaneously crossed the Rhine.

Immediately after the ground forces were committed,
328

troops of the First Allied Airborne Army were dropped behind the German lines and soon made contact with the troops which had crossed the Rhine. The operation was a spectacular success and one of the most highly coordinated large-scale movements of armies in history.

The capacity of the American Army to overcome a great river barrier was demonstrated in bridging the Rhine. A total of 62 bridges were thrown across the Rhine by the American armies alone. Five of these were railway bridges (four of them over 2,200 feet long), built in an average construction time of nine days and one hour. Forty-six tactical (ponton) and 11 fixed highway bridges (average length 1,256 feet) enabled us to throw our troops across the river in record time. In their construction we employed a total of 4,600 boats, 6,000 ponton floats, 100,000 tons of bridging equipment, 2,500 outboard motors, 315,000 feet of wire rope, and 8,000 feet of chain. Seventy-five thousand engineers were engaged in the crossing operation, assisted by 124 naval landing craft, 72 Sea Mules, and 370 DUKWs, manned by 893 naval ratings and 1,400 Army Transportation Corps troops.

Springing the Ruhr Trap

The 21st Army Group crossed the Rhine [*March 23, 1945*] on a 15-mile front between Rees and Wesel. Airborne troops dropped in conjunction with the crossing captured several bridges over the Ijssel River intact. German strength was concentrated in the north and progress on the 21st Army Group front was necessarily less spectacular than on the 12th Army Group front. At the end of the first day of operations in the north a firm bridgehead five miles deep had been established. British units reached Münster [*March 31, 1945*] and captured it [*April 3, 1945*]. From this point on operations of the 21st Army Group aimed at the liberation of Holland and capture of the great German ports of Bremen and Hamburg, and pinning down German forces in the north.

Operating on the flank of British units (as part of the 21st Army Group until April 3) the U. S. Ninth Army advanced to Lippstadt [*April 1, 1945*]. Here they made contact with elements of the U. S. First Army which had crossed

329

the Rhine south of Cologne and had swung westward and north to spring a trap around the Ruhr.

Meanwhile the 12th Army Group crossed the Rhine [*March 22–23, 1945*] on a front from Remagen to Oppenheim. The U. S. First Army which fought its way from the Remagen bridgehead reached the Sieg River at Eidorf [*March 26, 1945*]. The U. S. Third Army which crossed the Rhine near Oppenheim reached Frankfurt-am-Main [*March 26, 1945*] and began a house-to-house battle for its possession. After hard fighting at Paderborn [*March 30, 1945*], elements of the U. S. First Army made contact with Ninth Army troops at Lippstadt [*April 1, 1945*]. This completed the encirclement of the Ruhr, and although considerable fighting followed before the last German resistance in the Ruhr ended [*April 18, 1945*], a bag of about 400,000 German troops fell into Allied hands.

The Ruhr was the industrial heart of Germany and its capture ended Germany's ability to continue the war. Morale sagged in the German Army and many thousands of troops surrendered. Allied officers rightly described the encirclement and capture of the Ruhr as the greatest double-envelopment operation in history.

Advance into Germany

The 6th Army Group entered the campaign several days later than the Allied armies in the north. The U. S. Seventh Army captured Mannheim [*March 29, 1945*] and advanced toward Heidelberg. The French First Army crossed the Rhine [*March 30, 1945*] on a nine-mile front south of Speyer and reached the Neckar River south of Karlsruhe which was captured [*April 4, 1945*]. Fortified works of the Siegfried Line in this area made advances difficult and costly. Heilbronn was reached [*April 6, 1945*] but the Germans defended that town stubbornly for a week. A new crossing of the Rhine was made by units of the French First Army near Strasbourg [*April 13, 1945*] and led to the immediate capture of Kehl. Troops of the U. S. Seventh Army encircled Nürnberg [*April 15–18, 1945*], but resistance by German troops and civilians delayed the capture of the Nazi shrine city. It fell into our hands [*April 21, 1945*] almost completely destroyed. By this time German resistance in the south was crumbling. Stuttgart was occupied by the French First Army [April 22, 1945], and the general advance continued. Crossing the Danube, French troops reached the Swiss border near Donaueschingen [April 22, 1945], cutting off German garrisons in the Siegfried Line south of Breisach. Friedrichshafen was occupied by troops of the French First Army [April 30, 1945]. A crossing of the Austrian frontier was made [April 30, 1945] at the eastern end of Lake Constance.

After the Ruhr trap had been closed, its reduction was left to elements of the U. S. Ninth and First Armies. The rest of the Allied armies pushed on into Germany. The 21st Army Group advanced northward against strong opposition into Holland and the German coastal area. Its objective was to isolate the German forces in the Netherlands and take the great German ports of Bremen and Hamburg. The Canadian First Army captured Arnhem after heavy fighting [April 13, 1945] and reached the Ijsselmeer east of Amsterdam [April 18, 1945]. The British Second Army reached the vicinity of Bremen [April 8–9, 1945] but was held up by strong German resistance. On May 2, 1945, the British Second Army reached the Baltic. By this time the German Army in the West had reached the end of the road. Surrenders were taking place all along the front on a tremendous scale.

Kiel and Flensburg were declared to be "open cities" by the government of Admiral Doenitz [May 2, 1945], the same day that the British Second Army occupied Lübeck. Surrender negotiations were initiated by Admiral Von Friedeburg [May 3, 1945], who approached Field Marshal Montgomery with a request for terms. Oldenburg and Hamburg were surrendered to the British Second Army [May 3, 1945], and with Lübeck in British hands, the 21st Army Group was at the approximate line agreed upon with the Russians at Yalta.

Admiral Von Friedeburg surrendered all German naval and land forces in Holland, Northwest Germany, and Denmark to Field Marshal Montgomery [May 5, 1945] at 0800 hours.

It was on the 12th Army Group front that the most spectacular advances were made after closing the Ruhr trap. Kassel was captured [*April 4, 1945*]. Hanover fell to troops of the U. S. Ninth Army [*April 10, 1945*], the same day that the U. S. First Army reached Nordhausen and the Third Army attacked Erfurt. Great advances were made [*April 11, 1945*] when the U. S. Ninth Army reached the Elbe River near Madeburg after a 50-mile drive. Not to be outdone, the U. S. Third Army almost equalled this with a 46-mile advance to cross the Saale River near Jena. By April 15, the Ninth Army had two bridgeheads over the Elbe near Madeburg and had reached the Mulde River southeast of Leipzig, the First Army had reached the Mulde River south of Dessau, and the Third Army had captured Bayreuth and was closing in on Chemnitz.

The pace of operations slowed somewhat after April 15 because the U. S. armies had reached the approximate line agreed upon at Yalta. Halle was captured by troops of the U. S. First Army [*April 19, 1945*], and Leipzig was completely in American hands the following day [*April 20, 1945*]. The U. S. Third Army continued its advance through the Harz Mountains and reached the Czechoslovakian frontier near Tirschenreuth [*April 23, 1945*]. Munich was occupied by troops of the U. S. Seventh Army [*April 29–30, 1945*].

Junction of the Allied Armies

A junction of the Allied and Russian armies in the heart of Germany was one of the long-sought objectives of United Nations' strategy. It would symbolize the dismemberment of the Third Reich and set the seal on United Nations solidarity. In the last months of the struggle the only hope remaining to the Nazi leaders was that the Allies would fall to quarreling among themselves. At Yalta the Allies had set the future junction point on the Elbe River.

Foreseeing a possible junction of the Allied and Russian armies, Hitler issued a General Order [*April 16, 1945*] dividing the Reich into two defense areas. Hitler remained in command of the North Defense Area and apparently maintained his headquarters in Berlin until the last. The South Defense Area was entrusted to SS Chief and Minister of the

Interior Heinrich Himmler. This area included the mountainous district in southern Germany where the fanatical Nazis were expected to put up a last-ditch defense of the so-called "National Redoubt."

The "National Redoubt," like so many Nazi propaganda inventions, turned out to be a gigantic hoax. Himmler did not even stay in the South Defense Area but attempted separate peace negotiations with the Allies after Hitler's alleged death. He was finally arrested in civilian clothes with forged papers trying to escape the Allied dragnet after the surrender. Choosing suicide rather than face trial as a war criminal, Himmler took poison and died [May 23, 1945].

The actual meeting of the Allied and Russian armies took place on the banks of the Elbe River near Torgau [April 27, 1945] when a patrol of the 69th Infantry Division made contact with a patrol of the First Ukrainian Army. Germany was cut in two parts, and the end was near.

Disintegration and Surrender of the German Armies in the West

The Germans acknowledged that the end was near when Hitler divided the Reich into two defense areas. He made it even clearer in another General Order [April 19, 1945] calling upon Wehrmacht leaders to cease attacks on Allied strong points and concentrate on weak points. He stressed the desirability of waging small war on Allied communications and supply centers. Using the illustration of the success of the Russian partisans in 1942–44, he called upon German troops everywhere to wage guerrilla warfare. Dr. Goebbels' propaganda ministry created one last bogey-man. He now called upon all Germans behind the Allied lines to become "Werewolves" and kill Allied troops.

Since the 21st Army Group had reached its objectives [May 1, 1945], advances were thereafter confined to the 6th Army Group front. Passau was captured [May 2, 1945]. On the following day [May 3, 1945] Seventh Army troops crossed the Inn River and reached Innsbruck. Combat patrols of the U. S. 103rd Division made contact with the Fifth Army advancing from Italy toward the Brenner Pass. Junction was made at Vitipeno [May 4, 1945]. Fighting ended

333

on this front [*May 5, 1945*] with the surrender of German Army Group G.

The disintegration of the German armies in the West is illustrated by the rapidly increasing rate of prisoners taken from March onward. During the month of March the average daily bag of prisoners was 18,000. In the first two weeks of April the daily average of German prisoners taken rose to 42,500. These men did not surrender because they lacked weapons, ammunition, or food. They were short of gasoline for their armored units and planes, but they still were able to fight a delaying action. They surrendered because they knew the war was lost. The frantic Nazi propaganda campaign to keep the people and the army fighting had no effect upon them. They came in individually and in droves. By the end of April prisoners were coming into Allied cages in uncounted numbers. The grand total of military prisoners taken in the West [*March 1–May 5, 1945*] was 2,835,000.

With the Russian armies assaulting Berlin, Heinrich Himmler appealed [*April 23–24*] through Count Folke Bernadotte of Sweden to the governments of Britain and the U. S. asking for a separate peace. This was refused. On May 1, 1945, Grand Admiral Karl Doenitz announced to the German people that Adolf Hitler had died and that he had been designated as Führer. Surrender negotiations were again opened by Admiral Doenitz [*May 3, 1945*] who sent Admiral Von Friedeburg on a mission to see Field Marshal Montgomery. Admiral Von Friedeburg signed the surrender of the German forces confronting the 21st Army Group effective May 5, 1945. He then proceeded to Reims where he was joined [*May 6, 1945*] by Colonel General Alfred Jodl, Chief of Staff of the Wehrmacht. There [*May 7, 1945*] at 0230 hours, Jodl signed the act of surrender for the German high command. Lieutenant General Walter Bedell Smith signed for General Eisenhower, General Ivan Susloparoff for the Soviet high command, and General F. Sevez for the French. The text of the Reims surrender is given in Appendix IX.

On the following day [*May 8, 1945*] a second act of surrender was signed at Berlin by Field Marshal Wilhelm Keitel as Chief of the German high command in the presence

334

of Marshal Gregory Zhukov of the Soviet Union, Air Chief Marshal Sir Arthur Tedder, and General Carl Spaatz.

Order of Battle of the Allied Armies in Italy

After the Allied offensives in Italy during the autumn of 1944 which saw the U. S. Fifth and the British Eighth Armies advance from the Gothic Line [*September 1, 1944*] to a line running from Viareggio–Barga–Vergato–Faenza–Ravenna [*December 26, 1944*], the Allied command was reorganized. Field Marshal Sir Harold Alexander replaced Field Marshal Sir Henry Maitland Wilson as Supreme Allied Commander in the Mediterranean. Lieutenant General (now General) Joseph T. McNarney (appointed November 1, 1944) remained as Deputy Commander and as Commander of all American forces in the Mediterranean. Lieutenant General (now General) Mark W. Clark, formerly commander of the U. S. Fifth Army, became commander of the 15th Army Group.

15th Army Group, General Mark W. Clark
    U. S. Fifth Army, Lieutenant General Lucian K. Truscott.
    British Eighth Army, Lieutenant General Sir Richard L. McCreery
Allied Air Forces in the Mediterranean, Lieutenant General Ira C. Eaker
    U. S. Fifteenth (Strategic) Air Force, Major General Nathan F. Twining
    U. S. Twelfth (Tactical) Air Force, Major General John K. Cannon

Italy was long regarded by the Allied troops who fought and worked there as the "forgotten front." From the landings at Reggio di Calabria [*September 3, 1943*] and Salerno [*September 8, 1943*], through the bloody battles of the Gustav Line, Cassino, Anzio, Rome, and northward, the Allied forces had engaged a numerous, well equipped and well led enemy. Some of the bitterest fighting and severest hardships of the European war were the lot of the troops in Italy. If the gains measured in terms of miles did not seem great, the troops of the U. S. Fifth and British Eighth Armies had the satisfaction of knowing that their fighting kept an estimated 25 German divisions tied down in Italy while the decisive campaigns of the war were being carried out by Allied and Russian armies against the Reich itself. In the end they shattered the German forces in Italy.

The German Collapse in Italy

The German forces in Italy held the rich Po Valley with the populous industrial centers of Turin and Genoa. Under protection of German bayonets, Mussolini re-created the fiction of power by establishing a so-called Italian Socialist Republic. Marshal Rodolfo Graziani, defeated by Wavell in Libya, headed a handful of Italian Fascist divisions under the Germans. Until the spring of 1945, the German commander in Italy was Field Marshal Albert Kesselring. He was recalled to take command of the failing German defenses in the homeland and his place was taken by General Heinrich von Vietinhoff-Scheel.

The final Allied offensive began on the Italian front [April 9, 1945]. It coincided in point of time with a drive launched by French forces on the French-Italian frontier. The British Eighth Army drove forward toward Argenta [April 19, 1945] while the U. S. Fifth Army advanced toward Bologna which fell [April 21, 1945]. Porto Maggiore was captured by the Eighth Army [April 21, 1945], but repeated attacks on Ferrara failed to shake the German garrison.

Perhaps because they realized that the fate of the Reich had already been decided on the battlefields of Germany, the German troops in Italy then quit fighting in large numbers. They surrendered Ferrara, La Spezia, and Modena together with 40,000 prisoners [April 23, 1945]. The Allied armies thereupon advanced rapidly; both armies reached the Po River [April 23, 1945] and crossed it [April 25, 1945]. Troops of the U. S. Fifth Army entered Genoa [April 25, 1945]. Brescia, Vicenza, Padua, and Milan were entered by Allied troops [April 28–29, 1945].

Partisan troops arrested Mussolini in Como [April 28, 1945] and shot him. Other former Fascist leaders were rounded up and executed. April 30 was a great day of liber-

336

ation in northern Italy: Venice was freed by partisan troops and American forces entered Turin. British troops of the Eighth Army crossed the Piave River and the total bag of German prisoners captured in northern Italy rose to 100,000. General Mark W. Clark declared [*April 30, 1945*] that 25 German divisions in northern Italy had been destroyed and that German military power had practically ceased to exist on that front.

Contact was made [*May 1, 1945*] between patrols of the British Eighth Army and forces of Marshal Tito advancing westward from Trieste. The northward sweep of the U. S. Fifth Army reached to within two miles of the Swiss frontier [*April 29, 1945*]. At Vitipeno [*May 4, 1945*] contact was made between patrols of the U. S. Fifth Army and those of the U. S. Seventh Army. The campaign in northern Italy was now over.

Surrender negotiations covering the German forces in Italy were instituted by General Von Vietinhoff-Scheel [*April 26, 1945*]. Emissaries representing him and Obergruppenführer Karl Wolff, Chief of the SS and German General Plenipotentiary of the Wehrmacht in Italy, arrived by plane at Casserta [*April 28, 1945*], They signed an act of surrender covering all the German and Italian military forces in Italy and southern Austria. Hostilities ceased on this front [*May 2, 1945*] at 1200 hours.

IV. THE END OF THE LUFTWAFFE AND THE GERMAN NAVY

Order of Battle of the Allied Air Forces in Western Europe

From September 1, 1944, to May 8, 1945, the order of battle of the Allied Air Forces in Western Europe was as follows:

Great Britain
Marshal of the Royal Air Force: Sir Charles Portal
Commander in Chief of the Bomber Command: Air Chief Marshal Sir Arthur Harris
Commander in Chief of the Fighter Command: Air Marshal Sir R. Hill

Commander in Chief of the Second Tactical Air Force:
Air Marshal Sir Arthur Coningham
Commander in Chief of the Coastal Command: Air Chief
Marshal Sir William Sholto Douglas

United States

Commander of U. S. Strategic Air Forces in Europe:
General Carl Spaatz
Commander, U. S. Eighth Air Force: Lieutenant General
James Doolittle
Commander, U. S. Ninth Air Force: Lieutenant General
Hoyt S. Vandenberg

The prelude to the defeat of the Luftwaffe may be said to
have taken place [*February 20–26, 1944*] when the U. S.
Eighth Air Force carried out a series of heavy raids on German aircraft plants at Regensburg, Augsburg, Fürth, and
Stuttgart. These raids were aimed at two objectives: to
force German fighter planes to give battle; second, to strike
at German plane replacements in the manufacturing phase.
The February raids cut fighter strength considerably and
helped the Allied invasion. The contribution of Allied tactical air forces to the successful outcome of the battles of
France and Germany was very great. German generals have
testified to the effectiveness of Allied fighter bombers in dis-
rupting communications and tactical organizations.

Repeated raids by Allied heavy bombers had cut down the
manufacture of German planes, ball bearings, and aviation
fuel. By the autumn of 1944 Germany could still produce
planes, but she could no longer provide pilots, replacement
crews, ground crews, spare parts, fuel, and safe bases for the
continuous operation of all these planes. A considerable part
of Germany's air reserve was expended in the Rundstedt
offensive and the Battle of the Bulge. Speedy jet-propelled
fighters and fighter bombers, notably the Messerschmitt 262
and the Arado 234, were introduced but could not cope with
the overwhelming power of the Allied air forces because of
shortages of fuel and the breakdown of organization in the
Luftwaffe. Air Chief Marshal Douglas revealed that nearly
2000 serviceable German aircraft were found in the British
zone of occupation after the surrender.

338

Destruction of the Luftwaffe

As the battle line reached the German frontiers, the Luftwaffe was restricted to the use of airfields in Germany. It made a concentrated target. Unable to stave off the constant Allied attacks on its flying fields, the Luftwaffe's plane losses on the ground rapidly mounted. As the Allied strategic bombing program reached its final stages, the fighter planes, which hitherto escorted bombers, were now able to attack German flying fields. General Carl Spaatz announced [*April 15, 1945*] that the strategic air war against Germany had been successfully terminated. Henceforth U. S. heavy bombers were to be used for tactical purposes.

In eight days of relentless bombing and strafing [*April 10–18, 1945*] fighter bombers of the U. S. Eighth Air Force destroyed some 2,000 German planes on the ground. It was the greatest destruction of enemy air power achieved during the war. German plane losses in April were estimated at about 5,000 planes and most of them were destroyed on the ground. No air force in the world could stand such losses. Foreseeing the end, Reichsmarschal Hermann Goering resigned [*April 26, 1945*] as head of the Luftwaffe. He was replaced by Colonel General Robert Ritter von Greim, who committed suicide at Salzburg [*May 24, 1945*]. In the last days of the war the Luftwaffe ceased to be a factor of military importance. It simply dissolved in chaos. The largest organized unit, some 48,000 men, was captured in the American zone. Most of the Luftwaffe personnel were given rifles and hastily converted into infantry.

Allied Air Attacks on the Reich

It will be some time before the full extent of damage inflicted upon the Reich and its capacity to wage war by the Allied air forces can be accurately determined. All the leading German military and industrial prisoners taken in the last days of the war agree that strategic bombing contributed greatly to the final defeat of the Reich. Field Marshal Von Rundstedt, captured south of Munich [*May 1, 1945*] listed four main reasons for the military collapse of Germany:

(1) The Allies' tremendous air superiority, which hampered German troop movements.

(2) Lack of fuel for tanks and "the few planes we still had," resulting from the Allied air offensive against synthetic oil plants, and the loss of the Rumanian oil fields.

(3) The systematic destruction by the Allied air forces of the Reich's railway communications.

(4) The destruction by air of Germany's industrial centers, and the loss of Silesia, which prevented production of arms and ammunition.

Strategic bombing did not destroy all German industry; it knocked out key plants. Gasoline and oil were so scarce in Germany during the last weeks of the war that panzer units and planes were immobilized. A considerable amount of manufacturing was done in underground plants in Germany, but it was not enough to stave off defeat.

The main failure of the Luftwaffe was in not being able to fight off the strategic bombers of the Allied air forces. From the beginning of the war to May 8, 1945, British and American planes dropped a total of 2,453,595 tons of bombs on Germany and on German occupied targets in Europe. This was 315 times as great a tonnage of bombs as the Luftwaffe dropped on Britain during the same period. The RAF flew a total of 2,314,651 sorties in the war against the Axis in Europe. British and American bomber losses for the war in Europe amounted to 8,001. The U. S. Army Air Forces lost 7,165 fighter planes in Europe. RAF losses to V-E day in the European and Mediterranean theaters were 16,385 planes and 104,514 officers and men. Against these losses the Germans lost to the U. S. Army Air Forces alone an estimated 20,574 planes in the air and 12,337 on the ground. The table of Axis plane losses in Europe up to May 5, 1945 (excluding planes lost on the ground) kept by the British magazine *The Aeroplane,* lists a total of 31,298 planes destroyed.

In its operations up to May 8, 1945, the U. S. Eighth Air Force flew a total of 616,000 bomber and 260,574 fighter plane sorties. It destroyed a total of 11,439 enemy aircraft in the air and 4,207 on the ground. It dropped 701,300 tons of bombs on enemy targets, destroyed 4,660 locomotives, 6,038 freight cars, 1,449 tank cars, and 4,882 trucks. It damaged many more. The U. S. Ninth Air Force flew a total

340

of 400,000 sorties and destroyed 4,228 enemy planes. Its losses were 2,944 planes. The U. S. Twelfth Air Force flew a total of 377,069 sorties and dropped 198.042 tons of bombs on enemy targets. The U. S. Fifteenth Air Force flew a total of 280,987 sorties and dropped 380,047 tons of bombs. Further statistics on the operations of Allied Air Forces in Europe are given in Appendices VI, VII and VIII.

The contribution of Allied air forces to the victory in Europe did not end with the destruction of the German air force and with strategic bombing. Tactical aviation played a very great part in the destruction of the German Army. Transport planes aided enormously in the Rhine crossing and in supplying the fast-moving Allied armored forces in the drive into central Germany.

Field Marshal Sir Bernard Montgomery summed up the gratitude of Allied ground forces for the contribution of the air forces to the final victory by writing to Marshal of the Royal Air Force, Sir Charles Portal, as follows:

"At this historic moment I would like to express to you the deep sense of gratitude that we soldiers owe to you and your splendid force. The mighty weapon of air power has enabled us, first to win a great victory quickly, and secondly, to win that victory with fewer casualties than would otherwise have been the case. We are all deeply conscious of these facts."

The End of the German Navy

The German fleet had never possessed enough strength in surface vessels to challenge the Royal Navy. After losing several valuable ships in attacks on Allied convoys, the German fleet restricted its operations on the high seas. With the replacement of Grand Admiral Erich Räder [*January 30, 1943*] as head of the Navy by Admiral (later Grand Admiral) Karl Doenitz, the chief occupation of the German fleet was to support the U-boat war. After the destruction of the 26,000-ton Nazi battleship *Scharnhorst* [*December 26, 1943*] by ships of the Home Fleet under Admiral Sir Bruce Fraser, the German fleet undertook few sorties from German harbors. Individual German ships operated in the Baltic, the Channel, and in Norwegian waters, but they lived a dangerous existence and were constantly harassed by Allied air power.

In 1944 the most powerful German warship in commission was the 45,000-ton battleship *Tirpitz*. This vessel went into hiding in Tromsö Fjord, Norway, behind torpedo nets and antiaircraft screens. Damaged by repeated RAF attacks, the *Tirpitz* was sunk [*November 12, 1944*] by RAF Lancasters carrying six-ton "earthquake" bombs.

During the Russian advance along the Baltic, German surface ships occasionally operated against enemy ground forces, but as the amount of German-controlled territory dwindled, the ships of the German Navy were driven into their own or Danish harbors. Here they came under repeated heavy air attacks in the last days of the war. In April and early May all the German ships were scuttled, sunk by Allied action, or surrendered.

The 10,000-ton pocket battleship *Admiral Scheer* was sunk by planes of the RAF while at its dock in Kiel [*April 9, 1945*]. The 6,000-ton cruiser *Köln* was found sunk in dock at Wilhelmshaven. The cruisers *Admiral Hipper* and *Emden* were found damaged at Kiel along with 11 destroyers. The 10,000-ton pocket battleship *Lützow* was scuttled or sunk in Swinemünde harbor. The 26,000-ton battleship *Gneisenau* (sister ship to the *Scharnhorst*) was found sunk as a block ship in Gdynia harbor along with the old battleship *Schleswig-Holstein*. The incomplete 25,000-ton carrier *Graf Zeppelin* was damaged at Stettin. The 6,000-ton cruiser *Leipzig* was surrendered in a damaged condition at the Danish port of Aabenraa. The heavy cruiser *Seydlitz* was blown up in Königsberg. The only German surface vessels found in a condition to take the sea were the 10,000-ton cruiser *Prinz Eugen,* the 6,000-ton cruiser *Nürnberg,* and some 24 destroyers which surrendered to the Allies at Copenhagen.

German U-boats in harbor or at sea were included in the act of surrender signed at Reims. Up to the end of 1942, German U-boats took a heavy toll of Allied shipping, but they did not prevent the transfer of American military power to Europe. A total of 4,453,061 American troops were embarked from the United States to participate in the war against the European Axis. Of this total only 3,604 men were lost at sea from all causes including German U-boats. This amounted to .04 per cent of the troops shipped, as compared to .072 per cent lost at sea in the First World War. A grand total of 4,770 Allied and neutral ships aggregating 21,-140,000 gross tons was lost during the period of the European war. U-boats accounted for 2,770 of these vessels, aggregating 14,500,00 gross tons. The remainder were lost to mines, aircraft, surface vessels, accidents, and other causes. Details of Allied shipping losses are given in an appendix to this volume.

The final surrenders of German naval and military personnel in the Channel Islands and isolated French ports occurred [*May 9, 1945*] when Rear Admiral Frisius of the Dunkirk garrison signed an act of surrender covering a total of about 130,000 men in the French ports and Channel Islands.

35. VICTORY IN THE EAST

I. RED ARMY AUTUMN OFFENSIVES, 1944

The German Military Situation

In the autumn of 1944 Germany's military situation was hopeless. Her armies in the West were retreating to the Siegfried Line. Finland, Rumania, and Bulgaria had been knocked out of the war as a result of Russian victories. The Red Army had driven the Wehrmacht to the frontiers of East Prussia and the gates of Warsaw. Nazi leaders were feverishly preparing to defend Hungary and Austria. German hopes of European domination were shattered. Germany was isolated and her armies were stretched out from Norway to Crete, from Holland to Switzerland, and from the Baltic Sea to Belgrade. Her air force had been reduced to a remnant and her war industries and communications system were being reduced to rubble by Allied bombers. It was beyond Germany's power to defeat the armies of the United Nations or seriously damage their war industrial centers. Germany was defeated, but she could not make peace. Her leaders, facing death sentences as war criminals, could not surrender. Their only recourse was to continue the war in the hope that the United Nations might split.

On the pretext of "saving Europe from Bolshevism," German propagandists tried to sow discord among the United Nations. Fearing Russia because of their own barbarous conduct in Russian territory, the Germans concentrated their main ground forces on the Eastern Front. The German strategy of holding on to every inch of territory for political and ideological reasons produced the conditions of final defeat in the winter and spring of 1945. A greatly superior Red Army, striking first at one point and then at another along the immense Eastern Front, kept the German armies off balance and steadily drove them back to the heart of Germany. Only at certain points where prestige values were at stake were the Germans able to put up a prolonged defense of any area the Russians chose to attack. But Russian power overwhelmed the fanatical defenders of these hold-out points.

Order of Battle of the Soviet Armies

At the beginning of September 1944, the order of battle of the Red Army was as follows: Marshal of the Soviet Union, Joseph Stalin; Chief of Staff of the Red Army, Marshal A. M. Vassilievsky; Chief of the Red Army Artillery, Marshal N. Voronov; Chief of the Red Army Aviation, Marshal A. Novikov.

From north to south Soviet Armies or Army Groups were deployed as follows:

Leningrad Army, Marshal L. Govorov

Third Baltic Army, Colonel General I. S. Maslenikov

Second Baltic Army, General A. Yeremenko

First Baltic Army, Colonel General I. C. Bagramian

Third White Russian Army, Colonel General I. D. Chernyakovsky

Second White Russian Army, Colonel General M. Zakharov

First White Russian Army, General K. Rokossovsky

First Ukrainian Army, Marshal G. K. Zhukov

Fourth Ukrainian Army, Colonel General I. Y. Petrov

Second Ukrainian Army, Marshal R. Y. Malinovsky

Third Ukrainian Army, General F. Tolbukhin

The composition of these armies is unknown and their alignment changed during the ensuing campaigns. In some instances these units were in reality army groups. The Russian communiqués commonly referred to army fronts rather than armies or army groups as in the Western tradition. Thus Marshal G. K. Zhukov was in all probability commanding the 1st Ukrainian Army Group for we hear of Marshal I. S. Konev commanding the First Ukrainian Army under him.

The strength and composition of the German forces on the Eastern front are unknown but it has been estimated that over 2,000,000 men were detailed to defend the German front in the East. In the final stages of the war the Germans switched the numbers and names of divisions and battle groups so frequently that the preparation of a battle order of German units is impossible. Because of the lack of detailed information on operations of both the German and Russian armies, the account of the final campaigns on the Eastern front as given in this volume is necessarily brief and inadequate.

The Campaign in the Baltic and Poland

Advances of the Red Army on the northern front reached the Narev River [*September 5, 1944*] and cleared the eastern bank of the Bug River [*September 6, 1944*]. Operations of the Leningrad Army led to the capture of Tallinn [*September 22, 1944*], capital of Estonia, and freed the Gulf of Finland. A large-scale offensive mounted by the Third and Second Baltic Armies on a 160-mile front between Lake Peipus and the Dvina River [*September 16, 1944*] led to the investment [*September 26, 1944*] and the fall of Riga [*October 13, 1944*].

Immediate use of the port of Riga was denied the Russians by Germans garrisoning Oesel Island and by a large force left to hold a beachhead on Riga Gulf between Ventspils and Liepaja. Troops of the First Baltic Army attacked the Sworbe Peninsula on the southern end of Oesel Island [*October 19, 1944*] and forced a withdrawal of the German defenders [*October 23/24, 1944*]. The German Latvian beachhead was reduced in size by Russian attacks [*February 19-28, 1945* and *March 3-14, 1945*] but held out until the final German surrender [*May 8, 1945*]. The Red Army then announced that 146,000 German prisoners surrendered in the Latvian beachhead.

On the Polish front the Russian armies advanced in September to the Czechoslovakian frontier which was crossed [*September 13, 1944*] southwest of Przemysl. In central Poland troops of the First White Russian Army captured Praga [*September 14, 1944*] the eastern suburb of Warsaw. Here, despite the hopes of the Polish patriot forces which had risen in revolt under the leadership of General Bor (Lieutenant General Tadeusz Komorowski), the advance of the Russian armies halted after a frontal attack [*September 17, 1944*] failed to take the city. General Bor surrendered the Polish patriot army, which had been supplied by British and American planes, after sixty-three days of resistance [*October 2, 1944*].

The First Baltic Army launched an offensive toward the Baltic coast in Lithuania in October. This attack reached its objective sixteen miles north of Memel [*October 10, 1944*]. Further attacks by the First Baltic Army extended the breakthrough until a 70-mile front was established on the Niemen River [*October 23, 1944*]. Memel was held by the Germans until late in January 1945. It was occupied by the Red Army [*January 28, 1945*]. In the meantime the main direction of Russian attacks had changed.

East Prussia was invaded for the first time in the Second World War [*October 19, 1944*] when troops of the Third White Russian Army crossed the frontier below the Kaunas-Königsberg railway. After capturing Goldap [*October 23, 1944*] and Augustow [*October 24, 1944*], the line stabilized [*November 5, 1944*] after the Germans recaptured Goldap.

The Campaign in Hungary

Early in 1944 German troops occupied Hungary [*March 18-20, 1944*], and Field Marshal Doeme Sztojay was set up as a Nazi puppet ruler. He was succeeded by Bela Imredy, another Nazi puppet.

The withdrawal of Rumania and Bulgaria from the Axis

and their subsequent declarations of war on Germany radically changed the military situation on the southern front in September 1944. The Third Ukrainian Army invaded Yugoslavia and captured Belgrade [*October 20, 1944*]. The Germans slowly retreated in the south in order to prolong the escape corridor for their forces in Greece and Yugoslavia.

Aided by approximately 12 Rumanian divisions, the Fourth and Second Ukrainian Armies drove the Germans out of Transylvania [*September 28–October 5, 1944*] and crossed the Hungarian border east of Szeged [*October 6, 1944*]. Continuing their advance, forward elements of the Second Ukrainian Army reached Baja on the Danube River 84 miles south of Budapest [*October 21, 1944*]. After fluctuating battles in this area, the Red Army captured Alsó-Némedi, ten miles from Budapest [*November 3, 1944*]. The Germans put up a very stiff fight for the approaches to Budapest, and after the Russians had encircled the city, they fought a street-by-street battle which did not end until its complete capture [*February 13, 1945*]. As will be shown later, the Germans mounted their last great counteroffensive of the war in the Lake Balaton sector in an effort to relieve their forces in Hungary.

Hungary made an effort to get out of the war [*October 15, 1944*] when Regent Admiral Horthy appealed for an armistice. His appeal was renounced and he was overthrown by the pro-Fascist Red Arrow group under Ferenc Szalasy. Finally a Provisional Hungarian National Assembly was set up [*December 21, 1944*] at Debrecen. General Bela Miklos became Provisional Premier and appealed to the Russians for an armistice [*December 30, 1944*]. On the same day [*December 30, 1944*], the Provisional Hungarian Government declared war on Germany. Since Austria was a part of the Reich, this meant that Germany had lost all her former allies.

II. THE GREAT RED WINTER OFFENSIVE

The Drive in Central Poland

The front in central Poland had been relatively stable

since the Red Army had reached the Vistula and captured Praga [*September 14, 1944*]. The major fighting on the Eastern Front in the late autumn and early winter of 1944–45 had taken place in Hungary. Meantime the Red Army prepared for a great drive from Poland into East Prussia and Silesia. This drive was launched [*January 12, 1945*] by five Russian armies or army groups, the First, Second, and Third White Russian, and the First and Fourth Ukrainian. At the outset of the offensive the front in the East ran approximately from Memel–Gumbinnen–Augustow–Narev River–Vistula River–Wisloka River to the Dukla Pass.

After a tremendous artillery preparation [*January 12, 1945*], the great Russian winter offensive began. Immediate progress was made in the center. Warsaw was captured [*January 17, 1945*], and the First White Russian Army reached a position beyond Lodz [*January 19, 1945*]. Krakow was captured by the First Ukrainian Army on the same day [*January 19, 1945*].

The pattern of the Russian winter offensive was designed to exploit German weakness in the East. A drive toward Königsberg was launched directly from the Gumbinnen area, while two spearheads were driven northward from Poland aimed at cutting off East Prussia in the Danzig–Elbing area. As was customary in German military planning, their strongest resistance was offered on the northern and southern flanks of the Russian advance. Königsberg was defended stubbornly, and the Russian advance toward Elbing was slow and costly. But the Germans could not defend all areas. In the south the First Ukrainian Army broke through German defenses, crossed the Silesian border and captured Gross-Strehlitz [*January 22, 1945*]. Breslau was by-passed and under siege. The great German industrial area of Silesia was now directly threatened. The Oder River was reached by the First Ukrainian Army [*January 23, 1945*], and the following day [*January 24, 1945*] the industrial center of Oppeln fell into Russian hands. In the north the Second White Russian Army fought its way around Grudziadz [*January 28, 1945*] and captured Elbing after a street-by-street battle [*January 26–February 7, 1945*]. German flank forces having

348

been pushed back, it was now possible for the Russian armies in the center to make great progress.

Tremendous gains were made by the Russians in central Poland. The First White Russian Army advanced rapidly and by-passed Bydgoszcz, Poznan and Torun [*January 26–27, 1945*] where German garrisons held out for some time. The Germans reacted to these advances by withdrawing their Memel bridgehead [*January 28, 1945*] and by retreating to Königsberg, which came under close siege [*January 29–30, 1945*]. Further spectacular advances of the First White Russian Army brought it to the Oder River [*February 2, 1945*]. This advance was widened along the front Küstrin–Frankfurt–Fürstenberg [*February 3–4, 1945*]. Berlin was now only 45 miles distant from the Red Army Oder River positions. Early efforts of the Russians to cross the Oder in the Küstrin–Frankfurt area [*February 5–6, 1945*] failed. It became evident that the Germans were making their final defense of the Reich on the Oder and Neisse River line.

Preparations for the Final Assault on Berlin

In something more than a month [*January 12–February 18, 1945*], the Red Army had driven a tremendous salient into the Reich. The battle line now ran approximately from the Bay of Danzig at Elbing to Matawy–Chojnice–Eberswalde–Küstrin–Frankfurt–Crossen–Sagan–Namberg–Landau–Oppeln. Grudziadz, Ponzon, Glogau, and Breslau were holding out behind the Russian lines, as was Königsberg and the German beachhead in Latvia. After these great gains it was necessary for the Russians to widen the base of the salient before driving in on Berlin itself.

Meantime in Hungary the German garrison at Budapest had finally surrendered [*February 13, 1945*]. Despite the fact that Berlin itself was menaced, the Germans stubbornly continued the fight in northern Hungary and prepared to launch their final counteroffensive of the war in that area.

Operations of the Third and Second White Russian Armies in February and March were aimed at widening the salient in the north and effecting a new breakthrough to the Baltic Sea in the direction of Kolberg and Stettin. Russian attacks beginning February 19, 1945, gradually narrowed the German hold on the Königsberg–Danzig beachhead which was completely isolated when the First White Russian Army reached Kolberg [*February 26, 1945*]. Kolberg itself was not immediately captured by the Russians; it became another German "hedgehog" behind the advancing front. Neustettin was captured [*February 28, 1945*]; Grudziadz was reduced [*March 6, 1945*]; and Stolp was captured [*March 9, 1945*]. On the Bay of Danzig the Russian line reached Puck and the Hel Peninsula [*March 18, 1945*]. Stettin was under long-range attack and the battle front ran from the Gulf of Stettin along the Oder and Neisse to the Hron River.

The final German counteroffensives of the war were launched near Lake Balaton [*March 5, 1945*] in an effort to check the Red Army advance and possibly to recapture Budapest for prestige reasons. Some German gains were made northeast of Lake Balaton [*March 5–15, 1945*], but these advances were soon checked by Red Army attacks. The Third Ukrainian Army launched its own offensive [*March 23, 1945*] north of Lake Balaton and broke through the German line. This was a major thrust and reached Szombathely [*March 29, 1945*]. The important industrial city of Wiener Neustadt fell to the Red Army [*April 3, 1945*]. Without halting, the Third Ukrainian Army swung northeastward and reached the Danube River at Klosterneuberg [*April 7, 1945*], encircling Vienna. Some pretense was put up by the Nazi Propaganda Ministry that Vienna would be defended street by street, but the German garrison thought otherwise. The defense collapsed [*April 13, 1945*] when remnants of the garrison surrendered.

Meanwhile in the north Gdynia and Danzig surrendered [*March 29, 1945*], and Königsberg was captured by the Second White Russian Army together with 92,000 German prisoners [*April 9, 1945*]. The stage was now set for the final Russian advance on Berlin.

The Battle for Berlin

According to an interview given to Associated Press correspondents in Berlin [*June 10, 1945*] after the final victory,

Marshal Gregory K. Zhukov declared that the final battle for Berlin was won on the Oder front [*April 15–16, 1945*]. According to the Marshal, the Red Army massed 22,000 guns and mortars in preparation for the final breakthrough. Five thousand planes flew 15,000 sorties in twenty-four hours preceding the attack which was launched at night [*April 15–16*] on a wide front between Küstrin and Frankfurt. According to Marshal Zhukov's estimates, the Germans had concentrated half a million men to defend the Oder line.

In four days of fighting [*April 15–20, 1945*] the German Oder front was destroyed and according to Russian accounts 350,000 prisoners were taken. Troops of the First White Russian Army reached Jüterbog [*April 20, 1945*] and fighting began on the outskirts of Berlin [*April 22, 1945*]. The Elbe River was reached [*April 23, 1945*] near Meissen by elements of the First White Russian Army, and contact was made with patrols of the U. S. Ninth Army near Torgau [*April 26, 1945*].

While street fighting raged in the suburbs of Berlin, the First White Russian and the First Ukrainian Armies drew a steel trap around the city. It was closed [*April 28, 1945*], despite counterattacks of the German Twelfth Army which had left the American front on the Elbe and had raced eastward to defend the capital of the Reich.

Hitler's death was announced [*May 1, 1945*] by Grand Admiral Karl Doenitz over the Flensburg radio. This was a signal for the end. Remnants of the German Twelfth Army turned about face and attempted to reach the American lines in order to surrender. The Berlin garrison, some 130,000 men, surrendered to the Russians [*May 2, 1945*] at 1500 hours. The final act of surrender was signed in Berlin by Field Marshal Keitel [*May 8, 1945*].

Fighting continued in Czechoslovakia until May 11, 1945, when 374,000 German troops surrendered to the Americans and 26,000 to the Yugoslav forces. Breslau capitulated [*May 7, 1945*]. The German garrisons on the Hel Peninsula north of Danzig and on the island of Bornholm obeyed the surrender decree signed by Field Marshal Keitel. About one million prisoners were taken on the Eastern Front in the final operations of the war.

351

German Casualties

Final figures on German losses in the European war are not available. On account of the confusion existing in Germany at the end of the war losses may never be completely reported. A document captured in the home of General Hermann Reinecke of the Wehrmacht propaganda section set the German military losses to November 30, 1944, at 4,064,438 killed, wounded, and missing. Of these 1,709,-739 were listed as killed. German losses from November 30, 1944, to the end of the war have been conservatively estimated at over 500,000. This would bring the German casualty list to four and a half million. If the German prisoners taken by the Allied and Russian armies in the last days of the war are added, this accounts for seven and a half million men—approximately the total strength of the Wehrmacht and special troops.

36. BREAKING JAPAN'S INNER DEFENSES

I. OPERATIONS IN BURMA AND CHINA

Opening the Ledo Road to Kunming

After the capture of Myitkyina [*August 3, 1945*], Chinese and American forces in northern Burma pressed on toward the important road junction of Bhamo. Changes were made in the American command in the China–Burma–India Theater. General Joseph W. Stilwell was recalled to Washington [*October 28, 1944*] and subsequently became Commander of Army Ground Forces. Lieutenant General Daniel I. Sultan became American commander in the Burma–India Theater. The American command in China was assumed by Major General (now Lieutenant General) Albert C. Wedemeyer.

The basic plan of General Stilwell for opening a road from Ledo to Kunming remained in effect. The campaign in the north continued as Chinese troops captured Myothit, some 87 miles south of Myitkyina [*October 30, 1944*]. Lungling was occupied [*November 3, 1944*], and the advance on Bhamo continued. After meeting strong initial resistance at

Bhamo, the Chinese 38th Division captured it [*December 15, 1944*] after the Japanese suddenly withdrew their forces. There was a motor road running from Myitkyina to Bhamo. After it was repaired and put in condition for traffic, the Ledo Road was extended to a point where it joined the old Burma Road.

After the fall of Bhamo, Japanese forces in the northern Shan States retreated to Namkham from which they were driven by Chinese troops [*January 15, 1945*]. There was only one more Japanese road block on the old Burma road a few miles north at Wanting. It was cleared by Chinese and American troops [*January 17–18, 1945*]. Troops of the Y Force operating from China cleared the Japs from the town of Mongyu [*January 27, 1945*], and the route to Kunming was open. The first American truck convoy led by Brigadier General (now Major General) Lewis A. Pick, who built the Ledo Road, rolled into Kunming, China [*February 4, 1945*]. The long isolation of China was ended. Generalissimo Chiang Kai-shek renamed the Ledo–Burma Road "The Stilwell Road" in honor of General Stilwell.

The British Offensives in Burma

After the repulse of the Japanese offensives on the Arakan and Manipur fronts, the British Fourteenth Army under command of Lieutenant General Sir W. J. Slim assumed the offensive. Cooperating with the Chinese-American drive in the north, British troops captured Katha [*December 16, 1944*].

Amphibious operations of the Indian XV Corps led to the occupation of Akyab [*January 4, 1945*] which the Japanese had abandoned. Ramree Island was occupied by troops of the Indian 26th Division [*January 21–February 17, 1945*]. At the beginning of 1945 it became apparent that the Japanese were withdrawing to the Irrawaddy River in an effort to shorten their lines.

The British campaign to recapture Mandalay and Rangoon began with the capture of Shwebo [*January 9, 1945*] by troops of the British IV Corps. Troops of the XXXIII Corps crossed the Irrawaddy River in force near Myinmu [*February 26–March 3, 1945*] and reached Awa Bridge 10 miles southwest of Mandalay [*March 18, 1945*]. The Indian 19th Division left its bridgehead on the Irrawaddy River at Singan and reached the northern outskirts of Mandalay [*March 8, 1945*]. Farther south troops of the IV Corps captured Meiktila [*March 2, 1945*] cutting Japanese communications lines to the south. The Japanese put up a street-by-street battle for Mandalay [*March 8–22, 1945*]. Collapse of Japanese resistance came [*March 22, 1945*] with the capture by the Indian 22nd Division of Fort Dufferin, the principal Japanese strongpoint. Mopping up operations continued in the Mandalay area for some time.

Rangoon, the principal port of Burma, fell to elements of the British IV Corps [*May 2–4, 1945*]. Very little Japanese resistance was encountered and it now became clear that the enemy was withdrawing his forces across the Sittang River. Pockets of Japanese resistance near Pegu continued to give trouble, but the major campaign was over. Lord Louis Mountbatten announced [*May 4, 1945*] that the Japanese had suffered 347,000 casualties (of which 97,000 were counted dead) in Burma and that the campaign was at an end. Several thousand additional Japanese troops were killed on the Sittang River front before the Japanese surrender.

The Japanese Offensives in China, 1944

The only theater in which Japanese forces were on the offensive in 1944 was China. Here they undertook operations designed to gain control of the remaining railway line running south from Hankow to Canton. They also mounted offensives in Hunan, Kwangsi, Kwangtung, and Kiangsi Provinces to destroy the forward bases of the U. S. Fourteenth Air Force. In effect their objectives were defensive in character. They wished to protect their own shipping and coastal installations from the damaging attacks of the Fourteenth Air Force, and they wished to secure an inland route of supply to or retreat from their bases in Indo-China, Malaya, and Burma. As American air and sea power reduced the strength and operating zone of the Japanese Navy, they might eventually lose control of the China Sea.

The first major Japanese attack came southward along

the Hanchow railway toward Hengyang which was captured [*August 8, 1944*]. From Hengyang drives were mounted against the American air bases in Hunan, Kwangsi, and Kiangsi Provinces. At the same time drives based on Canton aimed at American airbases in Kwangtung and Kwangsi Provinces. Japanese landing parties captured the coastal cities of Wenchow [*September 20, 1944*] and Foochow [*October 5, 1944*]. It was apparent that a concerted Japanese effort was under way to discourage war-weary China, and protect herself against possible further reverses in other theaters.

Under the threat of multiple Japanese columns, one American airbase after another in southeastern China had to be abandoned. The Japanese advance from Hengyang forced the abandonment of Lingling [*September 8, 1944*] and of the great base at Kweilin [*September 17, 1944*]. Wuchow was destroyed by the U. S. Fourteenth Air Force [*September 22, 1944*]; Tanchuk was abandoned [*November 1, 1944*]; Luichow and Kweiping were evacuated [*October 10–13, 1944*]. Nanning fell to the Japanese [*November 26, 1944*]. Japanese columns operating out of Nanning met columns advancing from Indo-China [*December 10, 1944*], completing a Japanese-dominated route from Korea to Malaya.

Throughout all these operations the ill-equipped Chinese forces continued to resist the Japanese, and despite the loss of their forward bases the Fourteenth Air Force maintained constant pressure on the Japanese lines of communications and shipping. Major General Claire Chennault reported that as of February 1945 the Fourteenth Air Force had destroyed 2,194 Japanese planes, sunk 409 vessels of 859,000 tons, and damaged 169 vessels of 670,000 tons. China was painfully hurt by the losses of 1944 but she did not waver in her prosecution of the war.

Chinese Offensives in 1945

China's armies assumed the offensive on the southern front in the spring of 1945 and throughout the summer steadily reduced the Japanese hold on former American airbases and on certain coastal cities. They fought their way into Foochow [*May 13, 1945*] only to be driven out [*May 17, 1945*]. They recaptured Diongloh [*May 20, 1945*], Hochih and Mamoi [*May 21, 1945*]. The first American airbase in southern China to be recaptured was Nanning which fell [*May 27, 1945*].

At the end of May 1945 Lieutenant General Albert C. Wedemeyer said that the Allies were passing from the defensive to the offensive and that he was "very optimistic concerning future military developments in China." Wenchow was captured by Chinese troops [*June 19, 1945*], and Luichow fell [*June 22–30, 1945*]. A Chinese drive on the great American airbase at Kweilin began in July. Pingsiang was captured [*July 6, 1945*] and Tanchuk fell into Chinese hands [*July 9, 1945*]. As the Chinese drive neared Kweilin it threatened to wipe out the main Japanese gains made in 1944.

II. RECONQUEST OF THE PHILIPPINES

Invasion of the Palaus

An American return to the Philippines had long been the dream of General Douglas MacArthur and the troops of the U. S. Sixth Army (General Walter Krueger) under his command. With this objective in view they had fought their way from Australia up the coast of New Guinea. With this objective in mind the fleets and forces of Admiral Nimitz had fought their way through Jap strongholds in the Central Pacific and were firmly entrenched in the Marianas. There remained barring the route to the Philippines only the Japanese forces in the New Guinea–Halmahera group and strong Japanese garrisons in the Palaus. Against these barriers both forces moved in September 1944.

Operations of the Southwest Pacific Command looking forward to an invasion of the Philippines began [*September 7, 1944*] when landings were made on Soepiori Island off Biak in Geelvink Bay. Eight days later [*September 15, 1944*] troops of the 31st Infantry Division and the 126th Infantry Regiment of the 32nd Division under command of Major General John C. Persons landed on the southwestern coast of Morotai, the northernmost island of the Halmahera group. Conquest of these areas gave the Sixth Army airbases from which to dominate the approaches to the Philippines.

The attack on the Palaus began with a bombardment by units of the U. S. Third Fleet [*September 6–7, 1944*]. After heavy bombardment and repeated air strikes, troops of the 1st Marine Division (Major General William H. Rupertus) landed on the southwestern shore of Peleliu Island [*September 15, 1944*]. Strong Japanese resistance was encountered and progress was slow. Especially severe fighting raged around "Bloody Nose Ridge" where Japanese troops were sheltered in caves and pillboxes.

Two days after the initial landing on Peleliu, troops of the U. S. 81st Infantry Division (Major General Paul J. Mueller) landed on Angaur Island [*September 17, 1944*] and crushed all organized Japanese resistance in three days. Thereafter, until the end of organized Japanese resistance on Peleliu [*October 13, 1944*], 81st Division troops cooperated in the conquest of that island. They also occupied the small island of Garakayo [*October 11, 1944*]. Ngesebus and Kongauru, two small islands in the Palau group, were occupied without resistance by Marine troops [*September 28, 1944*]. Organized fighting ceased in the Palaus [*October 13, 1944*], although small numbers of Japs infested the islands for some time and mopping-up operations went on for several weeks. Total Marine and Army casualties in the Palau operations to October 9, 1944, were given as 1,105 killed, 6,439 wounded, and 245 missing. Japanese casualties amounted to 11,380 killed and 228 captured.

Preliminary Air Strikes and Fleet Operations

Liberators of the Far Eastern Air Force began the attack on Mindanao Island [*September 1–2, 1944*]. Carrier-plane strikes of the U. S. Third Fleet on the Mindanao area [*September 9, 1944*] sank or damaged 89 Japanese vessels and destroyed 68 enemy planes. Attacks of the Third Fleet carrier planes extended to Cebú, Negros, and Panay Islands in the Central Philippines [*September 12–14, 1944*]. In these operations 156 Japanese planes were destroyed in combat and 277 on the ground. Eighty-four enemy vessels were sunk or damaged. Task Force 58, commanded by Vice Admiral Marc A. Mitscher, joined in the pre-invasion assault on the Philippines. In a series of bold raids on Japanese shipping in Manila Bay [*September 21–22, 1944*] and on airfields around the capital, 103 Japanese ships were sunk or damaged and 405 enemy planes were destroyed or damaged. Switching their attack to the Central Philippines [*September 24, 1944*] planes of Task Force 58 sank 21 more Japanese ships and destroyed 36 enemy planes.

In October planes of the U. S. Third Fleet took over the job of keeping Japanese air power checked in the Philippines, while Task Force 58 steamed northward in a diversionary stroke at Formosa. Planes of the Third Fleet attacked Japanese airfields in Luzon [*October 14–17, 1944*]. Japanese feeder airfields on Formosa were struck by planes of Task Force 58 [*October 12–14, 1944*]. Admiral Mitscher's flyers had a rich haul on Formosa. They destroyed 437 Japanese aircraft and sank or damaged 113 Japanese vessels. The Japanese fleet took one look at Mitscher's armada off Formosa and fled. The Japanese propaganda machine covered this retreat by manufacturing a fake naval engagement off Formosa [*October 16–17, 1944*] in which they claimed the "annihilation of Task Force 58."

The American pre-invasion air attacks on the Philippines were more successful than the first reports indicated. After we had recaptured most of the islands, General George C. Kenney, commander of the Far East Air Force, declared that wrecks of nearly 3,000 Japanese planes littered the airfields of the Philippines. With Japanese air power in the Philippines reduced to a remnant, the American invasion was ready to begin.

Invasion of Leyte

The invasion of Leyte Island in the Philippines was carried out [*October 21, 1944*] by the U. S. Sixth Army, consisting of the X Corps (Major General Franklin C. Sibert) and the XXIV Corps (Lieutenant General John R. Hodge). The U. S. Seventh Fleet (Vice Admiral Thomas C. Kinkaid) was under the direct control of General (now General of the

358

Army) Douglas MacArthur. The U. S. Third Fleet (Admiral William F. Halsey, Jr.) operated in direct support.

After a heavy bombardment carried out by the fleet, the X Corps (24th Infantry Division and 1st Cavalry Division) landed south of Taclobán. The XXIV Corps (7th and 96th Infantry Divisions) landed near Dulag. A secure beachhead was established on both fronts by the night of October 21st, and troops moved inland aiming at a juncture. One combat team of the XXIV Corps landed on Panaon Island just south of Leyte. The two American beachheads on Leyte were joined [*October 25, 1944*], and troops pushed inland against light opposition by the Japanese 16th Division.

Troops of the 1st Cavalry Division invaded Samar Island and secured solid footholds on both sides of San Juanico Strait [*October 30, 1944*]. Samar Island was found to be without a Japanese garrison and its occupation was accomplished with little difficulty. By the end of October the Leyte plain extending from Carigara to Dulag had been occupied by American troops. It appeared that the end of the campaign for Leyte was in sight. The Japanese high command, however, determined to reinforce the Leyte garrison, and a long-drawn-out battle for control of the island followed. Additional American units sent to Leyte included the 32nd Infantry Division, the 77th and 38th Infantry Divisions, the Americal Division, the 11th Airborne Division, the 112th Cavalry Regimental Combat Team, the 503rd Parachute Infantry Regiment, the 20th Armored Group, and the 1st Filipino Infantry.

Naval Battles off the Philippines

The American invasion of the Philippines presented the Japanese Navy with a challenge that could not be ignored. Japanese spokesmen had long insisted that the Philippines were of decisive importance to a Japanese victory. If the American invasion was successful, Japanese communications to Indo-China, Malaya, and the Netherlands East Indies would be cut. The Japanese Navy as well as the Army was largely dependent on oil shipments from the Indies. It was a case of fight now or never. On October 23, 1944, the Japanese fleet steamed forth to give battle. A series of naval engagements [*October 23–26, 1944*] known as the Battle of Leyte Gulf followed. Three almost simultaneous engagements, called: the Battle of Surigao Strait, the Battle off Samar, and the Battle off Cape Engaño, took place as the Japanese attempted to strike at American transports in the Leyte Gulf area and destroy supporting American fleet units.

The Japanese fleet moved out in three columns. One (the southern force) entered Surigao Strait, one column (the central force) passed through the San Bernardino Strait, another (the northern force) moved southward from bases in the home islands. They converged on Leyte Gulf October 25.

American submarines and patrol planes had spotted the Japanese approach [*October 23, 1944*] and two heavy cruisers were sunk by the submarines *Darter* and *Dace*. Two additional cruisers were damaged by air attacks during the approach period.

Battle of Surigao Strait

The Japanese southern force consisting of two battleships, one heavy cruiser, and four destroyers entered Surigao Strait in the early hours of October 25, 1944. Rear Admiral (now Vice Admiral) J. B. Oldendorff, in tactical command of the U. S. Seventh Fleet units, stationed his forces so that the enemy was struck first by our PT boats, then by destroyer torpedo attacks, and finally as they reached the northern end of the Strait their battle line was met with our heavy cruisers and battleships. Admiral Oldendorff accomplished what few naval officers achieve in a lifetime of professional service— crossing the enemy's T. Before the Japanese could extricate themselves from their predicament they lost two battleships and three destroyers. The Jap heavy cruiser was sunk the following day by American planes. Thus almost the whole Japanese southern force was annihilated. The only damage sustained by Admiral Oldendorff's force was inflicted on the destroyer *Albert W. Grant* by Japanese gunfire.

Battle Off Samar

The Japanese central force heading for the Strait of San Bernardino consisted of 5 battleships, 8 cruisers, and 13 de-

360

stroyers. It was attacked [*October 24, 1944*] by carrier planes of the U. S. Third Fleet as it passed through Mindoro Strait. These attacks sank the new Japanese battleship *Musashi*, one cruiser and one destroyer. Damage must have been inflicted on other units of the central force because when it reached the eastern coast of Samar the force contained only 4 battleships, 5 cruisers, and 11 destroyers. This still powerful fleet fell upon a group of six American escort carriers, three destroyers and four destroyer escorts under Rear Admiral C. A. F. Sprague. Planes of the American carriers sank one enemy heavy cruiser and one destroyer, but in the surface engagements which followed the U. S. escort carrier *Gambier Bay*, the destroyers *Hoel* and *Johnston* and the destroyer escort *Roberts* were sunk by enemy gunfire. Damage by gunfire was inflicted on the escort carriers *White Plains* and *Kitkun Bay* and the escort carriers *Suwanee* and *Santee*. Enemy Kamikazes sank the escort carrier *Saint Lô* on the morning of October 25.

The strange thing about the Battle off Samar was that the Japanese fleet broke off the engagement after pounding the relatively weak American escort carrier force, ignored the American transports in Leyte Gulf, and retired through San Bernardino Strait. Here they were pursued by planes from Admiral Sprague's remaining carriers and by planes of the Third Fleet. Two additional enemy heavy cruisers and one destroyer were sunk as a result of American air attacks [*October 25–26, 1944*], while battleships sank one cruiser.

Battle Off Cape Engaño

The Japanese northern force consisting of 1 large and 3 light carriers, 2 battleships with flight decks, 5 cruisers, and 5 destroyers was discovered by American search planes [*October 24, 1944*] to be heading in the direction of the Philippines. Since this was the only Japanese force which included carriers, Admiral Halsey moved the Third Fleet carrier force to the attack. The first strike took place on the morning of October 25 at 0840 hours. Thereafter until 1800 hours our carrier planes struck repeatedly at the Japanese northern force. Cripples were finished off by American cruisers and destroyers. At the end of the day the Japanese northern force had lost four carriers, a light cruiser, and a destroyer. Damage had been inflicted on the Japanese battleships and other units.

Admiral Halsey then turned southward with most of his force before noon to relieve the hard-pressed ships of Admiral Sprague. Planes of the Third Fleet joined in the attack on the retreating Japanese central force, inflicting loss and damage on the remaining Japanese vessels.

The Battle of Leyte Gulf was an overwhelming American victory. The only American heavy unit lost was the fast carrier *Princeton*. The Japanese Navy suffered such heavy losses and damage as to be reduced to virtually "task force size." After that battle the Japanese fleet never attempted to interfere with an American landing operation except for the ill-fated cruise of the battleship *Yamato* in Okinawa waters.

Campaign on Leyte

By the end of October 1944 the Japanese had been driven from all of southern and northeastern Leyte with an estimated loss of 24,000 men. Instead of relinquishing Leyte, the Japanese high command decided to fight for it and sent in portions of the Japanese Thirty-fourth Army identified as the 1st, 30th, and 102nd Divisions under command of General Tomoyuki Yamashita. These reinforcements were shipped into Leyte via the port of Ormoc and their presence soon became felt on the northern front where both the X and XXIV Corps encountered strong opposition.

The general American plan of attack was centered around operations of the X Corps in the north and the XXIV Corps in the south. The 24th Infantry and 1st Cavalry Divisions had tough going in the difficult terrain near Pinamopoan, and the U. S. 32nd Division was sent in to reinforce that front. The U. S. 7th Division was facing strong Japanese opposition south of Albuera and the 77th Infantry Division was earmarked for support in that area.

Japanese air activity increased on the Leyte front as new planes were brought in to neighboring islands. Suicide attacks were made on American shipping in Leyte Gulf [*November 15–December 7, 1944*]. Japanese paratroops

362

were landed on American airstrips near Taclobán [*December 7, 1944*] in an attempt to destroy planes and disrupt our air operations.

A general advance on the X Corps front in the direction of Limon began [*November 15, 1944*]. Slow progress was made against strong opposition. The attack of the U. S. 7th Division in the south which made steady but slow progress against Albuera was suddenly aided by the landing of the U. S. 77th Infantry Division three miles south of Ormoc [*Decmber 6–7, 1944*].

The amphibious operation of the 77th Division must have surprised the Japanese command for they attempted to bring in several transports in Ormoc Bay at the same time as the American landing. Six Japanese transports laden with troops and supplies were sunk by our Navy on the night of [*December 6–7, 1944*]. Three additional transports were sunk northwest of Leyte [*December 12, 1944*], as the Japanese persisted in their attempts to reinforce Leyte.

Ormoc was captured by the 77th Division [*December 11, 1944*] and a junction was made on the same day with troops of the 7th Division which captured Albuera [*December 10, 1944*]. Advancing northward from Ormoc, the 77th Division captured Cogon [*December 16, 1944*] and occupied Valencia [*December 19, 1944*]. Junction was made with troops of the 1st Cavalry Division which had moved southward and captured Kananga [*December 20, 1944*]. In one of the final operations of the campaign, the 77th Division made an amphibious hop to Palompon on Christmas Day. Organized Japanese resistance was officially announced at an end [*December 26, 1944*]. Mopping up operations, however, continued for many weeks on Leyte.

Total Japanese losses on Leyte were estimated at 54,833 killed and 493 prisoners. American losses were 2,623 killed, 3,422 wounded, and 172 missing.

Invasion of Mindoro

Before the campaign on Leyte had reached an end, troops of the Western Visayan Task Force of the 24th Infantry Division and the 503d Parachute Infantry Regiment invaded Mindoro. In a brilliant movement, by-passing Japanese

363

troops on Panay, Cebú, Mindanao, and Negros, General MacArthur sent a convoy to the southwestern coast of Mindoro where troops landed [*December 15, 1944*]. Advancing inland against very light opposition, they secured the airstrip near San José [*December 16, 1944*]. When this airstrip was repaired and enlarged it afforded bases for planes covering the invasion of Luzon.

Invasion of Luzon

Leyte and Mindoro were but preliminaries to the great invasion of Luzon. It was on the island of Luzon that the American and Philippine Army had gone down to defeat in 1942. Luzon is the largest island of the Philippine group and seat of the capital. General MacArthur gave an ironical twist to the invasion by deciding to strike by the same route which the Japanese had used in 1941-42. His invasion armada steamed into Lingayen Gulf [*January 6, 1945*]. After three days bombardment by the fleet, troops of the Sixth Army landed [*January 9, 1945*]. They encountered unexpectedly little opposition and penetrated inland for seven miles [*January 11, 1945*]. The first serious Japanese resistance was met at Rosario [*January 11, 1945*]. By January 14 a firm American beachhead was established from Damortis on the east to Port Saul on the west.

Order of Battle in the Luzon Campaign

The order of battle of the U. S. Army in the first stages of the Luzon campaign was given in public sources as follows:

The U. S. Sixth Army, Lieutenant General (now General) Walter Krueger.
  I Corps, Major General Innis P. Swift.
    6th Infantry Division, Major General Edwin D. Patrick (Charles E. Hurdis)
    43rd Infantry Division, Major General Leonard F Wing
    25th Infantry Division, Major General Charles L Mullins
    32nd Infantry Division, Major General W. H. Gill

XIV Corps, Major General (now Lieutenant General) Oscar W. Griswold

37th Infantry Division, Major General Robert S. Beightler

40th Infantry Division, Major General Rapp Brush

1st Cavalry Division, Major General Verne D. Mudge

33rd Infantry Division, Major General P. W. Clarkson

11th Airborne Division, Major General Joseph M. Swing

Early operations on Luzon showed that the Japanese were not prepared to defend the central plain but were retreating to the mountains north and east of Rosario. There they put up a savage fight against the I Corps. Finding the central plain practically without Japanese defenders, the XIV Corps made rapid progress toward Manila. They reached Paniqui 37 miles inland [*January 18, 1945*]. Japanese forces in central Luzon retreated to the Zambales Mountains on the west and into the lower reaches of the Sierra Madre Mountains on the east.

Advance on Manila

On January 18, 1945, the U. S. I Corps occupied a line running from Rosario–Pozorrubbio–Binalonan–Urdaneta. The XIV Corps was developed in the area Paniqui–Santa Ignacia–Zambales Mountains to Balinao. The southward advance of the XIV Corps met with little resistance and reached Tarlac [*January 20, 1945*]. Fort Stotsenburg and Clark Field were reached [*January 25, 1945*]. Japanese troops which had retreated to the Zambales Mountains west of Fort Stotsenburg opened artillery fire on Clark Field after it came into American hands. The U. S. 40th Division was detailed to deal with these forces and the advance on Manila was resumed. Angeles was occupied by troops of the XIV Corps [*January 28, 1945*]. Manila seemed open to attack from the north.

Meanwhile units of the XI Corps (Lieutenant General Charles P. Hall) of the newly announced U. S. Eighth Army, commanded by Lieutenant General Robert L. Eichelberger, landed on the Zambales coast between San Narciso and San Antonio [*January 29*, 1945] with a mission to drive forward to the Subic Bay area and thence across the Bataan Peninsula to the northern shore of Manila Bay. The XIV Corps reached San Fernando [*January 29, 1945*]. The Rio Grande de la Pampanga was reached [*January 31, 1945*] at Calumpit and crossed by the XIV Corps on the following day.

In order to cut off Manila from the south, the U. S. 11th Airborne Division (then operating under the Eighth Army) was landed at Nasugbu in Batangas Province 50 miles southwest of Manila [*January 31, 1945*]. A race for the honor of entering Manila developed between the 37th Infantry Division which reached Bocaue fifteen miles from Manila [*February 3, 1945*] and the 1st Cavalry Division which reached Bustos on the same day. Both divisions reached the outskirts of Manila [*February 4, 1945*]. The 1st Cavalry Division immediately pushed into the city and freed 3,700 American prisoners in Santo Tomás University. They reached the northern bank of the Pasig River in the San Miguel district of Manila late that night. Advance of the 11th Airborne Division was held up by stubborn Japanese resistance south of Manila near Nichols Field. Under the cover of fires set in the city, Japanese troops withdrew beyond the Pasig River. There they elected to fight to the death. At the end of the first month of the Luzon campaign Japanese losses were estimated at 48,000. American losses were 1,600 killed, 5,276 wounded and 191 missing.

Clearing the Manila Area

Up to February 8, 1945, it appeared that the capture of Manila would be a relatively easy task. The Japanese commander, however, had deliberately withdrawn his troops into the southern section of the city and it was necessary to blast and burn them out yard by yard. The bitterest kind of fighting raged in the Intramuros, the port, and residential sections south of the Pasig River as the 37th Infantry, 11th Airborne, and 1st Cavalry Divisions closed in upon the Japanese defenders. It was a long-drawn-out struggle lasting from February 8 to 24, 1945.

While this siege went on, other operations were conducted to free the Manila Bay area from Japanese troops. The U. S. 6th and 25th Infantry Divisions pushed forward on

366

the eastern flank, capturing Muñoz, Rizal, and Lupszo [*February 8, 1945*]. Elements of the 6th Division broke loose on a long dash and reached the eastern coast of Luzon near Baler in Baler Bay [*February 12, 1945*]. Cavite naval base was occupied by troops of the 11th Airborne Division [*February 13, 1945*]. Fort McKinley was attacked by elements of the 11th Airborne Division [*February 14, 1945*] and fell after five days of fighting [*February 19, 1945*].

Troops of the U. S. 38th Infantry Division, commanded by Major General William C. Chase, landed in Mariveles Bay, Bataan Peninsula [*February 15, 1945*] and after mopping up Japanese resistance made a junction with troops of the XI Corps advancing from Subic Bay. Corregidor was invaded [*February 16, 1945*] by troops of the 503rd Parachute Infantry Regiment followed by landings from the sea by troops of the 34th Infantry Regiment. After six days of fighting the Japanese garrison on Corregidor was officially announced as being "practically destroyed." Twenty-three hundred Japanese dead were counted on Corregidor and many more were buried under the rubble of their pillboxes and caves. Japanese resistance in Manila was announced as at an end [*February 24, 1945*]. Twelve thousand Japanese dead were counted and great sections of the city were in ruins. A few Japanese suicide garrisons held out in such places as Caballo Island and Fort Drum, but they were burned out by pumping thousands of gallons of diesel fuel and gasoline into their defenses and setting fire to it. Caballo Island was thus reduced [*April 3–5, 1945*] and Fort Drum's concrete battleship was destroyed [*April 14, 1945*] by troops of the 2nd Engineer Special Brigade and by the 38th Infantry Division.

Freeing American and Filipino Prisoners on Luzon

One of the most satisfying aspects of the Luzon campaign was the fact that it enabled the U. S. Army to set free many American and Filipino prisoners long held by the Japanese. A force of 121 American rangers and 286 Philippine Scouts made a daring foray 25 miles inside the Japanese lines in eastern Luzon to free 513 prisoners from the Cabanatuan prison camp near Cabu [*January 30, 1945*]. The rescue force, from the 6th Ranger Battalion led by Lieutenant Colonel Henry A. Mucci, killed 532 Japanese during the operation.

Reference has already been made to the freeing of American and Filipino prisoners at Santo Tomás University [*February 7, 1945*]. A bold operation by American airborne and infantry troops aided by Filipino guerrillas freed 2,146 civilian prisoners from their prison camp at Los Baños, 35 miles south of Manila [*February 23, 1945*]. Two hundred and forty Japanese guards were killed. On April 18 about 7,000 civilians, mostly Filipinos, were freed in the Baguio area.

Operations in Central Luzon

The plan of the Japanese high command apparently was based upon a recognition of their inability to meet the American Army in force on the Luzon Plain. They avoided a decisive engagement with the Sixth and Eighth Armies and fought individual delaying actions on many fronts. Only in the north where the U. S. I Corps battled its slow way against strong Japanese forces and through some of the most heavily fortified mountain and hill positions in the Philippines did operations follow an orthodox pattern. The approximate front of the I Corps ran from Aringay–Rosario–Carranglan to Baler Bay.

There was a considerable pocket of Japanese troops holed up in the Zambales Mountains west of Fort Stotsenburg, and these troops were gradually wiped out by elements of the 40th, 43rd, and 38th Infantry Divisions.

East of Manila Japanese troops in considerable numbers occupied positions in the Marikina Valley and they occasionally shelled Manila from positions in the foothills. Operations against these forces were already under way by elements of the 6th Infantry Division. Montalban was captured by the 6th Division [*February 25, 1945*], but Antipolo held out against the 1st Cavalry Division until March 10, 1945. The U. S. 43rd Division relieved the 1st Cavalry Division [*March 14, 1945*] and captured Teresa [*March 17, 1945*]. The Japanese then withdrew into the San Mateo Mountains. Tanay was occupied by the 6th Infantry Division [*March*

368

19, 1945] and slow progress continued toward Bosoboco. In April the 43rd Division moved around the north side of Laguna de Bay [*April 6, 1945*], and met troops of the 1st Cavalry Division moving up from the south at Lumban. Ipo Dam, the principal source of Manila's water supply, and northern anchor of the Japanese Shimbu Line east of Manila, was captured [*May 18, 1945*], after more than a month of fighting. Wawa Dam and the remaining defenses of the Shimbu Line were captured [*May 28, 1945*]. Santa Ines, 23 miles northeast of Manila, was captured [*June 12, 1945*]. All organized Japanese resistance in central Luzon ended [*June 28, 1945*].

Clearing Southern Luzon

Japanese resistance in southern Luzon was wiped out in March and April. Troops of the 1st Cavalry Division, the 11th Airborne Division and the 158th Infantry Combat Team moved southward from the area of Lake Taal to Tanauan [*March 27, 1945*]. San Pablo was occupied [*April 1, 1945*]. The 11th Airborne Division was landed at Lucena [*April 6, 1945*], and the 158th Infantry Combat Team made a seaborne landing at Sorsogon on the southern tip of Luzon [*April 6, 1945*]. The 1st Cavalry Division and the 11th Airborne advanced to the line Lucban–Tayabas–Lucena [*April 8, 1945*]. Atimonan was captured [*April 10, 1945*], and on the same day the 158th Infantry Combat Team entered Legaspi. Calauag on the east coast of the Bicol Peninsula was captured by the 11th Airborne Division after a 30-mile hop [*April 12, 1945*]. This about ended Japanese resistance on southern Luzon.

Operations in Northern Luzon

Stubborn Japanese resistance met all efforts of the U. S. I Corps to advance northward toward Baguio. The U. S. 33rd and 37th Infantry Divisions attacked from Rosario in the direction of Baguio. The U. S. 32nd and 25th Infantry Divisions attacked along the Villa Verde Trail and Route No. 5. Balete Pass, one of the main Japanese defenses along this route, was captured [*May 15, 1945*] by the 25th Division and one regiment of the 37th Division. The intensity of

369

the fighting in this area can be judged by the fact that it required 25 days for the American troops to fight their way forward two miles. Filipino guerrillas now came to the aid of the American troops in spectacular fashion.

Infanta and Misua, two towns on the eastern coast of Luzon, were captured by Filipino guerrillas [*May 23, 1945*]. Santa Fé, guarding the entrance into the Cagayan Valley, was captured by American troops [*May 27, 1945*]. Aritao, ten miles north of Santa Fé, fell [*June 6, 1945*], and Bayombong was captured [*June 7, 1945*]. Bababag was entered after a nine-mile advance [*June 10, 1945*], and Orioung Pass was captured [*June 13, 1945*].

The slow grinding advance of the I Corps up the Cagayan Valley now began to produce big results. With Filipino guerrillas operating ever more openly in the north, the remnants of the Japanese Fourteenth Army, numbering around 20,000 men, were now trapped in the Cagayan Valley. A 22-mile advance was made by troops of the I Corps [*June 15, 1945*], freeing the towns of Santiago and Echague. Ipil, the first Jap airstrip to be captured in northern Luzon, fell to American troops [*June 16, 1945*]. Ilagan, the capital of Isabela Province, was occupied [*June 19, 1945*]. Japanese forces in northern Luzon were split into two parts [*June 20, 1945*] as Filipino guerrillas crossed the Cagayan River and occupied Tuguegarao, capital of Cagayan Province.

The north-south squeeze on the Japanese troops in the Cagayan Valley developed [*June 21, 1945*], as Filipino guerrillas and troops of the U. S. 11th Airborne Division captured Aparri, the last Jap escape port on Luzon. Lal-lo, 11 miles south of Aparri, was captured by the 11th Airborne Division [*June 24, 1945*]. Junction was made [*June 28, 1945*] between troops of the 37th Division moving northward and the 11th Airborne Division. This junction split the remaining Japanese forces into three parts.

General Douglas MacArthur announced [*July 5, 1945*] that the entire Philippine Islands were liberated and that the Philippine campaign could be regarded as "virtually closed." He estimated that 23 Japanese divisions were "practically annihilated" in the Philippines by 17 American divisions and their Filipino comrades. It was estimated that the Japa-

370

nese Army lost over 400,000 men in the Philippines. Isolated pockets of Japanese were still resisting in certain sections of northern Luzon and Panay at the end of the war.

Occupying Smaller Islands

Japanese resistance on the smaller islands of the Philippine group varied. On some such as Palawan and Cebú small pockets of Japanese troops resisted for considerable periods. On others there was little or no resistance.

Verde Island was occupied by units of the 24th Infantry Division [*February 26, 1945*].

Lubang Island was occupied by American troops [*March 2, 1945*].

Palawan Island was invaded by the 41st Infantry Division [*March 1–2, 1945*] near Puerto Princesa.

Romblon and Simara Islands were occupied [*March 11, 1945*].

Basilan, the northernmost island of the Sulu Archipelago, was occupied by American troops [*March 18, 1945*]. The near-by island of Malamaui was occupied on the following day [*March 19, 1945*].

Panay Island was invaded by elements of the U. S. 40th Infantry Division [*March 18, 1945*]. The principal town of Iloilo was occupied [*March 20, 1945*]. Guimaras Island off Iloilo was occupied [*March 22, 1945*].

Cebú Island was invaded by troops of the Americal Division [*March 26, 1945*]. Cebú City was captured [*March 27, 1945*], but pockets of Japanese resistance held out on the island until April 21, 1945.

Cauit and Mactan, two small islands near Cebu, were occupied by the Americal Division [*March 30, 1945*].

Negros Island was invaded by troops of the 40th Division [*March 29, 1945*], and resistance was virtually ended [*April 12, 1945*].

Sanga Sanga and Bongao, two small islands in the Tawitawi group, were occupied by troops of the 41st Division [*April 2, 1945*].

Masbate Island was occupied [*April 2, 1945*].

Tawitawi Island was occupied [*April 5, 1945*].

Jolo Island was occupied [*April 9, 1945*].

371

Bohol Island was occupied by troops of the Americal Division [*April 11, 1945*].

Rapu Rapu and Batan Islands off Legaspi were occupied [*April 13, 1945*].

Balabac Island, 45 miles north of Borneo, was invaded [*April 18, 1945*].

Invasion of Mindanao

Mindanao, the second largest island of the Philippine group, was invaded by troops of the U. S. 41st Infantry Division [*March 10, 1945*]. Landings were made on the westernmost tip of Mindanao island near Zamboanga. Light initial resistance was encountered and Zamboanga fell into American hands [*March 11, 1945*]. San Roque airstrip, four miles west of Zamboanga, was occupied on the same day. After five days of operations, the entire southern end of the Zamboanga Peninsula was announced as being in American control [*March 15, 1945*].

Troops of the 24th Infantry Division landed on the west coast of Mindanao between Parang and Cotabato [*April 19, 1945*] and captured Malabang. This division moved overland toward Davao, the capital city of the island. Naval forces shelled the shore installations near Davao [*April 30, 1945*] which was reached by troops of the 24th Division [*May 2, 1945*] and cleared of enemy opposition in two days of fighting [*May 4, 1945*]. Samal Island in the Gulf of Davao was occupied [*May 8, 1945*].

Units of the U. S. 31st Division landed in Illana Bay behind the 24th Division and moved toward a junction with troops of the 40th and Americal Divisions which landed [*May 10, 1945*] in Macajalar Bay near Cagayan. The 31st Division reached Malaybalay [*May 20, 1945*], and made a junction with troops of the Americal Division north of that city [*May 25, 1945*]. The Japanese garrison on Mindanao was now cut into several parts.

Japanese troops north of Davao launched counterattacks on American forces [*May 13, 1945*]. These were defeated and the Sasa airfield north of Davao was captured by American troops [*May 21, 1945*].

In an amphibious operation from the Davao area American
372

troops moved [*June 1, 1945*] to Luayon, 75 miles south of Davao. New landings were made [*June 5, 1945*] on Cape San Agustin on the southeast tip of Mindanao and on Balut Island, sealing the Gulf of Davao. On July 10, 1945, Japanese forces on Mindanao were still resisting, but they were split up and isolated. Mopping up operations continued.

The By-passed Japanese

With the American invasion of the Philippines, Australian and New Zealand troops assumed responsibility for the destruction of Japanese troops in by-passed areas. On February 12, 1945, a Navy spokesman in Washington estimated the Japanese garrisons on by-passed islands as follows:

Caroline Islands: Truk, 50,000; Ponape, 10,000; Yap, 10,000; Woleai, 6,000; Kusaie, 4,000; Puluwat, 3,000.

Marshall Islands: Wotje, Maloelap, Mili, and Jaluit, 12,-000–14,000.

Ocean and Nauru Islands: 4,000.

Marcus and Wake Islands: 10,000.

Solomons and New Guinea area: 100,000–120,000.

Palaus: Babelthuap, 30,000.

There has been no official estimate of the Japanese garrisons in the Netherlands East Indies.

Invasion of Borneo

Dutch and British Borneo are among the richest oil-producing areas in the world. Some of the best crude oil produced in Borneo can be used for fuel without refining. Its possession would simplify Allied supply problems. Australian troops invaded Tarakan Island off northeast Borneo [*May 1, 1945*] and had the island completely in control [*May 19, 1945*].

The main island of Borneo was invaded by Australian and Dutch troops in the Brunei Bay area [*June 10, 1945*]. Labuan Island was occupied [*June 16, 1945*]. New landings were made near Weston in the Brunei Bay area [*June 19–21, 1945*] and the oil refinery at Lutong was captured [*June 22, 1945*]. Miri was entered without opposition [*June 27, 1945*]. Australian troops landed in the oil-rich Balik-papan area [*July 2, 1945*] and captured the main part of Balikpapan city and its oil installations [*July 3, 1945*]. Con-

373

trol of Balikpapan Bay was secured [*July 10, 1945*]. Operations in this area continued. Samboja oilfield was captured July 18, 1945. Operations in Borneo continued until the Japanese surrender. Japanese casualties on Borneo to July 22, 1945, were estimated at 4,306 killed and 441 prisoners. Allied losses were 386 killed, 1,351 wounded and 12 missing.

III. THE CONQUEST OF IWO JIMA

Iwo Jima, the principal Japanese base in the Volcano Islands, lay athwart the route of the XXI Bomber Command's Superfortresses based in the Marianas on their long flight to Japan. From Iwo's two operating airfields Jap interceptor planes had been attacking the B-29s on their flight to and from the Jap homeland. Bombers based on Iwo had carried out occasional raids on our airfields on Saipan. In our advance against the Japanese home islands, Iwo Jima was of tremendous strategical importance. It was within fighter-plane range (750 miles) of Japan. In American hands it would enable us to escort B-29s on their flights over Japan. It would also provide a haven for B-29s damaged or in trouble.

Iwo Jima is a small island five and a half miles long and one and a half miles wide. It has no harbor and its rocky volcanic soil supports very little vegetation. There were no wells on the island and all water had to be brought in or caught in rain traps. The first Japanese territory that American troops assaulted in the war, Iwo Jima was heavily fortified and very well supplied with artillery and ammunition. There was a garrison of 22,000 troops under command of Lieutenant General Tadamichi Kuribayashi. He planned his defense around the use of artillery. Utilizing the lessons of Tarawa, Saipan, and Attu, General Kuribayashi ruled out Banzai attacks and grimly determined to make the American invaders pay heavily for every inch of ground.

Pre-invasion Bombardment

Iwo Jima and its installations were under periodic attack by American planes and ships from August 7, 1944, onward. Daily bombing missions against Iwo were flown from December 8, 1944 to February 19, 1945. Naval forces bombarded

374

the island [*January 5, 1945* and *January 24, 1945*]. For
three days prior to the landings, units of the U. S. Fifth Fleet
(Admiral R. A. Spruance) bombarded the island from close
range. Diversionary air strikes in the Tokyo area were carried out by carrier planes of Vice Admiral Marc A. Mitscher's
Task Force [*February 16–17, 1945*].

During the long pre-invasion bombardments it became
apparent that the Japanese defenders were busily engaged
in constructing new positions. Many of their batteries were
so well concealed that they were unmasked for the first time
when the fleet came in for close bombardment.

Order of Battle of the V Marine Amphibious Corps

Commander of U. S. Marine Forces in the Pacific: Lieutenant General Holland M. Smith

V Marine Amphibious Corps: Major General Harry
Schmidt

3rd Marine Division, Major General Graves B. Erskine
4th Marine Division, Major General Clifton B. Cates
5th Marine Division, Major General Keller E. Rockey

Capture of Mount Suribachi

Three important objectives on Iwo Jima were Mount
Suribachi, an extinct volcano on the southern tip of the
island, and Motoyama Airfields No. 1 and No. 2, located in
the northern and central section of the island.

At 0900 hours [*February 19, 1945*] troops of the 5th and
4th Marine Divisions landed on the western beaches of Iwo
Jima. Initial losses were light and by 1800 hours a line had
been built up across the island facing Motoyama Airfield
No. 1. To the southwest was the Japanese strongpoint on
Mount Suribachi. No sooner had the Marine forces pushed
inland, than Japanese mortar and artillery fire from both
front and rear began to fall on the beaches and on the troops
in the forward areas. Firing from concealed positions in pillboxes and caves, Japanese troops pinned the Marines down
and their fire raised havoc on the beaches where additional
men and supplies were coming in.

So strong was Japanese opposition that the U. S. 3rd
Marine Division in reserve was ordered ashore [*February 21,*

1945]. It took up a position in the line between the 4th and 5th Divisions. Mount Suribachi was finally reduced [*February 23, 1945*] but Japanese snipers concealed in the caves and pockets of the area continued to harass the Marines operating against Motoyama No. 1.

Capture of the Airfields

The main Japanese airfield, Motoyama No. 1, was reached by elements of the 5th Marine Division [*February 23, 1945*] after a savage fight in which they were supported by the 4th Marine Division. It was completely in American hands [*February 26, 1945*]. American planes began operating from Motoyama No. 1 immediately. Half of Motoyama No. 2 was in American hands [*February 26, 1945*] but the advance in that sector was bitterly contested by the Japanese who employed many new weapons for the first time in the Pacific war. The Marines were attacked by 380mm. mortars, rockets, and all types of artillery ranging from naval guns in concrete emplacements to antiaircraft guns. One hill with an area of less than 700 square yards was found to contain one large blockhouse, 20 pillboxes armed with medium and heavy machine guns, many caves with camouflaged firing slits, two medium tanks (47 mm. gun) dug in, two light tanks (37 mm. gun) dug in, one 75 mm. AT gun, three 75 mm. howitzers, four 47 mm. AT guns, twelve twin-mount 20 mm. machine guns, plus numerous Nambu- and Lewis-type machine guns.

Though the primary objectives were the airfields, the main fighting raged over hills such as 202 Able and 382 and the ridges commanding them. The third (uncompleted) Japanese airfield in the north was reached [*February 28, 1945*].

Elements of the 21st Marine Regiment reached the sea near Kitano Point [*March 6, 1945*] further cutting up the Japanese garrison. The end of the Iwo Jima campaign, which was essentially a battle of extermination, came officially [*March 16, 1945*] along with the announcement that Marine casualties amounted to 4,189 killed, 15,308 wounded, and 441 missing. The entire Japanese garrison was killed or captured.

Iwo Jima was the hardest and most costly operation in

the history of the Marine Corps, but a steady stream of B-29s began to use it as an intermediate base. Within three months after the capture of Iwo Jima 850 B-29s had made emergency landings there. Possession of Iwo Jima had thus saved the lives of 9,000 airmen in distress. American fighter planes based on Iwo made their first flight over Japanese territory [*April 7, 1945*] escorting a large force of Marianas-based B-29s against Tokyo and Nagoya.

IV. THE CONQUEST OF OKINAWA

Okinawa, the main island of the Ryukyu group, lies about 350 miles southwest of Japan. It is a mountainous island, some sixty miles long, varying in width from three to eighteen miles. Nakagusuku Bay on the southern half of the island was a former maneuver area for the Japanese Navy. There were six principal airfields on the island: Yontan, Katena, Machinato, Naha, Itoman, and Yonabaru. On near-by Ie Island was another airstrip. There was room on Okinawa for many new airfields. Naha harbor offered advantages for an advanced fleet and supply base. American possession of Okinawa would place the Japanese mainland within the range of our fighter planes, and would extend our air coverage to the China coast. American air and naval forces stationed in the island would cut Japanese lines of communication and supply to and from her southern empire. After it was developed by American engineers, Okinawa might provide an excellent advance base for operations against Japan itself.

Preliminary Attacks on the Ryukyus

Carrier-plane strikes and naval attacks on the Ryukyus in March prepared the way for the invasion of Okinawa. The U. S. Fifth Fleet (Admiral R. A. Spruance) carried out extensive attacks on Japanese shipping and airfields in the Ryukyus area [*March 19, 1945*]. The attack was renewed on Okinawa [*March 23, 1945*]. Elements of the U. S. 77th Infantry Division landed on islands of the Kerama group, some fifteen miles west of the southern tip of Okinawa [*March 26–27, 1945*]. On April 1, 1945, the newly announced U. S. Tenth Army landed on Okinawa.

377

Commander of the U. S. Tenth Army: Lieutenant General Simon B. Buckner, Jr.

U. S. XXIV Corps: Lieutenant General John R. Hodge
  27th Infantry Division: Major General George W. Griner
  77th Infantry Division: Major General Andrew D. Bruce
  96th Infantry Division: Major General James L. Bradley
  7th Infantry Division: Major General Archibald V. Arnold

U. S. III Marine Amphibious Corps: Major General (now Lieutenant General) Roy S. Geiger
  1st Marine Division: Major General Pedro A. del Valle
  6th Marine Division: Major General Lemuel C. Shepherd
  2nd Marine Division (in reserve): Major General Thomas E. Watson
  1 Reinforced Combat Team committed: Brigadier General (now Major General) LeRoy P. Hunt

Landing and Occupation of Northern Okinawa

Over 1,400 ships were involved in the Okinawa landing which took place on the western coast of the island between Yontan and Katena [*April 1, 1945*]. The III Marine Amphibious Corps landed on the northern flank and rapidly pushed across the narrow island [*April 3, 1945*]. It thereafter advanced northward against light resistance. The U. S. XXIV Corps landed on the southern flank and also reached the eastern coast of the island [*April 3, 1945*]. It advanced to Kuba [*April 4, 1945*] against increasing Japanese resistance. After reaching a position just north of Kinowan, the XXIV Corps was stopped short by savage Japanese resistance.

Meanwhile the III Marine Amphibious Corps rapidly pushed northward and occupied all the northern section of the island [*April 18, 1945*]. Eighty-five thousand Japanese civilians came under American military control. Engineers rapidly put airstrips into operation. Army units captured Ie Island against moderate resistance [*April 18–22, 1945*]. Ernie Pyle, the beloved war reporter, met his death on Ie Island [*April 19, 1945*]. Marine units occupied Yagahi, Kouri, and Heianza islands [*April 23–25, 1945*].

Air and Naval Engagements off Okinawa

The invasion of the Ryukyus could hardly go unchallenged by the Japanese Air Force and Navy. Repeated air attacks, including many by suicide planes, were made against American fleet units, shipping and supply installations. The *Baka* bomb, or piloted flying bomb, made its appearance on the Okinawa front. Very heavy losses were sustained by American ships, although only a small percentage of the suicide attacks was successful. It was estimated that around 4,000 Japanese planes were destroyed in the operations around Okinawa.[1]

Elements of the British Royal Navy attacked the Sakishima Archipelago [*April 6, 1945*], and this attack marked their first combat service in the Ryukyu area.

A small Japanese naval task force consisting of the new battleship *Yamato*, one cruiser and nine destroyers was sighted by American search planes steaming south from the vicinity of Kyushu [*April 7, 1945*]. It was promptly attacked by American carrier planes which sank the *Yamato*, the cruiser, and three destroyers. This was the last appearance of heavy Japanese naval units in the combat zone.

Clearing Southern Okinawa

The relatively easy progress of the initial operations on Okinawa gave rise to considerable optimism in public circles. Lieutenant General Mitsuru Ushijima, commander of the Japanese Thirty-second Army, however, had apparently planned his defense in the southern sector of Okinawa. He had a force of more than 100,000 men at his disposal. The principal Japanese units were the 24th and 62d Divisions and the 44th Independent Mixed Brigade. As on Iwo Jima, Japanese artillery fire was accurate and heavy. There seemed to be no shortage of ammunition. Japanese units counterattacked on occasion with vigor and excellent direction. Terrain difficulties and heavy mud impeded the Americans.

The XXIV Corps attacked from a line just north of Kinowan [*April 19, 1945*] after a very heavy bombardment

---

[1] Postwar reports show that the losses in ships and naval personnel at Okinawa were heavier than in any other engagement of the war.

from fleet guns and artillery weapons. For eight days [*April 19–27, 1945*] the attack was pressed relentlessly by the 27th, 96th and 7th Infantry Divisions. Total gains were limited to a mile and a half. Ishin fell to Army troops [*April 25, 1945*]. American losses averaged 913 men a day. Machinato Airfield on the west coast of Okinawa was captured [*April 29, 1945*].

The 1st Marine Division, freed from its responsibilities in the north, entered the line. Counterattacks accompanied by a landing behind the American lines were beaten off [*May 3–7, 1945*] with a loss of 3,000 Japanese. The U. S. 96th Division was relieved by the 77th Division and the attack, supported by the 6th Marine Division, was renewed [*May 8, 1945*]. Principal gains were made on the 6th Marine Division front where the advance reached the outskirts of Naha [*May 12, 1945*].

Fighting on Okinawa reached a new pitch of savageness in mid-May with certain areas such as Conical and Sugar Loaf Hills being retaken several times. Yonabaru airfield was captured [*May 14, 1945*]. Total American casualties on land to May 13 were given as 20,850, and casualties on the sea to May 12 as 6,853. Enemy losses to May 15 were given as 46,505 killed and 1,038 prisoners.

Chocolate Drop Hill was captured [*May 15, 1945*] by Marines after a five-day struggle. A first crossing of the Asato River was made on the same day [*May 15, 1945*]. The 6th Marine Division reached the outskirts of Naha, the island capital [*May 17, 1945*], but a savage fight lasting until June 7 followed. Sugar Loaf Hill had to be recaptured five times before the Japanese defenders finally gave up. The American advance reached the vicinity of the Shuri Line [*May 21, 1945*] but Shuri Castle was not captured until May 30. The U. S. 7th Division captured the ruins of Yonabaru [*May 22, 1945*]. Japanese tactics were to take shelter in caves dug in the reverse slopes of hills. When the Americans occupied the high ground Japanese artillery opened up and drove them off.

Naha airstrip was seized by the 6th Marine Division [*June 5–6, 1945*] after a landing from the sea behind the Japanese front. The 7th Division drove two miles forward on

380

the east coast to cut off the Chinen Peninsula [*June 5–6, 1945*]. Gushichan was captured [*June 7, 1945*], and the Oraku Peninsula on the southwestern side of the island was cleared of Japanese troops [*June 8–10, 1945*].

As the remnants of the Japanese garrison were being split up and hemmed in on the southern coast of Okinawa, General Buckner appealed to General Ushijima to surrender after his honorable defense of the island [*June 11, 1945*]. No reply to this request was received and the battle of annihilation continued. Yaeju Hill, the highest peak in southern Okinawa, was captured by troops of the 96th Division [*June 14, 1945*].

Though the Japanese position was hopeless, the enemy continued to resist and the bag of prisoners mounted. Lieutenant General Buckner was killed by a Japanese shell while observing operations [*June 18, 1945*]. His command was taken over by Major General (now Lieutenant General) Roy S. Geiger.

American forces reached the south coast of Okinawa [*June 19, 1945*], cutting the remaining Japanese forces into small pockets. Two days later [*June 21, 1945*] the campaign for Okinawa was officially announced as at an end. General Joseph W. Stilwell, former commander of Army Ground Forces, was made commander of the U. S. Tenth Army [*June 22, 1945*]. As of June 26, 1945, Japanese losses on Okinawa were given as 110,549 killed and 8,696 prisoners. By far the largest number of Japanese prisoners taken in the Pacific war surrendered on Okinawa. American losses through June 19 were 11,260 killed and 33,769 wounded.

Okinawa was a costly campaign, but it placed our Air Forces in a position to attack the Japanese home islands with heavy and medium bombers as well as fighter planes. The air war on Japan soon reflected this. Mustang fighters of the Far East Air Force flew their first mission against targets on the Japanese homeland [*July 3, 1945*].

V. AIR AND NAVAL ATTACKS AGAINST JAPAN

Japanese military leaders doubtless began the war in the belief that distance and the ring of Jap-held bases in the

Pacific would make it impossible for the U. S. Air Forces to strike directly at Japan's industrial heart. If this was the case, they did not count upon the long-range Superfortresses which the United States placed in operation in 1944. Based upon the experimental model XB-29 built in 1939, the design of the B-29 was decided upon in 1940. The Superfortress program was adopted in 1941 and the first three planes came off the assembly line in 1942. The XX Bomber Command was organized and trained its first crews in 1943. Five fields in India and four in China were built in 1944 by 700,000 native laborers. The first mission of the 58th Wing of the XX Bomber Command (Major General Curtis E. LeMay) was flown against Bangkok, Thailand [*June 5, 1944*]. Yawata, on the Japanese homeland, was bombed for the first time [*June 15, 1944*]. Palembang in Sumatra and Nagasaki on Kyushu Island were bombed [*August 10, 1944*] in the longest bombing operations in history.

The XXI Bomber Command of the Twentieth Air Force took up its base in the Marianas under Brigadier General H. S. Hansell. The first mission was flown from Isley Field on Saipan against Tokyo [*November 24, 1944*]. Major General Curtis E. LeMay succeeded Brigadier General Hansell in command of the XXI Bomber Command and Brigadier General Roger Ramey took over command of the XX Bomber Command. Five raids from Marianas bases were conducted against Tokyo in 1944, and 1,500 tons of bombs were dropped on military targets in the capital. Over a million tons of Jap shipping had been sunk in the Pacific area by the AAF to the end of 1944. Jap plane losses to the AAF up to December 7, 1944, were 6,422 planes. Navy and Marine Corps flyers accounted for many more. Their bag of Jap planes destroyed in the air and on the ground to July 11, 1945, was 17,000.

New Fleet Bases

The conquest of the Marianas enabled the U. S. Navy to build a vast advance fleet base and headquarters on the island of Guam. Another important fleet base was secured [*September 20-21, 1945*] when Ulithi atoll was occupied

382

without opposition by the 321st Regiment of the 81st Infantry Division. The occupation of Ulithi atoll passed almost unnoticed at the time, but it gave the Navy an advance fleet base capable of sheltering a thousand ships. Its principal islands, Falalop, Asor, and Mogmog, provided room for immense shore installations. Ulithi was 110 miles east of Yap and 400 miles southwest of Guam. Since it was 4000 miles nearer the combat zone than Pearl Harbor, it was of great value in the period when the war was brought to the doorstep of Japan.

The combination of our new advance bases, the fleet train, and the carrier task force, made it possible for the Allied fleets to mount carrier strikes against the Japanese homeland and ultimately to bombard her coastal cities.

Stepping Up the Air War in 1945

As American forces approached nearer the Japanese home islands, the pace of the air war increased. The U. S. Army Air Forces dropped a total of 10,503 tons of bombs on Japanese targets in the month of June 1944. By June 1945 the monthly rate reached well over 50,000 tons—an increase of 500 per cent. The first 100,000 tons of bombs to hit the Japanese homeland were dropped by July 4, 1945. By comparison the first 100,000 tons of bombs dropped on Germany by the AAF was reached on May 28, 1944—a few days before the invasion of France. It took the AAF until September 28, 1944, to drop its first million tons of bombs on enemy targets in all theaters, but its second million tons was dropped by July 9, 1945. With the ending of the European war, it became possible to transfer Air Forces units to the Pacific theater. The first planes redeployed from ETO were said to have reached the Philippines [*June 13, 1945*].

As fighter bases were established on Iwo Jima it became possible to coordinate the Superfortress raids with fighter plane sweeps and carrier attacks. When Okinawa bases were in operation it became possible to coordinate land-based medium and heavy bombers with B-29s, and with carrier- and land-based fighters. This pattern of attack developed in the summer of 1945.

383

Organization of the U. S. Air Forces in the Pacific (July 24, 1945)

Commander, U. S. Strategic Air Force: General Carl Spaatz

   Deputy Commander: Lieutenant General Barney M. Giles

   Chief of Staff: Major General Curtis E. LeMay

   Twentieth Air Force: Lieutenant General Nathan F. Twining

   Eighth Air Force: Lieutenant General James Doolittle

Commander, Far East Air Force: General George C. Kenney

   Fifth Air Force: Lieutenant General Ennis C. Whitehead

   Thirteenth Air Force: Major General Paul B. Wurtsmith

   Seventh Air Force: Brigadier General Thomas D. White

Commander U. S. Air Forces, China Theater: Lieutenant General George E. Stratemeyer

   Tenth Air Force (Burma-India): Major General Howard C. Davidson

   Fourteenth Air Force: Major General Claire L. Chennault (resignation announced July 14, 1945); Major General Charles B. Stone, III.

U. S. Naval Commander, Northern Pacific Area: Vice Admiral Frank J. Fletcher

   Eleventh Air Force (Aleutians): Major General John B. Brooks

Operations of the XX Bomber Command

As the Marianas bases came into use the XX Bomber Command confined itself to attacks on the perimeter of Japan's defenses. Bangkok, the capital of Thailand, was raided by B-29s of the XX Bomber Command on January 2; Shinchiku, on Formosa, was hit January 14 and 17; Saigon, in French Indo-China, was bombed January 27. Attacks against the drydock and harbor installations at Singapore were made February 1, along with diversionary raids on Penang Island. Rangoon was hit February 11; Singapore,

384

February 24 and March 12. The railway yards at Kuala Lumpur, in Malaya, were hit on March 10. Two raids were carried out against Rangoon on March 17 and 22. The transfer of the 58th Wing of the XX Bomber Command to the Marianas was made in April 1945. Its merger as part of the XXI Bomber Command was announced [*June 13, 1945*].

Operations of the XXI Bomber Command

The XXI Bomber Command announced the location of its new headquarters on Guam [*January 3, 1945*]. This powerful striking force assumed the main burden of strategic bombing against Japan. It carried out six heavy raids in January. Nagoya was hit January 3, 1945, Tokyo, January 9; Nagoya, January 14; Akashi, January 19; Nagoya, January 23; Tokyo, January 27.

Five large-scale raids were carried out in February. Tokyo was attacked February 10; Nagoya, February 15; Tokyo was hit in very great strength February 19 and 25; Hachijo was raided February 28,

Nine heavy raids were made by the XXI Bomber Command in March. The cities struck by heavy loads of incendiary bombs were: Tokyo, March 4 and 10; Nagoya, March 12; Osaka (2,000 tons), March 14; Kobe (2,500 tons), March 17; Nagoya, March 25; Omuta, March 28; Nagoya, March 31.

In April the XXI Bomber Command switched from its all-out attack on Japanese war industrial centers to pound airfields on Kyushu and Honshu Islands from which Japanese suicide planes were flying to attack our naval forces and shipping off Okinawa. The transfer of the XX Bomber Command from India and China to the Marianas increased the striking force of the XXI Bomber Command. A record number of missions were flown in April. Fifteen times in that month Marianas-based Superfortresses traversed the long route to Japan from their bases on Saipan, Tinian, and Guam. Tokyo was raided April 2; Shizuoka, Koizumi, and Tachikawa were hit April 4; Tokyo and Nagoya were bombed April 7; Kanoya and Kanoya East were hit April 8; Koriyama and Tokyo were raided April 12; Tokyo came in for repeated strikes April 14, 16, and 24. Japanese airfields on

Kyushu were raided April 18, 22, 23, 26, 27, 28, and 29. Airfields on Shikoku were hit April 26.

For the first ten days of May the XXI Bomber Command kept up the pressure on Japanese airfields. Targets on Kyushu were hit May 3, 4, 5, 9, and 10. Airfields on Honshu and Shikoku were also raided May 10. Large-scale raids were resumed against Japanese industrial centers in the second week of May. Nagoya was hit by "well over 500 planes" on May 14 and again on May 17. Tokyo was raided by a 550-plane force May 24 and by a similar force May 26. Great fires were set in the Japanese capital by the raids of May 24 and 26. One Japanese broadcast admitted that Tokyo was "literally scorched to the ground." Heavy losses were suffered by the XXI Bomber Command in these raids. Twelve Superforts were lost on May 24 and nineteen on May 26th. Yokohama was hit with 3,200 tons of incendiaries on May 28. At the end of May, Major General Curtis E. LeMay announced that 51 square miles of Tokyo had been burned out.

Raids against large Japanese cities continued until mid-June when the program of wiping out secondary industrial cities began. Osaka was hit with 3,000 tons of incendiaries June 1; Kobe received another 3,000 tons June 5; Osaka was raided again in force June 7. Attacks were made on Nagoya, Osaka, and Kobe June 9, and on Tokyo June 10. Osaka was hit again on June 15, the day on which General of the Army H. H. Arnold promised that beginning July 1, 1945, the USAAF would drop bombs at a rate of two million tons a year on Japan.

Raids on secondary Japanese industrial areas began in mid-June. Kagoshima and Omuta on Kyushu Island, and Yokkaichi and Hamamatsu on Honshu Island were raided June 18. Kure, Kamamigahara, Himeji, Akashi, and Tamashima were attacked June 22. Nagoya, Osaka, Akashi, and Gifu were bombed June 26. The Utsube River Oil Refinery on Honshu Island was attacked June 27, and the Kudamatsu Oil Refinery was bombed June 30.

July saw the air attack on Japan reach a new peak. In that month planes of the XXI Bomber Command joined with American and British carrier planes, with Okinawa-based fighters and bombers, and with Iwo-based fighters in bold strokes at Japanese airfields, naval installations and fleet units. For the first time in the war more than 2,000 American planes appeared over the Japanese homeland in a single day. As of July 5, 117 square miles of Japanese urban industrial area had been burned out by American raids. Generals Kenney and Doolittle threatened to strike Japan with 5,000 planes a day and turn Japan into a nation of nomads if the Japanese war lords did not surrender.

Carrier Strikes and Fighter-Plane Raids

American air operations against Japan were greatly aided by the carrier planes of the U. S. Third Fleet. The possession of a large force of swift carriers enabled us to throw as many as 1,000–1,500 planes at a single area. This force could be switched rapidly from one area to another. It could strike before the Japanese Air Force could react strongly. The record of carrier-plane strikes in 1945 gives some indication of the Fleet's range of action. On January 11, 1945, carrier planes made attacks in the Saigon and Camranh Bay area of French Indo-China, sinking 38 ships and damaging 104. Two days later [*January 13, 1945*] they appeared off Formosa and raided that island and the China coast for two days. Carrier planes again hit Formosa [*January 20, 1945*] destroying 140 Japanese planes.

As protection to the American invasion fleet off Iwo Jima, carrier planes of the Third Fleet raided the Tokyo Bay area [*February 16–17, 1945*] shooting down 332 planes and destroying 177 planes on the ground. They sank one destroyer, two destroyer escorts, damaged one escort carrier, and twenty-one coastal vessels. Carrier planes again raided the Tokyo area [*February 25–26, 1945*], destroying 158 enemy planes and sinking five small vessels. Carrier strikes against Japanese airfields on Kyushu and on shipping and naval units in the Inland Sea were carried out [*March 18–21, 1945*]. Destructive attacks were carried out against Japanese naval bases at Kobe and Kure. Six small ships were sunk. One battleship, two aircraft carriers, two light carriers, one heavy cruiser, one light cruiser, and four destroyers were

387

damaged. Two hundred eighty-one enemy planes were destroyed in the air and 275 on the ground.

Iwo-based Mustang fighters raided the Tokyo area [*April 19, 1945*], and they attacked Japanese airfields on Kyushu Island destroying 69 planes [*June 22, 1945*]. Okinawa-based Mustangs joined in attacks on Kyushu airfields [*July 3–4, 1945*], and Iwo-based fighters again raided the Tokyo area [*July 7, 1945*]. The air war against Japan began to reach its full stride [*July 10, 1945*] when 1,000 planes from the Third Fleet joined with 500 Marianas-based B-29s and 300 Okinawa-based Army and Marine planes to strike at Kyushu and Honshu. The stage was set for the direct bombardment of Japan by the fleet. Secretary of the Navy Forrestal said [*July 10, 1945*] "We now control the sea right up to Japan."

Closing in on Japan

The second half of July marked a new stage in the air and naval war against Japan. Repeated carrier plane strikes on Japanese airfields and installations had grounded the remnants of the enemy air force. The Far East Air Force had moved to new bases on Okinawa and was prepared to put medium and heavy bombers into operation. Airmen from the European theater joined in the assault on Japan [*July 16, 1945*]. British carrier and fleet forces were prepared to make their first attacks on the Japanese home islands. The Twentieth Air Force was about to be reinforced by the Eighth Air Force. General Carl Spaatz, commander of the Strategic Air Forces, had at his disposal the fighter planes based on Iwo Jima. Surface units of the U. S. Third Fleet under Admiral Halsey were now in a position to bombard the coastal cities of Japan. Though the operations of these various forces are described separately, they were, in fact, part of an over-all plan to bring Japan to her knees.

Carrier-Plane Attacks, July 11–August 14, 1945

Carrier planes of the U. S. Third Fleet carried out attacks on Japanese airfields and installations on Kyushu [*July 12, 1945*]. Two days later [*July 14–15, 1945*] they raided Japanese shipping and airfields on Honshu and Hokkaido in coordination with the naval bombardment of coastal cities.

388

These strikes sank 140 small Japanese ships, damaged 234 others, and destroyed or damaged 82 Japanese planes. British carrier forces joined with planes of the Third Fleet in attacks on the Tokyo area [*July 17, 1945*]. This was the first direct attack by British units on the Japanese homeland.

Heavy attacks were made by carrier planes on the Yokosuka naval base in Tokyo Bay [*July 18, 1945*]. The old battleship *Nagato* was damaged; one enemy destroyer was sunk and two were damaged in these attacks. Further blows at the Japanese fleet were struck [*July 24–25, 1945*] when carrier planes in great strength hit the Kure naval base on the Inland Sea. Here the remnants of Japanese naval strength were taking refuge. Final estimates of damage inflicted included one battleship, two aircraft carriers, three cruisers, and two destroyers seriously damaged; one battleship, one aircraft carrier, one destroyer moderately damaged; one battleship, one heavy cruiser, one escort carrier and one light cruiser slightly damaged. In addition 82 enemy merchant craft were sunk and 156 planes were destroyed. Carrier planes returned to the attack on Japanese fleet units in the Inland Sea [*July 28, 1945*] setting fire to the battleships *Haruna* and *Ise* and damaging seven other warships. Japanese resistance in the air was heavier than on the previous raids and 283 enemy planes were destroyed or damaged. Planes of the Far East Air Force followed up this attack with bomber and fighter sweeps over Kure [*July 28–31, 1945*] inflicting further losses on the Japanese fleet.

Switching to the Tokyo area 1000 carrier planes damaged 26 additional warships and 36 merchant ships in raids [*July 30, 1945*]. One hundred thirty-eight Japanese planes were destroyed or damaged in these attacks. Two days later [*August 1, 1945*] carrier planes raided the Nagoya area and made attacks on the Maizuru naval base. The attacks in July so reduced the Japanese fleet that Under Secretary of the Navy Artemus L. Gates declared [*July 30, 1945*] that the Japanese no longer had a single battleship fit for operations.

Pressure was maintained on the Japanese homeland during the period of negotiations by carrier strikes on northern

Honshu Island [*August 9–10, 1945*] and on the Tokyo area [*August 12–14, 1945*].

Operations of the Far East Air Force

General Kenney's Far East Air Force began attacks on the Japanese homeland in July. As new bases on Okinawa were put into operations the sorties flown rose from 200 [*July 15, 1945*] to 350 [*July 16, 1945*] when airmen from Europe joined in the attack. Japanese airfields outside Shanghai were hit with 290 tons of bombs [*July 17, 1945*]. These attacks were repeated [*July 19* and *22, 1945*]. Mitchell bombers from Okinawa followed up the carrier plane attacks on Kure [*July 29–31, 1945*] sinking or badly damaging an aircraft carrier and 100 merchant craft of various types. A total of 1,200 missions was flown in three days against targets in the Inland Sea area.

Enemy airfields on Kyushu were raided by planes of the Far East Air Force [*August 1, 1945*]. Nagasaki was hit with 250 planes [*August 2, 1945*] and 10 enemy ships were sunk. General Kenney announced the seven-month record of the Far East Air Force [*August 4, 1945*] as including 1,375 enemy planes destroyed and 2,846,932 tons of Japanese shipping sunk or damaged.

Flying through a typhoon [*August 6, 1945*] planes of the Fifth Air Force raided Takanabe on Kyushu Island. This was followed by a 400-plane attack on Tarumizu in southern Kyushu [*August 7, 1945*]. Kagoshima and Miyakonojo on Kyushu were hit with 360 planes [*August 8, 1945*]. Periodic strikes against targets on Kyushu were carried out [*August 10–14, 1945*].

Operations of the Strategic Air Force

The strategic bombing program against Japan came under the direction of General Carl Spaatz whose command included the Twentieth Air Force (Lieutenant General Nathan F. Twining) and the Eighth Air Force (Lieutenant General James Doolittle). The Twentieth Air Force headquarters, formerly in Washington, D. C., was moved to Guam [*August 1, 1945*], and the XXI Bomber Command, which had absorbed the personnel and planes of the 58th Wing of the

390

XX Bomber Command, then became in fact and name the Twentieth Air Force. Major General Curtis E. LeMay, who had long commanded the XXI Bomber Command and had brought its operations to a high state of efficiency, became Chief of Staff to General Spaatz.

In the period between July 15 and August 2 the operational strength of the Twentieth Air Force rose from the 600-plane level to a record strike of 820 Superforts. Continuing the program of attacks against secondary Japanese war industrial centers, Superforts raided Uwajima on Shikoku Island; Utsunomiya, Ichinomiya and Tsuruga on Honshu Island [*July 13, 1945*]. The Nippon Oil Company plant at Kudamatsu on southern Honshu was hit July 16. On the following day Hiratsuka and Kuwana on Honshu Island and Oita on Kyushu Island were attacked. A headquarters announcement of the Twentieth Air Force [*July 16, 1945*] stated that Superforts had carried out 261 missions against Japan and dropped 90,000 tons of bombs up to that date. These attacks had burned out 127 square miles in 26 industrial centers. The Twentieth Air Force lost 291 planes in these operations and shot down 760 Japanese interceptor planes. An additional 159 Japanese planes were destroyed on the ground.

On July 20 a force of 600 Superforts hit five industrial centers on Honshu Island: Choshi, Hitachi, Fukui, Oakasaki, and Amagasaki. Ube was raided July 23, and 600 planes struck the Osaka-Nagoya area on July 24. Twenty-two hundred tons of fire bombs were dropped on three widely separated targets: Omuta (Honshu), Matsuyama (Shikoku) and Tokuyama (Honshu) on July 27.

The Twentieth Air Force began the policy of warning certain Japanese cities of coming raids [*July 27, 1945*]. Leaflets were dropped warning eleven cities that they were next on the Superfort list for destruction. Citizens were urged to seek safety in flight. Six of these cities: Ichinomiya, Uwajima, Ujiyamada, Tsu, Ogaki, and Aomori were bombed within two days, on July 29. On July 31 leaflets were dropped warning twelve more Japanese cities of impending destruction by B-29 raids. A record raid of 820 planes was carried out against four industrial centers, Hachioji, Toyama, Na-

391

gaoka, and Mito, on Honshu Island on August 2. A total of 6,632 tons of bombs was dropped. On the same day a record long distance mining operation closed the Korean ports of Seisin and Rashin. The Twentieth Air Force had been mining Japanese ports for many weeks and on August 4 it was announced that all major Japanese ports had been mined by the B-29s and the Navy.

The first atomic bomb was dropped from a B-29 piloted by Colonel Paul W. Tibbets, Jr., on the Japanese military base of Hiroshima [*August 5, 1945*] (August 6 Japanese time). The second atomic bomb was dropped on Nagasaki [*August 9, 1945*]. Tokyo and Amagasaki were raided with incendiaries August 10. After the Japanese surrender offer was received, the planes of the Twentieth Air Force were held back from further attacks on Japan until August 13 and 14 when from 300–800 Superforts raided Kyushu. Statistics on B-29 attacks are given in Appendix XIII.

During this period fighter planes based on Iwo Jima made repeated air strikes at the Tokyo, Osaka, and Nagoya area in conjunction with Superfort and carrier plane assaults. Iwo Jima was used as a refueling base by B-29s on their flights to Japan as well as an emergency landing field for planes in distress. By refueling at Iwo Jima, the B-29s were able to carry a heavier bomb load. The average bomb load rose from 2.82 tons in January 1945 to 7.7 tons in July 1945.

Fleet Bombardment of Japan

Direct bombardment of the enemy's main industrial centers by surface vessels had occurred but rarely during the war. It was apparent by July 10 that the American fleet commanded the seas up to the coast of Japan. Admiral Halsey proved this [*July 14, 1945*] by shelling the Imperial Iron and Steel Works at Kamaishi on Honshu Island 275 miles northeast of Tokyo. American battleships and heavy cruisers lay off the coast and poured tons of high explosive shells into the city. Carrier planes covered the operation by sweeps over northern Honshu and Hokkaido Islands.

On the following day [*July 15, 1945*] units of the Third Fleet shelled the steel works and synthetic oil plant at Muroran while carrier planes attacked the car ferries running between Honshu and Hokkaido Islands. The absence of Japanese interference led Fleet Admiral Chester W. Nimitz to observe [*July 16, 1945*], "We have paralyzed the will and ability of the Japanese Navy to come out and fight."

For the first time in the Pacific war surface units of the British Navy joined American fleet units in the bombardment of the Japanese homeland [*July 17–18, 1945*]. Led by the battleships *Iowa* and *King George V*, heavy units of the U. S. Third Fleet shelled industrial plants and transport facilities around Hitachi, 50–85 miles northeast of Toyko. There was no enemy response to these attacks. The Japanese air force had apparently shot its bolt in the Okinawa campaign in which it lost more than 4000 planes. Repeated attacks on Japanese flying fields had grounded the remainder. Japanese news agencies attributed the absence of air attacks on the Third Fleet to a policy of "saving the Japanese air force" for the decisive period of the invasion.

American cruisers and destroyers boldly shelled the Nojima Cape area 50 miles south of Tokyo [*July 18, 1945*]. American destroyers attacked a convoy in Sagami Bay near Tokyo [*July 23, 1945*]. To add to the Japanese embarrassment, American cruisers and destroyers of the Northern Pacific Command shelled the southeast coast of Paramushiro Island in the Kuriles on the same day.

British and American fleet units returned to the attack [*July 30, 1945*], shelling the important industrial center of Hamamatsu on Honshu Island. Destroyers of the Third Fleet shelled Shimizu in Suruga Bay July 31. Fleet units again shelled Kamaishi [*August 10, 1495*]. The Japanese Air Force made a feeble effort to damage the Third Fleet [*August 13, 1945*] but lost 21 planes without inflicting any damage on the fleet.

The Third Fleet (Task Force 38) consisted of eight American and one British battleship, 16 American and four British carriers, 19 American and six British cruisers, 62 American and 17 British destroyers. In the final two and a half months of operations against Japan the Third Fleet destroyed or damaged 2,965 enemy planes, sank or damaged 1,600 warships and merchant vessels. It inflicted immense

393

damage on Japanese industrial war plants, airfields and other ground targets.

37. THE COLLAPSE OF JAPAN

Japan's Military Situation in 1945

The collapse of Germany left Japan waging a losing war against all the principal powers in the world except Soviet Russia. She had been steadily pressed back from her island bases in the Solomons to the very doorstep of Japan. Iwo Jima and Okinawa were in American hands. Carrier planes were ranging at will over her territory, blasting her airfields and installations. Superfortresses were burning out her war industrial centers one after another. Japanese troops had been driven out of nearly all of Burma. Their armies in the Philippines had been destroyed. The revitalized armies of China were assuming the offensive. Japan was cut off from the rich resources of the Netherlands Indies and Malaya. As the naval and air blockade around Japan tightened, she was virtually cut off from contact with Manchuria and the occupied territory in China. The raw materials of the home islands were insufficient to support a war against the most productive industrial nations in the world.

By August 1, 1945, Japan's air force and navy had been practically destroyed. The Japanese army remained unconquered, but its strategic position was curiously similar to that of the German army in the final days of the war. Japanese ground forces were strung out in a hopeless position from Manchuria to Malaya. Japanese garrisons were isolated on hundreds of islands in the Pacific. They could die in combat or from disease, but they could not change the course of the war. At best they could only prolong the resistance of Japan.

工 PSYCHOLOGICAL WARFARE AGAINST JAPAN

Weakness of Japan's Propaganda Policy

Japan doubtless went to war against Britain and America in 1941 on the assumption that the Axis would win the war in Europe. For the first two years of the war the Japanese government gave the people of Japan only reports of victories. The industrial strength and the fighting ability of the Allies were discredited. Japanese spirit was held up as superior to all eventualities. When reverses occurred the government pursued a policy of minimizing them. American advances in the Pacific were hailed as advantageous to Japan because they increased our supply difficulties and brought us closer to Japan where we could be destroyed the more easily. The Japanese fleet was said to have been conserved for the "golden opportunity" which would present itself when the Allied fleet approached the Japanese homeland. At that time the Japanese fleet and air force would destroy the enemy in one blow.

The cold facts of the war gradually undermined these promises. In July and early August 1945 the American and British fleets were operating boldly along the Japanese coast line. American planes were dominating the sky over Japan. Yet the Japanese fleet cowered in its Inland Sea bases and allowed itself to be destroyed without fighting. The Japanese air forces could not put sufficient planes into the air to stop either the Superforts or the carrier planes. A feeling of helplessness and frustration swept over the Japanese people.

By radio and by means of leaflets dropped over Japanese territories, the United States told the Japanese people of the predicament into which they had been dragged by their military leaders. Officially the Japanese government scoffed at the leaflet campaign, but it had an effect on the people.

The Twentieth Air Force Warning Program

A new departure in psychological warfare was instituted by the Twentieth Air Force [*July 27, 1945*] when it began to warn certain Japanese cities that they would be destroyed in the near future by the B-29s. Eleven cities were warned on July 27 and two days later six of them were heavily bombed. This was the clearest possible evidence to the Japanese people that their own air force could not protect them. Twelve more Japanese cities were warned of impending raids on July 31 and four of them were heavily bombed on August 2. These events proved that the American threats would be carried out and that no Japanese city was safe against destruction from the air.

The Potsdam Ultimatum

President Truman announced at the end of the war with Germany that unless the military leaders of Japan surrendered unconditionally Japan would be destroyed. He made it clear that we were not aiming at the destruction or enslavement of the Japanese people but at eliminating Japan's capacity to wage aggressive war.

The general conditions of a Japanese peace were stated at the Cairo Conference [*November 22–26, 1943*]. In his message to Congress [*June 1, 1945*] President Truman informed the world that the American forces in the Pacific would be more than doubled with more than 3,500,000 men who had fought in Europe to be thrown against Japan. He warned that if Japan did not surrender all her cities would be destroyed. Premier Kantaro Suzuki replied to this statement in an address to the Japanese people and Parliament [*June 9, 1945*] saying that "Japan would fight on to the last."

Italy declared war on Japan [*July 13, 1945*] adding one more nation to her list of adversaries. There were only a few nations which still maintained diplomatic relations with Japan. The sense of isolation in which Japan faced the last stage of the war lowered Japanese morale.

The decision of the United States Government in the *Awa Maru* case undoubtedly impressed the Japanese people. This vessel was sunk by an American submarine on April 15 while sailing under Allied safe conduct guarantee. The United States Government admitted responsibility for the sinking [*July 13, 1945*] and offered to replace the *Awa Maru* with a vessel of similar size. Reparations were to be taken up at the end of hostilities.

The meeting of the Big Three powers at Potsdam [*July 17–August 2, 1945*] provided another opportunity for Allied leaders to demand the surrender of Japan. The following ultimatum was delivered to Japan [*July 26, 1945*] by the leaders of Britain, China, and the United States.

396

(1) We—the President of the United States, the President of the National Government of the Republic of China, and the Prime Minister of Great Britain, representing the hundreds of millions of our countrymen—have conferred and agreed that Japan shall be given an opportunity to end this war.

(2) The prodigious land, sea and air forces of the United States, the British Empire and of China, many times reinforced by their armies and air fleets from the west, are poised to strike the final blows upon Japan. This military power is sustained and inspired by the determination of all the Allied nations to prosecute the war against Japan until she ceases to resist.

(3) The result of the futile and senseless resistance to the might of the aroused free peoples of the world stands forth in awful clarity as an example to the people of Japan. The might that now converges upon Japan is immeasurably greater than that which, when applied to the resisting Nazis, necessarily laid waste the lands, the industry, and the method of life of the whole German people. The full application of our military power, backed by our resolve, will mean the inevitable and complete destruction of the Japanese armed forces and just as inevitably the utter devastation of the Japanese homeland.

(4) The time has come for Japan to decide whether she will continue to be controlled by those self-willed militaristic advisers whose unintelligent calculations have brought the empire of Japan to the threshold of annihilation, or whether she will follow the path of reason.

(5) Following are our terms. We will not deviate from them. There are no alternatives. We shall brook no delay.

(6) There must be eliminated for all time the authority and influence of those who have deceived and misled the people of Japan into embarking on a world conquest. We insist that a new order of peace, security and justice will be impossible until irresponsible militarism is driven from the world.

(7) Until such a new order is established and until there is convincing proof that Japan's war-making power is destroyed, points in Japanese territory to be designated by the Allies shall be occupied to secure the achievement of the basic objectives we are here setting forth.

(8) The terms of the Cairo declaration shall be carried out and Japanese sovereignty shall be limited to the islands of Honshu, Hokkaido, Kyushu, Shikoku and such minor islands as we determine.

(9) The Japanese military forces, after being completely disarmed, shall be permitted to return to their homes with the opportunity to lead peaceful and productive lives.

(10) We do not intend that the Japanese shall be enslaved as a race or destroyed as a nation, but stern justice shall be meted out to all war criminals, including those who have visited cruelties upon our prisoners. The Japanese Government shall remove all obstacles to the revival and strengthening of democratic ten-

397

dencies among the Japanese people. Freedom of speech, of religion and of thought, as well as respect for the fundamental human rights, shall be established.

(11) Japan shall be permitted to maintain such industries as will sustain her economy and permit the exaction of just reparations in kind, but not those which would enable her to rearm for war. To this end, access to, as distinguished from control of, raw materials shall be permitted. Eventual Japanese participation in world trade relations shall be permitted.

(12) The occupying forces of the Allies shall be withdrawn from Japan as soon as these objectives have been accomplished and there has been established, in accordance with the freely expressed will of the Japanese people, a peacefully inclined and responsible Government.

(13) We call upon the Government of Japan to proclaim now the unconditional surrender of all Japanese armed forces, and to provide proper and adequate assurances of their good faith in such action. The alternative for Japan is prompt and utter destruction.

Premier Suzuki replied to the Potsdam ultimatum [*July 30, 1945*] saying that the Imperial Government of Japan would take no notice of the demands. The stage was then set for the atomic bomb attack on Japan.

II. THE ATOMIC BOMB ATTACK ON JAPAN

Development of the Atomic Bomb

Scientists had long been seeking the means to release the energy of the atom. German and Japanese scientists were known to be at work on the problem of utilizing atomic energy for military purposes. German researchers startled the world in 1939 with the announcement that they had succeeded in breaking up the uranium atom and in releasing incalculably greater energy than was used to disrupt it. Drs. Otto Hahn, F. Strassmann, and Luise Meitner were the leaders in this experiment. Nazi efforts to utilize these results were incomplete when the war ended in Europe.

Work began in the United States on the atomic bomb in 1941 under the supervision of the Office of Scientific Research and Development. President Roosevelt suggested to Mr. Clement Attlee [*October 11, 1941*] that Britain and the United States pool their resources and research facilities toward the solution of the problem. The program was trans-

398

ferred to the United States and a policy committee was set up under Mr. Henry Wallace, Secretary of War Stimson, General of the Army George C. Marshall, Dr. James B. Conant of Harvard University, and Dr. Vannevar Bush of Massachusetts Institute of Technology. The War Department assumed responsibility for the "Manhattan Project" and appointed Major General Leslie R. Groves to supervise it.

Three giant plants were set up in Oak Ridge, Tennessee, Pasco, Washington, and Santa Fé, New Mexico, employing more than 125,000 workers. The research and processing of the uranium element U-235 cost the staggering sum of two billion dollars. Among the notable scientists who collaborated in the project were: Niels H. Bohr, Enrico Fermi, Philip Abelson, John A. Wheeler, Robert J. Oppenheimer, E. O. Lawrence, A. H. Compton, Karl T. Compton, Richard C. Tolman, Sir James Chadwick, C. J. McKenzie, and many others.

The first test of the new atomic bomb was conducted at Alamogordo Air Base in New Mexico [*July 16, 1945*]. When the bomb exploded the steel tower on which it was suspended "vaporized." Clouds of smoke and dust rose 40,000 feet in the air. The force of the blast knocked down men standing five miles away, and the shock of the explosion was felt over a radius of 250 miles.

The Attack on Hiroshima

At 1045 hours [*August 6, 1945*] President Truman announced that sixteen hours earlier an American plane had dropped an atomic bomb on the Japanese army base at Hiroshima. The bomb was carried in the Superfortress *Enola Gay* piloted by Colonel Paul W. Tibbets, Jr. The bombardier who dropped the first atomic bomb was Major Thomas W. Ferebee. The bomb's designer, Captain William S. Parsons, accompanied the crew and supervised the handling of the new weapon.

The immediate effect of the bomb could not be estimated. Returning crew members spoke of a blinding flash and clouds of smoke and dust rising to a height of 40,000 feet. President Truman stated that the bomb had the explosive force of 20,000 tons of TNT. He said that it was to spare the Japanese people from utter destruction that the Potsdam Declaration had been issued. He added that if the Japanese leaders did not now accept our terms "they may expect a rain of death from the air, the like of which has never been seen on earth."

Early Japanese reports spoke of the terrible devastation caused by the bomb and admitted very heavy casualties at Hiroshima. Rail traffic in the area was suspended while an estimate of the damage was being made.

The Attack on Nagasaki

Following the Russian declaration of war on Japan [*August 8, 1945*], a second atomic bomb was dropped, this one on the Japanese naval base at Nagasaki [*August 9, 1945*]. The explosive effect of this bomb was said to have been somewhat greater than the one dropped at Hiroshima, but no immediate estimate of the damage was available.

The cumulative effect of atomic bombing and the Russian declaration of war prompted a Japanese offer to surrender on the terms of the Potsdam Declaration provided the sovereignty of the Emperor was not questioned. This offer was made over the Tokyo Radio [*August 10, 1945*]. Pending negotiations no atomic bombs were dropped on Japan.

III. THE RUSSIAN DECLARATION OF WAR ON JAPAN

Background of the Russian Declaration of War

Russian grievances against Japan date back to the Russo-Japanese War of 1904–1905. Border clashes on the Soviet-Manchurian frontier occurred in the period 1938–1939. Japan was said to have maintained a large military force in Manchuria called the Kwantung Army. The presence of this army was a constant threat to Russian communications with Vladivostok and the maritime provinces. Japan refrained from declaring war on Russia in December 1941, but she gave assistance to the enemies of Russia. The Soviet government denounced its five-year neutrality pact with Japan [*April 15, 1945*]. Marshal Stalin did not sign the Potsdam ultimatum but the official statement at the end of

400

the conference spoke of "military matters of common interest" having been discussed by the British, American, and Russian Chiefs of Staff.

The Russian Declaration of War

The Japanese government attempted to discount the Russian action in terminating the five-year neutrality pact. Official spokesmen in Tokyo assured the Japanese people that Russia was too involved in reconstruction problems to participate in the war against Japan.

These pretenses were shattered [*August 8, 1945*] when People's Commissar for Foreign Affairs of the U.S.S.R. Vyacheslaff M. Molotov handed Naotake Sato, the Japanese Ambassador to Russia, the following note:

> After the defeat and capitulation of Hitlerite Germany, Japan became the only great power that still stood for the continuation of the war.
>
> The demand of the three powers, the United States, Great Britain and China, on July 26 for the unconditional surrender of the Japanese armed forces was rejected by Japan, and thus the proposal of the Japanese Government to the Soviet Union on mediation in the war in the Far East loses all basis.
>
> Taking into consideration the refusal of Japan to capitulate, the Allies submitted to the Soviet Government a proposal to join the war against Japanese aggression and thus shorten the duration of the war, reduce the number of victims and facilitate the speedy restoration of universal peace.
>
> Loyal to its Allied duty, the Soviet Government has accepted the proposal of the Allies and has joined in the declaration of the Allied Powers of July 26.
>
> The Soviet Government considers that this policy is the only means able to bring peace nearer, free the people from further sacrifice and suffering and give the Japanese people the possibility of avoiding the dangers and destruction suffered by Germany after her refusal to capitulate unconditionally.
>
> In view of the above, the Soviet Government declares that from tomorrow, that is from Aug. 9, the Soviet Government will consider itself to be at war with Japan.

Order of Battle of Soviet Far East Forces

Commander of Soviet Far East Forces, Marshal Alexander M. Vassilievsky

First Far East Army (Maritime Provinces), Marshal Kirill Meretskoff

Second Far East Army (Khabarovsk area), Army General Maxim Purkayeff

Third Far East Army (Transbaikal area, Marshal Rodion Y. Malinovsky

The command and organization of the Japanese Kwantung Army is unknown.

The Invasion of Manchuria and Korea

Soviet forces crossed the Manchurian border at three widely separated points on the morning of August 9, 1945 (Far Eastern Time). The First Far East Army, operating from the Maritime province of Primorye, advanced fifteen kilometers on the first day in the general direction of Huchun and Harbin. Pogranichnaya, Tungning, Makiaoho and San-chakov were captured [*August 10, 1945*] after a total advance of thirty kilometers. Other units of the First Far East Army advanced betwen Hutow and Iman in the general direction of Kiamusze. In the Vladivostok area troops of the First Far East Army captured Matita [*August 11, 1945*] while other units farther north pushed forward to Mulingchau, Lishuchen, and Pankiehhotze. Hunchen and Mishan were captured [*August 12, 1945*], the same day on which the Korean ports of Yuki and Rashin were occupied by Russian landing parties. The advance toward Harbin continued with the capture [*August 13, 1945*] of Litzekow, Motaoshih, Linkow, and Tungan. When the announcement of the Japanese surrender came, troops of the First Far East Army had entered Seishen in Korea and Mutankiang on the road to Harbin. The continued to advance until Japanese representatives signed the formal surrender.

The Second Far East Army operated from the Khabarovsk and Blagoveshchensk areas. Troops in the Khabarovsk area advanced southward in the general direction of Kiamusze with a possible objective of effecting a junction with troops of the First Far East Army. These forces captured Tung-kiang and Lopei [*August 10, 1945*]. Fuchin was entered [*August 11, 1945*]; Tayako and Hwaitechen were captured [*August 12, 1945*]. Further advances on the following day brought Hamatungho and Hailu into Russian hands. In the final day of fighting before the Japanese surrender, Hsing-schanchen was captured [*August 14, 1945*].

Units of the Second Far East Army advancing from the Blagoveshchensk area crossed the Amur River, capturing Aigun and Taheiho [*August 10, 1945*]. Aigun Station and Sunho were reached [*August 13, 1945*].

Most spectacular advances were made by the Third Far East Army based in the Transbaikal region. Two wings of this army pushed forward in a concentric advance toward Hailar and Argun [*August 10, 1945*] and toward Kanchur, which fell to the Russian northern forces [*August 11, 1945*]. Further advances brought Korbunor and Yokoshih under Russian control [*August 12, 1945*]. The southern wing of the Third Far East Army reached Solun and Wangvehmiao [*August 13, 1945*]. A ninety-three mile advance was registered by the Third Far East Army [*August 14, 1945*] with the capture of Taonan, Lupeh, and Linsi. Advances continued until the formal act of surrender.

The Invasion of Japanese Sakhalin Island

With the invasion of Manchuria in full swing, Russian troops invaded the Japanese half of Sakhalin Island [*August 13, 1945*], capturing Keton. Simultaneously, Russian landing parties captured Ambetsu and Esutoru on the eastern coast of Sakhalin.

IV. THE SURRENDER OF JAPAN

The Japanese Surrender Offer

At 0735 hours Eastern War Time [*August 10, 1945*] the official Japanese Domei News Agency broadcast an announcement that the Government of Japan would accept the terms laid down in the Potsdam Declaration provided that the sovereignty of the Emperor was not questioned.

The text of the Japanese message delivered to the United States Government through the good offices of the Swiss Government read as follows:

In obedience to the gracious command of His Majesty the Emperor, who, ever anxious to enhance the cause of world peace,

403

desires earnestly to bring about an early termination of hostilities with a view to saving mankind from the calamities to be imposed upon them by further continuation of the war, the Japanese Government asked several weeks ago the Soviet Government, with which neutral relations then prevailed, to render good offices in restoring peace vis-a-vis the enemy powers. Unfortunately these efforts in the interest of peace having failed, the Japanese Government in conformity with the august wish of His Majesty to restore the general peace and desiring to put an end to the untold sufferings entailed by war as quickly as possible have decided upon the following:

The Japanese Government are ready to accept the terms enumerated in the joint declaration which was issued at Potsdam on July 26, 1945 [by] the heads of the Government of the United States, Great Britain and China and later subscribed [to] by the Soviet Government, with the understanding that the said declaration does not comprise any demand which prejudices the prerogatives of His Majesty as a sovereign ruler.

The Japanese Government hope sincerely that this understanding is warranted and desire keenly that an explicit indication to that effect will be speedily forthcoming.

The Allied Reply

After consulting with the other United Nations, Secretary of State James F. Byrnes sent the following message to the Japanese Government [*August 11, 1945*]:

With regard to the Japanese Government's message accepting the terms of the Potsdam Proclamation but containing the statement, "with the understanding that the said declaration does not comprise any demand which prejudices the prerogatives of His Majesty as a sovereign ruler," our position is as follows:

From the moment of surrender the authority of the Emperor and the Japanese Government to rule the State shall be subject to the Supreme Commander of the Allied Powers, who will take such steps as he deems proper to effectuate the surrender terms.

The Emperor will be required to authorize and insure the signature by the Government of Japan and the Japanese Imperial General Headquarters of the surrender terms necessary to carry out the provisions of the Potsdam Declaration, and shall issue his commands to all the Japanese military, naval and air authorities and to all of the forces under their control wherever located to cease active operations and to surrender their arms, and to insure such other orders as the Supreme Commander may require to give effect to the surrender terms.

Immediately upon the surrender the Japanese Government shall transport prisoners of war and civilian internees to places of safety, as directed, where they can quickly be placed aboard Allied transports.

The ultimate form of government of Japan shall, in accordance with the Potsdam Declaration, be established—by the freely expressed will of the Japanese people.

The armed forces of the Allied powers will remain in Japan until the purposes set forth in the Potsdam Declaration are achieved.

The Japanese Acceptance

At 1900 hours [*August 14, 1945*] the Japanese acceptance of the terms laid down in the Potsdam Declaration and the American note was announced. The text of the Japanese note was as follows:

With reference to the Japanese Government's note of Aug. 10 regarding their acceptance of the provisions of the Potsdam Declaration and the reply of the governments of the United States, Great Britain, the Soviet Union and China sent by American Secretary of State Byrnes under the date Aug. 11, the Japanese Government have the honor to communicate to the governments of the Four Powers as follows:

1. His Majesty the Emperor has issued an imperial rescript regarding Japan's acceptance of the provisions of the Potsdam Declaration.

2. His Majesty the Emperor is prepared to authorize and insure the signature by his Government and the Imperial General Headquarters of the necessary terms for carrying out the provisions of the Potsdam Declaration. His Majesty is also prepared to issue his commands to all the military, naval and air authorities of Japan and all the forces under their control, wherever located, to cease active operations, to surrender arms and to insure such other orders as may be required by the Supreme Commander of the Allied Forces for the execution of the above-mentioned terms.

Allied Instructions for Surrender

The following instructions were sent [*August 14, 1945*] to the Japanese government regarding the procedure of surrender:

1. Direct prompt cessation of hostilities by Japanese forces, informing the Supreme Commander for the Allied Powers of the effective date and hour of such cessation.

2. Send emissaries at once to the Supreme Commander with full information of the disposition of the Japanese forces and commanders, and fully empowered to make any arrangements directed by the Supreme Commander for the Allied Powers to enable him and his accompanying forces to arrive at the place designated by him to receive the formal surrender.

405

3. For the purpose of receiving such surrender and the carrying of it into effect, General of the Army Douglas MacArthur has been designated as the Supreme Commander for the Allied Powers, and he will notify the Japanese Government of the time, place and other details of the formal surrender.

Act of Surrender

The official instrument of surrender was signed aboard the United States battleship *Missouri* in Tokyo Bay [*September 2, 1945*]. Foreign Minister Magoru Shigemitsu signed on behalf of the Japanese Emperor. General Yoshijiro Umezu signed for the Japanese Imperial General Staff. The text of the surrender agreement read as follows:

1. We, acting by command of and in behalf of the Emperor of Japan, the Japanese government and the Japanese Imperial General Headquarters, hereby accept provisions in the declaration issued by the heads of the governments of the United States, China and Great Britain, July 26, 1945, at Potsdam, and subsequently adhered to by the Union of Soviet Socialist Republics, which four powers are hereafter referred to as the Allied Powers.

2. We hereby proclaim the unconditional surrender to the Allied Powers of the Japanese Imperial General Headquarters and of all Japanese armed forces and all armed forces under Japanese control wherever situated.

3. We hereby command all Japanese forces wherever situated and the Japanese people to cease hostilities forthwith, to preserve and save from damage all ships, aircraft and military and civil property and to comply with all requirements which may be imposed by the supreme commander for the Allied Powers or by agencies of the Japanese government at his direction.

4. We hereby command the Japanese Imperial General Headquarters to issue at once orders to the commanders of all Japanese forces and all forces under Japanese control, wherever situated, to surrender, unconditionally, themselves and all forces under their control.

5. We hereby command all civil, military and naval officials to obey and enforce all proclamations, orders and directives deemed by the supreme commander for the Allied Powers to be proper to effectuate this surrender, and issued by him or under his authority, and we direct all such officials to remain at their posts and to continue to perform their noncombatant duties unless specifically relieved by him or under his authority.

6. We hereby undertake for the Emperor, the Japanese government and their successors to carry out the provisions of the Potsdam Declaration in good faith, and to issue whatever orders and take whatever action may be required by the supreme commander for the Allied Powers or by any other designated repre-

sentative of the Allied Powers for the purpose of giving effect to that declaration.

7. We hereby command the Japanese Imperial Government and the Japanese Imperial General Headquarters at once to liberate all Allied prisoners of war and civilian internees now under Japanese control and to provide for their protection, care, maintenance and immediate transportation to places as directed.

8. The authority of the Emperor and the Japanese government to rule the state shall be subject to the Supreme Commander for the Allied Powers who will take such steps as he deems proper to effectuate these terms of surrender.

General of the Army Douglas MacArthur signed as Supreme Allied Commander. Fleet Admiral Chester W. Nimitz signed for the United States, General Hsu Yung-chang for China, Admiral Sir Bruce Fraser for the United Kingdom, Lieutenant General Kuzma Derevyanko for the Union of Soviet Socialist Republics, General Sir Thomas Blamey for Australia, Lieutenant General L. H. Van Oyen for the Netherlands, Colonel L. V. M. Cosgrave for Canada, General Jacques Leclerc for France, Air Marshal L. M. Isitt for New Zealand.

Immediately after the surrender was signed, General of the Army Douglas MacArthur, the Supreme Commander for the Allied Powers, issued General Order No. 1 to the Japanese General Staff, giving specific instructions for the surrender of Japanese troops and weapons. The text of General Order No. 1 is given in Appendix XIV.

APPENDIX I

Order of Battle of U.S. Forces

(The order of battle of our Allies is not shown below army level, except to show U. S. division under their operational control)

EUROPEAN THEATER OF OPERATIONS

(As of May 7, 1945)

Unit	*Commander*
SUPREME HEADQUARTERS ALLIED EXPEDITIONARY FORCES.............	GENERAL OF THE ARMY D. D. EISENHOWER
Northern Group of Armies	
(21st Army Group).............	FM Sir Bernard L. Montgomery
Canadian First Army.............	General H. D. G. Crerar
British Second Army.............	Lt. Gen. Sir Miles C. Dempsey
XVIII Corps (Airborne)......	Maj. Gen. Matthew B. Ridgway
5 Armored Division........	Maj. Gen. L. E. Oliver
7 Armored Division........	Maj. Gen. R. W. Hasbrouck
82 Airborne Division........	Maj. Gen. James M. Gavin
8 Infantry Division........	Maj. Gen. Bryant E. Moore
Central Group of Armies	
(12th Army Group)...........	General Omar N. Bradley
U.S. Ninth Army.................	Lt. Gen. William H. Simpson
XIII Corps	Maj. Gen. A. C. Gillem, Jr.
35 Infantry Division........	Maj. Gen. Paul W. Baade
84 Infantry Division........	Maj. Gen. A. R. Bolling
102 Infantry Division........	Maj. Gen. Frank A. Keating
XVI Corps	Maj. Gen. J. B. Anderson
29 Infantry Division........	Maj. Gen. C. H. Gerhardt
75 Infantry Division........	Maj. Gen. Ray E. Porter
79 Infantry Division........	Maj. Gen. Ira T. Wyche
95 Infantry Division........	Maj. Gen. H. L. Twaddle
XIX Corps....................	Maj. Gen. R. S. McLain
2 Armored Division........	Maj. Gen. Isaac D. White
8 Armored Division........	Maj. Gen. J. M. Devine
30 Infantry Division........	Maj. Gen. Leland S. Hobbs
83 Infantry Division........	Maj. Gen. Robert C. Macon
U.S. First Army	Gen. Courtney H. Hodges
78 Infantry Division........	Maj. Gen. E. P. Parker, Jr.
VII Corps	Lt. Gen. J. Lawton Collins
3 Armored Division........	Brig. Gen. Doyle O. Hickey
9 Infantry Division........	Maj. Gen. Louis A. Craig
69 Infantry Division........	Maj. Gen. E. F. Reinhardt
104 Infantry Division........	Maj. Gen. Terry Allen

Unit	Commander
VIII Corps	Maj. Gen. Troy H. Middleton
6 Armored Division	Brig. Gen. George W. Read, Jr.
76 Infantry Division	Maj. Gen. Wm. R. Schmidt
87 Infantry Division	Maj. Gen. Frank L. Culin, Jr.
89 Infantry Division	Maj. Gen. Thomas D. Finley
U.S. Third Army	Gen. George S. Patton, Jr.
4 Infantry Division	Maj. Gen. H. W. Blakeley
70 Infantry Division	Maj. Gen. A. J. Barnett
III Corps	Maj. Gen. J. A. Van Fleet
14 Armored Division	Maj. Gen. Albert C. Smith
99 Infantry Division	Maj. Gen. Walter E. Lauer
V Corps	Maj. Gen. C. R. Huebner
9 Armored Division	Maj. Gen. John W. Leonard
16 Armored Division	Brig. Gen. John L. Pierce
1 Infantry Division	Maj. Gen. Clift Andrus
2 Infantry Division	Maj. Gen. W. M. Robertson
97 Infantry Division	Brig. Gen. Milton B. Halsey
XII Corps	Maj. Gen. S. Leroy Irwin
4 Armored Division	Maj. Gen. William M. Hoge
11 Armored Division	Maj. Gen. Holmes E. Dager
5 Infantry Division	Maj. Gen. Albert E. Brown
26 Infantry Division	Maj. Gen. Willard S. Paul
90 Infantry Division	Maj. Gen. H. L. Earnest
XX Corps	Lt. Gen. Walton H. Walker
13 Armored Division	Maj. Gen. John Milliken
65 Infantry Division	Maj. Gen. S. E. Reinhart
71 Infantry Division	Maj. Gen. Willard G. Wyman
80 Infantry Division	Maj. Gen. H. L. McBride
U.S. Fifteenth Army	Lt. Gen. Leonard T. Gerow
66 Infantry Division	Maj. Gen. Herman F. Kramer
106 Infantry Division	Maj. Gen. Donald A. Stroh
XXII Corps	Maj. Gen. Ernest N. Harmon
17 Airborne Division	Maj. Gen. William M. Miley
94 Infantry Division	Maj. Gen. Harry J. Malony
XXIII Corps	Maj. Gen. Hugh J. Gaffey
28 Infantry Division	Maj. Gen. Norman D. Cota
Southern Group of Armies (6th Army Group)	General Jacob L. Devers
U.S. Seventh Army	Lt. Gen. Alexander M. Patch
12 Armored Division	Maj. Gen. Roderick R. Allen
63 Infantry Division	Maj. Gen. Louis E. Hibbs
45 Infantry Division	Maj. Gen. R. T. Frederick
100 Infantry Division	Maj. Gen. W. A. Burress
XXI Corps	Maj. Gen. Frank W. Milburn
101 Airborne Division	Maj. Gen. Maxwell D. Taylor
36 Infantry Division	Maj. Gen. John E. Dahlquist

409

Unit	Commander
XV Corps	Lt. Gen. Wade H. Haislip
20 Armored Division	Maj. Gen. Orlando Ward
3 Infantry Division	Maj. Gen. John W. O'Daniel
42 Infantry Division	Maj. Gen. Harry J. Collins
86 Infantry Division	Maj. Gen. Harris M. Melasky
VI Corps	Maj. Gen. Edward H. Brooks
10 Armored Division	Maj. Gen. W. H. H. Morris, Jr.
44 Infantry Division	Maj. Gen. William F. Dean
103 Infantry Division	Maj. Gen. A. C. McAuliffe
French First Army	Gen. J. J. de Lattre de Tassigny

SHAEF Reserve

First Allied Airborne Army	Lt. Gen. Lewis H. Brereton
13 Airborne Division	Maj. Gen. E. G. Chapman, Jr.
US Strategic Air Forces in Europe[1]	General Carl Spaatz
Eighth Air Force	Lt. Gen. James H. Doolittle
1 Air Division	Maj. Gen. Howard M. Turner
2 Air Division	Maj. Gen. William E. Kepner
3 Air Division	Maj. Gen. Earle E. Partridge
Ninth Air Force	Lt. Gen. Hoyt S. Vandenberg
IX Bomb Division	Maj. Gen. Samuel E. Anderson
IX Tactical Air Command	Maj. Gen. Elwood R. Quesada
XIX Tactical Air Command	Maj. Gen. Otto P. Weyland
XXIX Tactical Air Command	Brig. Gen. Richard E. Nugent

First Tactical Air Force

(Provisional)	Maj. Gen. Robert M. Webster
XII Tactical Air Command	Brig. Gen. Glenn O. Barcus
French I Air Command	Gen. de Brig. Paul Gerardot
IX Troop Carrier Command	Maj. Gen. Paul L. Williams

[1] Exercised operational control over Fifteenth Air Force shown under Mediterranean Theater of Operations.

MEDITERRANEAN THEATER OF OPERATIONS

(As of May 2, 1945)

Unit	Commander
15th Army Group	Gen. Mark W. Clark
U.S. Fifth Army	Lt. Gen. Lucian K. Truscott
II Corps	Lt. Gen. Geoffrey Keyes
10 Mountain Division	Maj. Gen. George P. Hays
85 Infantry Division	Maj. Gen. John B. Coulter
88 Infantry Division	Maj. Gen. Paul W. Kendall
IV Corps	Maj. Gen. W. D. Crittenberger
1 Armored Division	Maj. Gen. Vernon E. Prichard
34 Infantry Division	Maj. Gen. Charles L. Bolté
92 Infantry Division	Maj. Gen. Edward M. Almond

Unit	*Commander*
British Eighth Army	Lt. Gen. Sir R. L. McCreery
91 Infantry Division	Maj. Gen. William G. Livesay
U.S. Army Air Forces in MTO	Lt. Gen. J. K. Cannon
Twelfth Air Force	Maj. Gen. B. W. Chidlaw
XXII Tactical Air Command	Brig. Gen. T. C. Darcy
Fifteenth Air Force	Maj. Gen. N. F. Twining
XV Fighter Command	Brig. Gen. D. C. Strother

CHINA THEATER

(As of August 14, 1945)

HQ, U.S. FORCES, CHINA THEATER	LT. GEN. A. C. WEDEMEYER
U.S. Army Air Forces, China Theater	Lt. Gen. G. E. Stratemeyer
Tenth Air Force	Maj. Gen. H. C. Davidson
Fourteenth Air Force	Maj. Gen. Charles B. Stone, 3d

PACIFIC THEATER

(As of August 14, 1945)

GHQ, U.S. ARMY FORCES IN THE PACIFIC	GENERAL OF THE ARMY DOUGLAS MAC ARTHUR
U.S. Sixth Army	General Walter Krueger
40 Infantry Division	Brig. Gen. D. J. Myers
11 Airborne Division	Maj. Gen. J. M. Swing
I Corps	Maj. Gen. Innis P. Swift
25 Infantry Division	Maj. Gen. C. L. Mullins
33 Infantry Division	Maj. Gen. P. W. Clarkson
41 Infantry Division	Maj. Gen. Jens A. Doe
IX Corps	Maj. Gen. C. W. Ryder
77 Infantry Division	Maj. Gen. A. D. Bruce
81 Infantry Division	Maj. Gen. P. J. Mueller
XI Corps	Lt. Gen. C. P. Hall
43 Infantry Division	Maj. Gen. L. F. Wing
Americal Division	Maj. Gen. W. H. Arnold
1 Cavalry Division	Maj. Gen. W. C. Chase
U.S. Eighth Army	Lt. Gen. R. L. Eichelberger
93 Infantry Division	Maj. Gen. H. H. Johnson
96 Infantry Division	Maj. Gen. James L. Bradley
X Corps	Maj. Gen. F. C. Sibert
24 Infantry Division	Maj. Gen. R. B. Woodruff
31 Infantry Division	Maj. Gen. C. A. Martin

411

Unit	Commander
XIV Corps	Lt. Gen. O. W. Griswold
6 Infantry Division	Maj. Gen. C. E. Hurdis
32 Infantry Division	Maj. Gen. William H. Gill
37 Infantry Division	Maj. Gen. R. S. Beightler
38 Infantry Division	Maj. Gen. F. A. Irving
U. S. Tenth Army	General Joseph W. Stilwell
XXIV Corps	Lt. Gen. John R. Hodge
7 Infantry Division	Maj. Gen. A. V. Arnold
27 Infantry Division	Maj. Gen. George W. Griner
U.S. Army Forces, Middle Pacific	Lt. Gen. R. C. Richardson, Jr.
98 Infantry Division	Maj. Gen. A. M. Harper
U.S. Army Forces, Western Pacific	Lt. Gen. Wilhelm D. Styer
Far East Air Forces	General George C. Kenney
Fifth Air Force	Lt. Gen. E. C. Whitehead
Seventh Air Force	Brig. Gen. Thomas D. White
Thirteenth Air Force	Maj. Gen. P. B. Wurtsmith

U. S. ARMY STRATEGIC AIR FORCES

(As of August 14, 1945)

HQ, U.S. ARMY STRSTEGIC AIR FORCES

Commanding General	General Carl Spaatz
Deputy Commander	Lt. Gen. Barney M. Giles
Chief of Staff	Maj. Gen. Curtis E. LeMay
Eighth Air Force	Lt. Gen. James H. Doolittle
Twentieth Air Force	Lt. Gen. Nathan T. Twining

APPENDIX II

CAMPAIGNS AND BATTLES, U. S. ARMY

Battle participation stars have been awarded for the following campaigns. Battle participation credit for the campaigns noted by asterisks may be awarded by the appropriate theater commander to units or individuals who actually engaged the enemy in the combat zone after the closing date.

European—African—Middle Eastern Theater

Egypt-Libya .... June 11, 1942 to February 12, 1943
Air Offensive, Europe ...... July 4, 1942 to June 5, 1944

412

Algeria-French Morocco....November 8 to 11, 1942
Tunisia:
   Air ....November 8, 1942 to May 13, 1943
   Ground ....November 17, 1942 to May 13, 1943

Sicily:
   Air ....May 14 to August 17, 1943
   Ground ....July 9 to August 17, 1943

Naples-Foggia:
   Air ....August 18, 1943 to January 21, 1944
   Ground ....September 9, 1943 to January 21, 1944
Rome-Arno ....January 22 to September 9, 1944
Normandy ....June 6 to July 24, 1944
Northern France ....July 25 to September 14, 1944
Southern France ....August 15 to September 14, 1944
North Apennines ....September 10, 1944 to April 4, 1945
Rhineland ....September 15, 1944 to March 21, 1945
Ardennes ....December 16, 1944 to January 25, 1945
Central Europe ....March 22 to May 11, 1945
Po Valley ....April 5 to May 8, 1945

Asiatic-Pacific Theater

Central Pacific ....December 7, 1941 to December 6, 1943
Burma ....December 7, 1941 to May 26, 1942
Philippine Islands ....December 7, 1941 to May 10, 1942
East Indies ....January 1 to July 22, 1942
India-Burma ....April 2, 1942 to January 28, 1945
Air Offensive, Japan ......April 17, 1942 to September 2, 1945
Aleutian Islands ....June 3, 1942 to August 24, 1943
China Defensive ....July 4, 1942 to May 4, 1945
China Offensive ....May 5, 1945 to September 2, 1945
Papua ....July 23, 1942 to January 23, 1943
Guadalcanal ....August 7, 1942 to February 21, 1943
New Guinea ....January 24, 1943 to December 31, 1944*
Northern Solomons ....February 22, 1943 to November 21, 1944*

Eastern Mandates:
   Air ....December 7, 1943 to April 16, 1944*
   Ground ....January 31 to June 14, 1944*
Bismarck Archipelago .....December 15, 1943 to November 27, 1944*

Western Pacific:
   Air ....April 17, 1944 to September 2, 1945
   Ground ....June 15, 1944 to September 2, 1945
Southern Philippines ......October 17, 1944 to July 4, 1945*
Luzon ....January 9, 1945 to July 4, 1945*
Central Burma ....January 29, 1945 to July 15, 1945
Ryukyus ....March 26, 1945 to July 2, 1945

413

APPENDIX III

U.S. BATTLE CASUALTIES IN ETO

	World War II	World War I
Killed in action	98,812	34,785
Died of wounds	15,140	14,713
Wounded	373,018	205,690
Prisoners	24,783	4,480
Missing	42,278	1,609

APPENDIX IV

STATISTICS ON U.S. MILITARY EFFORT IN ETO

	World War II	World War I
Oil products used	7,108,718 tons	165,000 tons
Battle casualties	554,031	261,277
Deaths from disease	741	23,238
Motor vehicles		
(number)	710,650	80,395
(weight)	3,964,924 long tons	68,334
German prisoners handled	3,239,484	49,969
Artillery capacity at one round per gun	436 tons	102 tons
Army tonnage used in Europe	47,641,882 tons	8,346,342 tons

APPENDIX V

MERCHANT SHIPPING LOSSES OF ALLIED NATIONS TO MAY 8, 1945

Tonnage in thousands:

Sunk by	United States Number of Vessels	Gross Tons	British Empire Number of Vessels	Gross Tons	Other Allies Number of Vessels	Gross Tons	Gross Tons	Neutrals Number of Vessels	Total Number of Vessels	Gross Tons
U-boats	440	2,740	1,360	7,620	670	3,260	300	930	2,770	14,550
Mines	15	90	340	830	75	210	90	270	520	1,400
Surface craft	13	90	210	970	87	460	20	50	330	1,570
Aircraft	58	360	440	1,590	202	770	50	110	750	2,830
Other causes	12	30	220	370	138	330	30	60	400	790
Totals	538	3,310	2,570	11,380	1,172	5,030	490	1,420	4,770	21,140

414

APPENDIX VI

RAF SORTIES, MEDITERRANEAN AREA AND MIDDLE EAST

Year	Bomber Command	Fighter Command	Coastal Command	Tactical, Reconn., Army Cooper. Command	Miscel- laneous
1940	5,158	9,168	1,304	2,032	40
1941	14,850	33,211	4,845	3,554	568
1942	19,896	79,478	11,116	2,603	1,642
1943	18,968	107,671	—	2,681	13,631
1944	33,621	167,008	7,600	16,597	18,852
1945	15,959	57,245[1]	50	—	4,986
Total	108,452	453,781	24,924	27,467	39,728

[1] Figure includes operations for Tactical, etc., Command for year.

APPENDIX VII

RAF SORTIES FROM UNITED KINGDOM

Year	Bomber Command	Fighter Command	Army Cooper. Command	2d Tactical Air Force	Coastal Command
1939	591	3,217	—	—	41,001
1940	22,473	121,079	—	—	
1941	32,012	150,828	—	—	30,544
1942	35,338 (1,088)*	147,087	—	—	31,676
1943	65,068 (1,240)*	136,167	—	23,695	43,231
1944	166,844	122,136	—	214,592	66,362
1945	67,483	19,712	—	89,426	22,935
Total	389,809 (2,328)*	700,226	4,474	327,713	235,749

* Sorties made by Bomber Command aircraft operating under Coastal Command.

The total number of sorties made by aircraft under all commands in the Mediterranean, Middle East and United Kingdom theaters of operations from the beginning of the war in 1939 to June 16, 1945, was 2,314,651.

Bomb tonnage dropped in European war by RAF........955,044 tons
Mines laid by RAF.................................... 33,263 tons

SORTIES, AAF IN ETO

	8th AF	9th AF*	12th AF **	15th AF***
Prior to 1943..........	2,453		5,388	1,908
1943	54,207	9,722	142,063	26,500
1944	385,754	269,474	180,147	176,661
1945 through 8 May†...	137,904	114,473	49,471	75,918

TONNAGE

Prior to 1943..........	1,713		1,159	3,251
1943	47,475	8,186	49,258	44,765
1944	451,365	140,594	108,345	238,645
1945 through 8 May†...	220,988	102,697	39,280	93,386

* Includes all medium bombers in ETO and operations of the 1st Tactical Air Force.

** Includes mediums and fighters of the 9th (Middle East) Air Force.

*** Includes heavy bombers of the 9th (Middle East) Air Force.

† Figures for 1945 tentative.

APPENDIX IX

SURRENDER TERMS AT REIMS

The text of the German surrender terms, as signed at General Eisenhower's headquarters in Reims, France, on May 7 at 2:41 A.M., is given below.

(1) We, the undersigned, acting by authority of the German High Command, hereby surrender unconditionally to the Supreme Commander, Allied Expeditionary Force, and simultaneously to the Soviet High Command, all forces on land, sea, and in the air who are at this date under German control.

(2) The German High Command will at once issue orders to all German military, naval and air authorities and to all forces under German control to cease active operations at 2301 hours [11:01 P.M.] Central European Time on Eight May and to remain in the positions occupied at the time. No ship, vessel or aircraft is to be scuttled, or any damage done to their hull, machinery or equipment.

416

(3) The German High Command will at once issue to the appropriate commanders, and ensure the carrying out of any further orders issued by the Supreme Commander, Allied Expeditionary Force, and by the Soviet High Command.

(4) This Act of Military Surrender is without prejudice to, and will be superseded by, any general instrument of surrender imposed by, or on behalf of, the United Nations and applicable to Germany and the German Armed Forces as a whole.

(5) In the event of the German High Command or any of the forces under their control failing to act in accordance with this Act of Surrender, the Supreme Commander, Allied Expeditionary Force, and the Soviet High Command will take such punitive or other action as they deem appropriate.

Signed at Reims, France, at 0241 hours [2:41 A.M.] on the seventh day of May, 1945.

On behalf of the German High Command: JODL
  In the presence of:

On behalf of the Supreme Commander,
Allied Expeditionary Force: W. B. SMITH

On behalf of the Soviet High Command: IVAN SUSLO-
  PAROFF

On behalf of the French: F. SEVEZ

APPENDIX X

BERLIN DECLARATION

regarding the defeat of Germany and the assumption of supreme authority with respect to Germany by the Governments of the United States of America, the Union of Soviet Socialist Republics, and the United Kingdom, and the Provisional Government of the French Republic.

The German armed forces on land, at sea and in the air have been completely defeated and have surrendered unconditionally and Germany, which bears responsibility for the war, is no longer capable of resisting the will of the victorious Powers. The unconditional surrender of Germany has thereby been effected, and Germany has become subject to such requirements as may now or hereafter be imposed upon her.

There is no control Government or authority in Germany capable of accepting responsibility for the maintenance of order, the administration of the country and compliance with the requirements of the victorious Powers.

It is in these circumstances necessary, without prejudice to any subsequent decisions that may be taken respecting Germany, to make provision for the cessation of any further hostilities on the part of the German armed forces, for the maintenance of order in Germany and for the administration of the country, and to announce the immediate requirements with which Germany must comply.

The Representatives of the Supreme Commands of the United States of America, the Union of Soviet Socialist Republics, the United Kingdom and the French Republic, hereinafter called the "Allied Representatives," acting by authority of their respective Governments and in the interests of the United Nations, accordingly make the following Declaration:

The Governments of the United States of America, the Union of Soviet Socialist Republics and the United Kingdom, and the Provisional Government of the French Republic, hereby assume supreme authority with respect to Germany, including all the powers possessed by the German Government, the High Command and any state, municipal, or local government or authority. The assumption, for the purposes stated above, of the said authority and powers does not effect the annexation of Germany.

The Governments of the United States of America, the Union of Soviet Socialist Republics and the United

Kingdom, and the Provisional Government of the French Republic, will hereafter determine the boundaries of Germany or any part thereof and the status of Germany or of any area at present being part of German territory.

In virtue of the supreme authority and powers thus assumed by the four Governments, the Allied Representatives announce the following requirements arising from the complete defeat and unconditional surrender of Germany with which Germany must comply:

ARTICLE 1.

Germany, and all German military, naval and air authorities and all forces under German control shall immediately cease hostilities in all theaters of war against the forces of the United Nations on land, at sea and in the air.

ARTICLE 2.

(a) All armed forces of Germany or under German control, wherever they may be situated, including land, air, antiaircraft and naval forces, the S.S., S.A. and Gestapo, and all other forces or auxiliary organizations equipped with weapons, shall be completely disarmed, handing over their weapons and equipment to local Allied Commanders or to officers designated by the Allied Representatives.

(b) The personnel of the formations and units of all the forces referred to in paragraph (a) above shall, at the discretion of the Commander-in-Chief of the Armed Forces of the Allied State concerned, be declared to be prisoners of war, pending further decisions, and shall be subject to such conditions and directions as may be prescribed by the respective Allied Representatives.

(c) All forces referred to in paragraph (a) above, wherever they may be, will remain in their present positions pending instructions from the Allied Representatives.

(d) Evacuation by the said forces of all territories outside the frontiers of Germany as they existed on the 31st December, 1937, will proceed according to instructions to be given by the Allied Representatives.

(e) Detachments of civil police to be armed with small arms only, for the maintenance of order and for guard duties, will be designated by the Allied Representatives.

ARTICLE 3.

(a) All aircraft of any kind or nationality in Germany or German-occupied or controlled territories or waters, military, naval or civil, other than aircraft in the service of the Allies, will remain on the ground, on the water or aboard ships pending further instructions.

(b) All German or German-controlled aircraft in or over territories or waters not occupied or controlled by Germany will proceed to Germany or to such other place or places as may be specified by the Allied Representatives.

ARTICLE 4.

(a) All German or German-controlled naval vessels, surface and submarine, auxiliary naval craft, and merchant and other shipping, wherever such vessels may be at the time of this Declaration, and all other merchant ships of whatever nationality in German ports, will remain in or proceed immediately to ports and bases as specified by the Allied Representatives. The crews of such vessels will remain on board pending further instructions.

(b) All ships and vessels of the United Nations, whether or not title has been transferred as the result of prize court or other proceedings, which are at the disposal of Germany or under German control at the time of this Declaration, will proceed at the dates and to the ports or bases specified by the Allied Representatives.

ARTICLE 5.

(a) All or any of the following articles in the possession of the German armed forces or under German control or at German disposal will be held intact and in good condition at the disposal of the Allied Representatives, for such purposes and at such times and places as they may prescribe:

(i) all arms, ammunition, explosives, military equipment, stores and supplies and other implements of war of all kinds and all other war material;

(ii) all naval vessels of all classes, both surface and submarine, auxiliary naval craft and all merchant shipping, whether afloat, under repair or construction, built or building;

(iii) all aircraft of all kinds, aviation and antiaircraft equipment and devices;

(iv) all transportation and communications facilities and equipment, by land, water or air;

(v) all military installations and establishments, including airfields, seaplane bases, ports and naval bases, storage depots, permanent and temporary land and coast fortifications, fortresses and other fortified areas, together with plans and drawings of all such fortifications, installations and establishments;

(vi) all factories, plants, shops, research institutions, laboratories, testing stations, technical data, patents, plans, drawings and inventions, designed or intended to produce or to facilitate the production or use of the articles, materials and facilities referred to in sub-paragraphs (i), (ii), (iii), (iv) and (v) above or otherwise to further the conduct of war.

(b) At the demand of the Allied Representatives the following will be furnished:

(i) the labor, services and plant required for the maintenance or operation of any of the six categories mentioned in paragraph (a) above; and

(ii) any information or records that may be required by the Allied Representatives in connection with the same.

(c) At the demand of the Allied Representatives all facilities will be provided for the movement of Allied troops and agencies, their equipment and supplies, on the railways, roads and other land communications or by sea, river or air. All means of transportation will be maintained in good order and repair, and the labor, services and plant necessary therefor will be furnished.

ARTICLE 6.

(a) The German authorities will release to the Allied Representatives, in accordance with the procedure to be laid down by them, all prisoners of war at present in their power, belonging to the forces of the United Nations, and will furnish full lists of these persons, indicating the places of their detention in Germany or territory occupied by Germany. Pending the release of such prisoners of war, the German authorities and people will protect them in their persons and property and provide them with adequate food, clothing, shelter, medical

422

attention and money in accordance with their rank or official position.

(b) The German authorities and people will in like manner provide for and release all other nationals of the United Nations who are confined, interned or otherwise under restraint, and all other persons who may be confined, interned or otherwise under restraint for political reasons or as a result of any Nazi action, law or regulation which discriminates on the ground of race, color, creed or political belief.

(c) The German authorities will, at the demand of the Allied Representatives, hand over control of places of detention to such officers as may be designated for the purpose by the Allied Representatives.

ARTICLE 7.

The German authorities concerned will furnish to the Allied Representatives:

(a) full information regarding the forces referred to in Article 2 (a), and, in particular, will furnish forthwith all information which the Allied Representatives may require concerning the numbers, locations and dispositions of such forces, whether located inside or outside Germany;

(b) complete and detailed information concerning mines, minefields and other obstacles to movement by land, sea or air, and the safety lanes in connection therewith. All such safety lanes will be kept open and clearly marked; all mines, minefields and other dangerous obstacles will as far as possible be rendered safe, and all aids to navigation will be reinstated. Unarmed German military and civilian personnel with the necessary equipment will be made available and utilized for the above purposes and for the removal of mines, mine-

423

fields and other obstacles as directed by the Allied Representatives.

ARTICLE 8.

There shall be no destruction, removal, concealment, transfer or scuttling of, or damage to, any military, naval, air, shipping, port, industrial and other like property and facilities and all records and archives, wherever they may be situated, except as may be directed by the Allied Representatives.

ARTICLE 9.

Pending the institution of control by the Allied Representatives over all means of communication, all radio and tele-communication installations and other forms of wire or wireless communications, whether ashore or afloat, under German control, will cease transmission except as directed by the Allied Representatives.

ARTICLE 10.

The forces, ships, aircraft, military equipment, and other property in Germany or in German control or service or at German disposal, of any other country at war with any of the Allies, will be subject to the provisions of this Declaration and of any proclamations, orders, ordinances or instructions issued thereunder.

ARTICLE 11.

(a) The principal Nazi leaders as specified by the Allied Representatives, and all persons from time to time named or designated by rank, office or employment by the Allied Representatives as being suspected of having committed, ordered or abetted

424

war crimes or analogous offenses, will be apprehended and surrendered to the Allied Representatives.

(b) The same will apply in the case of any national of any of the United Nations who is alleged to have committed an offense against his national law, and who may at any time be named or designated by rank, office or employment by the Allied Representatives.

(c) The German authorities and people will comply with any instructions given by the Allied Representatives for the apprehension and surrender of such persons.

ARTICLE 12.

The Allied Representatives will station forces and civil agencies in any or all parts of Germany as they may determine.

ARTICLE 13.

(a) In the exercise of the supreme authority with respect to Germany assumed by the Governments of the United States of America, the Union of Soviet Socialist Republics and the United Kingdom, and the Provisional Government of the French Republic, the four Allied Governments will take such steps, including the complete disarmament and demilitarization of Germany, as they deem requisite for future peace and security.

(b) The Allied Representatives will impose on Germany additional political, administrative, economic, financial, military and other requirements arising from the complete defeat of Germany. The Allied Representatives, or persons or agencies duly designated to act on their authority, will issue proclamations, orders, ordinances and instructions for the purpose of laying down such additional

425

requirements, and of giving effect to the other provisions of this Declaration. All German authorities and the German people shall carry out unconditionally the requirements of the Allied Representatives, and shall fully comply with all such proclamations, orders, ordinances and instructions.

ARTICLE 14.

This Declaration enters into force and effect at the date and hour set forth below. In the event of failure on the part of the German authorities or people promptly and completely to fulfill their obligation hereby or hereafter imposed, the Allied Representatives will take whatever action may be deemed by them to be appropriate under the circumstances.

ARTICLE 15.

This Declaration is drawn up in the English, Russian, French and German languages. The English, Russian and French are the only authentic texts.

5 June 1945	Berlin
(Date and Year.)	(Place.)

1800

(Hours—Central European Time.)

Signed by the Allied Representatives:

U. S. A.   DWIGHT D. EISENHOWER, *General of the Army*

U. S. S. R.   ZHUKOV, *Marshal of the Soviet Union*

U. K.   B. L. MONTGOMERY, *Field Marshal*

FRANCE   DE LATTRE DE TASSIGNY, *General of the Army*

426

APPENDIX XI

AXIS U-BOATS SUNK IN THE EUROPEAN WAR

Sunk by:	U. S. forces and Other Allied Forces (except British Empire forces) under U.S. control	British Empire forces and other Allied forces (except U.S. forces) under British control	Total German U-boats assessed as sunk
Ships	30½	205½	236
Shore-based aircraft	45	179½	224½
Carrier-borne aircraft	32	18½	50½
Joint ship-shore-based aircraft	7½	21½	29
Joint ship-carrier-borne aircraft	6	4	10
Submarines	1	25	26
Bombing raids on U-boats afloat in enemy ports...	29	8	37
Total..............	151	462	613

APPENDIX XII

BRITISH EMPIRE CASUALTIES TO MAY 31, 1945

Total military and civilian casualties.........................1,424,634
  Dead 532,233
  Wounded 468,388
  Prisoners and internees..........330,523
Service deaths
  United Kingdom 233,042
  Canada 36,018
  Australia 21,415
  New Zealand 9,844
  South Africa 6,417
  India 23,295
  Colonies 6,741
Civilian casualties
  Dead 60,585
  Wounded 86,175
(British Information Service)

APPENDIX XIII

RESULTS OF B-29 INCENDIARY ATTACKS ON JAPAN

Place	Population	Number of Attacks	Square Miles Burned Out	Per Cent Destroyed
Tokyo area	9,094,600	6	110.80	39.9
Nagoya area	1,250,000	5	39.60	40.0

Nagasaki area	255,000	[1]	[1]	35.6
Osaka area	3,252,340	4	59.80	35.1
Kobe area	1,006,300	3	15.70	55.7
Kawasaki area	300,000	1	11.30	35.2
Yokohama area	866,200	[1]	20.20	57.6
Amagasaki	200,000	2	6.82	18.9
Hamamatsu	165,000	1	4.29	60.3
Kagoshima	181,000	1	4.87	63.4
Yokkaichi	102,000	1	3.51	33.6
Omuta	177,000	2	5.20	33.1
Fukuoka	323,217	1	6.50	24.1
Toyohashi	242,000	1	3.30	67.9
Shizuoka	212,000	1	3.50	66.1
Okayama	163,000	1	3.38	68.9
Sasebo	206,000	1	2.34	41.4
Moji	140,000	1	1.12	23.3
Nobeoka	80,000	1	1.43	25.2
Kure	238,000	1	3.26	41.9
Kumamoto	210,000	1	4.80	31.2
Shimonoseki	196.000	1	1.42	37.6
Ube	100,000	1	1.80	20.7
Takamatsu	111,000	1	1.80	67.5
Kochi	106,000	1	1.90	55.2
Himeji	104,000	1	1.92	49.4
Tokushima	120,000	1	2.30	85.2
Chiba	75,000	1	1.98	41.0
Akashi	47,750	1	1.73	50.2
Kofu	102,000	1	2.00	78.6
Shimizu	69.000	1	1.41	42.1
Sendai	223,630	1	4.53	21.9
Sakai	182,147	1	2.32	48.2
Wakayama	195,203	1	4.00	50.0
Gifu	172,340	1	2.60	69.6
Utsunomiva	88,000	1	2.75	43.7
Ichinomiya	50,000	2	1.28	56.3
Tsuruga	31,000	1	1.13	65.1
Uwajima	52,000	2	.93	54.2
Kuwana	42,000	1	.82	75.0
Numazu	55,000	1	1.40	42.3
Hiratsuka	43,000	1	2.48	48.4
Oita	76,000	1	2.20	28.2
Hitacha	82,000	2	1.38	72.0
Choshi	61,000	1	1.12	44.2
Fukui	100,000	1	1.90	86.0
Okazaki	84,000	1	.95	32.2
Matsuyama	120,000	1	1.67	64.0
Tokuyama	40,000	1	1.27	48.3
Tsu	68,000	1	1.48	69.3
Aomori	100,000	1	2.08	30.0
Ujiyamada	52,000	1	.93	41.3

428

Ogaki	35,000	1	1.38	39.5
Miyakonojo	54,000	3	[2]	26.5
Isezaki	33,000	1	[1]	56.1
Kumagaya	50,000	1	[1]	55.1
Hachioji	75,000	1	1.40	65.0
Toyama	27,000	1	1.88	95.6
Nagaoka	70,000	1	1.33	64.9
Mito	66,500	1	2.20	68.9
Saga	50,000	1	1.20	44.2
Maebashi	87,000	1	2.36	64.2
Nishinomiya-Mikagae	300,000	1	9.1	11.9
Imabari	55,000	1	.94	63.9
Yawata	243,500	1	5.78	21.2
Fukuyama	57,000	1	1.20	80.9

[1]Figure not released.
[2]Only minor damage.

APPENDIX XIV

Text of General Order No. 1 [*September 2, 1945*] issued by Japanese Imperial General Headquarters for the orders of the Supreme Allied Commander:

I. The Imperial General Headquarters by direction of the Emperor, and pursuant to the surrender to the supreme commander for the Allied Powers, of all Japanese armed forces by the emperor, hereby orders all of its commanders in Japan and abroad to cause the Japanese armed forces and Japanese-controlled forces under their command to cease hostilities at once, to lay down their arms, to remain in their present locations and to surrender unconditionally to commanders acting on behalf of the United States, the Republic of China, the United Kingdom and the Britsh Empire, and the Union of Soviet Socialist Republics, as indicated hereafter or as may be further directed by the supreme commander for the Allied Powers.

Immediate contact will be made with the indicated commanders, or their designated representatives, subject to any changes in detail prescribed by the supreme commander for the Allied Powers, and their instructions will be completely and immediately carried out.

(*a*) The senior Japanese commanders and all ground. sea, air and auxiliary forces within China (excluding Manchuria), Formosa and French Indo-China north of

16 degrees north latitude shall surrender to Generalissimo Chiang Kai-shek.

(b) The senior Japanese commanders and all ground, sea, air and auxiliary forces within Manchuria, Korea north of 38 degrees north latitude and Karafuto shall surrender to the commander in chief of Soviet forces in the Far East.

(c) The senior Japanese commanders and all ground, sea, air and auxiliary forces within the Andamans, Nicobars, Burma, Thailand, French Indo-China south of 16 degrees north latitude, Malaya, Borneo, Netherlands Indies, New Guinea, Bismarcks and the Solomons shall surrender [copy garbled here—probably to the supreme Allied commander, Southeast Asia Command, or to the commanding general, Australia, to be arranged between them and the details of this paragraph then prepared by the supreme commander for the Allied powers].

(d) The senior Japanese commanders and all ground, sea, air and auxiliary forces in the Japanese mandated islands, Ryukyus, Bonins and other Pacific islands shall surrender to the commander in chief, U. S. Pacific Fleet.

(e) The Imperial General Headquarters, its senior commanders, and all ground, sea, air and auxiliary forces in the main islands of Japan, minor islands adjacent thereto, Korea south of 38 degrees north latitude, and the Philippines shall surrender to the commander in chief, U. S. Army Forces in the Pacific.

(f) The above indicated commanders are the only representatives of the Allied Powers empowered to accept surrender and all surrenders of Japanese forces shall be made only to them or to their representatives.

The Japanese Imperial General Headquarters further orders its commanders in Japan and abroad to disarm completely all forces of Japan or under Japanese control, wherever they may be situated, and to deliver, intact, and in safe and good condition, all weapons and equipment at such time and at such places as may be described by the Allied commanders indicated above.

Pending further instructions, the Japanese police force

in the main islands of Japan will be exempt from this disarmament provision.

The police force will remain at their posts and shall be held responsible for the preservation of law and order. The strength and arms of such a police force will be prescribed.

II. The Japanese Imperial General Headquarters shall furnish to the supreme commander for the Allied Powers within [time limit] of receipt of this order complete information with respect to Japan and all areas under Japanese control as follows:

(a) Lists of all land, air and antiaircraft units showing locations and strengths in officers and men.

(b) Lists of all aircraft, military, naval and civil, giving complete information as to the number, type, location and condition of such aircraft.

(c) Lists of all Japanese and Japanese-controlled naval vessels, surface and submarine and auxiliary naval craft in or out of commission and under construction giving their position, condition and movement.

(d) Lists of all Japanese and Japanese-controlled merchant ships of over 100 gross tons in or out of commission and under construction, including merchant ships formerly belonging to any of the United Nations now in Japanese hands giving position, condition and movement.

(e) Complete and detailed information, accompanied by maps showing locations and layouts of all mines, minefields and other obstacles to movement by land, sea and air and the safety lanes in connection therewith.

(f) Locations and descriptions of all military installations and establishments, including airfields, seaplane bases, antiaircraft defenses, ports and naval bases, storage depots, permanent and temporary land and coast fortifications, fortresses and other fortified areas.

(g) Locations of all camps and other places of detention of United Nations prisoners of war and civilian internees.

431

III. Japanese armed forces and civil aviation authorities will insure that all Japanese military and naval and civil aircraft remain on the ground, the water or aboard ship until further notification on the disposition to be made of them.

IV. Japanese or Japanese-controlled naval or merchant vessels of all types will be maintained without damage and will undertake no movement pending instructions from the supreme commander for the Allied Powers. Vessels at sea will remove explosives of all types to safe storage ashore.

V. Responsible Japanese or Japanese-controlled military and civil authorities will insure that:

(a) All Japanese mines. minefields and other obstacles to movement by land, sea and air, wherever located, be removed according to instructions of the supreme commander for the Allied Powers.

(b) All aids to navigation be reestablished at once.

(c) All safety lanes be kept open and clearly marked pending accomplishment of *(a)* above.

VI. Responsible Japanese and Japanese-controlled military and civil authorities will hold intact, and in good condition, pending further instructions from the supreme commander for the Allied Powers the following:

(a) All arms, ammunitions, explosives. military equipment, stores and supplies and other implements of war of all kinds and all other war material (except as specifically prescribed in Section IV of this order).

(b) All land. water and air transportation and communication facilities and equipment.

(c) All military installations and establishments including airfields, seaplane bases, antiaircraft defenses, ports and naval bases, storage depots, permanent and temporary land and coast fortifications, fortresses and other fortified areas together with plans and drawings of all such fortifications, installations and establishments.

(d) All factories, plants, shops, research institutions, laboratories, testing stations, technical data, plans, drawings and inventions designed or intended to produce or facilitate the production or use of all implements of war and other material and property used or intended for use by any military or part-military organizations in connection with its operations.

VII. The Japanese Imperial General Headquarters shall furnish to the supreme commander for the Allied Powers within [time limit] of receipt of this order complete lists of all the items specified in paragraphs *(a)*, *(b)* and *(d)* of Section VI above, indicating the numbers, types and locations of each.

VIII. The manufacture and distribution of all arms, ammunition and implements of war will cease forthwith.

IX. With respect to United Nations prisoners of war and civilian internees in the hands of Japanese or Japanese-controlled authorities:

(a) The safety and well-being of all United Nations prisoners of war and civilian internees will be scrupulously preserved to include the administrative and supply service essential to provide adequate food, shelter, clothing and medical care until such responsibility is undertaken by the supreme commander for the Allied Powers.

(b) Each camp or other place of detention of United Nations prisoners of war and civilian internees together with its equipment, stores, records, arms and ammunition will be delivered immediately to the command of the senior officer designated representative of the prisoners of war and civilian internees.

(c) As directed by the supreme commander for the Allied Powers prisoners of war and civilian internees will be transported to places of safety, where they can be accepted by Allied authorities.

(d) The Japanese Imperial General Headquarters will furnish to the supreme commander for the Allied Powers within [time limit] of the receipt of this order

complete lists of all United Nations prisoners of war and civilian internees indicating their location.

X. All Japanese and Japanese-controlled military and civil authorities shall aid and assist the occupation of Japan and Japanese-controlled areas by forces of the Allied Powers.

XI. The Japanese Imperial General Headquarters and appropriate Japanese officials shall be prepared, on instructions from Allied occupation commanders, to collect and deliver all arms in the possession of the Japanese civilian population.

XII. This and all subsequent instructions issued by the supreme commander for the Allied Forces of other Allied military authorities will be scrupulously and promptly obeyed by Japanese and Japanese-controlled military and civil officials and private persons.

Any delay or failure to comply with the provisions of this or subsequent orders, and any action which the supreme commander for Allied Powers determines to be detrimental to the Allied Powers, will incur drastic and summary punishment at the hands of Allied military authorities and the Japanese government.

434

MAPS

MAP 1. Europe After World War I.

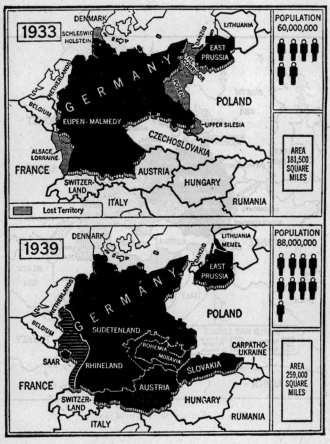

MAP 2.   Expansion of Germany: 1933-39.

MAP 3. Blitzkrieg in Poland: 1939.

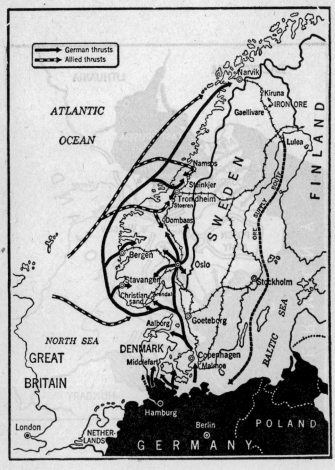

MAP 4. German Invasion of Denmark and Norway: 1940.

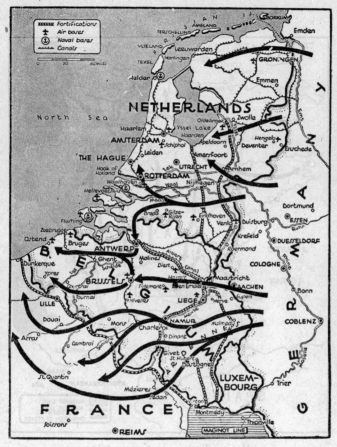

MAP 5. German Attack on the Low Countries and France: 1940.
(From *The War in Maps*, by Francis Brown; New York: Oxford
University Press, 1944. Reproduced by permission.)

441

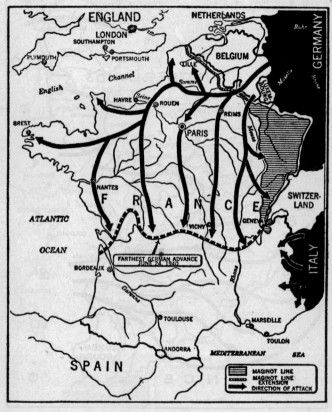

Map 6. Blitzkrieg in France: 1940.

442

MAP 7. The Balkan Theater: 1940. (From *The War in Maps*, by Francis Brown; New York, Oxford University Press, 1944. Reproduced by permission.)

443

BELGIUM

ATLANTIC

FRANCE

OCEAN

SWITZER-
LAND

Venic

Spezia

Lisbon

Madrid

CORSICA
Fr.

PORTUGAL

SPAIN

Sp.
Balearic Is.

Terranc

SARDINIA
It.

Br.
Gibraltar

Cagliari

1140 Miles

Mediterranean

Castellamm

SP. MORCCCO

90 MI.

Pante
It.

Tunis

FR. MOROCCO

ALGERIA
Fr.

TUNISIA
Fr.

THE AXIS POWERS
OCCUPIED BY GERMANY
■ BRITISH NAVAL BASES
△ ITALIAN NAVAL BASES

MAP 8. The Mediterranean Theater: 1939-42.

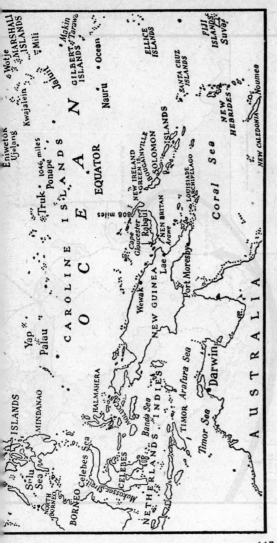

MAP 9. – The Pacific Theater: 1941.

447

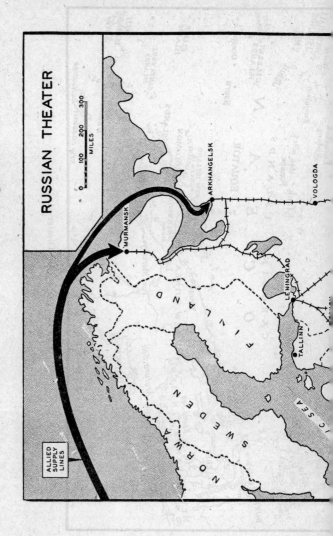

RUSSIAN THEATER

MILES
0 100 200 300

ALLIED
SUPPLY
LINES

ARKHANGELSK

VOLOGDA

MURMANSK

FINLAND

LENINGRAD

TALLINN

SWEDEN

NORWAY

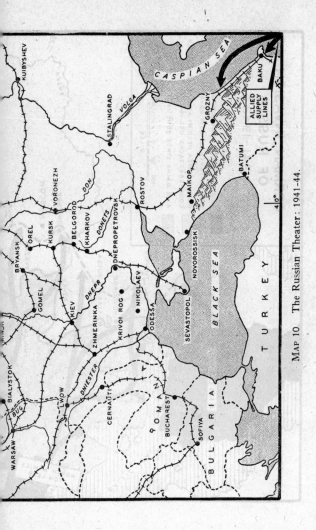

Map 10. The Russian Theater: 1941-44.

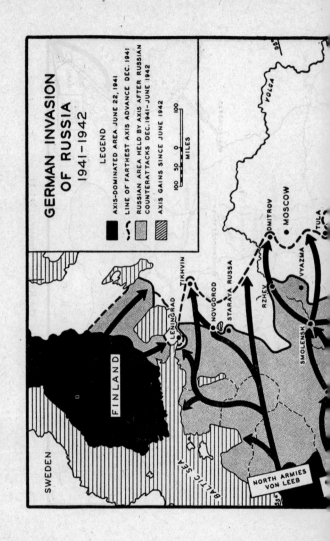

GERMAN INVASION
OF RUSSIA
1941–1942

LEGEND

- AXIS-DOMINATED AREA JUNE 22, 1941
- LINE OF FARTHEST AXIS ADVANCE DEC. 1941
- RUSSIAN AREA HELD BY AXIS AFTER RUSSIAN COUNTERATTACKS DEC. 1941–JUNE 1942
- AXIS GAINS SINCE JUNE 1942

MILES
100   50   0   100

SWEDEN

FINLAND

BALTIC SEA

LENINGRAD

TIKHVIN

NOVGOROD

STARAYA RUSSA

RZHEV

DMITROV

MOSCOW

VYAZMA

SMOLENSK

TULA

VOLGA

NORTH ARMIES
VON LEEB

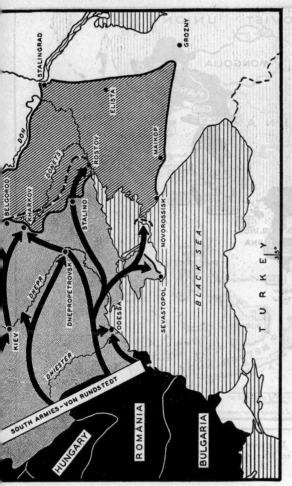

MAP 11. The German Invasion of Russia : 1941-42.

451

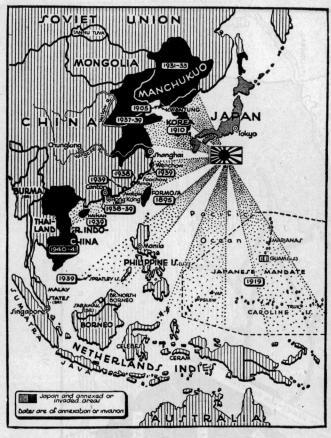

MAP 12. Japanese Conquests in Asia Before Pearl Harbor. (From *The War in Maps,* by Francis Brown; New York: Oxford University Press, 1944. Reproduced by permission.)

Legend:
- Japanese attacks
- Railways
- Motor Roads
- Boxes show dates of Japanese landings

THAILAND
SINGORA
PATANI
Setul
PERLIS
Changun
Yala
ALOR STAR
Betong
GEORGETOWN
PENANG
Krian
Grik
Taiping
Kuala Kangsar
Ipoh
Sungei Siput
7,159 Ft.
Lumut
Telok Anson
6,987
6,914 Ft.
Tanjongbalai
Kuala Kubu
KUALA LUMPUR
Port Dickson
MALACCA
SUMATRA

Muda
Tanah Merah
Kuala Krai
Kuala Trengganu
Kuala Dungun
7,183 Ft.
Kuala Lipis
Tembeling
Kuantan
Temerloh
Pekan
Gemas
Endau
Tampin
Mersing
Mawai
Johore Bahru
SINGAPORE
Str. of Singapore
BATAM
BINTAN

SOUTH
CHINA
SEA

1 DEC. 8 — Kota Bharu
2 DEC. 9
3 JAN. 6
4 JAN. 27 — TIOMAN
5 FEB. 8, 1942

STR. OF MALACCA

0   50   100 MILES

MAP 13. The Japanese Conquest of Malaya: 1941-42. (From *The War in Maps*, by Francis Brown; New York: Oxford University Press, 1944. Reproduced by permission.)

453

Map 5. The Japanese Conquest, December 1941–1942. From *The War in Asia*, by Francis Brown, New York: Oxford University Press, 1942. Reproduced by permission.

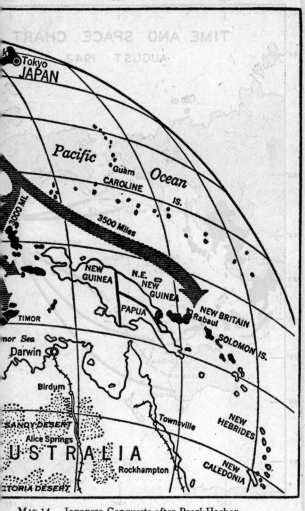

MAP 14. Japanese Conquests after Pearl Harbor.

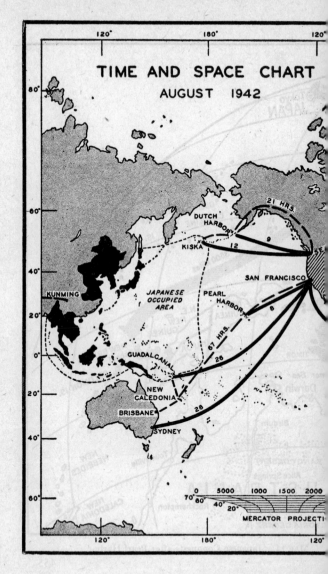

TIME AND SPACE CHART
AUGUST 1942

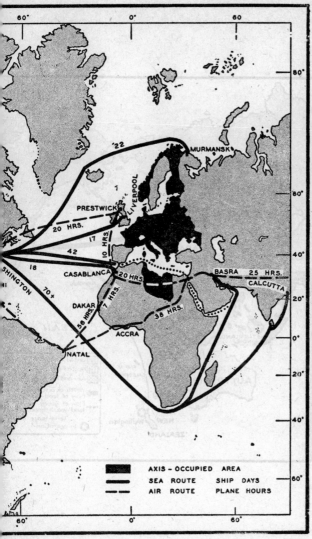

MAP 15. American Supply Lines: Time and Space Chart.

457

Within the image:

SOVIET UNION
ALASKA
CHINA
INDIA
Dutch Harbor
Vladivostok
JAPAN
Tokyo
Chungking
MIDWAY
PHILIPPINES
GUAM
CAROLINE IS.
NETHERLANDS INDIES
PACIFIC
Honolulu
OCEAN
FIJI IS.
NEW CALEDONIA
AUSTRALIA
Sydney
NEW ZEALAND
Wellington
C A
UNIT

Legend:
United Nations
Neutral areas not eligible fo
Axis and occupied areas
Nonbell
Width of arrows suggests
Flow of lend-lease goods
Flow of goods made from
lend-lease goods
lend-lease mission
In operation

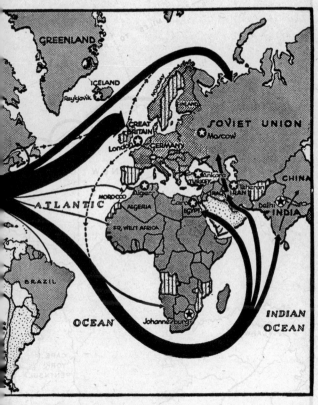

MAP 16. American Lend-Lease Supply. (From *The War in Maps*, by Francis Brown; New York: Oxford University Press, 1944. Reproduced by permission.)

459

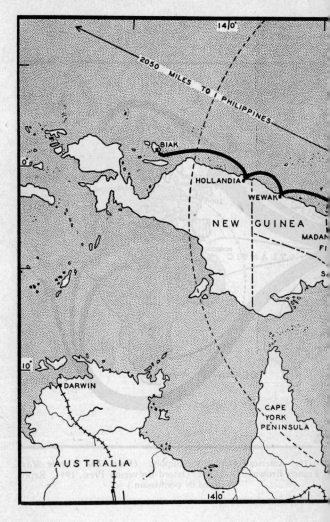

460

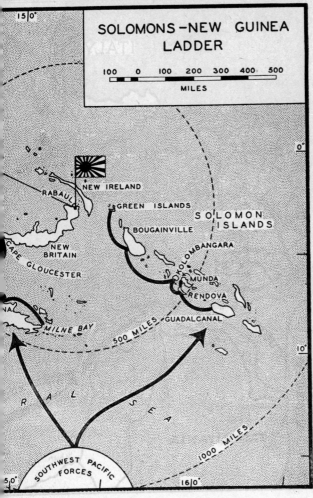

MAP 17. The Solomons—New Guinea Ladder.

461

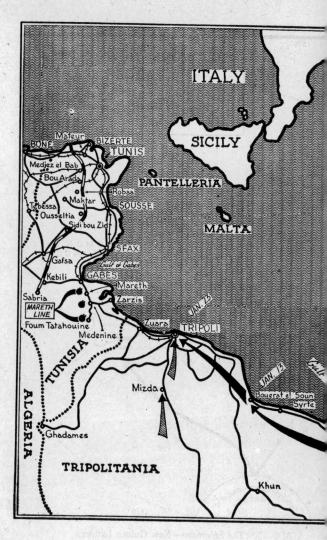

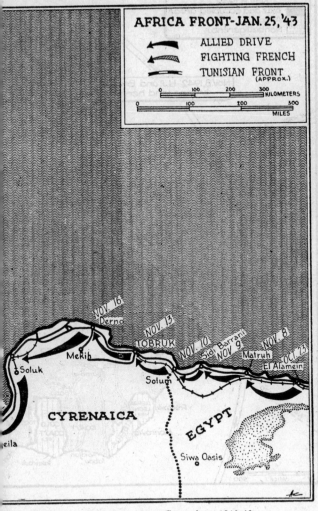

AFRICA FRONT—JAN. 25, '43

ALLIED DRIVE
FIGHTING FRENCH
TUNISIAN FRONT
(APPROX.)

0   100   200   300
KILOMETERS
0   100   200   300
MILES

NOV. 16
Derna
NOV. 13
TOBRUK
NOV. 10
Mekih
NOV. 9
Sidi Barrani
Matruh
NOV. 8
OCT. 23
El Alamein
Soluk
Solum

CYRENAICA

EGYPT

eila

Siwa Oasis

MAP 18.   The North Africa Campaign: 1942-43.

463

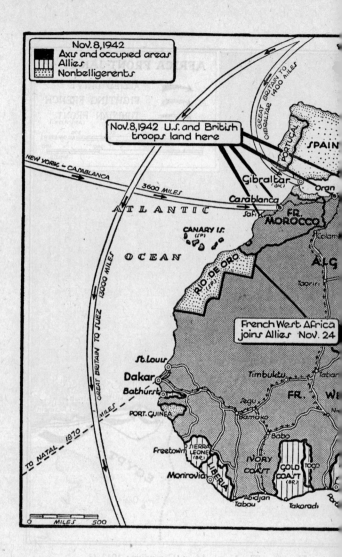

Nov. 8, 1942

- ▉ Axis and occupied areas
- ▥ Allies
- ▤ Nonbelligerents

Nov. 8, 1942 U.S. and British troops land here

GREAT BRITAIN TO GIBRALTAR 1400 MILES

NEW YORK — CASABLANCA

3600 MILES

GREAT BRITAIN TO SUEZ 13000 MILES

TO NATAL 1870 MILES

PORTUGAL

SPAIN

Gibraltar (BR.)

Oran

Casablanca

ATLANTIC

Safi

FR. MOROCCO

Colomb

CANARY IS. (SP.)

OCEAN

RIO DE ORO (SP.)

ALG

Taorirt

French West Africa joins Allies Nov. 24

St. Louis

Dakar

Timbuktu

Tabor

Bathurst

FR. W

PORT. GUINEA

Segu

Bamako

Babo

N

Freetown

SIERRA LEONE (BR.)

IVORY COAST

GOLD COAST (BR.)

TOGO

Monrovia

LIBERIA

Abidjan

Tabou

Takoradi

Port

EGYPT

0   MILES   500

464

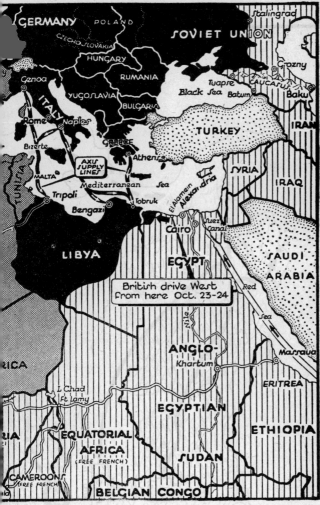

MAP 19. American Landings in North Africa: 1942 (From *The War in Maps*, by Francis Brown; New York: Oxford University Press, 1944. Reproduced by permission.)

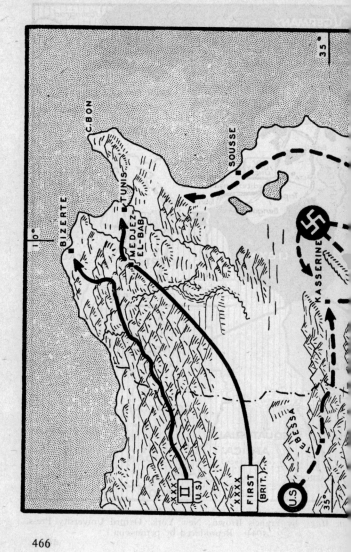

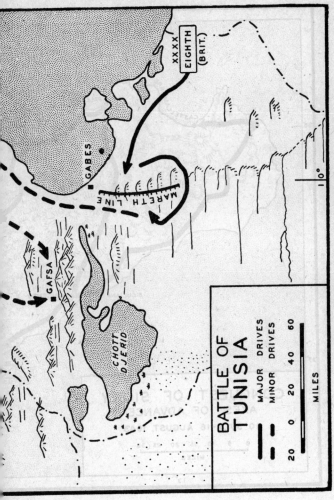

MAP 20   The Battle of Tunisia : 1943.

467

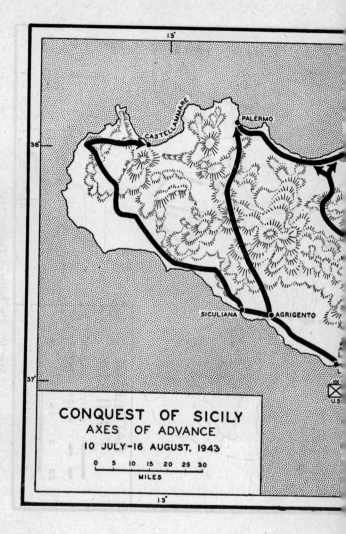

CONQUEST OF SICILY
AXES OF ADVANCE
10 JULY—16 AUGUST, 1943

0 5 10 15 20 25 30
MILES

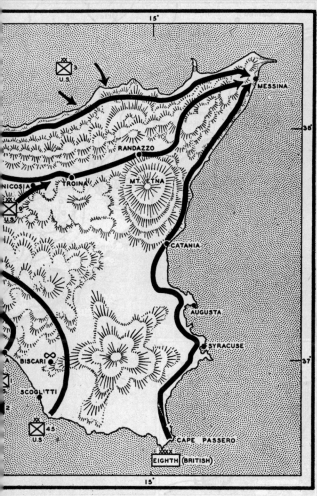

MAP 21. The Conquest of Sicily: 1943.

469

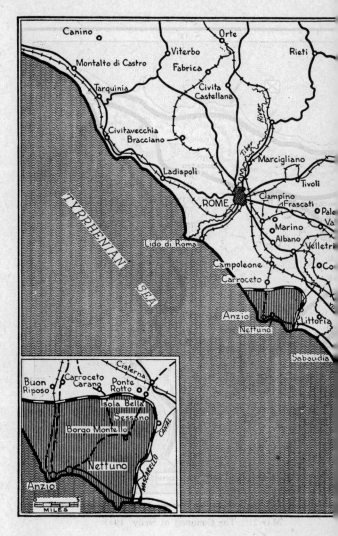

MILES

470

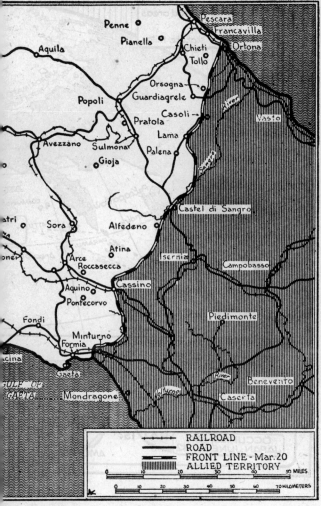

MAP 22. The Early Italian Campaign: 1943.

Japan and dominated areas
⚓ Naval bases
Distances are statute miles

SOVIET UNION

APPROXIMATE

o Bodaibo
Okhotsk
Anac

MONGOLIA
MANCHURIA
CHINA
VLADIVOSTOK ⊚
KOREA

Petropavlovsk KAMCHATKA
Komsomolsk

765 —— ATTU
2005

⚓ PARAMUSHIRU

Area of inse

IBER
COMMANDE
Kiska

JAPAN
Nagasaki o
⊚ TOKYO

ATTU
NEAR IS.
AGATTU

RETAKEN BY
U.S. FORCES
JUNE 2, 1943

180 MILES
BULDIR

RETAKEN BY AMERICA
& CANADIANS AUG. 15, 19

Kiska Harbor
SEMISOPOCHNOI
KISKA
RAT IS.

OCCUPIED BY
JAPAN JUNE 6-7 '42

58 M.

AMCHITKA

472

Map 23. The Aleutians Campaign: 1943. (From *The War in Maps*,
Francis Brown; New York: Oxford University Press, 1944. Reproduced by permission.)

Southeast
EUROPE

0   100   200   300   400

474

MAP 24. Southeast Europe: December 1943.

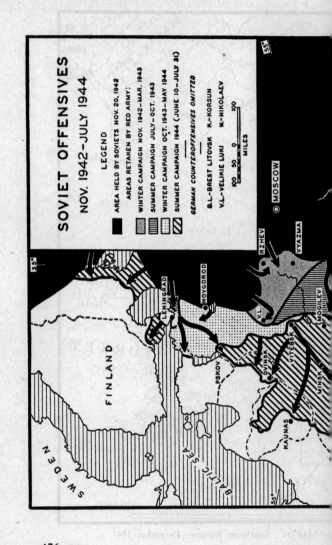

SOVIET OFFENSIVES
NOV. 1942–JULY 1944

LEGEND

AREA HELD BY SOVIETS NOV. 20, 1942

AREAS RETAKEN BY RED ARMY:

WINTER CAMPAIGN NOV. 1942–MAR. 1943

SUMMER CAMPAIGN JULY–OCT. 1943

WINTER CAMPAIGN OCT. 1943–MAY 1944

SUMMER CAMPAIGN 1944 (JUNE 10–JULY 31)

GERMAN COUNTEROFFENSIVES OMITTED

B.L.–BREST LITOVSK   K.–KORSUN
V.L.–VELIKIE LUKI   N.–NIKOLAEV

MILES
100 50 0   100

MOSCOW

RZHEV

VYAZMA

NOVGOROD

LENINGRAD

PSKOV

DVINSK

VITEBSK

MOGILEV

MINSK

KAUNAS

FINLAND

SWEDEN

BALTIC SEA

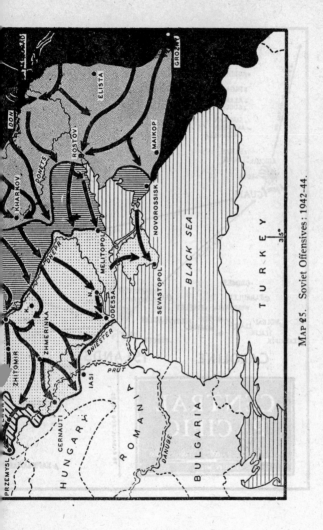

MAP 25. Soviet Offensives: 1942-44.

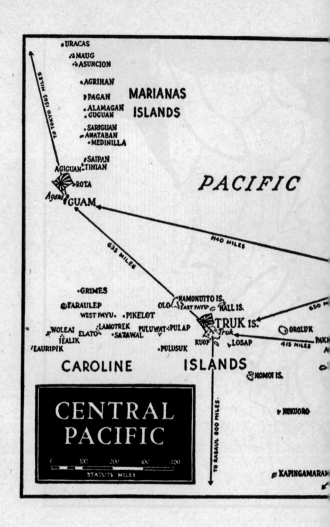

MARIANAS ISLANDS

PACIFIC

URACAS
MAUG
ASUNCION
AGRIHAN
PAGAN
ALAMAGAN
GUGUAN
SARIGUAN
ANATABAN
MEDINILLA
SAIPAN
AGIGUAN TINIAN
ROTA
Agana GUAM

1565 MILES TO TOKYO

3140 MILES

635 MILES

GRIMES
FARAULEP
WEST FAYU PIKELOT
WOLEAI LAMOTREK PULUWAT PULAP
ELATO SATAWAL
IFALIK
EAURIPIK PULUSUK

CAROLINE ISLANDS

NAMONUITO IS.
OLO EAST FAYU HALL IS.
TRUK IS.
Truk
KUOP LOSAP
OROLUK
PONAPE
650 MI.
415 MILES

NOMOI IS.

NUKUORO

KAPINGAMARANGI

TO RABAUL 800 MILES

CENTRAL PACIFIC

0 100 200 300 400
STATUTE MILES

478

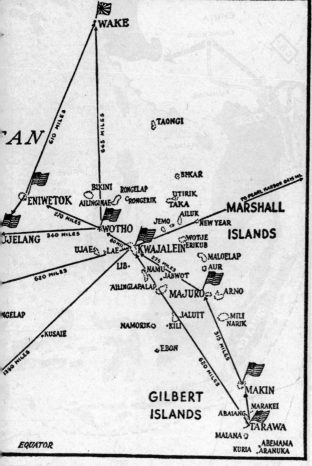

MAP 26. The Central Pacific: March 1944.

479

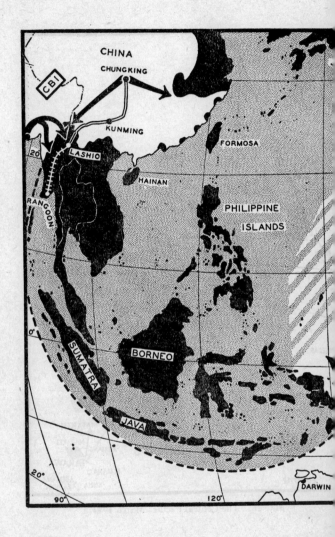

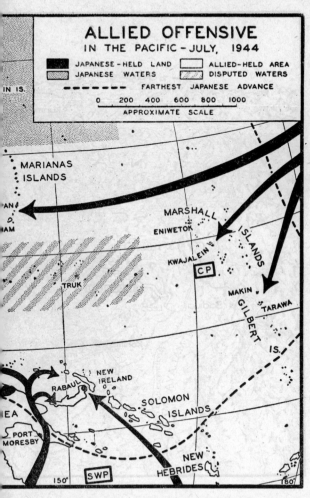

MAP 27.   Allied Offensive in the Pacific: July 1944.

481

MAP 28. Campaigns in Burma: 1943-44. (From *The War in Maps*,
Francis Brown; New York: Oxford University Press, 1944. Reproduced by permission.)

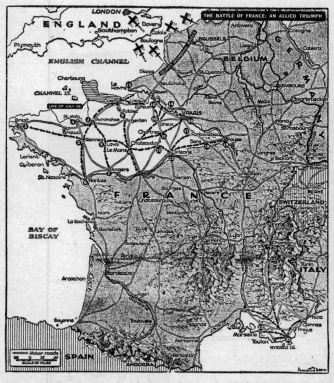

MAP 29. The Battle of Normandy: 1944. (From *The New York Times* of August 27, 1944. Reproduced by permission.)

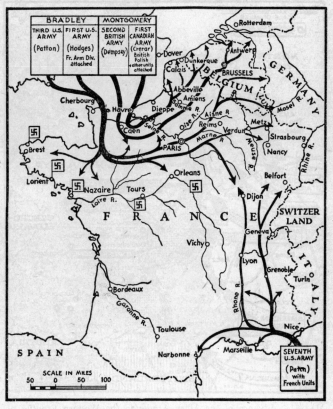

MAP 30.   The Battle of France: 1944.

485

MAP 31. Advance of the Allied Armies to the Western Frontier of Germany: 1944. (From *The New York Times* of September 17, 1944. Reproduced by permission.)

486

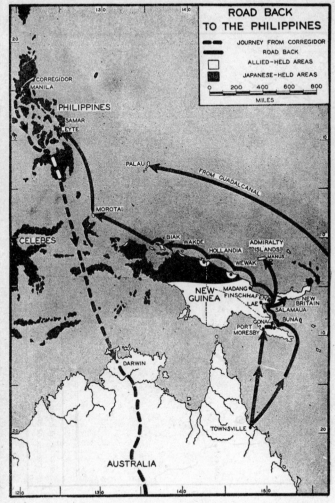

MAP 32. The Road Back to the Philippines: October 1944.

487

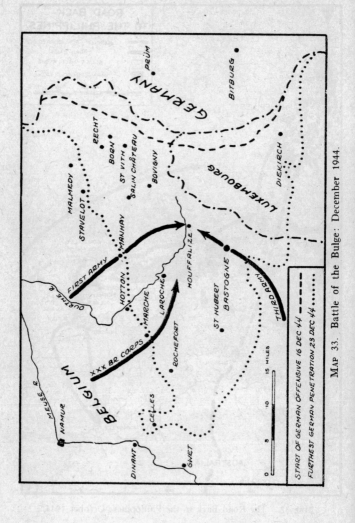

MAP 33. Battle of the Bulge: December 1944.

GERMANY

BELGIUM

LUXEMBOURG

BITBURG

PRÜM

RECHT

BORN

ST VITH

SALM CHÂTEAU

BOVIGNY

DIEKIRCH

MALMEDY

STAVELOT

MANHAY

OURTHE R.

FIRST ARMY

HOTTON

MARCHE

LAROCHE

HOUFFALIZE

BASTOGNE

ST HUBERT

THIRD ARMY

XXX BR CORPS

ROCHEFORT

MEUSE R.

NAMUR

CELLES

DINANT

GIVET

START OF GERMAN OFFENSIVE 16 DEC 44 ━━━

FURTHEST GERMAN PENETRATION 23 DEC 44 ·······

MILES

0   5   10   15

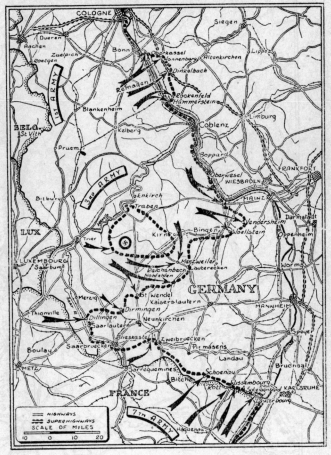

MAP 34. The Remagen Bridgehead.

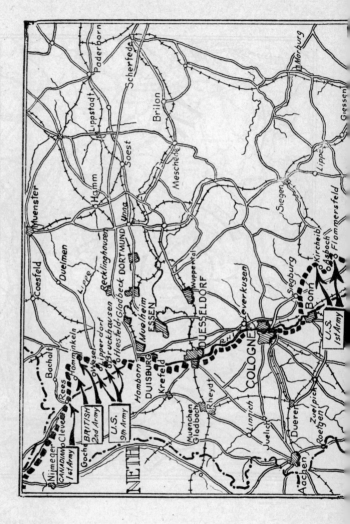

490

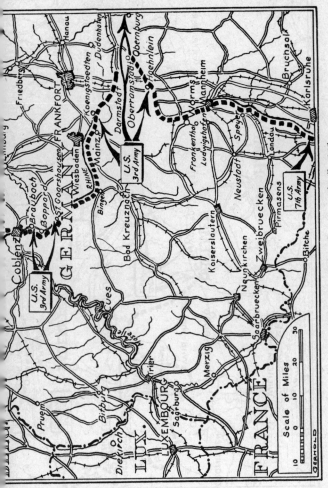

MAP 35. The Rhine Crossings, April 1945.

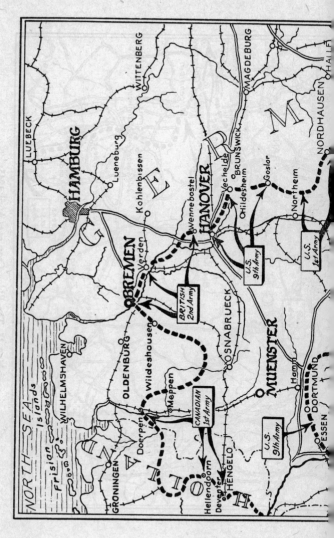

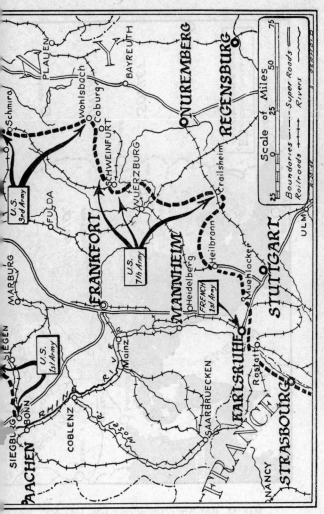

MAP 36. The Ruhr Trap and the Advance East.

493

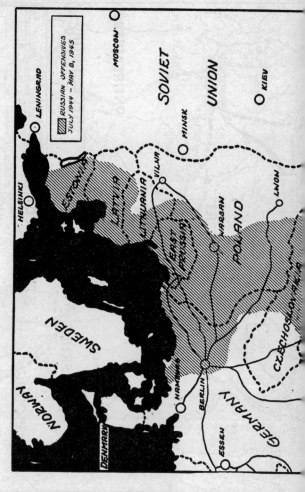

MAP 37. Red Army Offensives: July 1944–May 1945.

SEVASTOPOL
BUCHAREST
ISTANBUL
TURKEY
SMYRNA
BULGARIA
SOFIA
CRETE
SALONIKA
GREECE
BELGRADE
ALBANIA
YUGOSLAVIA
ITALY
PALERMO
NAPLES
SICILY
ROME
GENOA
TUNISIA

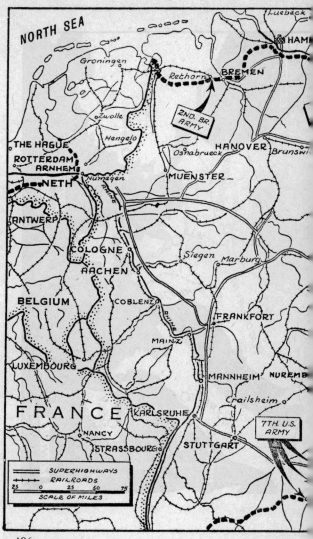

MAP 38. Junction of Allied Armies.   497

MAP 39. Allied Operations in Western Europe:

June 6, 1944 to May 8, 1945.

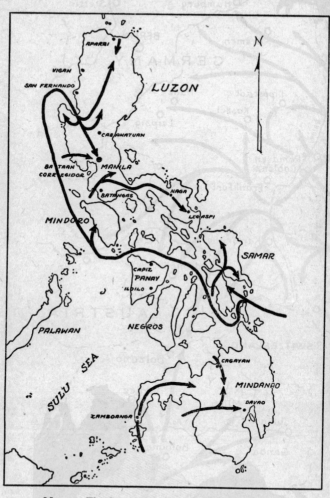

MAP 40. The Campaign in the Philippines: 1944-45.

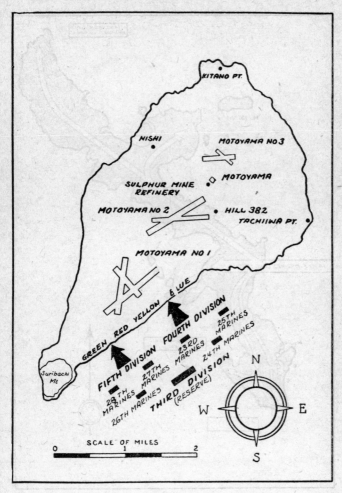

MAP 41. Invasion of Iwo Jima.

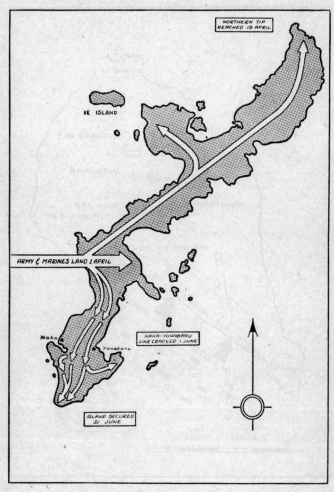

NORTHERN TIP
REACHED 19 APRIL

IE ISLAND

ARMY & MARINES LAND 1 APRIL

Naha

Yonabaru

NAHA-YONABARU
LINE CRACKED 1 JUNE

ISLAND SECURED
21 JUNE

MAP 42. Invasion of Okinawa.

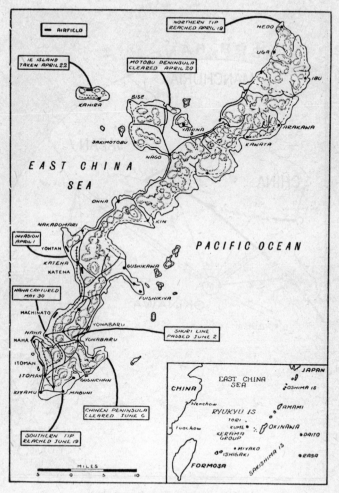

MAP 43. The Okinawa Campaign.

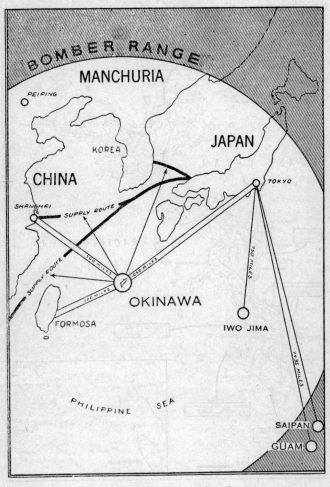

MAP 44. The Air War Against Japan.

INDEX

505

506

507

508

Brécy, 309
Breda, 320
Breisach, 331
Bremen, 329, 331
Brenner Pass, 333
Brereton, Lt. Gen. Lewis H., 176, 269, 314, 318, 325
Brescia, 336
Breskens, 320
Breslau, 251, 348, 351
Brest, 52, 310ff
Brest-Litovsk, 40, 85, 276ff
Breton, USS, 239
Brett, Lt. Gen. George H., 114
Brighton, 56
Bristol, 59
Britain. See Great Britain
British Army. See also Great Britain
  Borneo invasion, 373ff
  Burma offensives, 353ff
  Colonial troops in Africa, 68
  Dieppe casualties, 291
  Greece campaign, 76
  Hong Kong, strength at, 112
  Middle East, defense of, 68
  British First Army, 188
  Canadian First Army, 316ff, 325, 331
  British Second Army, 296ff, 317ff, 325
  British Eighth Army, 73, 157ff, 181ff, 214ff, 288ff, 335
  British Fourteenth Army, 353ff
  Imperial III Corps, 113ff
  British III Corps, 247
  British IV Corps, 246, 353ff
  British X Corps, 222ff, 227ff
  Indian XV Corps, 353ff
  British XXXIII Corps, 353ff
  New Zealand Corps, 228
  1st Airborne Division, 221, 314, 318
  2d New Zealand Division, 228
  3d Canadian Division, 297ff
  4th Indian Division, 189ff, 228
  5th Indian Division, 245
  6th Airborne Division, 296ff
  6th Armored Division, 189ff

6th Australian Division, 173ff, 234ff
7th Armored Division, 73, 297ff
7th Australian Division, 173ff, 233ff
7th Indian Division, 245
9th Australian Division, 233ff
9th Imperial Division, 113
11th Imperial Division, 113
17th Indian Division, 246
19th Indian Division, 354ff
22nd Indian Division, 354ff
23d Indian Division, 246
26th Indian Division, 353ff
50th Infantry Division, 188, 297ff
51st Infantry Division, 189ff, 324
70th Armored Division, 73
Indian Division, 73
New Zealand Division, 73, 189
South African Divisions, 73
18th Australian Brigade, 173ff
British Guiana, 66
Brittany, 269, 307ff
Broadway, 245
Brolo, 217
Brooks, Maj. Gen. John B., 384
Brown, Admiral Wilson, 126
Brozovich, Josip. See Tito, Marshal
Bruce, Maj. Gen. Andrew D., 381, 378
Bruges, 319
Brunei Bay, 373
Brunswick, 266ff
Brush, Maj. Gen. Rapp, 365
Brussels, 318
Bryansk, 84, 93-94, 160, 202, 250
Bucharest 277
Buckner, Lt. Gen. Simon B., 377ff, 381
Budapest, 347, 349
Budyenny, Marshal Semion, 84, 87ff, 94
Bug River, 40, 80, 87, 151, 255, 275ff, 345
Buka Island, 233
Bukhovina, 80
Bulgaria, 75, 277ff

509

510

511

512

514

518

521

522

523

526

527

530

533

534

535

537